Jews and Samaritans

Jews and Samaritans

The Origins and History of Their Early Relations

GARY N. KNOPPERS

OXFORD
UNIVERSITY PRESS

Oxford University Press is a department of the University of Oxford. It furthers
the University's objective of excellence in research, scholarship, and education
by publishing worldwide. Oxford is a registered trade mark of Oxford University
Press in the UK and certain other countries.

Published in the United States of America by Oxford University Press
198 Madison Avenue, New York, NY 10016, United States of America.

© Oxford University Press 2013

First issued as an Oxford University Press paperback, 2019

All rights reserved. No part of this publication may be reproduced, stored in
a retrieval system, or transmitted, in any form or by any means, without the
prior permission in writing of Oxford University Press, or as expressly permitted
by law, by license, or under terms agreed with the appropriate reproduction
rights organization. Inquiries concerning reproduction outside the scope of the
above should be sent to the Rights Department, Oxford University Press, at the
address above.

You must not circulate this work in any other form
and you must impose this same condition on any acquirer.

Library of Congress Cataloging-in-Publication Data
Knoppers, Gary N., 1956–
Jews and Samaritans : the origins and history of their early relations / Gary N. Knoppers.
pages cm
Includes bibliographical references.
ISBN 978-0-19-532954-4 (cloth : alk. paper) | ISBN 978-0-19-006879-0 (paper : alk. paper)
1. Samaritans—Relations—Judaism—History. 2. Judaism—Relations—
Samaritans—History. 3. Lost tribes of Israel. I. Title.
BM915.K56 2013
296.8'17—dc23
2012039515

In memoriam Frank Moore Cross
13 July 1921–17 October 2012

Contents

Preface — ix

1. Samaritans, Jews, and the Contested Legacy of Classical Israel — 1
   I. So Much in Common, Why So Far Apart? — 3
   II. The Search for the "Ten Lost Tribes" — 5
   III. The Agenda of this Work — 8

2. The Fall of the Northern Kingdom and the Ten Lost Tribes: A Reevaluation — 18
   I. The Case for Devastation and Massive Bidirectional Deportations — 21
   II. Questioning the Consensus — 26
   III. The Case for a Reduced Israelite Presence in the Region of Samaria — 28
   Conclusions — 42

3. God and Country: The Revival of Israelite Religion in Postexilic Samaria — 45
   I. Give Me that Old-Time Religion — 49
   II. The Old-Time Religion Reborn — 54
   III. Those Descendants of Jacob Who Do Not Worship Yhwh — 57
   IV. Rooting Out the Old-Time Religion — 62
   Conclusions — 65

4. The Fall of the Northern Kingdom as a New Beginning in Northern Israelite–Southern Israelite Relations — 71
   I. The Tale of the Good Samarians — 75
   II. Renaissance and Reformation under Hezekiah — 82
   III. "Following in the Ways of David": Cultic Purity and Unity under Josiah — 92
   Conclusions — 97

5. A Distinction without a Difference? Samarian and Judean Cultures during the Persian and Early Hellenistic Periods ... 102
   I. Samaria from the Late Neo-Assyrian Period to the Early Hellenistic Period ... 103
   II. Cultural Continuities ... 109
   III. New Evidence about Cultic Affairs in Persian/Hellenistic Period Samaria ... 120
   IV. Archaizing, Piety, and Identity in the Mt. Gerizim Cult ... 125
   Conclusions ... 131

6. Ethnicity, Communal Identity, and Imperial Authority: Contextualizing the Conflicts between Samaria and Judah in Ezra-Nehemiah ... 135
   I. Samarian Opposition to Nehemiah's Building Campaign in the Mid-5th Century ... 140
      A. The Enemy Without ... 142
      B. The Enemy Within ... 153
   II. "Déjà Vu All Over Again?": Nehemiah's Second Term ... 160
   Conclusions ... 165

7. The Torah and "the Place[s] for Yhwh's Name": Samarian-Judean Relations in Hellenistic and Maccabean Times ... 169
   I. The Rise of the Pentateuch and Judean-Samarian Relations in the Late Persian–Early Hellenistic Period ... 178
   II. Location, Location, Location: Different Ways of Reading the Same Book ... 194
   Conclusions ... 212

8. An Absolute Breach? ... 217
   I. Catalysts toward Deteriorating Relations in Early Roman Times ... 220
   II. Religious Development and Cultural Exchange ... 228
   Conclusions ... 237

Bibliography ... 241
Jewish Scriptures ... 295
Author Index ... 311
Subject Index ... 319

Preface

MY INTEREST IN the history of Samaritan-Jewish relations began during the years of my doctoral program at Harvard some three decades ago. My *Doktorvader*, Frank Moore Cross, showed a keen interest throughout his long and illustrious career in the history of Samaria, especially during the Persian, Hellenistic, and Maccabean periods. His research into the textual development of the Hebrew text, including the witness of the Dead Sea Scrolls and Samaritan Pentateuch, was extraordinarily helpful to me as I studied the history of Samaria and Judah in postmonarchic times. Although we occasionally disagreed on certain issues, he nevertheless encouraged me to pursue my own line of research. It was my original intention to dedicate this monograph to him in his honor. Given his recent death, the volume is now dedicated to Frank Moore Cross in memoriam of his singular contributions to the field.

Two other professors in ancient Near Eastern and Jewish studies at Harvard significantly influenced my research. Paul Hanson helpfully stressed the importance of postexilic Judean literature for developing a deeper grasp of the diversity of social movements in ancient Israelite history. James Kugel's emphasis on reception history, the different ways late biblical authors creatively appropriated and recast older texts, was quite useful for gaining a better grasp of the various interpretive tropes employed in Persian and Hellenistic Judean literature.

In developing a monograph on a major topic that involves a long history of development within the southern Levant, I have found it to be advantageous to consult with a wide variety of active historians, biblical scholars, classicists, Judaic studies scholars, and Samaritan studies specialists. Within the academy, a large number of scholars have supported my work and I am most appreciative of their good counsel. At different stages in the development of this project, Joseph Blenkinsopp, Israel Eph'al, Sara Japhet, and Hugh Williamson have encouraged my interest in postexilic literature and Samarian history. To them I owe a debt of gratitude. Within the Canadian Society of Biblical Studies/Le société canadienne des études bibliques, Mark Boda, Ehud Ben Zvi, John Kessler, Christine Mitchell, and David Vanderhooft have been most willing to offer insightful critiques of my work. Within the Society of Biblical Literature, Reinhard Achenbach, Sidnie White Crawford, Ronald Hendel, Jan Joosten, Louis Jonker, Bernard Levinson, Oded Lipschits, Peter Machinist, Christophe Nihan, Steven McKenzie, Thomas Römer, and John Wright have provided me with insightful counsel. Among my colleagues in the Société d'Études Samaritaines, I would like to express a special word of thanks to Ingrid Hjelm, Magnar Kartveit, Menachem Mor, Stefan Schorch, Abraham Tal, József Zsengellér, and last, but certainly not least, Reinhard Pummer for their keen interest in and valuable comments on various aspects of my research. To the two anonymous readers at Oxford University Press, I extend my appreciation for their invaluable suggestions and commentary. The religion editor at Oxford, Cynthia Read, waited all too long for the delivery of this manuscript. For her patience and good-natured support, I am most grateful.

The present project has been generously supported by a number of different institutions. A fellowship in 2006 from the Canadian Society of Biblical Studies/Le société canadienne des études bibliques allowed me to spend several weeks at the École biblique et archéologique française de Jérusalem. I wish to thank the faculty and staff of the École biblique, including its able librarian, Pawel Trzopek, for all of their wonderful cooperation during my residence there. Among the institutions supporting my research, the Pennsylvania State University has been, of course, first and foremost. I appreciate, in particular, a residency fellowship from the Institute for the Arts and Humanities in the fall of 2010, which enabled me to devote focused attention on this project. A sabbatical leave in the fall of 2011 allowed me to spend approximately a month at the Albright Institute of Archaeological Research in Jerusalem. Heartfelt thanks go to the director, Sy Gitin; the manager, Nadia Bandak; and the librarian, Sarah Sussman, for their kind hospitality during my residence at their fine institution. Led by the indefatigable Daniel Mack, the library personnel of the university were absolutely terrific in assisting me to gain access to obscure scholarly monographs and journal articles that were unavailable in our own library collections. Among the graduate students in the departments of History and Classics and Ancient Mediterranean Studies at Penn State, I would like to single out Deirdre Fulton, Jonathan

Greer, Sara Hoffman, Kenneth Ristau, Jeffrey Rop, and Eric Welch for their timely and helpful assistance during various phases of this project.

I would like to extend my special gratitude to my colleague in Classics, Paul Harvey, because he graciously read the last two chapters of this work and offered very useful commentary on my research. Thanks go to my other colleagues in biblical and ancient Near Eastern studies—Baruch Halpern, Ann Killebrew, Donald Redford, Aaron Rubin, and Gonzalo Rubio—for their insights at various points in the preparation of the present manuscript. Finally, I sincerely thank my wife, Laura, for her wonderful support during every phase of this project. Given the arcane nature of my academic interests, I am amazed that after all these years she still shows no visible hesitation in reading and providing feedback on any aspect of my work.

Gary N. Knoppers

Jews and Samaritans

I

Samaritans, Jews, and the Contested Legacy of Classical Israel

IN A WELL-KNOWN passage from the Gospel of John, Jesus converses with a Samaritan woman at Sychar, near Shechem (modern-day Nablus) about a series of subjects, including Jewish-Samaritan relations. Explaining why the Samaritan woman is amazed that Jesus is even talking with her, the narrator (or a later scribe) comments: "Jews do not share (things) in common with Samaritans" (John 4:9).[1] Later in the dialogue the Samaritan woman tells Jesus, "Our ancestors worshiped at this mountain, but you (Jews) say that the place at which God must be worshiped is in Jerusalem" (John 4:20). "This mountain" is nearby Mt. Gerizim in central Israel, the site of the Samaritan temple, which had been destroyed by the Judean (Maccabean) leader John Hyrcanus over a century before (ca. 111–110 BCE). The Jewish insistence that "God must be worshiped in Jerusalem" refers, of course, to the Jewish temple located there. The conversation between the Samaritan woman and Jesus reflects the strained relations between Samaritans and Jews in the first centuries of the Common Era. In line with the demands of the Torah (Deuteronomy 12), both Samaritans and Jews advocated centralization—the firmly held tenet that the God of Israel had to be worshiped only at one location—but differed strongly about where that worship was to be centered (Mt. Gerizim vs. Mt. Zion).

There are fewer than 800 Samaritans living today, a distinct change from antiquity.[2] During the Neo-Babylonian (626–539 BCE), Persian

---

1. That the explanation, οὐ γὰρ συγχρῶνται Ἰουδαῖοι, is lacking in some important textual witnesses (Uncials Sinaiticus, Bezae Cantabrigiensis, etc.) suggests that it is a later addition.
2. This figure represents a distinct improvement over against the figure tabulated in the census of the early 20th century, when the number of Samaritans had dipped below 150.

(538–332 BCE), and early Hellenistic (332–164 BCE) eras, there were probably, as we shall see, more Samarians than Judeans residing in Palestine. The area of ancient Samaria suffered during the Assyrian invasions during the 8th century BCE, but gradually recovered afterward. Unlike the area of Judah, the area of Samaria does not seem to have experienced massive destructions at major sites during the Babylonian conquests of 598 and 586 BCE. During the Neo-Babylonian and Persian periods, the Samarians were a force to be reckoned with in the southern Levant, even though Samaria and Judah were both under foreign domination. The province of Samaria was larger, more populous, and wealthier than its neighbor to the immediate south. In assessing the significance of Samaritan-Jewish relations, one must distinguish, therefore, between the contemporary historical situation and that of two and a half millennia ago.

Although interactions between Jews and Samaritans had become contentious by the 1st century CE, the two major groups actually shared much in common. The groups shared a belief in monotheism, an attachment to the land of Israel, and the same ancestral tongue (Hebrew). Both claimed descent from the same first progenitor (Adam), the same chain of ancestors (Abraham and Sarah, Isaac and Rebekah, Jacob and Rachel and Leah), the same priestly tribe originating in the patriarch Levi, and the same priestly pedigree originating in the succession of Aaron, Eleazar, and Phinehas. Samaritans and Jews practiced a number of similar rituals, festivals, and feasts, and the groups shared an overlap in holy scriptures—the Pentateuch, or Five Books of Moses. Each kept similar but not identical calendars.

Both groups could be found both in the land and outside of the land in diasporic communities. Each group developed its own synagogues, which were so similar architecturally that it can be challenging to tell them apart.[3] Members of both groups professed a pedigree in the same eponymous ancestor (Jacob/Israel). Samaritans claimed to be descendants of the northern tribes of Joseph, representing Jacob's progeny of Ephraim and Manasseh (*'eprayim* and *mĕnaššeh*), while Judeans (*yĕhûdîm*) claimed to be descendants of the southern tribes, most notably Jacob's progeny of Judah (*yĕhûdâ*). Indeed, it is probably no accident that the encounter between Jesus and the Samaritan woman occurred at Jacob's well, "by the

---

3. See Pummer 1998a, 1999; Hachlili 2001, 2009; Fine 2005; Magen 2008c.

plot of land that Jacob had bequeathed to his son Joseph" (John 4:5–6). Jacob's Well, although not specifically mentioned in the Hebrew Bible (cf. Gen 33:18), was an important site in Samaritan and Jewish (and later Christian and Muslim) tradition.

I. So Much in Common, Why So Far Apart?

But, if Jews and Samaritans shared important beliefs and practices, why is the Samaritan woman in the story of John so surprised that Jesus is even conversing with her? One factor is that in a traditionally patriarchal society Jesus, as a man, is speaking to "a woman of Samaria" in an open public place (John 4:9). Hence Jesus's disciples were astonished to find their leader "communicating with a woman" (John 4:27). Another factor has to do with ethnicity. In traditional Jewish interpretation, the Samaritans were the descendants of immigrants imported into the land from foreign territories (e.g., ancient Babylonia). Employing the biblical account of the (northern) Israelite exile in 722 BCE (2 Kings 17) as a key source, Jews claimed that Samaritans were of foreign origin or at best had a mixed pedigree.[4] According to this influential paradigm, the Samaritans were the descendants of the polytheistic foreign settlers whom the Assyrians had imported into the land in the late 8th century BCE to replace the departed Israelites. In this common understanding, Samaritans were either foreigners or the offspring of intermarriages between foreigners and the few Israelites who managed to survive and remain in the land. The question of poor relations did not have to do, therefore, so much with the observance of particular rituals as with genealogy, history, and blood.[5]

In one early Jewish interpretation, already attested in the work of the 1st century CE Jewish historian Josephus, the Samaritans are Cutheans, descendants of one of the five peoples said to be imported into the land by the Assyrian authorities from *kûtâ* in southern Babylonia (2 Kgs 17:24).[6] In rabbinic times, a minor tractate, *Kutim* (כותים), was devoted to the subject of the Samaritans.[7] In advising Jews on how to conduct

---

4. See chapters 2–3.
5. Some rabbis conceded, for instance, that when it came to *halakah* (religious practice), the Samaritans were quite strict and in some cases could be judged to be more righteous than the Jews (*t. Pesaḥ.* 2.3; *b. Ḥul.* 4a; *b. Nid.* 56b; *b. Giṭ.* 10a).
6. Josephus *BP* 1.63; *Ant.* 9.279, 288–91; 10.184; 11.302. Pummer (2009: 67–76) provides a useful discussion.
7. The tractate ascribes to the Samaritans a marginal status. In some respects, the practices of the Cutheans are to be regarded like those of Gentiles, but in other respects like those of

their relations with Samaritans, the tractate refers to earlier rabbinic discussions—for example, in the Mishnah, a very important written compilation of Jewish oral law dating to the early 3rd century CE (*m. Šeqal.* 1:5; *m. Abod. Zar.* 1:5, 7, 15b), and in the Tosefta, a collection of early additions or supplements to the Mishnah (*t. Demai* 3:3; *t. Abod. Zar.* 3).

In some instances, scholars have cited another rabbinic expression to refer to the Samaritans. The Samaritans are called "lion proselytes" (גרי אריות), as opposed to "genuine proselytes" (גרי אמת). The usage plays on the story of 2 Kgs 17:25–28 in which Yhwh sends marauding lions (האריות) among the foreign immigrants settling in Samaria, because "they did not worship [literally, fear] Yhwh."[8] According to this calculation, the foreign settlers did not convert to Yahwism so much out of their own free volition as out of a situation of acute distress. The dire circumstances cast some aspersions on the circumstances of the conversion. Yet one must employ the rabbinic material carefully. As Schiffman (1985: 327) observes, the rabbinic dispute about lion converts as opposed to true converts is an Amoraic creation in reference to earlier Tannaitic disputes. The expression "lion converts" does appear in a baraita (a Tannaitic statement not found in the Mishnah) appearing in both Talmuds (*y. Qidd.* 65; *b. Yebam.* 24b; cf. *y. Giṭ.* 1:4; *b. Qidd.* 75a–b), but in neither case are the Samaritans mentioned.[9] Moreover, there are some instances in rabbinic discourse in which the Samaritans are referred to in a nonderogatory manner simply as Samaritans (שמריין; *y. Abod. Zar.* 39c, 44d; *Gen. Rab.* 32).[10]

If the Samaritans were not Israelites (in Jewish perspective), what happened to the northern Israelites? If the Jews of the 1st centuries CE thought that virtually all of the northern Israelites had been banished from the land many centuries earlier, what did they believe about the fate of those exiled Israelites? Considering that northern Israelites in biblical lore represented most of demographic Israel—traditionally numbering

---

Israel. The latter is more often the case than the former (*Kutim* 1.1). Incidentally, Samaritans do not view Jews as foreigners or as descendants of foreigners. Rather, Samaritans view Jews as descendants of the patriarch Judah, son of Jacob/Israel. The quarrels Samaritans have with Jews have to do, therefore, with other issues (e.g., the site of the central sanctuary).

8. See *y. Giṭ.* 43c; *y. Qidd.* 65b; *b. B. Qam.* 38b; *b. Ḥul.* 3b; *b. Nid.* 56b; *b. Qidd.* 75a–76a; *b. Sanh.* 85b).

9. Montgomery's treatment (1907: 165–203) is dated, but still useful in providing an overview of the complex Talmudic evidence. Schiffman's careful analysis (1985) traces a shift to a more hostile stance from the time of the Tannaim to that of the Amoraim. Hjelm (2000: 104–238) provides a detailed overview of recent discussions.

10. I wish to thank Abraham Tal (personal communication) for these references.

ten out of twelve tribes—their dislocation represented a monumental loss. One part of this book will be devoted to discussing this complex question from a critical, historical standpoint. I shall argue, in fact, that the common assumption of a comprehensive northern exile needs to be rethought. To be sure, tens of thousands of Israelites were deported by the Assyrians to foreign territories and were forced to adjust to living in cultures considerably different from their own. But many others continued to reside in their ancestral homeland, albeit under foreign rule.

II. The Search for the "Ten Lost Tribes"

For the moment, however, it is important to discuss the avid interest of many writers (both Jewish and Christian) through the ages in those members of the northern tribes who were forcibly deported to other lands. Because of the widespread popular interest in what became of Israel's "lost tribes," it may be helpful to deal briefly with this matter before proceeding to discuss the central task of this project. Following the narrative of one influential biblical source (2 Kings 17) we have already discussed, many modern interpreters have followed early interpreters in assuming that virtually all northern Israelites were killed or were forced to leave their homeland for parts unknown. In postbiblical tradition, the deported northern Israelites are often referred to as "the ten lost tribes." Given the lack of documentation relating to the fate of the northern exiles, later writers referred to those dispersed to obscure locations within the (former) Assyrian empire as "lost." The number "ten" is given, because this number represented the traditional number of northern tribes (e.g., 1 Kgs 11:29–38). In the case of the later exiles of Judahites to Babylon (ca. 598 and 586 BCE), there is significant historical literature pertaining to the return or, more accurately, the returns of some Judahites back to their homeland in the centuries that followed.[11] With one important exception, referring to the resettlement of exiles from Manasseh and Ephraim in

---

11. See, e.g., Isa 44:24–28; 45:1–8; 2 Chr 36:22–23; Ezra 1:1–4; 2:1–70; 5:13–16; 7:1–28; 8:1–14; Neh 1:1–2:11; 5:14–16. It is clear, however, that only some of the deported Judahite population returned to the land. Other Judahites remained in the eastern Diaspora, having successfully settled into their new environment. On this matter, the continuing publication of the Al-Yahudu ("town of Judah") cuneiform tablets, dating to Neo-Babylonian and (mostly) Persian times, is of great interest (Joannès and Lemaire 1999; Pearce 2006; Abraham 2005–6; 2007). On the Judean military colony in Elephantine, Egypt, see Porten 1968; Lozachmeur 2006; Lemaire 2011. In the wake of the Babylonian exiles (ca. 598 and 586 BCE), a major development thus

Jerusalem (1 Chr 9:3; Knoppers 2000b), there are no comparable biblical accounts of the exiled residents of the former northern kingdom.[12]

The interest in the ten lost tribes is certainly not without merit. Indeed, recent scholarship has discovered scattered references to Samarians in Assyrian sources (Zadok 1988, 1995, 2002, 2008; Younger 1998, 2003b; Galil 2009). Such epigraphic documentation of Samarians and of individuals with Yahwistic names is important, because it confirms the continuing survival of northern Israelites far from their original homeland. The presence of Yahwistic names in business, legal, and administrative documents furnishes scattered bits of information about the location and fate of exiled northern Israelites in the decades following their deportation to foreign lands. Less clear is what all happened to these expatriates in later Neo-Assyrian and Neo-Babylonian times.

The deportees (and others) also figure in a variety of prophetic oracles in the Hebrew Bible that speak of a future gathering together of God's people, a reunification of all Israelites, and a return of all expatriates back to the land (Coggins 1975; Fuller 2006; Knoppers 2011b).[13] Such oracles in Jeremiah, Ezekiel, Zechariah, and other books hardly speak with one voice, but they assume the survival of Israelites and Judahites in a variety of territories and prophesy their reconfiguration in some new political form within their ancestral land. But such prophetic passages are wishfully directed to the future; they do not refer in a past historical sense to something that has already occurred. According to the prophets, the deported northern groups never returned to the land of Israel.

The question thus arises: what happened to these people? What became of those exiled northern Israelites in later times? In the many centuries that followed the biblical era, the mystery of what happened to "the ten lost tribes" spawned a whole popular literature. The interest intensified in recent centuries, when European explorers, missionaries, and colonizers visited new and exotic lands. The operative assumption among many, but by no means all, travelers was that the northern tribes were lost but not extinct. These groups may have changed and adapted

---

occurred in the history of traditional Israelite/Judahite religion. Judaism became an international religion.

12. In medieval Samaritan tradition (e.g., *Abū 'l Fatḥ* 60,71–79,94), northern deportees were eventually repatriated, along with some Judeans. The accounts presuppose that the northern tribes were exiled along with the southern tribes in the time of Nebuchadnezzar (!).

13. Such a hope is also found in the Torah itself (Deut 30:1–10). The promises in Deut 4:25–26 and Leviticus 26 are more circumspect.

to local circumstances, wherever those local circumstances were said to be, but the common assumption was that the tribes or, at least remnants thereof, had somehow survived and remained relatively intact. To be sure, there was some debate already within late antiquity about this very matter. In one discussion recorded in the Mishnah, Rabbi Aqiba declared that the ten tribes would not return (*m. Sanh* 10.3). In so doing, he cited Deut 29:27, "and He [Yhwh] cast them to another land, as is still the case today." But Rabbi Eliezer countered: "As the day grows dark and then becomes light, so also for the ten tribes for whom it grew dark, it will [again] become light."

Over the past several centuries, the ten lost tribes have been purportedly found in all sorts of different places. The speculation continues in contemporary times. The former northern tribes have been located in a surprisingly wide range of geographic locales all over the world. Since the Middle Ages, remnants of the exiled Israelites have been identified with a variety of peoples in Asia, such as the Pathans of Afghanistan, the mountain Jews of Dagestan (in the eastern Caucasian mountains west of the Caspian Sea), the "Beit Shalom" community in Burma, and the Makuya sect in Japan.[14] Identifications in the continent of India have included the Cochin, living on the Malabar Plain south of Calcutta in southern India, and the Shinlung groups living in Mizoram in northeastern India (Benjamin 2001; Gonen 2002: 170–76; Asa-El 2004: 205–6).[15]

Within the continent of Africa, members of the ten lost tribes have been associated with the Jews in Djerba (an island off the Tunisian mainland), the Beta Israel (or Falashas) of Ethiopia, and the Lemba tribe of South Africa, Zimbabwe, and Mozambique (Asa-El 2004: 209–15).[16]

---

14. See, for instance, Law 1992; Gonen 2002: 53–123; Asa-El 2004: 195–203. The whole issue is complicated by the different definitions of Israel, Judean, Jew, and Judaism (see below).
15. Identifications (or guesses) made by modern travelers to Asia and India were sometimes made with a view to a particular tribe or tribes. The Pathans of Afghanistan were connected to the tribe of Gad, the Jews in Djerba were associated in local legend to the seafaring sodality of Zebulun, the Shinlung groups in northeastern India were connected to the tribe of Manasseh, and the Beta Israel of Ethiopia were tied to the tribes of Dan and Gad.
16. In the case of the Beta Israel of Ethiopia, some 30,000 made aliyah (immigrated) to Israel in the late 20th century by means of a series of secret airlifts organized by the Israeli government. Their identity as Jews was, however, the subject of some debate, because the Beta Israel were largely unacquainted with Mishnaic and Talmudic teachings. Such ignorance is understandable, given the fact that the Beta Israel groups developed quite early within late antiquity and in isolation from ongoing developments in Jewish life and literature, such as the compilation of the Mishnah, the composition of the Jerusalem and Babylonian Talmuds, and the writing of the medieval commentaries. The national discussion in Israel was affected, but not conclusively settled, by the insistence of Israel's second president, Yitzhak Ben-Zvi (1884–1963), that the

In the early modern and modern eras, the lost tribes have been found in even more far-flung places.¹⁷ In the Americas, the lost Israelite tribes have been linked to the native Americans in South America, the native Americans in North America, and the Eskimos in northern Canada, and also the Mormons in the United States (Gonen 2002: 145–68). Last, but not least, some regarded the inhabitants of the British isles as the long-lost descendants of the ancient northern Israelites. A 19th-century movement in Great Britain called "British Israel" proclaimed the British themselves to be the descendants of Israel's wandering lost tribes (Gonen 2002: 125–43). Such movements testify, among other things, to the enduring allure of the name Israel and the desire of groups in a surprising diversity of lands to identify themselves with being God's chosen people.

It is not the task of this book to sort out and assess all of these far-ranging claims. Such a critical assessment would require a full-length monograph (or two). It should be pointed out, however, that the claims, no matter how diverse, implicitly presuppose the dispersal of all the northern tribes from their homeland. It is this common presupposition that needs to be thoroughly reexamined. Hence, the task of this work is to return to basic historical issues. The interest of the present study lies much more with those northern Israelites who survived the Assyrian invasions and remained within their ancestral territories than it does with those northern Israelites who were scattered to other lands (including Judah).

III. The Agenda of this Work

This book revisits the fate of northern Israelites in the late 8th century BCE and beyond. Several decades ago, this would have been a most difficult undertaking, because of the paucity of available evidence. Aside from a few biblical allusions, references in later Jewish and Samaritan sources, and rudimentary information provided by a few archaeological

---

Beta Israel were part of the Jewish people and by the official ruling given by the Sephardic chief rabbi, Ovadiah Yosef, in 1973 that affirmed a historic connection between the Beta Israel and the tribe of Dan (Gonen 2002: xv–xxii, 39–44, fig. 3). The ruling was affirmed by Chief Rabbi Yosef's successor. Hence, in this case, an explicit link was drawn between an expatriate group and one of the northern tribes.

17. Such inquisitiveness on the part of travelers was fuelled not simply by native curiosity but also by theological beliefs about a future ingathering of Israelites from all the ends of the earth (see above). In this respect, the search for the ten lost tribes tells us as much about the seekers as it does about the actual peoples they encountered.

excavations (primarily at Samaria and Shechem), there was not much to go on. Fortunately, things have changed and there is now much more information available from which to reconstruct Samarian history. Unprecedented modern textual discoveries (e.g., the Dead Sea Scrolls), new archaeological excavations at a variety of major sites (especially the temple complex at Mt. Gerizim), the conclusion of major archaeological site surveys in the hills of Manasseh and Ephraim, the discovery and publication of important epigraphic finds (e.g., the Samaria papyri and the hundreds of fragmentary inscriptions found at Mt. Gerizim), and advances in numismatics (the analysis of coins) enable us to revisit basic issues. My work does not jettison, by any means, the textually based approaches that have traditionally dominated the debates about ancient Samaria. Quite the contrary; there are some neglected literary sources that bear upon the central questions at hand. Yet this book brings traditional literary approaches together with analyses of the many new material finds.

The present work has seven chronologically organized chapters. Chapters 2–4 deal with the origins of the Samaritans, their links to the traditional northern Israelite tribes, and literary accounts of the early relations between these people(s) and Judah. Chapter 2 draws upon archaeological reports, site surveys, and Assyrian royal inscriptions to argue for both discontinuity (destruction layers at most major sites, significant depopulation) and continuity (persistence of local pottery traditions, survival of Samaria, and relatively few signs of upheaval in rural areas) in the material record. Not all areas of the northern realm were affected in the same way by the Assyrian conquests and deportations. Areas in the northern Transjordan and in the Galilee were very hard hit by the western campaigns of the Assyrian king Tiglath-pileser III, but the areas in the region of Samaria (the reduced northern kingdom) were less severely affected by the western campaigns of Shalmaneser V and Sargon II in the late 8th century. There are notable signs of an elite Assyrian presence at several sites, but not of a complete cultural transformation in the land, witnessing to the presence of several new alien nations. My work concludes that of those who survived and remained in the land, the majority were Israelite. Significantly, then, portions of "the ten lost tribes" were never lost.

Analysis of the material remains allows for a fresh consideration of the literary remains. The third chapter closely examines the long Deuteronomistic commentaries found in Kings on demographic developments in northern Israel, following the northern exile (722 BCE) and the later interventions in the former northern kingdom by the late-7th-century monarch, Josiah of Judah (640–609 BCE). My study argues that the extensive Deuteronomistic commentary on the adjustments made by Assyrian state-sponsored immigrants in the northern territories (2 Kgs 17:24–41) shows multiple layers of composition and is polyvalent. On the surface, it posits radical upheaval and displacement—centuries of infidelity are followed by massive destruction, complete deportation, and the replacement of an indigenous Israelite population by imported foreign settlers from a variety of lands. The post-Assyrian-invasion residents of the region are thus distanced—literally and figuratively—from their Israelite forbears. But the authors also acknowledge that the new community was led in its religious functions by a repatriated Israelite priest and that the new cult observed by the immigrants replicates the old Israelite state cult in every important respect. Other voices in the text lambaste the northern inhabitants, but do so on the assumption that they are descendants of Jacob. In short, careful analysis of this text argues against simplistic readings. On one level, the writers argue for total discontinuity. On another level, they concede substantial continuity. Similar things can be said about Josiah's northern reforms (2 Kgs 23:15–20). On the surface, this rare southern intervention into northern affairs rectifies centuries of wrongdoing stretching back to the founding of the northern kingdom itself. On a more profound level, however, the very account of these reforms presumes that the inhabitants of the northern areas affected by Josiah's actions are fundamentally Israelite in character.

The fourth chapter of this study explores the implications of a series of neglected texts in Chronicles that posit a continuous northern Israelite presence in the land, despite the Assyrian deportations. The authors of Chronicles selectively employ a version of Samuel-Kings in their own writing, but creatively rewrite, rearrange, and supplement this older work with their own material (Knoppers 2004a). According to this alternate account of Israel's monarchic past, members of the northern tribes were familiar with ancestral traditions shared with the southern tribes, retained their tribal structures, enjoyed recourse to Yahwistic prophecy, worshiped the same deity as the Judahites did, and maintained contacts with their southern kin. Both groups were familiar with and were held accountable to the same historic standards. Given that the text of Chronicles, like Kings, was written in Judah, this shows both that the Judean community was hardly monolithic in character and that there were some in Judah who viewed the (Yahwistic) residents of Samaria as co-religionists, rather than as representatives of alien faiths.

Chapters 5–7 address Judean-Samarian relations during the Neo-Babylonian (626–539 BCE), Persian (538–332 BCE), Hellenistic (332–164 BCE), and Maccabean (164–63 BCE) periods. In discussing the history of Samaria and Yehud in the Achaemenid era, some scholars assumed that these two entities were substantially unlike one another. In fairness, there was until recently little hard evidence to go by, aside from scattered remarks made in various biblical writings and in the works of the 1st-century CE Jewish historian Josephus. It is now possible to make crucial progress on this front. Site surveys and available excavation reports show that Samaria had a substantially larger and more well-to-do population than Yehud did during the Neo-Babylonian and Persian periods (chapter 5). Some leading archaeologists estimate that the city of Samaria was one of the largest in Palestine during the Persian period. In other words, the province of Samaria was not an insignificant backdrop to Judah during the historical era under review.

Analysis of scripts, personal names on papyri, bullae, coins, and seals, cultic figurines (or the absence thereof), and bilingualism (the elite use of Hebrew alongside the Aramaic vernacular), shows many common cultural features, as well as some differences, between the two provinces during the Persian and Hellenistic periods. The same chapter engages one of the most recent archaeological discoveries pertaining to the relations between Judeans and Samarians. Over nineteen seasons of excavations at Mt. Gerizim (near Shechem) have revealed a monumental, well-built Samarian temple, dating to Hellenistic times, as well as a smaller sanctuary predating it, stemming from Persian times (mid-5th century onward). The new finds are extremely significant, because they indicate that the Jerusalem Temple had a Yahwistic rival to the north significantly earlier than most scholars had assumed, basing their reconstructions on the testimony of Josephus.

Chapter 6 returns to the literary evidence, focusing on the depiction of Samaria in the book of Ezra-Nehemiah. This chapter pays close attention to the stories about tensions and conflicts between the Jerusalemite authorities, in particular the governor Nehemiah, and the Samarian authorities, in particular the governor Sanballat. The stress found in Ezra-Nehemiah on the need to focus on Judah itself—rebuilding its institutions and its infrastructure—is quite important. The unabashedly and aggressively independent stance espoused by Nehemiah vis-à-vis Yehud's regional neighbors represents a new and influential development. The repeated references to "the Judeans" (היהודים), as opposed to "the children of Israel" (בני-ישראל) in the first-person accounts of Nehemiah is telling in this respect. The question is, however, whether Nehemiah's position should be privileged as historically representative of the entire Persian period. The larger picture needs to be kept in view. During the late 6th–4th centuries, the Achaemenid kings controlled a huge expanse of land, stretching from the border of India in the east to Egypt and the Mediterranean littoral in the west. The Achaemenid authorities encouraged trade, commerce, and travel among the far-flung realms they ruled. Many regions, including the Levant, benefited from international commerce.

Despite what some biblical scholars have claimed, no large-scale schism between Samarian Yahwists and Judean Yahwists can be traced to this era. Quite the contrary, the same work (Ezra-Nehemiah) acknowledges numerous contacts between Samarians and Judeans, especially between their elites. The pattern of intermarriage between the leading houses of Jerusalem and Samaria, condemned by Nehemiah, seems to have continued after he left office (so Josephus). Cooperation between Samarian and Jerusalemite leaders is documented in the Elephantine papyri (late 5th century BCE). In my judgment, the struggles depicted in Ezra-Nehemiah testify to internal Judean debates about identity, ethnicity, and nationality. The very definition of "Israel" becomes a contested topic in a world in which a number of communities, whether more narrowly or more broadly defined, claim to continue the legacy of the descendants of Jacob.

The book's penultimate chapter discusses both cooperation and increasing estrangement between Samaria and Judah during the Hellenistic and early Maccabean eras. It is important to acknowledge the 2nd and 1st centuries BCE as times of increasing distrust, tension, and conflict. The gradual rise in Maccabean control over Samaria, the Galilee, Idoumea, and areas of the Transjordan witnessed a recalibration of power relations in the southern Levant. If Samaria was a dominant regional power in the early Achaemenid period, Judah became a dominant regional power in the 2nd century BCE. For Yahwistic Samarians, the destruction of their temple and town on Mt. Gerizim in 111–110 BCE by the Maccabean leader John Hyrcanus was a signal event, leading to (or confirming) hostile relations.

Yet, if the 2nd and 1st centuries represent a period of increasing estrangement, the 4th and 3rd centuries represent, I argue, a much more complex situation. The traditional model of a continuous downward spiral in postmonarchic times construes relations between Samarians and Judeans too much in a binary fashion and ignores contrary evidence. There were likely more high-level contacts and occasions of cooperation between the two elites than many have acknowledged. In this respect, the publication of the Dead Sea Scrolls has afforded new insights into the editing and transmission of the Pentateuch, claimed by both Judeans and Samarians, in the last centuries BCE. Chapter 7 examines the text-critical evidence available from the Dead Sea Scrolls, the (Jewish) Masoretic text, the Septuagint (the ancient Greek translation of the Pentateuch), and the Samaritan Pentateuch to contest the view that the genesis of the Samaritan Pentateuch with its distinctive set of theological readings dates to early postmonarchic times. Rather, it may be argued with other scholars that the rise of a distinctive Samaritan Pentateuch occurred sometime in the 2nd and 1st centuries BCE. In short, both Judah and Samaria possessed versions of the Pentateuch in the Hellenistic age, although the text of the Pentateuch was not yet set in all of its details.

That Yahwistic Samarians and Judeans cherished a basic set of common sacred writings points to a history of at least intermittent cooperation between Judean and Samarian scribes over a considerable period of time prior to the Maccabean expansion. In other words, the appearance of a distinctive Samaritan Pentateuch points back to the existence of an older forbearer in earlier Hellenistic times. Members of each group could read basically the same scriptures with their own practices, beliefs, and institutions in view. But the later addition of a thin layer of sectarian readings in the Pentateuch of the Samarians and, to a lesser extent, the addition of the occasional reading in the Pentateuch of the Judeans in the 2nd and 1st centuries BCE effectively transformed the Pentateuch in both communities. What had previously functioned, albeit somewhat unusually, as a fundamental source of fraternal unity now became a fundamental source of division.

From this picture, it would be tempting to infer that the Roman era was one in which Samaritan-Jewish relations had deteriorated to the point of outright hatred, jealousy, factionalism, and absolute schism. Yet, as the Gospel story with which we began and other literary evidence suggests (chapter 8), such a sweeping historical conclusion would be too far-reaching. Even in Roman times, there are signs of occasional interaction, communications, and respect. Both groups developed similar religious symbols (menorahs, mezuzot), institutions (*miqva'ot*, synagogues), and literary genres, such as the Targum (Aramaic translations and paraphrases of the Scriptures). Such developments could be explained by the phenomenon of competitive emulation, but the practice of competitive emulation indicates a good knowledge of the very institutions that are being emulated and hence some substantial contacts between the parties in question. In this respect, ancient polemics mask some continuing interaction between the two communities.

At the end of this introduction, it is necessary to say a few things about the difficult issue of ethnic nomenclature. Readers will have noticed that I have been referring to Samarians (or Yahwistic Samarians) and Judeans, rather than to Samaritans and Jews in speaking of these two peoples during the Neo-Babylonian, Persian, and Hellenistic periods. There are a number of reasons for this. The periods under view predate the consolidation of classically distinctive Samaritan and Jewish identities. Hence, one must come to grips with multiple stages in the history and development of both groups. If one thinks, for example, of Samaritans as a particular people embracing a historical heritage in ancient Israel, a distinct set of scriptures (the Samaritan Pentateuch), the principles of monotheism and the unity of God, the firm belief that Moses was God's only designated prophet, the sanctity and centrality of Mt. Gerizim, and a day of vengeance and recompense, the designation "Samaritans" is largely anachronistic for the eras addressed by this book.[18]

Similar, but not identical, problems exist in employing the nomenclature "Jews" for the periods under view. As ethnographers remind us, *ethnē* (peoples) change over time in response both to internal developments and to external challenges. Indeed, the important indices by which a particular group defines itself may shift as a result of historical and social changes, including imperial impositions. In dealing with antiquity, scholars (e.g., Cohen 1999; Blenkinsopp 2009) have traced the gradual shift from a strong association of Judean identity with the land toward classifications of identity that are more associated with a particular way of life, an international presence, and religious practices. Yet this shift is affected by local conditions and does not occur uniformly in all geographic areas. In this respect, ethnic classifications attempt to capture complex, moving targets. If one thinks of "Jewish" as primarily an ethno-religious classification of

---

18. J. Macdonald 1964; Montgomery 1907; Gaster 1925; Egger 1986; Pummer 1987b, 2009; Macchi 1994a; Nodet 1997, 2011; Zsengellér 1998; Hjelm 2000; Faü and Crown 2001; Kartveit 2009; Dušek 2012a, 2012b.

someone who, among other things, embraces monotheism, the heritage of the Israelite people, an attachment to the ancestral land of Israel, the international identity of his/her people, and the Torah, Nevi'im, and Kethuvim (Tanakh, or Hebrew Bible), the Targums, the Mishnah, Tosefta, and the Talmud as the written sources of his/her identity, the ethnicon is anachronistic for the periods under view. Hence, we prefer the term Judean for the Neo-Babylonian, Persian, and Hellenistic periods.

There are other problems with the "Samaritan" designation. The name given to a people may reflect an insider (emic) viewpoint, or it may be one assigned to that people by others (an etic classification). However much the members of a particular group may resist, their group identity may be profoundly affected by external forces, such as foreign invasions, wars, forced migrations, military service, taxes, and regulations. In the case of the people in question, the title "Samaritans" is basically one that non-Samaritans gave to this group. The terminology is based on the rare usage *hā-šōmĕrōnîm*, "the Samarians," appearing in 2 Kgs 17:29, translated in the Greek Septuagint (LXX) as οἱ Σαμαρεῖται, "the Samaritans."[19] As such, the term is basically geographical in orientation. Yet *šōmĕrōnîm*—in this, the one and only case in which the ethnicon appears in the Hebrew Bible—ironically refers to the residents of the area of Samaria prior to the time of the northern exile. It does not refer, as is often thought, to the foreign immigrants, whom the Assyrian authorities imported into the land. Similar usage can be found in the primary textual witnesses to 2 Kgs 18:11. In summarizing the collapse of the northern kingdom, the Hebrew reads: "The Assyrian king exiled Israel (את־ישראל) to Assyria." In this passage in the Septuagint, the Greek translator renders his Hebrew source (which may not have been identical to the Masoretic text) as "The Assyrian king exiled the Samarians (τὴν Σαμάρειαν) to Assyria." It is clear, then, that "the Samarians" in LXX 2 Kgs 18:11 refers to the Israelites who remained in the reduced kingdom of Israel/Samaria prior to its final downfall and dislocation.

The designation "Samaritans" is largely shunned by the Samaritans, who prefer to call themselves northern Israelites, the "community of the Samarians" (עדת השומרים), "the Samarian Israelites" (בני ישראל השמרים; Pummer 2002: 6–7), or the "community of the Samarian Israelites" (עדת בני ישראל השמרים).[20]

---

19. To complicate matters, earlier in Kings, the city name *šōmĕrōn* ("Samaria") is tied to *šemer* ("Shemer"), the original owner of the site (1 Kgs 16:24).
20. The title "the "community of the Samarians" (עדת השומרים) is popular in the late Samaritan Chronicle of Adler-Séligsohn, e.g., 1210 [28 3309]; 1213 [36 3544]; 1217 [35 3772], while the titles "Samarian Israelites" (בני ישראל השמרים) and the "community of the Samarian

Or, playing on the Hebrew root *šāmar* שמר), "to guard, keep, observe," they refer to themselves as *šāmĕrîm*, "guardians" (= שמרים), that is, guardians of the Torah.[21]

There is another drawback in employing "Samaritans" for the ethno-religious people under view. As Dušek (2012a: 71) points out, the term "Samaritan" (Σαμαρίτης) technically refers to a citizen of the 3rd-century BCE Seleucid province of Samaritis (Σαμαρῖτις). Such precise usage is certainly appropriate for residents of this administrative district during the Seleucid period, but the title does not differentiate between Yahwistic and non-Yahwistic residents of this geopolitical entity.

The issue of appropriate terminology is difficult, but I am referring to the residents of Yehud and Samerina (Samaria) during the Neo-Babylonian, Persian, and Hellenistic periods as Judeans and Samarians to distinguish them from the later Jews and Samaritans of the later Roman period. In both cases, one can see lines of continuity from one period to the next. Some distinguish between general residents of the district of Samaria, called Samarians, and those specific residents of Samaria who worshiped Yhwh, called proto-Samaritans. Calling for some such distinction is warranted, because it is clear that at least from the Hellenistic period onwards many residents in the capital city of Samaria were Macedonian immigrants and, therefore, non-Yahwistic in religious orientation.[22] I prefer

---

Israelites" (עדת בני ישראל השמרים) are popular in another late Samaritan Chronicle, e.g., Macdonald II.69 [C.A*], 70 [G*.12], 71 [E.C*], 85 [H.H*], 85 [I.C.7; D.12]; 87 [J.D*], 88 [L.G.*], 89 [M.M*], 91 [N.K*].

21. Within antiquity, this usage of שמרים is acknowledged already by Origen (*Comm. in. Joh.* 20.35.312; *Hom. in Ezek.* 9.1). See also Eusebius (*Chron.* 2.ann.1270), Jerome (*Comm. in Isaiam* 21.11.12; *Comm. in Ezek.* 16.8c.9; *Epist.* 45.6; 46; 75 [*Subscriptio*]; 108.12); *De nominus Hebraicis* 66.3; Epiphanius (φύλακες; *Haer.* 9.1); *b. Ḥul.* 6a (Pummer 2002: 7–8, 123, 188–89; 2009: 4–7). There may be a much earlier allusion in late biblical lore (noted but not developed by Montgomery 1907: 318). In the Chronistic depiction of the dual monarchies, King Abijah of Judah pointedly announces to his northern counterparts and enemy in battle, "Jeroboam and all Israel": "Indeed, we are observing (שמרים אנחנו) the charge (את־משמרת) of Yhwh our God" (2 Chr 13:11). It would seem that Chronicles is punning on a traditional self-designation of the Samarians, insisting that the southern Israelites, and not the northern Israelites, are properly keeping the responsibilities Yhwh entrusted to his people. One could object that the postexilic text is coincidentally referring to general piety, but Abijah's signal speech (2 Chr 13:4–11) is filled with detailed references to Judahite cultic practices, corresponding to Pentateuchal (mostly Priestly) precedent. The same oration details how the northern Israelites are departing from such authoritative precedents (Knoppers 2005). When God is the object of *mišmeret*, the reference is normally to keeping divine commandments and, by implication, guarding against violations (Gen 26:5; Lev 8:35; 18:30; 22:9; Num 9:19, 23; 18:7–8; Deut 11:1; Josh 22:3; 1 Kgs 2:3; Neh 12:45; Ezek 44:16; 48:11; Zech 3:7; Mal 3:14; 2 Chr 13:11; 23:6; Milgrom, Harper, and Fabry 1998).

22. It is doubtful, of course, whether all residents of Judah in the Neo-Babylonian, Persian, and Hellenistic periods were Yahwistic Judeans, but this matter cannot be pursued here.

the terminology Yahwistic Samarians over against proto-Samaritans, not only because it circumvents the erroneous assumption that Yhwh worship was a relatively late development or arrival in Samaria, but also because it avoids terminology that the people in question themselves largely eschew.

To be sure, traditional usage dies hard. Adopting one nomenclature and completely ignoring others is impossible, because the usage of Samaritan and Jew is longstanding and pervasive both in popular and in scholarly parlance (and hence is retained in the title of this book). Moreover, in referring to the work of scholars who employ the traditional terminology, one has to respect such usage and quote this work according to the customs it follows. Readers will thus find multiple designations appearing in this book, but I shall attempt to clarify in my citations of other scholars whether the references pertain to earlier (Samarian, Judean) periods or to later (Samaritan, Jew) periods in the histories of Judah and Samaria.

Engaged with previous scholarship and bringing to bear new material and literary evidence, this book offers a new understanding of the history, identity, and relationship of Samaritans and Jews. While the focus has traditionally been on the "ten lost tribes" and on long-held antagonisms between Jews and Samaritans, close examination of a wider array of evidence reveals important continuities and convergences between Judeans and Samarians in the ancient world. Departing from the oppositional framework governing older interpretations, the new more complex and shifting picture forces us to reassess theories of the "ten lost tribes" and of the "empty land" and to reconfigure our sense of identity, religion, and ethnicity in the ancient world with implications even for contemporary times. To this "lost history" of Samaritans and Jews we now turn.

2

The Fall of the Northern Kingdom and the Ten Lost Tribes

A Reevaluation

THE OPENING NARRATIVE of 2 Kings 17 presents the fall of the kingdom of Israel briefly, but with a sense of finality. After Israel's last king, Hoshea, had broken his pact with Assyria by withholding tribute and sending emissaries to the king of Egypt, the Assyrian king captured Hoshea and imprisoned him. The Assyrian monarch later moved against the heart of the Israelite state itself.

> The Assyrian king came up against the whole land and came up against Samaria, besieging it for three years. In the ninth year of Hoshea's reign, the Assyrian king captured Samaria and exiled Israel to Assyria. He settled them in Halah, by the [River] Habur, [by] the River Gozan, and [among] the cities of the Medes. (2 Kgs 17:5–6)

These definitive statements conclude the coverage of the northern kingdom. If the chapter's opening narrative depicts watershed events rather laconically, the Deuteronomistic commentary that follows is anything but laconic. The writers denounce the northern kingdom in considerable detail, attributing its demise to the repeated failure of its monarchs and people to depart from the influential cultic policies established by their founding king—Jeroboam I—centuries earlier (2 Kgs 17:7–23). The text goes on to speak of the Assyrian-sponsored importation of new settlers, drawn from other parts of the Assyrian empire, into the territories once occupied by northern Israel (2 Kgs 17:24–41). The result is a land completely transformed—depleted of Israelites and filled with foreign immigrants.

Although most scholars recognize the accusations leveled at the Israelites in 2 Kings 17 as Deuteronomistic propaganda, many have nonetheless accepted the basic picture of a radical metamorphosis in the land. In this reconstruction, the defeat, destruction, and dislocation associated with the Assyrian western campaigns were nothing short of catastrophic. What occurred after Israel's fall marked both an end and a new beginning. The state's ruination coupled with the people's deportation brought northern Israel to a tragic end. The division of the former kingdom into a number of different Assyrian provinces coupled with the importation of peoples from other lands profoundly changed the land's ethnic and political character.[1]

In many treatments, the origin of the Samaritans is to be found here. The Samaritan people are said to be the offspring of the foreign settlers imported into the former northern kingdom by a succession of Assyrian monarchs. Some early Jewish texts speak of the Samaritans as Cutheans, that is, as descendants of one of the five groups of foreign colonists who settled in the territories vacated by the banished Israelites.[2] However much it is recognized to be tendentious, the Deuteronomistic version of events has held sway over a range of early and modern interpreters. Accordingly, most histories of ancient Israel terminate their coverage of northern Israel with the Assyrian exile. The late 8th century BCE marks the terminus of attention paid to Samaria's history until the Persian period (538–332 BCE), when the interaction of Nehemiah and others in Yehud with leading figures in Samaria, such as Sanballat, rekindles an interest among scholars in north-south relations.

Yet it is debatable whether this broad consensus on the effects of Israel's demise is warranted. One may begin with the Deuteronomistic picture of the northern kingdom's fall. If this text and others in Kings are theological reflections to be dated to later times, how reliable are they for reconstructing detailed events in the 8th century? Presenting both the Assyrian exile of the late 8th century and the Judahite exile of the early 6th century as completely devastating creates, ironically, a direct parallel between them. Over the course of less than 200 years, all of the Israelite tribes were forced to exit the land. But many questions have been raised about whether the picture of an "empty land" in Judah depicted at the end of Kings reflects actual historical reality.[3] Material evidence attests to not only tremendous

---

1. E.g., Orlinsky 1960: 86–87; Donner 1977: 434; 1986: 311–16; Bright 1981: 275–76; Herrmann 1981: 250–52; Ahlström 1993: 665–80; Kuhrt 1995: 2.468–69.
2. Hjelm (2000) and Kartveit (2009) provide references and a detailed overview of recent discussions.
3. E.g., Carroll 1992, 2001; Barstad 1996, 2003; Grabbe 2000, 2004; Kiefer 2005; Lipschits 2005, 2011; Middlemas 2005.

destruction but also some continuity of occupation in certain areas, such as the Benjamin region. Should not similar sorts of questions be raised about the northern kingdom's collapse? Was there no postexilic Israel?

Drawing parallels between the demise of Israel and that of Judah 135 years later raises its own set of issues. Should the Assyrian campaigns and the Babylonian campaigns be viewed as comparable? Were there not important differences between them? In the last three decades much archaeological work has been carried out in Syria-Palestine. Does this attention to the material remains confirm a cataclysmic end for the ten northern tribes? What does one make of the testimony of the Samaritans themselves? In their literature, they claim Israelite status as descendants of Joseph (the tribes of Ephraim and Manasseh) and Levi (Dexinger 1992; Hjelm 2000: 76–103; Kartveit 2009). These Samaritan documents date to much later times, but what should one make of their claims?

In this chapter, I would like to revisit the archaeological and epigraphic evidence relating to northern Israel's demise. As we shall see, the general use of this evidence to assert Israel's disappearance from the land is questionable. We shall also examine the minority of scholarly opinion, which contends that the upheaval caused by the Assyrian conquests was temporary and localized to major urban centers. The Assyrian exile purportedly affected only a small portion of society—the elite. My concern in what follows is not with particular matters such as whether Shalmaneser V or Sargon II was primarily responsible for the capture of Samaria.[4] Rather, my interest lies with the overall nature, goals, and results of the Assyrian campaigns. To what extent do we find discontinuity or continuity? Having summarized the traditional case for utter devastation and forced population exchange, I shall bring to the fore some additional material evidence not hitherto addressed. As we shall see, the prevailing theory commendably attempts to engage the archaeological and epigraphic remains in a comprehensive way, yet it does so to reach a largely foregone conclusion that conforms to the testimony of one influential biblical text. In spite of its popularity, the cultural exchange hypothesis oversimplifies matters and exhibits debilitating flaws. The history of the late 8th century is not simply one of destruction and dislocation, but also of survival and cultural continuity.

---

4. Timm (1989–90) and Tappy (2007) provide useful analyses of the relevant material and epigraphic remains.

I. The Case for Devastation and Massive Bidirectional Deportations

To assert that a people was forced to leave its land for a variety of foreign destinations only to be replaced by a variety of foreign peoples, who were themselves forced to leave their lands, is a tremendous claim to make. The dominant maximalist theory follows 2 Kings 17 (or one portion thereof) closely in positing a massive case of population exchange.[5] Yet it involves more than biblical evidence, engaging epigraphic remains, Assyrian reliefs, the Babylonian Chronicle, and various sorts of archaeological evidence. Assuming a strong link between statehood and ethnic identity, commentators speak of a series of devastating blows to the infrastructure of the Israelite state. For the sake of convenience, we may trace four major events said cumulatively to have sealed Israel's fate.

The first major event was the western campaign of Tiglath-pileser III (744–727 BCE) in 733–732 BCE that resulted in the defeat of the House of Omri, the loss of territory, and the destruction of many towns in the Galilee, the northern Transjordan, and the northern coastal region (2 Kgs 15:19, 29; 16:5–9; cf. 1 Chr 5:6, 25–26; H. Tadmor 1999). The Assyrian king boasts, "The land of the house of Omri […its] auxillary army […] all of its people […] I carried off [to] Assyria" (H. Tadmor 1994a, Summ. 4.15´b–17´a). According to 2 Kgs 15:29, Tiglath-pileser destroyed a series of sites in upper Galilee: Ijon, Abel Beth-Maachah, Janoah, Kedesh, and Hazor.[6] The Annals of Tiglath-pileser speak of the conquest of towns in lower Galilee: Hinatuna, Yatbite, Aruma, and Marum.[7] Another Assyrian source may allude to the conquest of the towns of Gilead and Abel Shitim, although both of these readings are contested.[8] Stern (2001: 7) speaks of a "generalized destruction to all settlements." His recent work (2001: 7, 9, 50) lists the following sites as razed during this time: Dan,

---

5. On the tensions and strains within 2 Kgs 17:24–41, see the following chapter.
6. There is reason to believe that by the time the Assyrian king reached these sites, they had already long passed from Israelite to Aramean control (Miller and Hayes 2006: 380–83; Na'aman 1995b). The biblical text is somewhat ambiguous at this point, but it seems that it presents the sites' conquest to indicate Israel's ongoing decline.
7. Cf. Josh 11:1, 5; 19:14; 2 Kgs 21:19; 23:26. Some of the names in the Annals are uncertain due to the fragmentary condition of the inscriptions (H. Tadmor 1994a, Ann. 18.3´–13´; 24.3´–10´; Na'aman 1995c).
8. Probably one of Tiglath-pileser III's Summary Inscriptions (Younger 2000c: 288). On "the city of Gil[ead]," see H. Tadmor 1994a, Summ. 9.3´. Regarding fragmentary "Abil […]," Tadmor argues for restoring Abel-Shitim, rather than Abel Beit-Maachah (1994a, Summ. 4.6´). For another view (Abila), see Oded 1997: 110.

Hazor, Chinnereth, Bethsaida, Tel Hadar, ʿEn Gev, Beth Shean, Kedesh, Megiddo, Yoqneʿam, Qiri, Akko, Keisan, Shiqmona, and Dor.[9] Some settlements were purportedly abandoned and did not recover for many years: Bethsaida, Tel Hadar, Kedesh, Beth Shean, and ʿEn Gev (Stern 2001: 7).

Conquest in war is one thing, but enforced population displacement is quite another. According to the prevailing hypothesis, a second blow to the Israelite state came in the form of unidirectional extraditions enforced by Tiglath-pileser, who practiced "deportation on an unprecedented scale" (Cogan and Tadmor 1988: 177). Second Kings 15:29 claims that "he came and took (*wayyiqaḥ*)...Galilee, Gilead, and all of the land of Naphtali and exiled them (*wayyiglēm*) to Assyria."[10] The Assyrian king's annals mention the mass deportation of 13,520 prisoners taken from the towns of lower Galilee (H. Tadmor 1994a, Ann. 24.13′). This disastrous scenario, drawn mostly from written sources, may be supplemented by recourse to the material remains. The swath of destruction was particularly severe in the regions of Galilee and the northern Transjordan. Gal (1992) conducted a decade-long survey of the lower Galilee region. Based on his field survey and study of individual sites, he concludes that the peak occupation of this region occurred in the 10th century BCE and that a large gap in occupation began in the late 8th century.[11] The lower Galilee was practically abandoned and Tel Qarnei Hittin and Tel Hannathon were destroyed.[12] Stern (2001: 7, 46–47) speaks of a similar occupation gap for sites in upper Galilee (e.g., Tel Chinnereth, ʿEn Gev, Tel Hadar).[13] Yet one of these sites—Tel Chinnereth—witnesses some rebuilding and resettlement during the Iron II period.[14] Other sites that seem to have survived without destruction

---

9. Whether all of the sites should appear in this list is another matter. See further below. Perhaps to be added to his list are Kh. Marjameh, Tell er-Rumeith (= Ramoth-gilead), and Tell Rehov.
10. "Galilee" and "Gilead" are likely later additions (Würthwein 1984: 383; Cogan and Tadmor 1988: 174). For a different view, see Galil 2000.
11. But the destruction of Ḥorvat Rosh Zayit and Tel Gath-Ḥepher has been dated to the early or mid-9th century (Gal 1992: 36–53; Gal and Alexandre 2000: 198–201), rather than at a later time.
12. Tel Mador (Kh. Abu Mudawer ʿI'blin) is sometimes mentioned in this context. The site was destroyed and not reoccupied until the Persian period (mid-6th to mid-5th century). The remains suggest that new settlers stemming from the west, most likely the Phoenician coastal plain, began to occupy these rural areas. But the time of abandonment was the mid-9th century, not the late 8th century (Gal 1992: 41).
13. At Hazor, Stratum IV (late 8th century) represents an unfortified settlement, while Strata III–I represent a series of Assyrian (citadel and palace), Persian, and Hellenistic citadels. If the remains from Area M (on the slope) belong to this late layer, Stratum IV was more substantial than earlier believed (Ben-Tor 2008: 1775).
14. After the late-8th-century destruction of Tel Chinnereth, part of the town (in the northwest corner) was rebuilt (Stratum I), perhaps to serve as a local or secondary Assyrian

include Tel Par, Rosh Ha'ayin, 'En Ḥaggit, and Ḥorvat Eli (Wolff 2008; Bloch-Smith 2009: 37). But these were all relatively small settlements.

If Tiglath-pileser did indeed deport 13,520 prisoners from northern Palestine, this may have represented much of the 8th-century population of the region. Gal's survey (1992: 109) of the region intimates that less than 18,000 people resided here during the early 8th century BCE. Broshi and Finkelstein's figure (1992: 50) for lower Galilee is higher: 22,500. Unfortunately, such demographic estimates are only guesses, so it is impossible to be sure about how many people were left behind. What one can say, based on archaeological studies, is that the Assyrian campaigns caused devastation and severe depopulation in the region.

The third major blow to Israel adduced in the maximalist view was the capture of Samaria itself, presumably by Shalmaneser V (727–722/721 BCE) in 722/721 BCE after a two- or three-year siege (2 Kgs 17:1–5; 18:10).[15] Shalmaneser died in 722/721 BCE, but in 720 BCE a new insurrection developed involving the cities of Ḥamath, Arpad, Ṣamirra, Damascus, Ḥatarikka, and Samaria and the new Assyrian king Sargon II marched west to end it.[16] Sargon apparently recaptured Samaria, and he (or his predecessor Shalmaneser) conquered a number of major sites.[17] Over the latter course of his reign (722/21–705 BCE), Sargon also implemented a series of bidirectional deportations. This policy of forced population exchange represented a fourth blow to Samaria (Na'aman and Zadok 1988; Na'aman 1993). In Nimrud Prisms D and E, we read:

> 4.25–41. [The inhabitants of Sa]merina, who agreed [and plotted] with a king [hostile to] me, not to render service and not to bring tribute [to Aššur] and who did battle, I fought against them with

---

administrative center (Building 737; Dubovský 2006: 215–16). Fritz (2008) thinks that the site was abandoned ca. 700 BCE, but Knauf (2003) contends that Stratum I continued for some time. There is some confusion in scholarly references to Tel Chinnereth (Kinneret). For the sake of clarity, I am referring to the site as Chinnereth (Tell el-'Oreimeh), on the western shore of the Sea of Galilee. In speaking of Kinneret(h), some scholars mean a very small archaeological site near Kibbutz Kinneret (B. Mazar 1993).

15. There are no inscriptions surviving from his reign. The Babylonian Chronicle (I i.27–28) may allude to a two-year siege resulting in the taking of Samaria, but the city itself is not explicitly mentioned (Grayson 1975: 73). Second Kings 17:5 mentions a three-year siege.

16. H. Tadmor 1958; Timm 1989–90; Fuchs 1994, 2.3:23–24; Younger 1999: 71–73, 2003a.

17. Second Kings 17:5 and 6a may telescope two discrete events (Cogan and Tadmor 1988: 200). Cogan and Tadmor think that the capture of Samaria is to be credited to Shalmaneser, while the exile is to be credited to Sargon II. Na'aman (1990) holds that the conquest of Samaria is to be credited simply to Sargon II. Younger (1999) and Tappy (2007) provide helpful overviews.

the might of the great gods, my lords. I counted 27,280 people as spoil, together with their chariots, and (the) gods in which they trusted. I formed a unit with 200 of [their] chariots for my royal force. I settled the rest of them in the midst of Assyria. (Gadd 1954: 197–80, pls. xlv–xlvi)[18]

This text is interesting not only because it speaks of triumph and the capture of a very large number of prisoners, but also because it speaks of the integration of a Samarian chariot contingent into the conqueror's army (Dalley 1985). We shall return to this matter later.

In the maximalist theory, the interventions of Sargon II represented the undoing of the northern kingdom, because his deportation of Israel's inhabitants and the import of foreign peoples drawn from other sectors of the Assyrian empire are said to have resulted in a comprehensive demographic and religious transformation (2 Kgs 17:5b–41; 18:9–12; 18:31–32// Isa. 36:16–17). Here, archaeological evidence is employed to buttress certain biblical claims. Kings mentions that the peoples entering the land brought along their own gods and cultural customs (2 Kgs 17:24–41). This picture of intrusive foreign religious elements has proved influential: "The religious pollution of Israel symbolizes, perhaps more than anything else, its final fall" (T. C. Mitchell 1991: 344).

Although drawn primarily from written sources, the maximalist portrait of widespread destruction and upheaval has been supplemented by studies of the material remains. The Assyrian conquests have been cited to explain late 8th century destruction layers at many sites (e.g., A. Mazar 1990: 544–47; Stern 2001: 3–41). According to Stern (2001: 7–9, 49–50), the "total destruction" of the region of Samaria is reflected in excavations and surveys conducted at Taʿanach, Dothan, the city of Samaria, Tell el-Farʿah (North), Gezer, Shechem, and Bethel.[19] Looking further afield within the Levant, Assyrian reliefs depict the conquest of Ashtaroth, Ekron, Gibbethon, Gezer, Lachish, and Raphia (Franklin 1994).[20] Creating lists of sites serves more than archival purposes. The compilations of destroyed or abandoned settlements are said to demonstrate a larger point, namely, that the Assyrian campaigns were thoroughgoing and

---

18. My translation basically follows that of Younger (2000b: 295).
19. But the settlement history of Bethel in the Iron II–III era is under new scrutiny, significantly complicating the older reconstruction (see further below).
20. In the case of Gezer, a cuneiform tablet evinces a "battlefield sketch," showing the Assyrian attack on one of its city gates (Dever 2007: 86).

ruinous to Israel's infrastructure. The long process of repopulation begins under Sargon II and is said to continue under Sennacherib, Esarhaddon, and Ashurbanipal.[21]

In brief, the claims of a major population exchange in Kings are aligned with a maximal reading of destruction in the archaeological evidence to contend that the Assyrians created havoc within the Levant. To be sure, those holding to the cultural exchange theory would not assert that all Israelites exited the land. All acknowledge that some Israelites survived, but they claim that the population exchanges sponsored by the Assyrians were so massive and thorough to alter the character of the local population: "It seems that as a result of this bi-directional movement of the deportees, great changes occurred in the ethnic composition of the population during the Assyrian domination of Megiddo and Samaria" (Stern 2001: 43). There are thus two essential components in the dominant interpretation. One is the pervasive damage caused by the invasions of Tiglath-pileser III, Shalmaneser V, and Sargon II, while the second is the transformative effects of the Assyrian unidirectional and bidirectional deportations. One of the two components would not be enough by itself to sustain the thesis. Indeed, the argument is cumulative in its application. The damage resulted from the actions of more than one king. The effect of Assyrian onslaughts was to refashion the demographic, ethnic, and religious landscape of Israel in the course of just a few generations.

Information about the post-720 BCE phase of Samarian history is not easy to come by, but scholars have pointed to some bits of evidence to buttress their claim for fundamental discontinuity. During and after the Assyrian campaigns, the former northern kingdom was divided into different administrative districts. Two of the regional capitals were located in Megiddo and Samaria. The names of at least some of the Assyrian governors of Megiddo and Samaria are known (Cross 1998). Some have argued for the existence of other administrative districts in Dor and Gilead.[22] Whatever the case, the argument is that the dismantling of the northern kingdom and its replacement by a system of Assyrian

---

21. The book of Ezra alludes to Assyrian-sponsored immigrations during the reigns of Esarhaddon (*ēsar ḥaddōn*; Ezra 4:2) and Ashurbanipal (*'osnappar*; Ezra 4:10). In both cases, however, the immigrants were located in a variety of areas (and not only in Samaria).
22. Some have argued against the proposition that Gilead constituted a separate province (e.g., Younger 1998: 205). The case for Dor's provincial status is clearer (Stern 1994a: 131–45; Na'aman 2009b).

provinces destroyed distinctive Israelite elements within the land. As an Assyrian province, Samaria's territorial reach extended over only a fraction of the former northern kingdom. Assyrian influence is reflected in Assyrian-type palaces, residencies, cuneiform inscriptions, seals, pottery, and metal artifacts (Barkay 1992: 351–53; Na'aman and Zadok 1988, 2000). The import of settlers, specifically Arabian settlers, is mentioned in Sargon's annals (M. Tadmor 1983: 5; Younger 1998: 226–27; 2000a: 293; 2003b). There may be some evidence that the very understanding of who a Samarian was could vary, depending on the situation. In this context, the publication of some nonliterary Assyrian documents from Samaria and Gezer may be relevant. In these texts, written during the post-720 BCE period in Akkadian and Aramaic, "Samarian" can carry more than one connotation (Eph'al 1991: 41; Kelle 2002). When taken together, the material and literary remains seem to buttress the view of a wholesale cultural metamorphosis in northern Israel during the 8th century.

II. Questioning the Consensus

The predominant theory of massive destruction and major bidirectional deportations has not gone uncontested, but the number of scholars questioning the consensus is small. Nevertheless, the arguments of the minority minimalist position merit closer attention than they have received. Much of their case is presented by citing literary, chiefly biblical, evidence. Some attention, mostly negative, has also been given to the archaeological and epigraphic evidence. In the minority view, the damage caused by the Assyrian invasions was of limited duration and concentrated in major urban centers. One aspect of the minimalist theory involves taking issue with the Assyrian versions of western conquest. The number of 27,280 (or 27,290) northern exiles during the time of Sargon II is said to be an exaggeration, an example of literary hyperbole (Schur 1989: 20). Rather, the countryside was largely left untouched by the Assyrian invasions, and "the overwhelming majority of the population" remained in the land (Coggins 1975: 18; Schur 1989: 21). Demographically speaking, the Assyrian exile primarily affected the elite of society (Schur 1989: 20). In the opinion of Coggins (1975: 17), the group of northern exiles only amounted to somewhere between 3 and 4 percent of the total population. Hence, the effects of the Assyrian conquests were hardly as revolutionary as one would make out from the biblical and Assyrian accounts.

The importation of foreign settlers by Sargon II is not denied, but is said to be concentrated in the city of Samaria itself (Schur 1989: 21–23). In Schur's treatment, this datum mitigates the prospect of a demographic transformation in the region as a whole, because the foreign immigrants are said to be located primarily in one location. Coggins (1975: 18–20) offers, however, a more nuanced view. While not arguing that the foreign settlers were all confined to one area, he disputes that foreign settlers mixed with native Israelites to form a new amalgam and syncretistic religion. Yahwists were able to conduct an independent religious life within Samaria. In this respect, Coggins's view recalls that of Alt (1953a; 1953b), who contended that the communities established by the landed immigrants were largely separate from those of the surviving northern Israelites and remained so for centuries. The former consisted of the imported elite, while the latter consisted of the lower classes left in the land. The former was much more powerful politically than the latter, but the latter managed to maintain its own distinctive cultural profile.

Scholars in the minority camp have focused much of their attention on the testimony of various biblical writings. The Kings account is said to be partisan, a clear case of special pleading by Judahite authors eager to denounce the northern kingdom and its many failings. Judging the Kings account as biased and tendentious, they offer counterevidence from other biblical texts as germane to the larger discussion. One is the testimony provided by the author of Chronicles, who posits continuous inhabitation of the land by remnants of the northern tribes, in spite of the Assyrian exile.[23] Another is the testimony provided by the major prophets, all but ignored by those adhering to the cultural exchange model. As Coggins (1975: 28–37; cf. Schur 1989: 23) well points out, these prophetic texts all stem from Judah, but they continue to speak of Israel as a larger tribal entity. The prophetic writings associated with Jeremiah and Ezekiel (early 6th century) repeatedly refer to specific northern Israelite sodalities. They make no mention of strange peoples having displaced the ten northern tribes. They may express sorrow over the fate of Israel and denounce its shortcomings, but they do not speak of the Israelites as having all departed the land, become contaminated by alien blood, or come to naught. On the contrary, some express aspirations for the reunification

---

23. Myers 1965: 176; Coggins 1975: 19–22; Japhet 1989; Williamson 1977b; Cogan 1988; Willi 1995. See further chapter 4.

of north and south (Knoppers 2011b). These authors would not express sentiments expressing a desire for reunification if a whole series of tribes had already been eliminated and no longer existed.

To sum up, the minority (minimalist) theory holds that the long-term effects of the Assyrian invasions were not nearly as radical as the (maximalist) population exchange theory asserts. The Assyrian policy of bidirectional deportations affected only Israel's elite. In spite of military damage and political upheaval, the vast majority of Israelites continued to live within their territories and practice their traditional religion. The presence of Assyrian-sponsored colonists is not denied, but the arrival of these newcomers is said to have had little or no effect on the lives of average Israelites.

III. The Case for a Reduced Israelite Presence in the Region of Samaria

In presenting my own position, I shall be taking issue with some aspects of both of the aforementioned theories. It may be helpful to begin with some remarks about the minority hypothesis. The Deuteronomistic commentary on Israel's fall reveals much about what a series of biblical writers thought about the fate of the northern tribes, but the presuppositions and aims of these writers warrant closer scrutiny.[24] The cessation of coverage for the northern tribes in Kings following the collapse of the northern realm reflects a literary and theological decision on the part of the biblical authors and, as such, cannot do justice to the actual situation in the north following the Assyrian campaigns. Similarly, the points made by Coggins about the prophetic texts in the Hebrew Bible are well taken. If these writers thought that the northern tribes were entirely defunct and no longer had any tangible presence in the land, they do not say so. As we have seen, those scholars holding to the minority (minimalist) theory (section II above) point out that the prophets largely do not assert that a variety of foreign peoples replaced the ten northern tribes in the land. Prophetic works, such as Jeremiah and Ezekiel, acknowledge, of course, past catastrophes and hardly speak with one voice about the configuration of Israel's restoration, but they do portray a pan-Israelite restoration.

---

24. Coggins (1975: 14–15) stresses that neither the authors of 2 Kgs 17:7–23 nor the authors of 2 Kgs 17:24–41 evince any anti-Samaritan bias, even though the former lambaste the northern kingdom and the latter decry the revitalization of the Bethel cultus.

Similarly, Coggins's brief discussion of Chronicles is on the mark. The Chronistic writing, often neglected in this context, asserts that a remnant survived the Assyrian onslaughts and remained in the land. These northern Israelites retained familiarity with their own traditions and maintained their long-established tribal structure. Such insights may be developed and extended (chapter 4). Additional linguistic and literary evidence buttresses points made by those holding that the Assyrian campaigns did not have utterly transformative effects in northern Israel. The case for the survival and development of northern Hebrew as a distinct dialect into the Persian period has been argued largely on the basis of linguistic evidence found within the Hebrew scriptures (e.g., Ginsberg 1982; Rendsburg 1991b). The continuation of this dialect, sometimes called Israelian Hebrew, would be highly unlikely if there were no longer any northern Israelite presence in the land. Scholars have long thought that some poems and stories in other biblical books, such as Genesis, Deuteronomy, Joshua, Judges, Hosea, and Psalms, originally stemmed from northern Israel before they were reworked and (re) edited in their new literary frameworks.[25] It could be countered that such a literary transmission must have occurred fairly early, when the northern kingdom collapsed and some northern refugees streamed south into Judah.[26] Certainly, such a process in the mid- to late 8th century is quite plausible, given the upheaval and devastation caused by the Assyrian invasions, but it hardly seems likely that the process of literary transmission accompanying such a demographic shift was a one-off phenomenon. Rather, the literary and linguistic diversity inherent in these literary works, dating to different times, makes it more likely that the process of northern Israelite and Judahite communications continued in later centuries. Indeed, there is material evidence to suggest that when the areas of the southern Levant (Samaria, Judah, and neighboring areas) were all under Assyrian control in the 7th century, contacts and trade increased (e.g., Zimhoni 1990).

Some of the arguments made in minimalist proposals about the material remains are, however, less tenable. It is too strong a generalization to say that the Assyrian exile affected only the elite, a tiny portion (3–4 percent) of the total population. To be sure, the Assyrian policies

---

25. E.g., Burney 1918; Alt 1953b; Otto 1979; Ginsberg 1982; Rendsburg 1990, 2002; Knauf 1994; Brettler 2002; Rofé 2002; Schorch 2011.
26. Broshi 1974; Finkelstein 2008b. For a counterargument, see Na'aman 2009a.

of population exchange targeted the upper crusts of subject societies, but the policies were not limited to skilled artisans, military personnel, and native leaders. Under Shalmaneser III, Tiglath-pileser III, Sargon II, and (especially) Sennacherib, the Assyrians claim to have deported hundreds of thousands of people (Oded 1979: 20; Limet 1995). All told, the various Assyrian monarchs may have forcibly displaced some 1.2 million people during the course of their empire.[27] Whole communities were dislocated (Oded 1995: 209–212). Assertions about forced migrations affecting only a small part of the population are predicated on inflated and outmoded population estimates for the northern kingdom in the 8th century. De Vaux (1965: 66), for example, spoke of there being 800,000 Israelites in the land during the 8th century. More recent estimates, informed by the results of archaeological site surveys, have drastically reduced such high numbers (e.g., Broshi and Finkelstein 1992: 47–60; Na'aman 1993). The assertion of Sargon II that he made Samaria more populous than it was before, if this is indeed what he claims, may be a hyperbole.[28] With one possible exception, the Assyrians do not seem to have undertaken any major construction at the site (Tappy 2001: 571–79; 2007). Nevertheless, there is no reason to think that the Sargonic figure of 27,280 (or 27,290) prisoners from Samaria is a great exaggeration.[29] Nor is there any clear evidence that the foreign exiles brought into Samaria were confined to the city itself. Indeed, there is clear counterevidence to this claim. To begin with, the town of Megiddo (Stratum III), as the administrative center for the province of the same name, clearly bears witness in architecture and material finds to an elite Assyrian presence. Second, the southern Levant was home to a series of small Assyrian forts and administrative centers at a variety of sites situated in strategic locations (Stern 2001;

---

27. The figure only accounts for cases in which the actual number of deportees is listed. In other cases, no specific number is given. If the 43 cases (out of 157) are representative of the total, the overall figure would climb to approximately 4.5 million (Oded 1979: 20).

28. Nimrud Prisms D and E can be read in more than one way (cf. the Annals of Sargon II; Fuchs 1994, 2.3:10–16). I am following Dalley (1985: 36), who reads a hendiadys, *uttir...ušēšib*. Hence, she reads the verbs *watāru*, "to increase" (in number or size), and *(w)ašābu*, "to settle, reside," rather than *târu*, "to return, restore" and *ewû* (*emû*), "to become." In older treatments (e.g., H. Tadmor 1958: 34), one finds the translation, "I made it greater than before." See further, Fuchs (1994, 2.3:3), who prefers the older reading, and Younger (2000b: 295–96), who follows Dalley.

29. De Odorico's detailed study (1995: 52, 70, 86) suggests that the number is authentic (contra Gray 1970). The total likely includes exiles from both the city and the surrounding district (Na'aman 1993: 106–8; Younger 1998: 218–19).

Parker 1997; Dubovský 2006; Fantalkin and Tal 2009).[30] Whether the garrisons and forts were staffed by locals or by Assyrians is a matter of debate, but they attest to an imperial projection of power.[31] Third, some of the Assyrian (or Assyrian-imitation) material remains (architecture, glyptics, burial artifacts, etc.) discovered have been found at sites outside of the capital of Samaria. Fragmentary cuneiform tablets, for instance, were found in Samaria, Tel Hadid, Gezer, and Qaqun. Interestingly, one such document, a Neo-Assyrian contract dating to 698 BCE found at Tel Hadid contains a number of Akkadian names and only one possible West-Semitic name (Na'aman and Zadok 2000). Such evidence contradicts the notion that the foreign presence was concentrated at a single site.

It seems that scholars holding to the minimalist position may have substantially underestimated the impact of the Assyrian campaigns on the southern Levant. Given the congruence of some of the archaeological findings with the epigraphic and biblical evidence pertaining to the late 8th century, the time in which Tiglath-pileser, Shalmaneser, and Sargon achieved a series of impressive victories, those holding the maximalist interpretation are justified in some of their claims. Where the case for massive cultural exchange may be genuinely faulted is not so much in the evidence that is cited as in the assumptions it makes and how it employs material evidence in support of sweeping conclusions. Archaeologically, the maximalist approach is fundamentally tell-centered and oriented toward the Israelite kingdom as a whole. Presuming close linkages between text and history, state and people, politics and cult, center and periphery, scholars collect sites showing destruction layers and cite the total as proof for the cataclysmic end of northern Israel's existence in the land. One may question, however, whether scholars should either assume or assert such close linkages. In spite of the attention given to matters of epigraphy and archaeology, there is no clear evidence that the dismantling of the northern kingdom and its replacement by a system of Assyrian provinces were intrinsically fatal to native cultures. Such a proposition effectively equates a centralized political authority with the cultural and demographic realities of all the geographic areas it claims to control. In

---

30. Zertal (2003: 386–95) points to a number of such possible structures in the Manasseh region, but some caution must be registered. It is unclear whether all of these sites date to the Assyrian period or are indeed military centers.
31. The former possibility is more likely, given the ceramic remains (Fantalkin and Tal 2009).

a rural society, the state should be seen as one institution among others that seeks to impose its authority upon those whom it considers to be its subjects. How effective or ineffective such control may be depends on the economic, political, and military power of the state; how well it communicates its policies; and how well it can defend its interests in the hinterland. Human culture is a larger, much more complex, and more enduring phenomenon than any one political institution can represent.

In this context, there is no compelling evidence that the Assyrians systematically imposed their own culture or religious practices upon subject peoples.[32] For the most part, as long as subject peoples remained loyal to the Assyrian crown and paid their tribute and taxes, the Assyrian authorities did not interfere with local customs and practices. Even the authors of 2 Kings 17 do not claim that the Assyrian authorities imposed their own culture and religion upon subject peoples. On the contrary, the author of 2 Kgs 17: 24–34a presents an unnamed Assyrian monarch as working to ensure a revival of traditional religion at Bethel following the arrival of state-sponsored Assyrian colonists. Whatever one makes of this odd passage, it is clear that the author did not view the Assyrian crown as demanding that local populations abandon their native customs and religious practices (chapter 3).

There is, moreover, other important archaeological, literary, and epigraphic evidence that should be brought to bear in addressing the larger historical questions. To begin with, some archaeological field surveys are not given significant attention. To be sure, the data provided by these surveys cannot be considered in isolation from the material evidence pertaining to individual tells, but the surveys are relevant in testing claims of significant depopulation, especially in discerning the number and size of settlements in a given region during a particular era. We shall return to this matter later. Second, there is no widespread evidence that the Assyrian campaigns of Tiglath-pileser, Shalmaneser, and Sargon systematically destroyed small towns, villages, and farmsteads. Rather, they concentrated on targeting strategically located fortified sites and administrative centers (Bloch-Smith 2009). The damage they inflicted on these sites varied. Some were utterly devastated, while others were physically compromised by the selective destruction of fortifications, public structures, and

---

32. So McKay 1973, Cogan 1974, 1993, Dalley 1985: 41–42, Day 2000: 232–33, Berlejung 2012. Spieckermann (1982: 212–21) and Parpola (2003: 100–101) argue the opposite view.

domestic buildings. In other words, the destruction inflicted was discriminating, rather than systematic.

Third, closer attention must be given to the individual regions within Israel that were affected by the Assyrian campaigns. There are, as we have seen, cases in which archaeological excavations and site surveys indicate fundamental disruption of settlement and great depopulation. The areas of Galilee and northern Transjordan stand out in this respect. But questions may be raised whether this pattern holds true for all regions within the Israelite kingdom. In pointing to severe depopulation, long occupation gaps, and site abandonment, one must inquire as to the precise geographic area or location addressed by the claim. The part should not be taken for the whole. In this context, it may be best to decouple the western campaigns and unidirectional-deportation policies of Tiglath-pileser from those of his immediate successors. The damage done in Galilee by Tiglath-pileser was not commensurate with the damage done in the Samarian hill country by Shalmaneser and Sargon. This becomes evident when one revisits the list of sites razed (or partially destroyed) by the Assyrians. In service to the cultural exchange hypothesis, the documentation of destruction is extremely important, because such evidence contributes to a larger picture of devastation and displacement. But the locations of these sites should be kept in mind. Those sites with evidence for both conflagration and abandonment (or conflagration and a long occupation gap) include Bethsaida, Tel Hadar, Tel Qarnei Hittin, Tel Hannathon, Beth Shean, Kedesh, and ʿEn Gev.[33] At least two of these are disputed. Bethsaida in Area A (Southern Section, Level 5) shows clear evidence of a destruction dated by the excavators to the late 8th century, but the site was not abandoned.[34] Similarly, Beth Shean shows a partial, albeit poor and temporary, restoration in the years following the Assyrian conquest (B. Mazar 1993; A. Mazar, 2008). All of these sites are situated in Galilee, the northern Transjordan, and the northern coastal region at some distance from Samaria itself.

Fourth, in assessing the Assyrian damage, it is important to pay close attention not only to razed and abandoned settlements but also to razed

---

33. The list differs somewhat from Stern's tabulation (2001: 7, 9, 46–51). On Tel Mador, Tel Chinnereth, and Hazor, see above.
34. In his report on Bethsaida (et-Tell), the excavator stresses that this was a substantial two-tiered Iron II walled settlement with a gateway. Level 4 represents the Iron III period (732–540 BCE). The site, although reduced in occupation, was not abandoned at the end of the Iron Age (Arav 1999: 15–31, 84, 102–4; 2008).

and restored settlements. Sites that evince both destruction and restoration include Akko, Bethsaida, Dan, Dor, Dothan, Gezer, Shiqmona, Tell el-Farʿah North (= Tirzah; Chambon 1984), Shechem,[35] Tel Keisan, and Yoqneʿam.[36] The evidence from these sites presents some problems for the cultural exchange hypothesis, because it does not comport well with notions of complete dislocation. To be sure, most were not rebuilt to their earlier size, but the settlement continuity is itself important, suggesting that some residents at these locations were not permanently uprooted.

Fifth, even granting the validity of the tell-centered nature of traditional archaeology, there are some sites that show continuity in material culture throughout the 8th century. It has to be conceded, however, that such sites are not many in number: Bethel, Kh. el-Ḥammam, Tel Qiri, Tell Jezreel, and Taʿanach.[37] Of these, Bethel requires some special comment. In the view of the original excavator, Bethel underwent destruction at the end of the 8th century, but the site was purportedly reoccupied in the 7th century, perhaps toward the end of the Assyrian period (Kelso 1968, §§143–45, 150, 206). Both the southern town wall and a tower allegedly underwent reconstruction during the 7th century (Kelso 1968, §§42, 47). Fresh analysis reveals that the site enjoyed a period of substantial growth in the 8th century, but experienced a time of decline in the late 8th century or the early 7th century (Finkelstein and Singer-Avitz 2009: 38–45). No clear evidence of destruction at this time is attested (Finkelstein and Singer-Avitz 2009). The site did decline at the end of the Iron IIB period (late 8th or early 7th century), but it is impossible to say whether this resulted from Assyrian activities. In the 7th century, Bethel was small and sparsely inhabited.

Ceramic remains suggest that settlement (rather small in the late Iron Age) at Tel Jezreel continued from the time of a major destruction in the late 9th century BCE up to 1948 (Ussishkin and Woodhead 2008: 1837–39). Similarly, Kh. el-Ḥammam, a fortified town in the northwestern Samarian hills, was continuously inhabited from the 11th/10th century to the 2nd/early 1st century BCE (Zertal 1993). Tel Qiri, an unfortified agricultural village 2 km south of Tel Yoqneʿam, was continuously occupied

---

35. The remains from Shechem Stratum VI (Tel Balâṭah) indicate a partial resettlement in the 7th century (Campbell 1991; 2002: 295–99).
36. In addition, Tell Hadid witnesses the construction of what may be an unfortified (Assyrian?) administrative center, comprising three building complexes, in the 7th century (Stern 2001: 16–21; Beit-Arieh 2008).
37. Zertal (2003) adds a number of other small sites to this list.

in the Iron Age, except for a slight disruption between Strata VIII and VII (Ben-Tor 1987, 1997). Taʿanach, a fortified town at the southern end of Jezreel Valley, exhibits limited Iron II remains. Its occupation continued into the 5th century BCE (Glock 1993). The residents in these settlements may have temporarily abandoned their sites, offered only nominal resistance to the invading Assyrians, or peacefully surrendered.

Sixth, there are sites that experienced only limited or very limited destruction. One important example is Megiddo, and another is Samaria itself. In constructing their buildings at Megiddo (Stratum III), the Assyrians built over and reused sections of the earlier 8th-century Stratum IVA (Chicago) level.[38] The major public buildings and the water tunnel remained. The Assyrians used the same offset-inset wall (Stratum IVA) for their own defenses. There is some evidence of an internal, probably controlled, destruction by fire in the domestic quarters at the site in the late 8th century, which formed the basis for Assyrian rebuilding activities (Joffe, Cline, and Lipschits 2000; Halpern 2000; Finkelstein and Ussishkin 2000). Yet there is no clear evidence that the forces of Tiglath-pileser, Shalmaneser, or Sargon destroyed Megiddo, even though the Assyrians clearly took over the location and rebuilt sections of the site according to their own design (Macchi 1994b; Peersmann 2000: 526–27; Finkelstein, Ussishkin, and Halpern 2006). The defenders may have simply surrendered the site.

The site of Samaria exhibits several Iron Age layers. If, as estimated, the area of Iron II Samaria was approximately 70 hectares, Samaria was larger than Jerusalem in the same period (Avigad 1993: 1302).[39] A layer of ashes has been attributed to the Assyrian conquest, but neither Shalmaneser nor Sargon seems to have destroyed the city's fortifications, which continued to be used. In Tappy's recent study of Kenyon's excavation notes, he points out that there are relatively few traces of Assyrian destruction (Tappy 2001: 351–441; 2007: 266–75; so also Naʾaman 1990: 209; Dalley 1985). There are some Assyrian remains, but there is no evidence of a major razing dating to this time. Moreover, some of the ceramic evidence cited by Kenyon in favor of Assyrian destruction in the late 8th century actually dates to several different periods. Tappy (2001:

---

38. Three phases in Assyrian construction can be discerned at the site: Levels H-3, H-2, and H-1 (all Stratum III; Joffe, Cline, and Lipschits 2000).

39. Zertal (2001: 49) speculates that its population was around 17,000 people. The estimate of Broshi and Finkelstein (1992: 51) seems to be much higher, even though they estimate Samaria's area as 60 hectares.

440) comments: "I have not encountered a blanket of destruction debris across the B[uilding] P[eriod] V remains at the site; rather, diverse layers dating from many time periods and extending as late as the Late Roman period have emerged." In other words, Samaria lacks a coherent destruction level that dates to the time of Tiglath-pileser III, Shalmaneser V, and Sargon II. Some new types of pottery appear at the site (Kenyon 1957: 97–98). There are also Assyrian remains, including a fragment of a stela attributed to Sargon II, but these Assyrian remains are not abundant (Tappy 2001: 572). There is a fundamental material continuity in the Iron II period at Samaria, in spite of whatever political discontinuity the Assyrians introduced. The site's walls continue in use for a long period, and the city itself survives into the Babylonian and Persian periods (Crowfoot 1957a: 3–5). Such evidence of continuing inhabitation belies two critical claims in the prevailing hypothesis about Israel's demise, namely, that the Assyrians caused generalized destruction of all settlements and that they deported the inhabitants of these communities. One wonders whether much of the newer archaeological evidence unearthed over the past three decades has been forced into the service of upholding an older interpretive paradigm.

In this context, it is relevant to pay close attention to what Assyrian and Babylonian scribes claim (and do not claim) about the taking of the city of Samaria. The Babylonian Chronicle speaks of Shalmaneser as having "broken" the city.[40] As for Sargon, he claims to have "besieged and conquered" Samaria (Fuchs 1994, 2.4:23–27). The Assyrian and Babylonian scribes do not assert that Shalmaneser and Sargon razed the city, thus decimating it. The Mesopotamian sources speak of siege and conquest, not of devastation. Similarly, 2 Kgs 17:6 speaks of the unnamed Assyrian monarch as having "captured" (*lākad*) the city. It is true that Sargon claims to have taken tens of thousands of Samarians as prisoners, but Sargon also boasts that the annual income to the crown remained the same as in the time of his predecessor (Fuchs 1994, 2.4:27). The latter would be impossible if the land's infrastructure had been thoroughly ruined. Dalley (1985: 34–35) observes that Sargon never claims to have taken any booty from Samaria, aside from its people and its gods.

---

40. The translation of *ḫepû* in this context (Babylonian Chronicle I i.28) is disputed (Grayson 1975: 73). I am following Becking (1992: 25), Dalley (1985: 33), and Younger (1999: 464–68) in taking the basic meaning as "to break" or "to ruin." Na'aman (1990: 211) takes *ḫepû* in this context to indicate pacification. Cf. CAD H173.

One may also ask whether a scorched-earth policy would be in keeping with the strategic goals of Assyrian imperial policy. There are economic consequences to dismantling local infrastructure and implementing a policy of widespread destruction. To lay lands waste means denuding those territories of people who could bring income to the imperial treasury. Sargon claims to have received as much tax, on an annual basis, from Samaria after its fall as the tribute received before its fall. That Samaria was made into a provincial capital would be most unlikely if Sargon's geopolitical and military aims in dealing with the region were simply punitive. The king's assertion that he absorbed a contingent of 200 chariots from Samaria into his forces suggests that he did not relegate Samaria to a pariah status during his time. Quite the contrary, the integration of select foreign military units into the king's military may be considered both as a self-serving and as a benevolent imperial policy toward select subject peoples (Lanfranchi 1997; Kaplan 2008; Galil 2009).

Returning to the archaeological surveys, we have seen that these have been cited (e.g., Galilee) as confirming the radical effects of the Assyrian deportations. The results of surveys conducted in the Manasseh hill country show, however, less revolutionary results. In the systematic surveys conducted by Zertal (1990, 2004, 2008), the Iron II period marks the settlement peak. Only the Byzantine era is more populous. The number of sites during the Iron II period, defined by Zertal as the 10th–late 8th centuries, is more than double the number attested during the Iron I period. There is a steep decline during the Iron III period, especially in the Wadi 'Iron–Wadi Shechem region and in the eastern valleys, before the area experiences a strong recovery during Persian times.[41] The number of Iron III sites is approximately 33 percent the number of Iron II sites.[42] Faust (2003a) points to a large number of farmsteads, as well as some hamlets and villages, which have been excavated in the Samaria highlands. Almost all of these Iron Age rural sites exhibit continuity into the Persian period. Zertal (2001: 44) estimates that the number of prisoners taken as booty by Sargon II (27,290) might have represented about one-third of the state's total population. If the higher estimate of Broshi and Finkelstein (1992:

---

41. Not so in the 'Iron-Shechem area, the eastern valleys, and the desert fringes (Zertal 2003: 400–404; 2008: 85–92). There, both the Persian and the Hellenistic periods are relatively sparsely inhabited. By contrast, the Persian era represents the time in which northern Samaria is the most densely populated of all periods.
42. The earlier figures provided by Zertal (1990: 11–16; 1997) are being revised as Zertal completes his studies (2001: 41–44; 2003; 2004; 2008).

50–51) for Samaria's population in the 8th century is closer to the mark, the number of prisoners taken as booty by Sargon II might have represented about one-quarter of the (reduced) state's total population.[43]

The Iron II period witnessed a major increase of settlements in western Samaria. In the subsequent period, there seems to be a decline (Dar 1986, 1992). Faust (2006) observes that most Iron Age rural sites excavated in the Samarian foothills—that is, the westernmost slopes of Samaria (above the alluvial valley)—continued to exist through the Persian and early Hellenistic period. The date of their destruction/abandonment is not entirely clear, but seems to have taken place in the 2nd century BCE. A recent archaeological survey confirms that the agricultural farms in western Samaria were more extensive than previously recognized during the Iron IIC period (Magen 2008c: 8).[44] In his survey of southern Samaria, Finkelstein also points to the Iron II period, defined by him as the 10th–early 6th centuries, as a time of unprecedented level of settlement, with the northern area being the most intensively settled (Finkelstein 1988–89; Finkelstein, Lederman, and Bunimovitz 1997; Watkins 1997). During the Iron II era, the 8th century marks the peak of occupation. Only the Bethel plateau showed a decrease in sites during the Iron II period. Compared with the Iron II period, the Persian period witnesses a sharp decline in the number of sites. The number of Achaemenid-period sites (90) is approximately 47 percent the number of those that existed during the Iron II period (190). During this time of decline there is a shift in settlement toward the western coastal plain.[45]

In brief, site surveys and salvage excavations confirm the late 8th century as a time of real settlement decline in certain parts of the Samaria hill country. By the same token, the archaeological remains point to meaningful continuity in settlement. In this respect, one has to distinguish the archaeological work in Galilee and the northern Transjordan from the archaeological work in the hills of Manasseh and Ephraim. The former shows severe depopulation with only nominal reinvestment of resources by the Assyrians.[46] The latter shows mixed results—both discontinuity

---

43. The estimate (102,500) only includes the areas of Gilboa, Carmel, northern Samaria, and southern Samaria. It does not include any part of Galilee, the Huleh Valley, or the Jordan Valley.
44. Indeed, the survey reveals the existence of a number of new agricultural settlements in central Samaria, dating to the 7th century BCE.
45. A recovery occurs in the Hellenistic period (Finkelstein 1993).
46. Much of their economic effort was probably expended on areas to the south and southwest of the province of Magiddu (Finkelstein and Ussishkin 2000: 602; Stern 2001: 46–51).

and continuity. Hence, in spite of Sargon's forced deportation of some 27,290 prisoners, the vast majority of those who endured the Assyrian invasions continued to reside in the land.

To this line of argumentation, an objection may be made. The site surveys showing significant continuity of inhabitation may be misleading, because one has to take into account the bidirectional nature of the Assyrian deportations during the time of Sargon II. If, for example, Sargon's reign witnessed both Israelite deportations to various areas in the Assyrian empire and importations of many émigrés from elsewhere into Samaria, the degree of settlement continuity evinced by site surveys may mask the true degree of population exchange. If a bidirectional deportation occurred, the continuity reflected in settlement surveys might occlude the true degree to which the Assyrian campaigns negatively affected the Israelite population. Three points may be made in response to this objection. First, we do not know how many foreigners were transported to Samaria by Sargon and other Assyrian monarchs. There is no reason to doubt that Sargon drew settlers from different geographic areas, but it is unclear how many he imported into the region. This is a critical consideration in assessing the extent of cultural change introduced by the Assyrians. Second, Assyrian records present a complex picture of the aftermath of Samaria's conquest. On the one hand, they speak of conquest and deportation. On the other, the texts speak of maintaining an equal amount of income from Samaria and of the integration of a Samarian chariot contingent into Sargon's army. In short, Sargon's royal inscriptions indicate subjugation and integration, rather than utter devastation and disintegration.

Third, if Sargon deployed vast numbers of immigrants to the former northern kingdom, one would expect to find confirmation of this enormous population exchange in the material record. But local pottery traditions continued. Even though the former Aramean and Israelite territories were transformed into a system of Assyrian provinces, local pottery types changed only minimally (Amiran 1970: 191–92; Zertal 2003; Bloch-Smith 2009: 36). The importance of this point should not be underestimated. In Syria, Iron Age pottery types remained almost unchanged until the mid-7th century BCE (Lehmann 1998). Assyrian hegemony did not result in large amounts of Mespotamian pottery being shipped into areas west of the Euphrates. This is not to deny the possibility that some new pottery types were introduced by Assyrian-sponsored immigrants. Zertal (1989), for instance, argues for a new "Cuthean" style of pottery in the hills of Samaria. But this assessment has been vigorously contested by London (1992), who argues that the pottery type in question is attested elsewhere outside northern Israel and has been mislabeled. The bowls have a utilitarian function as graters, are not distinctive of Mesopotamia, and are common in villages, because food-processing equipment is often found in villages and farms in which food preparation is a regular activity. Even if one were to grant, for the sake of argument, the validity of Zertal's theory, there is little cause to posit any substantial influence by incoming immigrants on local material conditions. There is no evidence that the traditional culture in the hill country of Ephraim and Manasseh was suddenly displaced by a single foreign culture or by a variety of foreign cultures. In this context, Stern (2001: 45) makes a major concession:

> It seems, however, that this major change in the region's population [following the Assyrian conquest] left but a modest mark in the archaeological record. Almost nothing has been uncovered that can be attributed to the countries of the different groups of deportees, who are said to come from the Iranian plateau or Elam. Even in the capital cities of the two Assyrian provinces, only a handful of finds can be attributed to them.[47]

Especially in rural areas, the basic pottery repertoire (e.g., cooking pots, storage jars, amphorae) changed little in the 8th century.[48] Had there been a major influx of state-sponsored immigrants from major Babylonian cities and certain Aramean, Chaldean, and Elamite areas (2 Kgs 17:24), one would expect to find some clear evidence of their inhabitation. That one does not find such material remains in any significant number compels us to revisit the basic questions.

In discussing the relevance of the material remains for different historical reconstructions, consideration of larger geopolitical factors is pertinent. During the reigns of Sargon and his successors, the expansion of Assyrian control in Syria, Lebanon, and Israel encouraged the development of more trade with the Phoenician cities, Cyprus, Arabia, Egypt,

---

47. Stern (2001: 45) acknowledges that "this is difficult to understand," but at this point he prefers to follow the "historical sources," rather than to question some of their claims.
48. This situation may be contrasted with that pertaining in the Cizre Plain of the (then) recently established Mešennu province of the Upper Tigris region during the reign of Tiglath-pileser III (Parker 2001). During this era, Neo-Assyrian ceramic wares became dominant and a variety of new settlements dotted the landscape.

and various sites in the west. By defeating the Aramean and Israelite states and reducing others, such as Judah, to client status, the Assyrians enlarged their markets for trade. The selective use of forced population movements served a variety of imperial purposes: conscription into the armed forces, weakening or stabilizing local regions (depending on the situation), staving off desolation, providing labor in areas where it was needed, enforcing state control over newly conquered peoples, maintaining psychological control over previously rebellious states, integrating far-off regions into the Assyrian empire, and securing the southwestern border of the Assyrian empire over against the Philistines and the Egyptians (Oded 1979: 33–68; Younger 1998: 225–27; Thompson 2001: 102–3; Liverani 2005).

There is no doubt that Tiglath-pileser and Sargon both employed such deportations of northern Israelites to their advantage in conquering the land of the House of Omri. The question is how many foreign exiles Sargon imported into the highlands of Samaria. Three considerations suggest that the numbers were not high. First, as we have seen, the archaeological remains point to both significant depopulation and to the relative lack of cultural indicators for deportees stemming from the Iranian plateau or from Elam. Second, it would serve no demonstrable strategic purpose to import tens of thousands of foreign settlers into the Samarian hill country. Or, to put matters somewhat differently, those arguing that the Assyrians actually did so have not made a compelling case for why the Assyrians would want to deploy so many colonists in the former northern kingdom. In an agricultural economy, natural resources and labor are precious commodities, and there is no clear evidence to indicate that the Assyrian imperial regime dispatched large groups of immigrants into peripheral areas randomly. Most of the Assyrian (or Assyrian-sponsored) building activities in the southern Levant are concentrated in the coastal region, including southern Philistia and the border with Egypt. Sending a significant number of settlers into border areas close to Egypt is quite understandable, because the presence of such émigrés in southern Philistia and the western Negev would serve a critical purpose in safeguarding imperial interests in a sensitive, economically important, and contested geographic area. But dispatching tens of thousands of foreign immigrants into the central hill country is another matter. The general pattern in both Israel and Judah (in the time of Sennacherib) is one of deportation rather than importation.

Third, a significant disparity in the number of exiles in two-way deportations involving Israelites and forced immigrants would be broadly consistent with Assyrian imperial policy. The Assyrian authorities typically sent far more people from the periphery toward the core areas of their empire than vice versa (Liverani 2005). In fact, in about 85 percent of the cases in which the destinations of the deportees are stipulated, the destinations are the principal cities of Assyria—Ashur, Calah, Nineveh, and Dur-Sharrukin (Oded 1979: 28). Such a great imbalance in population transfers enabled a succession of Assyrian monarchs to build up the main urban centers at the core of their empire (Oded 1979: 27–32, 60–62; 2000: 91–103). Deportees were also profitably used to reclaim marginal regions for agriculture and to develop new ones. Such considerations have a bearing on the larger point in question. All three indicate that of those who resided in the districts of Samerina and Magiddu—Israelites, Assyrians, and immigrants—the clear majority were Israelites.

Conclusions

The results of our investigation are at odds with the presentations found in standard histories. Both of the main theories—the dominant maximalist and the minority minimalist—on the Assyrian exile are at some variance with the material evidence. Study of the archaeological remains suggests a more complex situation. In the regions of Galilee and the northern Transjordan, the Assyrian invasions caused widespread devastation. It is within these areas that one finds many sites both destroyed and abandoned. Other locations evince long occupation gaps. Site surveys indicate a process of extreme depopulation in the late 8th century. Historically, one may associate this devastation with the western campaigns of Tiglath-pileser III in 734–732 BCE, which eliminated the kingdom of Damascus, greatly reduced the size of the Israelite state, and led to mass deportations.

Analysis of the material remains from the hill country of Ephraim and Manasseh suggests a mixed picture. Some sites either were destroyed and abandoned during the late 8th century or evince long occupation gaps. A few locations, showing no traces of destruction, evince continuity in occupation. Some major sites, including Megiddo and Samaria itself, show only limited or minimal signs of destruction. Yet other sites evince destruction and some rebuilding. Archaeological surveys indicate a process of significant depopulation in the late 8th century. Historically, one may associate these developments with the western campaigns of Shalmaneser V and

Sargon II, which overthrew the Israelite state and transformed Samaria into an Assyrian province.

What one finds in the Samarian hills is not the wholesale replacement of one local population by a foreign population, but rather the diminution of the local population. Widespread abandonment does not occur as in parts of Galilee and Gilead, but significant depopulation does occur.[49] Among the causes of such a decline one may list death by war, disease, and starvation; forced deportations to other lands; and migrations to other areas, including south to Judah. There is no reason to deny the arrival of state-sponsored immigrants in Samaria as both the Assyrian royal inscriptions and the authors of Kings maintain. But the numbers of such foreign transplants do not appear to be high. Whatever exiles from foreign states were forcibly imported into the Samarian highlands, most seem to have been gradually absorbed into the local population. An enduring, but significantly reduced, Israelite presence in the land would explain three major features of the material remains. First, it explains why there is a continuity in material culture in both the city of Samaria and in the Samarian hill country, in spite of the Assyrian invasions. Such continuity would be unlikely, if not impossible, were there either an empty land or a land filled with foreign *émigrés*. Second, it clarifies what features of a foreign presence do appear in the material record. There are indications of an elite Assyrian presence in select sites, but such signs of foreign occupation coexist with signs of indigenous material culture. Neither the Assyrian themselves nor the immigrants they sponsored arrived in sufficient numbers to replace the Israelites.

Third, the Assyrian selectivity in dealing with the House of Omri— conquering some strategically located sites while minimizing the damage to others of lesser importance, deporting some Israelites while leaving many others in the land, establishing an imperial presence while having indigenous residents carry on their work—explains why the region of Samaria made a swifter recovery after the Assyrian campaigns than Judah did after the Babylonian invasions in the early 6th century BCE (Stern 2001: 49–51). Much of the area grew and prospered during the 7th century BCE. Under Nebuchadnezzar the Babylonians took a much more devastating approach to dealing with rebellions in the southern Levant than Shalmaneser V and Sargon II did. One does not have to embrace

---

49. The situation in south-central Transjordan is, however, complex, because Assyrian destructions remain largely undocumented (Dever 2007: 81–82).

the myth of the empty land to acknowledge that the Babylonian forces inflicted tremendous damage on the economic infrastructure of various coastal city-states and to Judah as well (Vanderhooft 1999). Excavations in Jerusalem indicate that the Babylonians did massive injury to the city's fortifications and major buildings (Lipschits 2001, 2003, 2005; Faust 2004). The contrast with the relatively lenient treatment given centuries earlier to the city of Samaria is striking. Both the Assyrians and the Babylonians were punitive, but the Assyrians were much more interested in directing the resources of their far-flung empire toward exploiting the possibilities for trade and commerce in the southern Levant than the Babylonians were. This brings us back to the question with which we began: What happened to the "ten lost tribes?" A significant portion of the "ten lost tribes" was never lost. In the region of Samaria, most of the indigenous Israelite population—those who survived the Assyrian onslaughts—remained in the land.

One must reckon, then, with a reduced but continuing northern Israelite presence in the land from the period of Assyrian domination onward. Clearly, this surviving community (or communities) was not static or fossilized. Rather, it continued to evolve and develop over the course of time under Assyrian and later Babylonian political domination. The results of our investigation thus warrant reexamining both the available material remains of Samaria dating to later periods and the available literary remains pertaining to the population of Samaria during the Neo-Assyrian, Neo-Babylonian, and Persian eras. The next few chapters will be devoted to addressing these issues.

At the beginning of this chapter, we saw that one particular text (2 Kings 17) has been enormously influential in shaping ancient and modern perceptions of the loss of Israel's ten northern tribes. The complexities in this long text and others in Kings pertaining to the former northern kingdom deserve close scrutiny. As we shall see in the next chapter, the multilayered Deuteronomistic commentary on Israel's fall (2 Kgs 17:7–41) does not speak with one voice about postexilic Samaria. Writers within Judah wrestled with the phenomenon of continuing Yahwistic practices in northern Israel. Indeed, I shall argue that there is indirect literary evidence both within this chapter and elsewhere in Kings attesting to a continuing Israelite population in the land.

3

God and Country

THE REVIVAL OF ISRAELITE RELIGION IN POSTEXILIC SAMARIA

THE LONG DISCUSSION of Israel's exile in 2 Kings 17 presents some very unusual features. The chapter contains not only a summary of Israel's fall to the Assyrians (2 Kgs 17:1–6) and a series of Deuteronomistic reflections on the causes of the northern kingdom's decline (2 Kgs 17:7–23) but also a series of Deuteronomistic stories about conditions in the land following Israel's deportation (2 Kgs 17:24–41). The presence of lengthy editorials explaining Israel's defeat does not occasion any great surprise, because the Deuteronomistic writers characteristically editorialize on major transitions in Israelite history. As has been long recognized, such summarizing speeches, prayers, and reflections punctuate the larger narrative and give it meaning (Noth 1943; Weinfeld 1972). The text of 2 Kings 17 may be atypical in the number of such reflections it contains, but the presence of at least some commentary is to be expected.[1]

---

1. In one reflection, the demise of the northern kingdom is attributed to the repeated failure of its monarchs and people to depart from the influential cultic policies established by their founding king—Jeroboam I—centuries earlier (2 Kgs 17:7aα, 18, 21–23). In another much longer (probably later) reflection, Israel's demise is traced to the people's rejection of Yhwh's commandments and Israel's desire to follow the customs of the surrounding nations (2 Kgs 17:7b–17). The latter commentary, which largely consists of a catalogue of cultic infractions ranging from astral worship to child sacrifice, blames the people themselves for their sorry fate. Scholars debate whether the material in 2 Kgs 17:19–20, which links the fate of Judah to that of Israel, belongs to the longer reflection in 2 Kgs 17:7b–17 or represents a later editorial insertion. There are other ways of understanding the breakdown of 2 Kings 17 (e.g., J. Macdonald 1969–70; Dietrich 1972, 2000; Becking 1992, 1997, 2000; Fritz 2003). In Brettler's analysis (1995), one finds several layers of composition, dating to different times. Similarly, Jones (1984: 542) speaks of a "long and tortuous process of composition." The case for unity is argued by Viviano (1987) and Long (1991). The short study of Rösel (2009) contends that most, if not all, of the Deuteronomistic editorialization in 2 Kgs 17:7–23 is secondary or late.

What is unusual is the amount of attention paid to the postexilic history of Samaria. If the ten tribes were all evicted from their land in the latter part of the 8th century BCE (and replaced en masse by waves of Assyrian-sponsored foreign immigrants), the story might be expected to end there. One of the defining characteristics of Deuteronomistic ideology is its intense focus on the land. The Deuteronomistic depiction of the past is landlocked. The work begins with the whole people encamped on the Plains of Moab (Deuteronomy) preparing to enter the land. The history proper begins with the people's conquests in the land (Joshua) and continues with the turbulent period of the chieftains (Judges 1–1 Samuel 12); the rise and fall of the united monarchy of Saul, David, and Solomon (1 Samuel 12–1 Kings 11); and the time of the divided monarchy (1 Kings 12–2 Kings 17). Commensurate with the existence of two kingdoms, the work has two endings—one for the northern monarchy (2 Kings 17) and the other for the southern monarchy (2 Kings 25). In each case, the people exit the land en masse for various destinations in faraway lands.

The interests of the authors are historical, typological, and theological. The divine bequest to Israel is a "good land" (Deut 1:35; 3:25; 4:21, 22; 6:18; 8:10; 9:16; 11:17; Josh 23:13, 15, 16; 1 Kgs 14:15). To reside in the land is both a gift and a blessing (Deut 4:21; 15:4; 19:10; 20:16; 21:23; 24:4; 26:1; 25:19; 1 Kgs 8:36). To leave it is both a punishment and a curse (Weinfeld 1972: 346–49). Indeed, in such a scenario, Israel itself "will become a proverb and a byword among all the peoples" (Deut 28:37; 1 Kgs 9:7), "a desolation and an imprecation" (2 Kgs 22:19). Although the writers acknowledge that Israel consists of a number of distinct groups, their approach to these sodalities is typological. The people either exist in the land or are forced at some point to leave it. The option of distinguishing between the fate of certain families within a tribe as opposed to the fate of others within the larger body politic is largely not entertained. The literary work deals typologically with the people (and its leaders) as a whole.

The very fact that the writers feel compelled to discuss the aftermath of the Assyrian exile is significant, because it departs from the standard trope. To take one example, 2 Kgs 15:27–29 mentions that the residents of various sites in Gilead and the Galilee, "the entire region of Naphtali," were deported by Tiglath-pileser III (2 Kgs 15:29).[2] In the subsequent

---

2. "Gilead and Galilee" likely represents a later addition to the text (Würthwein 1984: 383; Cogan and Tadmor 1988: 174).

narratives dealing with the northern kingdom, these exiled Israelites are never heard from again. To take a second example, the authors mention Yhwh's dispatching bands of Chaldeans, Edomites, Arameans, Moabites, and Ammonites against Judah during the final decades of the Judahite kingdom (2 Kgs 24:2). The attacks by these groups indicate the troubles that the Judahite monarchy faced as it neared dissolution. Nevertheless, the text does not discuss what happens to these foreign elements after the Judahites are forced to leave their homeland (cf. 2 Kgs 23:26–27; 24:3; Weinfeld 1972: 347). Typologically presenting the final course of history as actualizing covenant curses, the Deuteronomistic authors portray the effects of the foreign invasions and deportations as definitive.[3] The cessation of coverage for the northern and southern tribes following the collapse of the northern and southern kingdoms thus reflects a conscious decision on the part of the authors. The very structure and definition of their work reflects complex judgments about the connections among deity, land, and people. The only exception to this pattern that I am aware of is the short appendix to Kings dealing with the mercies afforded to the exiled King Jehoiachin in Babylon (2 Kgs 25:27–30).[4] Given the normal Deuteronomistic pattern of beginning the story with the people's entrance into the land and ending the story when the people leave the land, one would expect that coverage of northern affairs would terminate with the fall of the northern kingdom. In Kings, exile is not simply the nadir of history but also its end. Or so it would seem.

The usual practice of limiting historical coverage to life in the land makes the anomaly in 2 Kings 17 all the more intriguing. Why relate a strange anecdote about Yhwh sending ravenous lions against the foreign settlers (2 Kgs 17:24–26)? What does this tell us about how Judahite writers perceived the relationship between the God of Israel and the land? And why recount the story of the repatriated Israelite priest, who is commissioned by no less an authority than the Assyrian king to teach the foreign immigrants how to revere the neglected god of the land (2 Kgs 17:27–34a)? Why include another account insisting that the residents do not worship Yhwh (2 Kgs 17:34b–40)? If the Samarians are non-Israelites, why should this matter? Finally, if the northern Israelites were replaced

---

3. On the threat of exile, see Deut 4:25–28; 6:13–15; 28:36–37, 63; 29:26–27; Josh 23:13, 15, 16; 1 Sam 12:25; 1 Kgs 9:7; 14:11, 15. Most of these curses have to do with worshiping other gods (Deut 6:14–15; 28:36–37, 63–68; 29:17–27; Josh 23:15–16; 1 Kgs 9:7; 14:11, 15).
4. Often thought to be an epilogue or late addition to Kings (e.g., Fritz 2003: 425). Some, however, view the piece as an original part of the Deuteronomistic History (e.g., Noth 1943: 108).

by waves of Assyrian-sponsored immigrants in the late 8th century, why does Judah's preeminent reformer king (Josiah) launch a series of massive cultic reforms in Samaria (2 Kgs 23:15–20) approximately a century later? Normally, a reform presupposes the existence of an earlier form; but, in this instance, what is the standard the foreigners are supposed to follow?

That the highly-slanted and multilayered Deuteronomistic commentary stigmatizes the residents of the former northern kingdom seems clear. But in this chapter I would like to explore the nature of the polemic and the different views of Samarian religion and ethnicity embedded within the conflicting accounts of Kings. In what follows, I shall focus on three texts dealing with postexilic northern history (2 Kgs 17:23–34a, 34b–40; 23:15–20), comparing these texts with each other and with earlier Deuteronomistic claims about northern religion.[5] How does what these passages say about postmonarchic practices comport (or not comport) with what Kings elsewhere asserts about monarchic practices? What do these texts assert about postexilic northern religion and its relations to southern religion?

My study will demonstrate that the writers present conflicting accounts of Samarian life. The first text (2 Kgs 17:23–34a) has attracted the bulk of attention from antiquity to modern times, yet it has often been treated in isolation as an independent story, sufficient to explain the peculiar origins and religious practices of the Samarian people without recognition of the larger context of the Deuteronomistic portrayal of the northern monarchy. The passage assumes the Israelite exile depicted in 2 Kgs 17:6, but portrays the religion adopted by the incoming immigrants—whatever their land of origin—as remarkably conservative. That is, on the level of ethnicity the text suggests total discontinuity, but on the level of religious practice the text asserts substantial continuity. The second text (2 Kgs 17:34b–40) disputes one of the central points made by the earlier passage (2 Kgs 17:23–34a) about Yahwistic worship in Samaria, but paradoxically does so by recourse to Israel's longstanding covenant with Yhwh. This second text assumes a connection between the residents of the former northern kingdom and the descendants of Jacob. The third text, the account of Josiah's northern reforms (2 Kgs 23:15–20), seems to redress the issue of

---

5. There is a fourth text mentioning the Assyrian exile (2 Kgs 18:9–12) that resembles 2 Kgs 17:3–6. The placement of this passage in the context of Hezekiah's tenure suggests that the Assyrians also posed a tremendous threat to Judah. Jeremiah (3:6–11; 7:15) and Ezekiel (4:1–8; 16:44–63; 23:1–49) likewise link the fate of Judah to the fate of Israel.

idolatrous and syncretistic worship in Samaria, as portrayed in the first text (2 Kgs 17:24–34a), but raises new questions about the ethnicity of Samaria's population.

In short, the Deuteronomistic remarks about the identity and religious practices of the Samarians are discordant and polyphonic. My work will argue that the divergences within the Deuteronomistic commentary on postexilic life in Samaria reveal that the historical situation in northern Israel presupposed by the writers of 2 Kings 17 is more complex than many historians have imagined it to be. The issue is not, as many have supposed, a complete cultural transformation in Samaria within the late 8th and early 7th centuries BCE, but rather the survival of native culture in modified form within this region. Recognizing that some form of Yahwistic religious belief and practice continued in Samaria after the fall of the northern kingdom, a succession of Judahite writers struggled to explain this survival. Some thought that the continuity in Yahwistic worship was to be explained by the foreign immigrants' adoption of native customs, while others disputed on the basis of Yhwh's covenant with Israel that the surviving northern Israelites did, in fact, truly worship Yhwh. A long-term Israelite presence in Samaria is also presupposed in the idealized presentation of Josiah's northern reforms in the late 7th century. In what follows, my procedure will be to discuss each of the Kings accounts separately before addressing their historical ramifications for understanding Samarian history.

I. Give Me that Old-Time Religion

Second Kings 17:24–34a depicts a complete demographic transformation of the area once occupied by the northern kingdom. Israel's massive dislocation is followed by alien immigrations into the land. Assyrian-sponsored settlers, drawn from various sectors of the Assyrian empire, are transported into the territories vacated by the Israelites. The post-Assyrian-invasion residents of the region are thus distanced—literally and figuratively—from their Israelite forbears. Typologically, the sequence of events represents the reversal of the process whereby Israel first entered the land in Joshua's time. Instead of the autochthonous nations being removed from the land in favor of the allochthonous Israelites, the autochthonous Israelites are removed from the land in favor of allochthonous Babylonians, Cutheans, Avvites, Hamathites, and Sepharvaites (2 Kgs 17:24). The legacy of the Assyrian campaigns is thus a land transformed—emptied of natives and filled with foreigners.

What should one make of this presentation? One common interpretation (e.g., Burney 1903: 333) is that the text constitutes anti-Samaritan polemic. The Israelites are replaced by "total aliens, a mixed multitude of idolatrous peoples" (Astour 1988: 9). The result is a new "mongrel race" (Bewer 1933: 285). The "foundation for the later rejection of the Samaritans is laid here" (Fritz 2003: 356). The declaration of a metamorphosis in the land coupled with the depictions of the idolatrous and polytheistic customs practiced by the landed immigrants are designed to "exemplify the new detestable state of affairs" (Fritz 2003: 354). The late 8th century BCE marks the beginning of the "syncretistic" religion of the Samaritans (Ringgren 1975: 98–99). The cultic system adopted by the postexilic residents of Samaria has been variously described as a "heathen eclecticism" (Montgomery and Gehman 1951: 471),[6] a "wretched religion" (Pfeiffer 1948: 399), and a mixed religion with a "pagan nucleus" and a "Yahwistic veneer" (Talmon 1981: 61).[7]

Although the anti-Samaritan hypothesis has dominated scholarship, this line of interpretation has its critics (e.g., Coggins 1975: 13–15; Schur 1989: 20–21; Jobling 2003). The Deuteronomistic writers narrate a number of parallels among the religious practices of the old northern state religion, Samarian religion, and Judahite religion. Many of the Judahite kings allowed, if not sponsored, similar practices to those attributed to the Samarians including idolatry, worship at the high places, and worship of other gods (Hoffmann 1980: 40–42, 74–77; Barrick 2002). In fact, Kings posits more cultic heterogeneity in the south than it does in the north.[8] That those passages dealing with postexilic Samarian religion highlight the high places only underscores the parallels between south and north, because the high places are a consistent theme in the Deuteronomistic critique of Judahite worship practices.[9] If one views the perspective(s) of

---

6. Historically, Montgomery (1907) disagrees avidly with the characterization found in the text.
7. Nevertheless, Talmon's position (1981: 57–75) is more nuanced. The composition of 2 Kings 17 "arose from the post-Exilic author's intent to prevent integration (with)...the disreputable Ephraimite version of the Israelite religion" (Talmon 1981: 61). Talmon recognizes that what is at stake in this chapter is one version of Israelite religion being pitted against another.
8. The basic offenses that plague northern history are Jeroboam's counter cultus, Baal worship, and the manufacture of an asherah. But Ahab's asherah (1 Kgs 16:33) is a relatively minor theme in the Deuteronomistic treatment of the northern kingdom. Some ten cultic offenses plague Judahite history, including worship at the high places, the sculpting of standing stones and asherahs, astral worship, Baal worship, Asherah worship, divination, sorcery, and child sacrifice (Hoffmann 1980).
9. Auld (1994: 86–88) points out that the high place theme culminates in the account of Josiah's reforms. The most thorough treatment is Barrick 2002.

2 Kings 17 as anti-Samaritan, what should one call the Deuteronomistic critique of Judahite worship? Given the tremendous cultic heteropraxis attributed to Judah, does this make the writers anti-Judean? Moreover, if the point is to label the Samarians as un-Israelite, why continue the story at all? If the residents of the former northern kingdom were all foreigners and the cult they practiced was no more than a "wretched religion," there would be nothing for the biblical writers to comment upon. The story would simply end with Israel's expulsion from the land.

That the narrative contains tales about the foreign settlers shows that there are more complications to the ethnographic and religious situation in the former northern kingdom than one might initially surmise. When viewed in the context of the larger presentation, the difficulties encountered by the landed immigrants are fascinating. In Deuteronomistic thought, there is a strong connection between deity and land. The tie is so basic that the Deuteronomists consistently speak of exile as being cast away from God.[10] The commentary on Israel's fall repeatedly underscores the point: "And Yhwh became very angry with Israel and turned them away from his presence until there was none remaining, only the tribe of Judah by itself" (2 Kgs 17:18).[11] Second Kings 17:23 puts things similarly: "Yhwh turned Israel away from his presence, as he spoke by the hand of all his servants the prophets." Alluding to the dislocations of both Israel and Judah, 2 Kgs 17:20 declares, "And Yhwh rejected all of the seed of Israel, afflicted them, and consigned them to plunderers until he cast them away from his presence." The close linkage between God and land is also evident in a critical text anticipating the fall of Judah. In announcing (to the reader) Yhwh's decision to deport the residents of Jerusalem and Judah in the future because of King Manasseh's sins, the author of 2 Kgs 21:9 writes that "Manasseh led the people to do more evil than the

---

10. The divine announcement of (northern) Israel's reduction appears in 2 Kgs 10:32–33. A reprieve is granted during the Aramean conflicts (2 Kgs 13:3–5): "And Hazael king of Aram oppressed Israel all the days of Jehoahaz. But Yhwh had compassion on them and was merciful to them and God turned [toward them] for the sake of his covenant with Abraham, Isaac, and Jacob. He was not willing to destroy them and he was not willing to cast them out from his presence until now" (2 Kgs 13:22–23). In 2 Kgs 14:25–27 the survival of a decimated Israel is linked to Yhwh's concern that "the name of Israel" not be blotted out "from under heaven."
11. Of all the assertions made about the Israelite exile (2 Kgs 17:6, 18, 20, 23; 18:9–12), this one is the most explicit about a (temporarily) empty northern land. The comprehensive declaration influenced later tradition. Hence, Josephus (*Ant.* 9.278) speaks of the Assyrian monarch bringing "all of the people (*panta ton laon*) to Media and Persia."

nations did whom Yhwh had destroyed before the Israelites."[12] The implication seems to be that the God of the land would prefer a Judah-less land, rather than having Judahites continue to commit more iniquity than the indigenous residents did before the Israelites entered the land centuries earlier (2 Kgs 21:11). The very judgment presupposes an indelible connection between Yhwh and the land, a connection that predated Israel's occupation of the land.

In this context, the remark that Yhwh sent lions to attack the new colonists in Samaria is important, because it shows that Yhwh has not relinquished his claim to the territory once inhabited by Israel (Cohn 2000: 120). Indeed, it is curious that in sending lions to kill some colonists, Yhwh uses a time-tested and rather successful means of gaining the attention of the northern Israelites (1 Kgs 13:20–26; 20:35–36; Strawn 2005). Given the continuing loss of settlers, a crisis ensues both for the immigrants and for the imperium that sent them (2 Kgs 17:25; cf. 1 Kgs 13:24). The lifestyle maintained by the immigrants, who do not worship—literally "fear" (*yārāʾ*)—Yhwh, is deemed to be unacceptable, because they do not know "the custom (*mišpāṭ*) of the god of the land" (2 Kgs 17:24–26). Alerted to this crisis, the Assyrian king repatriates an exiled Samarian priest to teach the foreign settlers the custom of the neglected god of the land (2 Kgs 17:27). Led by this northern priest, the colonists reform their religious practices. This strategy proves successful insofar as the Israelite priest teaches the strangers "how to worship Yhwh" (2 Kgs 17:28).[13] But what does it mean to worship Yhwh? What exactly is this repatriated official telling the immigrants? We gain a vital clue from the fact that the priest takes up residence at one of the (former) major state-sponsored sanctuaries in Israel, the shrine at Bethel (2 Kgs 17:28). I would stress that the cultic practices acquired by the colonists from their new guide do not inaugurate a new mongrel religion, but rather replicate traditional northern Israelite practices in most details.[14]

---

12. Manasseh is the worst Judahite monarch in Deuteronomistic perspective (Cross 1973: 274–89; van Keulen 1996; Eynikel 1997; Halpern 1998). On the differences among the MT, the LXX, and the Old Latin of 2 Kgs 21:4–9, see Trebolle Barrera 1989: 206–7 and Schenker 2005. For another perspective, see van Keulen 1996: 55–59.
13. In Josephus' retelling (*Ant.* 9.290), the conversion was even more successful than in the biblical account: "They worshiped him with great zeal." Interestingly, the Josephus account lacks reference to 2 Kgs 17:19–20, 29–41 (Pummer 2009: 68–74).
14. In other words, the point is not that "the pre-exilic priests of the northern kingdom (and, by implication, its people) practiced the true religion of Yahweh" (Astour 1988: 11). Quite the contrary, the implication is that the preexilic northern priests practiced a syncretistic religion,

As presented earlier in Kings, the development of a distinctive northern cult has everything to do with the formative innovations of its first independent monarch, Jeroboam I. Upon being elected king in the late 10th century, Jeroboam embarked on a series of initiatives designed to counter the influence and attraction of the Solomonic sanctuary (1 Kgs 12:26–28). Seen over against the earlier establishment of a national cultus in Jerusalem (1 Kgs 6:1–9:3), Jeroboam's maneuvers were comprehensive, involving sanctuaries, priesthood, theology, iconography, pilgrimage, and calendar.[15] The new potentate invests two principal shrines at the southern and northern tiers of his large state—the sanctuaries at Bethel and Dan.[16] A related charge leveled against Jeroboam is that he established high places at various unspecified locations throughout his realm (1 Kgs 12:31; 13:32). The northern iconography, involving the manufacture of two golden calves and the installation of these calves in the state-sponsored sanctuaries at Bethel and Dan, is perhaps the most infamous aspect of Jeroboam's reforms.[17] Although the northern king associates the calves with the God of the Exodus, the Deuteronomists associate the creation and deployment of these symbols with idolatry and worshiping other gods (1 Kgs 12:28; 14:10; 2 Kgs 10:29). Another royal innovation was to "appoint priests from all sectors of the people who were not from the descendants of Levi" (1 Kgs 12:31). Jeroboam thus opens the sacerdocy to those who did not qualify before.

To be sure, Jeroboam's actions do not go unchallenged. A prophet from Judah fortuitously arrives at Bethel, denounces Jeroboam's innovation, and predicts the demise of the Bethel cultus (1 Kgs 13:1–9). Similarly, an old

---

one that (from a Deuteronomistic perspective) combined Yahwistic practices with idolatrous and polytheistic practices.

15. The pilgrimage following the golden calves to their new shrines (1 Kgs 12:30) and the institution of a "feast on the 15th day of the 8th month, like the feast which is in Judah" (1 Kgs 12:32) are not, however, productive themes in the Deuteronomistic coverage of northern Israel. On the textual criticism of 1 Kgs 12:30, see Knoppers 1994: 25–27.

16. Only the cultus (and altar) at Bethel are productive themes in the subsequent evaluation of the northern monarchy. Little if any attention is paid to the fate of the cultus at Dan or to the golden calves themselves. Instead, the text targets the Bethel altar, the high places, and their priests. By narrowing the issues, the writers establish a continuity of northern religious practice, despite Israel's exile, extending to the late 7th century (Halpern 1988: 249–50).

17. That the polemic against Bethel is not confined to the Deuteronomistic History (e.g., Amos 4:4–5; 5:4–5; Hos 4:15; 9:15; 10:5; 12:12; cf. 13:2) suggests that the Bethel shrine was an avid concern of a succession of Jerusalem scribes. How long the Bethel shrine survived is much debated (Blenkinsopp 2003; Koenen 2003; Gomes 2006; Knauf 2006). That Bethel continued into early Achaemenid times seems unlikely, given the recent reexamination of the relevant material remains (Finkelstein and Singer-Avitz 2009). The shrine itself (which was not found in the excavations) is another matter (Na'aman 2010).

prophet from Bethel, after engaging in a remarkable series of exchanges with the anonymous man of God, comes to second the prophecies against the Bethel cultus, and includes the high places in Samaria for good measure (1 Kgs 13:11–32). Nevertheless, these objections have only a negative effect: "And he [Jeroboam] again made priests of the high places from the ranks of the people" (*wayyāšob wayya'aś miqṣôt hā'ām kōhănê bāmôt*; 1 Kgs 13:33). Whoever "wished to become ordained (*heḥāpēṣ yĕmallē' 'et-yādô*) became a priest of the high places" (1 Kgs 13:33). Presented in this way, the new state cultus becomes immortalized as "the sin(s) of Jeroboam," a perversion of an established orthopraxis.[18] Set within a culture that valued antiquity and suspected religious novelty, Jeroboam's maneuvers appear as unauthorized departures from divinely sanctioned tradition. The southern cultus perpetuates the ancient institutions of sacrifice, priesthood, ark, and festival (1 Kings 8), while the northern cultus creates an idolatrous and syncretistic new alternative. Yet over the centuries Jeroboam's actions prove formative, creating their own influential traditions of religious practice.[19]

II. The Old-Time Religion Reborn

Some consideration of Jeroboam's counter cultus is helpful in appreciating the contours of the cultus (re)established by the repatriated Yahwistic Samarian priest in the former northern kingdom. That this officiant settles in Bethel upon his restoration can be no accident. The ancient Bethel shrine takes on a new life in changed political circumstances. The priestly initiatives recreate the basic features of Jeroboam's state cult. After making the golden calves, the founding father declared, "Behold your gods (*'ĕlōhêkā*) O Israel" (1 Kgs 12:28).[20] Like this first king, who was charged by the prophet Ahijah with "having made other gods" (*watta'ăśeh-lĕkā*

---

18. In Deuteronomistic perspective, the northern iconography revives and perpetuates aspects of the golden calf cult established by Aaron at Sinai (Exod 32:1–35; Deut 9:13–21; Knoppers 1995). The Deuteronomists implicitly concede the antiquity of the northern cultus and acknowledge that the differences between the southern and northern cults were longstanding. That the golden calf cultus was attributed to such a major figure of high standing and antiquity as Aaron indicates that the authors realized that the rivalry between Bethel and Jerusalem was an inner-Israelite issue.
19. He not only sinned, but also "caused Israel to sin" (1 Kgs 14:16; 15:26, 30, 34; 16:13, 19, 26; 22:53; 2 Kgs 3:3; 10:29, 31; 13:2, 6, 11; 14:24; 15:9, 18, 24, 28; 17:21; 23:15). No king "turned from the sin(s) of the house of Jeroboam" (2 Kgs 3:3; 10:29, 31; 12:4; 13:2, 6; 14:4; 15:4, 18, 35; 17:22; Knoppers 1994: 13–20).
20. On the pl. translation of *'ĕlōhêkā*, see my earlier work (1994: 26–27).

ĕlōhîm ʾăḥērîm; 1 Kgs 14:9), each of the new immigrant peoples "were making its own gods" (*wayyihyû ʿōśîm gôy gôy ʾĕlōhāyw*; 2 Kgs 17:29).

One of Jeroboam's innovations was to establish a system of high places (*wayyaʿaś ʾet-bêt bāmôt*; 1 Kgs 12:31).²¹ The shrines of the high places, located in the towns of Samaria (*kol-bātê hā-bāmôt ʾăšer bĕʿārê šōmĕrôn*), were decried by the old prophet from Bethel (1 Kgs 13:32).²² Having been instructed by the Samarian priest, the Assyrian state-sponsored settlers revive this centuries-long tradition of dispersed cult places by "making shrines of the high places for themselves" (*wayyihyû ʿōśîm lāhem bēbêt hā-bāmôt*; 2 Kgs 17:32). Just as Jeroboam installed his golden calves in the Bethel and Dan sanctuaries, the immigrants installed their gods in "the shrines of the high places (*bēbêt hā-bāmôt*) that the Samarians had made in the towns in which they resided" (2 Kgs 17:29).²³ The settlers revived royal policies in yet another respect. Just as Jeroboam "appointed priests from all ranks of the people" (*wayyaʿaś kōhănîm miqṣôt hāʿām*; 1 Kgs 12:31), so the foreign émigrés "appointed priests of the high places for themselves from their own ranks" (*wayyaʿăśû lāhem miqṣôtām kōhănê bāmôt*; 2 Kgs 17:32).

---

21. Understanding *bêt hā-bāmôt* as a composite pl. (GKC, §124r) or as a pl. of a genitival group (Joüon 1923, §§136m-o). Joüon notes that in those rare cases in which only the second noun appears in the pl., the single noun in this construction is almost always *bêt* (e.g., *bêt ʾābôt*; Joüon 1923, §136n). For the locution *bêt hā-bāmôt* in 1 Kgs 12:31, the LXX and Vg. reflect *bātê hā-bāmôt*. Similarly, in 2 Kgs 17:29, 32 the MT has *bēbêt hā-bāmôt*, while the LXX^L and the Vg. reflect *bēbātê hā-bāmôt*. The latter lemmata congrue with *bēbātê hā-bāmôt* and *kôl-bātê bāmôt* in 2 Kgs 23:19 and 1 Kgs 13:32. Thinking that that the LXX (and Vg.) readings are earlier, Schenker (2000: 105–6, 115–20, 142–46) contends that the MT's *bêt hā-bāmôt* constitutes a superlative, reflecting an anti-Samaritan and an anti-Mt. Gerizim polemic in Hellenistic, and perhaps more specifically Maccabean, times. In a manner of speaking, the opposite argument has been made by Talmon (1981: 63). The references to *bātê bāmôt* attempt "to undermine the singularity of the northern *Reichsheiligtum* in Bethel and to relegate it to the status of just one other *bāmāh*."
22. The restricted scope of the prophecy to "the towns of Samaria" is deliberate, because it reflects the reduced size of the (later) region of Samaria in comparison with the size of the earlier northern kingdom. A continuity in recreancy is thus created from the 10th century BCE to the 8th-7th centuries BCE.
23. The only overt reference in the Hebrew Bible to "the Samarians" (*hā-šōmĕrōnîm*) refers to the former inhabitants of the northern kingdom, specifically those Israelites who lived in the region of Samaria. The term does not apply to the post-Assyrian exile residents of the same area. Interestingly, the term Samaria (*šōmĕrôn*) as a reference to more than the capital of Samaria is not widespread within the Hebrew Bible (e.g., 1 Kgs 21:1; 2 Kgs 1:3; Jer 31:5; Amos 3:9; 4:1; 6:1; Hos 10:7; Obad 19). Two of these references are to the "king of Samaria" (*melek-šōmĕrôn*; 1 Kgs 21:1; 2 Kgs 1:3), that is, the monarch who ruled over the reduced northern kingdom, headquartered in the capital of Samaria. References to "the land of Samaria" or to "the city of Samaria" are common in relevant Neo-Assyrian royal inscriptions (Ephʿal 1991; Kelle 2002). The lone biblical mention of "the Samarians" reflects a time in which it made sense to speak of the former residents of an area (Samaria), rather than of a much larger kingdom.

The verbal parallels between Jeroboam's system of worship and the immigrants' system of worship are too many and too close to be accidental. The overall point seems clear. The state cultus inaugurated by Jeroboam experienced a dramatic renascence after the Israelites were forcibly expelled from their territory. Whether with respect to shrines, priesthood, or iconography, the settlers revive and perpetuate the old-time religion of northern Israel. The repatriated priest has done his work well. The reinvigoration of northern worship (2 Kgs 17:27–33) ironically (re)creates the conditions under which the ancient prophecies of the man of God from Judah (1 Kgs 13:2) and the old prophet from Bethel (1 Kgs 13:31–32) can still be realized. To be sure, the royal sponsor changes from the Israelite monarchs to the Assyrian monarch, and the practitioners change from the Israelites to the colonists, but the basic features of the religion remain constant. The result is not so much a new "mongrel" cult as the old cult in a new form. Given the settlement of the Israelite priest at Bethel (2 Kgs 17:28), one may assume the continuing vitality of this sanctuary as well.

The foreign-colonists tale thus involves a series of paradoxes. First, the text underscores an ineluctable association between God and country to such an extent that it follows not the story of the ten lost tribes who were forcibly deported to various locales in the Assyrian empire but the story of the various non-Israelite peoples who were relocated to Samaria. Within the world of the biblical text, the fate of the Israelite expatriates is lost to the reader. There is no mention of a chariot of Yhwh, as there is in Ezekiel (1:1–27; cf. 8:1–19:14), traveling with the deportees to a far-off foreign territory. Instead, Yhwh remains active in the land itself. The destiny of the ten lost tribes becomes grist for the mills of early and modern interpreters.[24] By contrast, the deity of Israel becomes an adopted deity of the non-Israelites who reside en masse in a land bereft of all Israelites, save one.[25] The foreign émigrés thus take on a hybrid or double identity.

---

24. On the fate of the Israelite deportees, see the previous chapter and the references listed there.

25. Only one priest from Samaria is specifically mentioned in 2 Kgs 17:27–28, but pl. verb forms appear in two instances within MT v. 27 (followed by the LXX^B): "Let them go (וילכו) and let them settle (וישבו) there and let him teach them the custom of the god of the land." Similarly, Josephus (*Ant.* 9.289–90) speaks of "priests" (*hiereis*) being repatriated to Samaria. In 2 Kgs 17:27–28, I would be inclined to read consistently the sing. with the LXX^L, Syr., Vg., Arm., and Eth. (*lectio difficilior*). In any case, perhaps the pl. forms appearing in the MT (and the LXX^B), coupled with specific mention of the repatriated Israelite priest(s), may be partly the basis for the later tradition that the Samaritans were a mixed population. The juxtaposition of two different passages (2 Kgs 17:24–34a; 34b–40) may have also contributed to this view (see below).

They are non-Israelites ethnically, but Israel-like religiously. Inasmuch as the settlers learn how to fear Yhwh, they stand in an ongoing relationship to him.[26]

Second, the Assyrian exile ends up barely changing the religious landscape in northern Israel. The humiliation of Samaria and the forced Israelite deportations caused profound political and ethnic upheaval. Second Kings 17:6 unequivocally claims that the king of Assyria "exiled Israel to Assyria." Yet, if the Assyrian campaigns find the writers stressing political and ethnic revolution, it also finds them stressing profound religious conservatism. Immediately after attributing Israel's exile to its stubborn allegiance to perpetuating Jeroboam's sins, the text declares that these sins prevail in radically altered circumstances (2 Kgs 17:24–34a). The persistence of older practices is, in fact, so strong that it undercuts the claim made of complete demographic discontinuity. The close comparability of preexilic Israelite religion with postexilic Samarian religion belies the claim of a complete Israelite dislocation to Assyria. On one level, the text presents a picture of total transformation, but on another level the text presents a picture of fundamental continuity.

Third, the Deuteronomistic work upholds certain ideals, such as the importance of the Deuteronomic statutes, the principle of centralization, the Jerusalem temple, the Davidic dynastic promises, the worship of Yhwh, and the avoidance of other gods. Yet, in this case, it acknowledges that reviving the old-time religion was critical to pacifying conditions in the former northern realm. It is only after the aliens learn to practice autochthonous religion that the lion attacks cease (cf. 2 Kgs 17:24–26). At this point, it would seem that the god of the land is satisfied. The very sins that ultimately doomed the northern kingdom ironically saved the settlers. The writers seem to concede, in this case, that syncretistic Yahwistic worship is better than no Yahwistic worship at all.

III. Those Descendants of Jacob Who Do Not Worship Yhwh

The text of 2 Kings 17 does not speak with one voice about ethnic and cultic life in postexilic Samaria. The author of 2 Kgs 17:34b–40 disputes whether the residents of the former northern kingdom truly worship

---

26. And, in this case, the story continues in later generations (2 Kgs 17:41).

Yhwh.[27] Introducing his commentary through the use of the literary technique of inverted citation, the writer of the second passage (2 Kgs 17:34b–40) declares: "They do not worship Yhwh and they do not act according to their statutes and their custom—the teaching and the commandment that Yhwh commanded the children of Jacob, whose name he [Yhwh] changed to Israel."[28] This text (2 Kgs 17:34b–40) is commonly understood as an addendum to 2 Kgs 17:24–34a, further condemning the postexilic inhabitants of Samaria already excoriated in earlier verses.[29] From this viewpoint, the northerners do not worship Yhwh, because they do not keep the covenant Yhwh made with them when he brought them up from Egypt (17:35–36). As such, the text refutes the earlier claim that the northern residents worship Yhwh. Their cult did not conservatively replicate the old state cult but radically departed from Israel's covenant.

Admittedly, this exegesis of 2 Kgs 17:34b–40 is not without its problems, because the passage seems to assume that the land's residents are responsible for keeping Yhwh's covenant.[30] To assert, as this passage does, that "they did not listen but rather acted according to their former custom" (v. 40) is to acknowledge that these people were subject at some point to a communication from Yhwh about what worship of Yhwh entailed (vv. 34b–39).[31] Otherwise, the criticism would be baseless. Is this a case of confusion or mistaken identity? Or are readers expected to recognize hyperbole in earlier text of foreign settlers completely displacing the Israelites (Ben Zvi 1995: 102)? Or should one imagine an altogether different scenario (Cogan 1978, 1988; Cogan and Tadmor 1988: 213; Brettler

---

27. On the division of these verses and their separation from vv. 24–34a, see Stade 1886: 167–70; Burney 1903: 333–37; Noth 1943: 85–86; Gray 1970: 655–56; Nelson 1981: 64–65; Jones 1984: 555; McKenzie 1991: 140–42; Walsh 2000: 318–19.
28. Instead of the MT's משפט in v. 33, Tg. Jonathan has *nimôsā*, "law" (cf. Greek *nomos*). Similarly, in the following verses, the Tg. has *gĕzērā*, "decree" instead of the MT's חוק. The usage likely reflects an interpretation by the Targum writers that the "custom(s)" and "statutes" refer to non-Israelite regulations (Harrington and Saldarini 1987: 298).
29. See Stade 1886: 156–89; Noth 1943: 85n5; Montgomery and Gehman 1951: 471–80; Gray 1970: 655–56; Würthwein 1984: 401; O'Brien 1989: 211; Eynikel 1996: 94. Whether this text is a late Deuteronomistic addition (e.g., Jones 1984: 555–56) or a post-Deuteronomistic interpolation that mimics Deuteronomistic language (Würthwein 1984: 401; Macchi 1992: 92; 1994a: 67–69; Fritz 2003: 348–57) is not my present concern. Rather, my concern is to demonstrate that vv. 34b–40 react to the claims made earlier (vv. 24–34a).
30. Hence, Macchi (1992: 92) compares the perspective with that of Chronicles and the perspective of vv. 24–34a with that of Ezra-Nehemiah.
31. The reader is not to suppose that "the children of Jacob" (17:34b) are distinct from the northern residents (*pace* Rudolph 1951: 213–14). Rather, the reader is to suppose that the northern residents are to be associated, ethnically at least, with "the children of Jacob" (Ben Zvi 1995: 102).

1995: 112–34, 208–17; Walsh 2000), namely, that 2 Kgs 17:34b–40 concerns northern Israelites deported from their land to various Assyrian locales? In this view, 2 Kgs 17:34b picks up the story from 2 Kgs 17:23, bringing the focus back to the Israelites who were residing in exile.

There is some evidence to indicate that vv. 34b–40 refer to Israelites, because the text speaks of the exodus and of Yhwh's covenant with Israel. The covenantal obligations of Torah are mentioned three times (vv. 34, 35, 37). Nevertheless, there are also some strong connections between vv. 34b–40 and the preceding story (vv. 23–34a).[32] The nearest antecedents to the plural third person masculine pronoun and participle (*hēm ʿōśîm*), "they are acting," in v. 34a and the plural third person masculine participles with the inflected negative particle *ʾên* (*ʾênām yěrēʾîm, ʾênām ʿōśîm*), "they are not worshiping, they are not acting," in v. 34b are the plural third person perfects and participles (*hāyû yěrēʾîm, hāyû ʿōbědîm*) in v. 33, "they were worshiping, they were serving," referring to the Samarians. In other words, the very placement of v. 34 after v. 33 suggests a relationship between the two passages.

Indeed, closer examination reveals that the latter passage (vv. 34b–40) has been framed to refute the conclusion of the earlier pericope (vv. 24–34a), namely, that the northerners worshiped Yhwh. The writer of 17:34b–40 introduces his material by the literary technique known as inverted citation (Beentjes 1982) from v. 34b, "[until this day] they are acting according to their former custom" (a: *hēm ʿōśîm*; b: *kammišpāṭām hāriʾšōn*)"[33] to the end of v. 40, "according to their former custom they are acting" (b: *kěmišpāṭām hāriʾšōn*; a: *hēm ʿōśîm*).[34] The insertion of new material itself calls attention to the editor's engagement with a preexisting narrative. In short, the author of vv. 34b–40 rebuts the claim that the postexilic northern population worships Yhwh, yet assumes that this population stands in continuity with the northern Israelites. In other words, the writer does not view the Samarians ethnically as non-Israelites.[35]

---

32. The matter is admittedly complex (Knoppers 2007).
33. Reading the sing. "former custom" with the LXX and the Vg. The MT has "former customs" (cf. Tg. "former laws"). Cf. v. 40.
34. A later editor, who compiles a brief update, has added v. 41, reasserting the thrust of vv. 24–34a by returning to the statement in v. 34a and quoting it according to the same technique (inverted citation)—v. 34 "until this day they are acting" (a: *ʿad hā-yôm hā-zeh*; b: *hēm ʿōśîm*); v. 41: "they do so until this day" (b: *hēm ʿōśîm*; a: *ʿad hā-yôm hā-zeh*). The editor clearly has the earlier pericope in view, because he speaks of "these nations" (*hā-gôyîm hāʾēlleh*), referring to "the nations" (*hā-gôyîm*) in vv. 26 and 29.
35. Alternatively, one could argue that the colonists from Assyria are now being held responsible for observing the covenant traditionally observed by the Israelites (Cohn 2000: 122). In this scenario, the colonists take on the historical identity of the departed Israelites.

The interpolated text begins with the assertion that *'ênām yěrē'îm 'et-yhwh*, "they do not worship Yhwh," thus both citing and contesting the repeated declaration in v. 33 (and elsewhere in the earlier passage), that *'et-yhwh hāyû yěrē'îm*, "Yhwh they were worshiping" (cf. 17:29, 32). Unlike the earlier text, this text (vv. 34b–40) associates the postexilic northern inhabitants with the Israelites by making reference to Israel's obligation, under the terms of the covenant, "not to worship, bow down to, serve, or sacrifice to other gods" (17:35). Significantly, the thrice-repeated admonition not to worship other deities (17:35, 37, 38)—quoted as part of a direct speech from Yhwh to the people (17:35–39)—both assumes a direct communication from Israel's God to this people and presents worship as an either/or proposition. Citing the repeated use of the verb *yārā'* ("to fear, to worship") in his source, the writer of this later text disputes its Yahwistic application to the postexilic residents of Samaria.[36] Remembering "the covenant that I [Yhwh] cut with you" means that "you are not to worship other gods; but, rather Yhwh your God you are to worship" (17:38–39). The adversative *kî 'im* is strategically placed in the middle of this chiastic construction:

ולא תיראו אלהים אחרים
כי אם־
את־יהוה אלהיכם תיראו

By this logic, the residents of the former northern kingdom fail to worship Yhwh precisely because they also worship other gods. The basis for the argument is revealing. The connection of the subject of this passage with the Israel whom Yhwh brought out of Egypt (17:36) critically undermines the earlier claim that the subject was a group of foreign peoples whom the Assyrian king imported into the southern Levant. The admonition to Jacob's descendants not to forget the covenant that "I [Yhwh] cut with you" (17:38) and "not worship other gods (*lō' tîrĕ'û 'ĕlōhîm 'ăḥērîm*)" intimates that Jacob's descendants did indeed forget the

---

36. The use of the verb "to fear" (ירא = worship) with Yhwh as object appears in the earlier text (17:24–34a) in 17:32 (*bis*) and 33 and in the later text (17:34b–40) in 17:39. The same verb is used in a negative sense with Yhwh as object in 17:34b. The use of the verb with other gods as the object appears three times in the later text (17:35, 37, 38). Elsewhere in 2 Kings 17, the verb appears with "other gods" in 2 Kgs 17:7 and with Yhwh as object in the summary of 17:41. Elsewhere within Deuteronomy and the Deuteronomistic work, the verb often refers to loyal service and piety (Deut 4:10; 14:23; 17:19; 31:12, 13; Josh 4:24; 1 Sam 12:14, 24; 1 Kgs 8:40, 43; Weinfeld 1972: 83, 322, 332–33). The chief exception is 2 Kings 17.

covenant and worshipped other gods.[37] The declaration that Yhwh would have delivered the people from their enemies if the people had worshiped Yhwh (2 Kgs 17:39) assumes both that Yhwh revealed this obligation to this people in the past and that they themselves were responsible for their later problems. The implication is that things could have been otherwise. If the descendants of Jacob had followed the example of their eponymous ancestor (Gen 35:1–12) and the example of other Israelites (e.g., Judg 10:16–11:33; 1 Sam 7:3–14) and put away their foreign gods, history would have taken a different course.[38] From this perspective, the behavior of the descendants of Jacob, unlike that of their ancestor, was self-destructive. The Israelites were thus themselves to blame for their ill fortunes. Indeed, their sad fate itself indicates that they did not worship Yhwh. The conclusion that "they did not listen, but rather acted according to their former custom" (2 Kgs 17:40) is predicated on the people having been part of a long-term, albeit troubled, relationship with the God of Jacob.

The point is not that this writer is less critical of the northerners than the previous writer is. Indeed, he may be more severe in his judgment, yet the second writer brings a different ethnographic understanding to the situation from that of the first. The earlier writer depicts the residents as foreigners and thus lacking any association with the name Israel. The second writer views the ancestors of Samaria's residents as descendants of Jacob, but charges these inhabitants with not worshiping Yhwh according to the terms that he thinks are normative for all who would identify with the name Jacob. He asserts that the (surviving) Israelite residents of Samaria were fundamentally unchanged by the Assyrian conquests.[39] They stubbornly clung to their ways and failed to worship Yhwh, just as their ancestors failed to worship Yhwh.

The text of 2 Kings 17 has often been viewed as presenting a univocal perspective on Samarian origins, but the situation is more complex. The chapter presents two fundamentally different understandings of Samarians—one as foreign and the other as Israelite.[40] These two conceptions, along with the view that the Samarians were somehow an ethnic

---

37. Reading with the MT and the Tg. (*lectio difficilior*). The LXX and Vg. have the 3rd masc. sing.
38. The indebtedness of 2 Kgs 17:34b–40 to a select group of earlier texts will be the topic of a future essay.
39. Hence, the writer(s) of this passage, like the writer(s) of 17:24–34a, posits continuity. But, in this case, the continuity resides in nonworship of Yhwh.
40. The latter is, of course, also the Samaritan view. The Samaritans see themselves as descendants of the sons of Joseph (Pummer 1987b:2–5; Hjelm 2000: 76–103; Faü and Crown 2001: 7–15).

conglomeration of native Israelites and foreigners—have dominated scholarly discussions from antiquity to modernity.[41] Indeed, the juxtaposition of the two passages (17:24–34a and 17:34b–40) creates its own impression on readers. Taken together, the two texts have functioned as a kind of metanarrative in the history of the interpretation. "The resultant composite of the two distinct documents presents the Samaritan religion as a heathen eclecticism, and this presentation has swayed subsequent opinion to regard that sect as utterly perverse, so that 'the good Samaritan' appears as a surprise" (Montgomery and Gehman 1951: 471).

IV. Rooting Out the Old-Time Religion

At first glance, it might seem that many of the issues raised in the first passage (2 Kgs 17:24–34a) about postexilic Samaria (ca. late 8th century BCE) are resolved in the account of Josiah's reforms in the late 7th century BCE (2 Kgs 23:15–20). It is true that Josiah's northern campaign, following his many southern reforms (2 Kgs 23:4–14), solves the problem of the ongoing northern cultus as presented in the first narrative (2 Kgs 17:24–34a). Indeed, there are so many parallels among the stories about the establishment of Jeroboam's state cultus, the revival of that cultus in the aftermath of the Assyrian campaigns, and Josiah's northern reforms that some scholars have spoken of a particular source employed by the Deuteronomist(s) in composing this narrative.[42] Whatever the case, Josiah's campaigns do not reconcile all of the inconsistencies in the earlier narratives. Far from it—the story of his reforms raises new complications regarding ethnicity and religiosity.

To be sure, the king desecrates the Bethel altar, burns the asherah, tears down the high places, burns their altars, and slaughters all of the northern priests upon the high place altars (2 Kgs 23:15–20). Predicated upon

---

41. The antique view that the Samaritans were Cutheans or Cuthites from the region of Cutha (Greek *Xouthos*; cf. MT 2 Kgs 17:24 *kûtâ*) whom the Assyrian king brought to Samaria is already attested in Josephus (*BP* 1.63; *Ant.* 9.279, 288–91; 10.184; 11.302; Pummer 2009: 67–76).
42. Or as an addition or a layer secondary to the composition of the primary work. See Talmon (1981); Macchi (1992; 1994a); and, most recently, Van Seters (2000: 119–34), who views 1 Kgs 12:33–13:33, 2 Kgs 23:15–20 (and probably 2 Kgs 17:24–34 as well) as the work of a post-Deuteronomistic (postexilic) narrator, who interpolated all of this material into Kings. It seems likely that one can discern the work of a succession of writers in the relevant texts, although situating each of the texts within a specific time frame is difficult. One should also pay some credence to Van Seters' own plea (ironic, in this instance) not to deal death to the Deuteronomistic work by endlessly multiplying redactions.

a remarkable constancy in the northern cultic practice over the course of some three centuries, the story maintains the historical and prophetic ties that bind the fate of north and south. Judah's greatest reformer decisively eradicates Jeroboam's sins and fulfills the prophecies delivered against the Bethel altar and the northern high places shortly after the Bethel cultus was inaugurated by northern Israel's founding monarch (1 Kgs 13:1–3, 32–34; Knoppers 1994: 196–15). Yet one has to ask some basic questions about the assumptions governing this text. When Josiah travels northward in the late 7th-century, approximately a century after the northern monarchy's fall, he is not traveling to the northern kingdom but to an erstwhile Assyrian province. According to the earlier narrative dealing with events in the late 8th century, non-Israelites populate Samaria. Nevertheless, Josiah readily converses in Hebrew with locals in the Bethel area (2 Kgs 23:17–18). Moreover, when Josiah asks the locals, "What is the sign that I am seeing?" (2 Kgs 23:17), the men of the town respond: "The grave of the man of God, who came from Judah and predicted these deeds, which you are performing against the Bethel altar" (2 Kgs 23:17). What happened to the foreigners populating the area of the former northern kingdom? Have they disappeared or have "these nations" (*hā-gôyîm hā'ēlleh*; 2 Kgs 17:41) inhabiting Samaria's towns somehow become Israelite in the intervening century since the Assyrian invasions? Significantly, the men of Bethel know the story about the old prophet and the man of God and apply the prophecy perceptively to King Josiah (2 Kgs 23:18; cf. 1 Kgs 13:1–3).[43] Either the teaching of the repatriated Israelite priest in the late 8th century was remarkably detailed or the story of Josiah's reforms presupposes that he is dealing with his northern kin.[44]

---

43. And one has to suppose either that nothing had essentially changed since the late 10th century BCE or that the repatriation of the Israelite priest led to the revival of this site as a northern sanctuary in its traditional form.

44. It is also relevant that Kings mentions two cases of Judahite kings marrying northern brides in the late 8th and 7th centuries. One of Hezekiah's wives hails from Jotbah (*yoṭbâ*; 2 Kgs 21:19) in Lower Galilee (probably Kh. Yifât), while one of Josiah's wives hails from Rumah (*rûmâ*; 2 Kgs 23:36), also in Lower Galilee (Kh. er-Rûmah). It may be too much to assert that there was "settled policy of connubium with the north after the time of Hezekiah" (Albright 1939: 184–85). Some caution is called for as there may also be a Rumah in the Judean Hills, although this theory assumes that Dumah (MT and Tg. Josh 15:52; Eusebius, *Onomasticon* 78; Jerome, *Liber Locorum* 79) should be read as Rumah (so some Heb. MSS and a few LXX witnesses, assuming a *rêš*/*dālet* confusion). Some (e.g., Aharoni 1979: 354; Kallai 1986: 389) associate Dumah with Kh. ed-Deir Dômeh southwest of Hebron. In any case, the continuing connections between the Judahite royal house and certain northern families augur against the supposition that there was no longer an active Israelite community in the former northern kingdom (Oded 1987: 42; Cogan and Tadmor 1988: 275; Barrick 2000: 566; Dutcher-Walls 2007: 213–17).

As for Josiah, he treats the Bethel shrine, the Bethel altar, and the high places as if they were all Israelite in character. There are a series of parallels between Moses' incineration and pulverization of the golden calf (Exod 32:20; Deut 9:21) and the manner of Josiah's southern and northern reforms (2 Kgs 23:4–20; Friedman 1981; Knoppers 1994). Hence, like Moses, Josiah seems to be waging an inner-Israelite battle. He enforces the Deuteronomic statutes of centralization—the removal of all non-Yahwistic and Yahwistic altars (apart from the Yahwistic Jerusalem temple altar)—in support of one divinely elect sanctuary for all Israelites (Deut 12). Similarly, his sacrificing the northern priests upon the high place altars and his burning of their bones upon these altars treats these officiants as if they were rebellious Israelites advocating the worship of other gods (cf. Deut 13:2–19).[45] The statutes of Deut 13 mandate such summary executions, without recourse to a normal judicial review, for prophets (vv. 2–6) and anyone else within the covenant community who agitates for the worship of other gods (vv. 7–12; Levinson 1995, 1996). But these statutes pertain, of course, to Israelites.[46]

The king's extirpation of northern cultic sites raises further questions about the ethnicity of Samaria's residents. If Josiah extended his centralization campaign to the towns of Samaria by contaminating the Bethel sanctuary and other northern shrines, where would those who remained be expected to worship? If they followed Josiah's example, they would worship at the central sanctuary in Jerusalem. But this raises the larger issue of whether the northerners of Josiah's time should be regarded as Israelite in character.[47] The accounts of northern religion (2 Kgs 17:24–34a) and Josiah's northern reforms (2 Kgs 23:15–20) exhibit many interesting verbal and thematic parallels, but it is ironically the historical and ethnic understanding of the northern residents presupposed in the second

---

45. To his credit, Cogan (2004) recognizes this problem and asserts that Josiah's northern campaign was only directed at Israelite inhabitants of Samaria. Josephus (*Ant.* 10.68) makes a similar claim, stating that Josiah campaigned against the Israelites who survived the Assyrian invasions. But the text does not make any such distinction.

46. The same point can be made another way. If the text assumed that the people of the north were foreigners, one could conceivably imagine the Deuteronomists portraying Josiah as a new Joshua, who intervenes against indigenous peoples (Deut 20:1–18). But Josiah is not portrayed in this manner. Rather, the focus is on the high place priests, who led the Israelite people in worshiping other gods.

47. They certainly appear as such in Chronicles, which reuses the text of Kings. The Chronistic treatment is a subject in and of itself (chapter 4), but it is surely relevant that the Chronicler understood his *Vorlage* of Kings as indicating that the northerners in Josiah's time were Israelite in character.

account of postexilic Samarian religion (2 Kgs 17:34b–40) that seems to be operative in Josiah's northern campaign. The commentary on the land's ethnic revolution (2 Kgs 17:24–34a) insists that Samaria's postexilic residents were outsiders, but Josiah's reforms suggest otherwise. In the latter case, there is every indication that the Judahite monarch is waging an inner-Israelite battle.

Conclusions

In his detailed treatment of 2 Kings 17, Brettler (1995: 133) comments that "because the reason that the north was exiled was of tremendous ideological importance for the Judeans, the story of the exile of the north acted as a magnet, collecting an unusually large number of traditions and reflections." Brettler helpfully calls attention to the sustained Judahite interest in the Assyrian exile. Yet surely the questions arising for Judahite writers did not have to do simply with the causes of the Israelite deportations, but also with the phenomenon of continuing Yahwistic worship in the former northern kingdom. Given the northern monarchy's end, the dislocation of Israelites to various sites in the Assyrian empire, and the passage of many generations, how should one account for the continuation of Yahwism in Samaria? To this question, writers in the Deuteronomistic tradition did not provide univocal, much less simple, answers.

The very fact that there are a variety of positions within a single literary work is itself revealing, because it suggests that the issues of identity, religious practice, and national origins were ongoing issues in elite Judahite circles. The complications and tensions in the three accounts we have discussed suggest that the practice of some form of Yahwism in the north challenged and strained a series of Deuteronomistic principles, such as the linkages among deity and geography, people and land, genealogy and nationality, ethnicity and practice. The tensions and strains were undoubtedly exacerbated by the fact that Judahite conceptions of northern identity had a direct bearing on how the writers viewed their own Judahite identity (Macchi 1992; 1994a: 59–135; Jobling 2003). The strong tie between God and country could lead one to assert that Yhwh demanded obedience from foreign immigrants, even though these immigrants had no earlier ties to the Israelites. One could embrace a comprehensive concept of Israel, as opposed to a restrictive one, and yet debate whether continuity in Israelite identity was to be found outside the land in exile or inside the land in religious beliefs and practices (Linville 1998:

212–18). One could insist on a comprehensive northern forced migration, yet also insist that over the centuries northern religious practices remained fairly stable. One could concede that the northerners were biological descendants of Jacob, but dispute that they truly worshiped Yhwh. One could marginalize northern affairs after the Assyrian conquests by restricting coverage to Judah, but insist that northern Israel remained an object of divine concern by having Judah's greatest reformer right northern wrongs.

Modern scholars have tried to tidy up the discordant statements about northern history found in Kings, but the Deuteronomistic writers may have held to more pliant and elastic notions of Israelite identity than we have recognized.[48] For these literati, religious practice and inhabitation of the land may have carried more weight than simply the factor of strict genealogy. Or, to put matters somewhat differently, genealogy was ultimately tied to centuries of inhabitation of the land, language, social mores, and worship practices. Such writers may have allowed for the development of a kind of Israelite identity in the land over time even though they deplored the practices of the very people who adopted these ancestral rites. In any case, the tensions and strains in Kings should caution us against simplifying the Deuteronomistic work's depiction of northern history in the aftermath of the Assyrian campaigns. The three passages in question demonstrate that there was significant diversity of opinion within elite circles. These Judahite writers belonged to a living and developing tradition, rather than to a static and monolithic school. Their views are important not least because they tell us what different Jerusalemite scribes, writing at various times, thought about postexilic northern history.

Such views have to be sifted and carefully evaluated before they are employed in the service of historical reconstruction. To be sure, attempts have been made to reconcile the disparate viewpoints expressed in the compositional history of Kings. In one common theory, the Samarians are indeed deemed to be foreigners, but ones who became more Israelite over time.[49] This interpretation aims to account for the continuation (or reemergence) of Yahwism in Samaria by integrating

---

48. Especially if one follows the sequence from 2 Kgs 17:24–34a to 23:15–20. The shift is not as abrupt if one moves from 2 Kgs 17:34b–40 to 23:15–20. But note that 2 Kgs 17:41 reiterates the basic point of 2 Kgs 17:24–34a.
49. E.g., Kuenen 1875: 206–8; Kaufman 1960: 130–31, 286–87, 300–301; Cogan 1974: 107–10.

the testimony of 2 Kgs 17:24–34a with the later references in 2 Kgs 23:15–20.[50] The Samarians initially remained non-Israelites with respect to national-historical identity, but they abandoned their pagan ways after centuries of settlement in Israel among the remaining, nondeported Israelites. As the generations passed, the immigrants became more and more Israelite in their actions. The diverse conglomeration of groups eventually melded together into a new reality (proto-Samaritans or Samaritans).

Another interpretation, less common than the first, stipulates that the immigrant communities were separate from those of the surviving Israelites and remained so for several centuries (Alt 1953b, 1959; Schur 1989: 21–23; cf. Coggins 1975: 18–20). The former consisted of the imported elite, while the latter consisted of the lower classes remaining in the land. The former were much more powerful politically than the latter, but the latter managed to maintain their own distinctive religious profile. During the course of their history, the northern Israelites became more exclusively Yahwistic and developed their own notable standards of piety, including the concept of cult centralization. Indeed, according to Alt (1953a), Ginsberg (1982), Schorch (2011), and others, proto-Deuteronomy was a predominately northern document that made its way south in the hands of northern refugees and influenced events in the southern kingdom during Josiah's late-7th-century reforms.[51] Hence, the northern and southern Yahwistic communities did not exist in complete isolation from one another. There was some important interaction between the two. Centuries later, the northern Yahwistic group adopted the Torah and became known as the Samaritans.[52]

There is something to be said for certain elements in both of these reconstructions. There is, as we have seen (chapter 2), some evidence of a limited elite Assyrian presence in the land. There is also some evidence for the continuation of Yahwism in the north long after the time of the Assyrian deportations. Yet both of these reconstructions have debilitating flaws and are unnecessarily complicated.[53] Whatever the precise number of foreign settlers may have been, most seem to have been integrated into

---

50. And in some cases with Ezra 4:2, 10 (but not with 2 Kgs 17:34b–40).
51. Ironically, then, proto-Deuteronomy's own doctrine of centralization was turned against northern sanctuaries by a later southern king.
52. In Alt's reconstruction, the elite upper class also evolved over the centuries and oversaw the construction of the Mt. Gerizim temple (mostly for the use of the lower classes).
53. In particular, see the sharp critique of Alt's theory by M. Smith (1987: 147–53).

native society over the course of the generations.[54] In this respect, one has to be careful not to take the typologically driven and theologically laden presentation of Kings too literally (Oded 2003). The blanket statements about the utterly transformative effects of bidirectional deportations cannot be taken at face value for historical purposes. The historical realities affecting the former Israelite kingdom were likely not so dramatic, much less convoluted. The numbers of northern Israelites remaining in the land far outnumbered the population of the resident Assyrians and Assyrian-sponsored immigrants. For this reason, only scattered material remains attest to a foreign presence. It was not a matter of some surviving Israelites intermarrying with and absorbing a much larger foreign presence. Rather, the opposite scenario held true. A substantial number of Israelites gradually absorbed a minor foreign presence within their ranks over the course of several generations.

The continuity within Samaria, in spite of the Assyrian conquests, deportations, and depopulation during the late 8th century, helps to explain the later literary reflections about the settlers found in Kings. The very insistence of the first Kings account that the religious practices of the new settlers quickly came to resemble the older form of Israelite state religion observed for centuries before the settlers arrived suggests that the Assyrian conquests caused less long-term upheaval for the region of Samaria than the blanket statements of dislocation (2 Kgs 17:6, 18, 20, 23) might initially indicate. The claim that the new northern religion quickly reverted to its earlier Israelite form represents a southern scribal attempt to explain substantial stability in northern practices. Even the later writer (2 Kgs 17:34b–40), who disagrees with the opinion found in the immigrants tale (17:24–34a), concedes the larger point about ethnicity. His argument is not predicated on the northerners being foreigners. Quite the contrary—his argument is predicated upon the northerners having a genealogical link to the patriarch Jacob. On this basis, he contends that they have departed from their historical roots and do not practice proper (exclusive) Yahwistic worship. They may be linked genealogically to Jacob, but they do not conform to the terms of the divinely initiated covenant with Jacob's descendants.

Similar considerations come into play when one grapples with the assumptions inherent in the stories about Josiah's northern reforms. That

---

54. It is also possible that some left with the decline in the Assyrian empire in the late 7th century.

this material has the king encountering northerners in the late 7th century who know the old legends about the man of God from Judah and the prophet from Bethel should occasion no great surprise. The story's presupposition is that the Judahite ruler was dealing with Israelites. For this very reason, it was vitally important (in Deuteronomistic perspective) for the southern monarch to reclaim part of the legacy of the united monarchy and reinstate, however temporarily, Jerusalem's cultic sovereignty over northern Israelites. However much the first writer distances the landed immigrants ethnically from the Israelites but links them religiously to the Israelites, the writer of the Josiah account has the reformer waging an inner-Israelite struggle.

This study has larger implications for our understanding of the development (and interaction) of Israelite and Judahite literature in the First Temple period. Scholars have long puzzled over the presence of northern traditions in a variety of biblical books. If the northern kingdom was decimated in the 8th century and its inhabitants deported to foreign lands, how did ostensibly northern writings, such as Hosea, find their way into the canons of southern literature? If the Israelite kingdom was exiled, how did Kings come to include so many stories about northern prophets, such as Elijah and Elisha? One common explanation, as we have seen, is that northern refugees brought such literature to Judah in the late 8th century BCE, when they fled south before the advancing Assyrian armies. While it is certainly possible that such migrants brought traditional lore with them to Judah, it seems precarious, historically speaking, to posit one single moment as the occasion for the origin of all Israelite literature in Judah. Each of the relevant biblical writings has its own complex history of composition and editing. As many have acknowledged, the late 8th century may well be too early a time for all of the literature associated with northern circles to have been revised, edited, and interpolated into southern writings. One has also to deal with the distinct possibility that the Bethel sanctuary served for some time as a conduit of northern traditions to the south (Blenkinsopp 2003; Knauf 2006; Na'aman 2010).[55]

Recognition that Yahwism in northern Israel continued and evolved during Neo-Assyrian and Neo-Babylonian times provides a more historically viable and complete explanation for how northern traditions made

---

55. The sanctuary at (or near) Bethel seems to have fallen into desuetude in the late Neo-Babylonian or early Persian period, but by this time it lay within the boundaries of Yehud (Stern 2001; Lipschits 1998, 2005).

their way into southern literary works. Northern Israel was hard hit and significantly depopulated during the Assyrian occupation, but endured in reduced circumstances. Communications between north and south continued, because Judahites and Israelites shared much in common in spite of their historical and cultural differences. In times of foreign occupation, it was not normally in the best interests of either geographically contiguous unit to ignore the other. Notions of a larger pan-Israelite tribal entity to which the Yahwistic members of each community ultimately belonged survived, but were transformed to address new circumstances. The transmission of literary traditions from Samaria to Judah (and vice versa) was, therefore, not a one-off phenomenon, but rather an ongoing dynamic in the history of relations between the two evolving communities.

4

The Fall of the Northern Kingdom as a New Beginning in Northern Israelite–Southern Israelite Relations

SCHOLARS LONG VIEWED the Chronistic treatment of the former northern kingdom (and, by implication, the Samaritans) as largely an update and extension of one of the views found in Kings (2 Kgs 17:24–34a). Interpreting Chronicles-Ezra-Nehemiah as a single work written sometime in the Persian period (538–332 BCE), scholars concluded that Judah and Samaria were perpetually at loggerheads with one another. The mutual animosity theory was so common that many commentators in the 19th and 20th centuries simply assumed that the rivalry between Jews and Samaritans dominated the religious, social, and political life of postexilic Judah. Wellhausen (1885: 188) stated that in the portrayal of the division following Solomon's death, the Chronicler demonstrates his belief that "Israel is the congregation of true worship...connected with the temple at Jerusalem, in which of course the Samaritans have no part." Similarly, in von Rad's view (1930: 31), Judah and Benjamin constitute "the true Israel" over against their neighbors to the north. Presupposing a highly contentious atmosphere, Pfeiffer (1961: 202) opined, "In the days of the Chronicler the Samaritan community was to Judaism a more serious adversary than heathenism."

In an even stronger version of this view, some contended that the Chronicler engaged in a strident polemic, depicting northern Israel as a pagan or abandoned people.[1] From this perspective, the Samarian community and the Judean community were judged to be

---

1. See, e.g., Torrey 1909: 157–73, 188–17; 1954: xviii–xix; Galling 1954: 15; Plöger 1968: 37–38; Rowley 1955–56: 166–98; Mosis 1973: 169–71, 200–201.

two fundamentally different ethnic enclaves. Thus, the Chronistic depiction of the northern kingdom was a thinly disguised attempt to address present problems by rewriting the past. According to de Wette (1806–7: 1:126–32), the Chronicler wrote to express his "love for Judah and his hatred toward Samaria" ("Vorliebe für Juda und Häß gegen Israel"). Similarly, Bewer (1933: 294) wrote: "The [northern] Israelites were no better than the heathen. Judah alone was God's people." Pfeiffer claimed that the Chronicler's portrayal of the northern tribes was a guise for a diatribe against the Samaritans, whom the author regarded "ethnically as alien rabble (Ezra 4:1–3, 7–11; 5:3, 6; 6:6) and religiously as semiheathen (II [2 Chr] 13:4–12), Godforsaken (II 25:7–10) mobs, over whom the divine wrath rests because of their abominations (II 28:9–15)."[2]

Recent scholars have strongly reacted against this long-established and forceful anti-Samaritan line of interpretation by attacking the central premises upon which it was based.[3] Calling into question the widely held assumption that the Chronicler wrote Chronicles and Ezra-Nehemiah, Japhet (1968, 1983, 1989, 1993), Williamson (1977b, 1982, 1989), and others argued that the author of Chronicles was not anti-Samaritan in orientation. Far from it—the Chronicler displays a very open and conciliatory attitude toward residents of the north whom he unequivocally regards as Israelites. The work espouses a comprehensive understanding of the nature of Israel, comprising twelve or more tribes, all of whom are linked genealogically to each other by means of a shared ancestry to the patriarch Jacob/Israel (1 Chr 2:3–8:40; Japhet 1989; Willi 1994, 1995; Knoppers 2004a). To be sure, Ezra-Nehemiah provides a much more hostile perspective toward the northern community and presents very different ideas about ethnicity, national identity, and the people's role in an international imperial context. In this respect, the older view may be judged to have some merit. But even here, the situation is more complicated than previously acknowledged (J. L. Wright 2004; Knoppers 2007). In any case, the many differences between Ezra-Nehemiah and Chronicles are telling. The emphatic reassertion of pan-Israelite identity found in Chronicles would not make much sense in a cultural setting in which it was universally

---

2. "Behind the mask of the ancient kingdom of Israel, he [the Chronicler] portrayed the detested Samaritan community" (Pfeiffer 1948: 811).
3. Including the supposition that the Samaritan Pentateuch was an early postexilic work (chapter 7).

accepted that the Samarian and Judean communities were ethnically, historically, and religiously distinct.

The anti-Samaritan theory has thus been dealt a series of serious blows. Yet, if scholars have been guilty of retrojecting later disputes into earlier times, what should one make of Judean-Samarian relations during the Achaemenid occupation?[4] Viewing recent scholarly developments as healthy correctives to the extreme views promoted in past generations, I have no desire to return to the dominant theories of the 19th and early 20th centuries. Nevertheless, several salient issues remain. How do the Chronistic claims about ethnic, religious, and national constitution compare with the assertions about postexilic northern practices expressed in Kings? What are the important differences between the two works, and what are the similarities? Granted that Chronicles espouses a comprehensive notion of Israelite identity, what are the practical implications of such a view? Is there any hierarchy in its depiction of pan-Israelite identity, or is its ideology inherently egalitarian? Ethnographers speak of multiple and sometimes overlapping indices of ethnic identity, such as ties to an ancestral homeland, a common language, collective genealogy, a single religion, and shared history. Are the assertions about shared ancestry and historic ties to the land balanced or offset by assertions of Judahite distinctiveness and privilege?[5] In relating the Chronistic perspective to its social context, how significant is the issue of Judahite-Ephraimite relations? Given the paradigmatic and typological traits exhibited by the writing, how might its portrayal of Israelite-Judahite contacts during the monarchy shed light on Samarian-Judean relations in the late Persian/early Hellenistic era?[6]

At the outset, it should be observed that Chronicles includes many north-south incidents in its portrayal of the Judahite monarchy. In fact, the work includes every instance of Judahite-Israelite encounters found in Kings, save one (2 Kings 3). In addition, the book depicts many important encounters not mentioned in Kings. In what follows, I would like to focus on three critical stories about Judah's relations with its northern neighbor

---

4. The issue of terminology is difficult, but I am referring to the residents of Yehud and Samaria during the Persian and early Hellenistic periods as Judeans and Samarians to distinguish them from the later Jews and Samaritans of the Maccabean and Roman periods. In both cases, I see lines of continuity from one period to the next.
5. Such distinctions are evident in the genealogical prologue to the book in which three sodalities—Judah, Levi, and Benjamin—receive the bulk of coverage and pride of place (Kartveit 1989; Oeming 1990; Knoppers 2004a).
6. Recently, Schweitzer 2007, with references.

in the latter stages of the Judahite monarchy. The case studies involve the story of the good Samarians (2 Chr 28:8–15) in the time of King Ahaz (743–728 BCE), the Passover and cultic reforms of King Hezekiah (727–699 BCE), which include the estranged northern tribes (2 Chr 30:1–26), and the account of Josiah's pan-Israelite reforms (641–610 BCE; 2 Chr 34:1–35:19).[7] The first two incidents, unique to Chronicles, tell us a great deal about what the writer wanted his readers to know about northern Israel in the centuries following the Assyrian conquests. In the third case, Josiah's reforms, Chronicles presents a strikingly variant account to that found in Kings.

The fact that the work provides its readers with so many north-south stories is remarkable. The presence of a significant Yahwistic population to the north of Yehud illumines why, in my view, Chronicles revisits aspects of northern history. It must be emphasized that for reasons of coverage and temporal context, the author was not compelled to do so. The factor of coverage is relevant, because the Chronicler does not include independent northern history in his own story of the monarchy. Regarding both the kingdom and the cult of the northern tribes as inherently rebellious, he does not provide an independent history of the northern realm (Knoppers 1990, 1993a). Kings provides a synchronistic history of Israel and Judah, but Chronicles concentrates on Judahite history and only mentions northern Israel when it depicts contacts between the two realms. The factor of temporal context is relevant, because the author lived during the late Persian/early Hellenistic period, a time in which the northern monarchy had already been extinct for some four centuries. Given the temporal distance from the events depicted, the writer did not have to go out of his way to engage northern Israel's populace, social structure, and religious practices. That the author evidently felt the need to discuss northern leadership, life, and cult suggests that these issues were not only historical in nature but also in some way current. Indeed, the separate existence of the provinces of Yehud and Samaria may have spurred the Chronicler to reflect on the original division of Judah and Israel. If one looks at the different eras in ancient Israelite history as they are presented in the Pentateuch and the Former Prophets, the separation between Israel and Judah during the divided monarchy was the most analogous to the separation of Samaria

---

7. On the chronological challenges in correlating the biblical information about regnal years with extrabiblical epigraphic data, see Miller and Hayes (2006: 393–98).

and Yehud in his own era. Some of the writer's hopes and aspirations for his own time would thus likely be evident in his depiction of the Judahite monarchy. In any case, the work's depiction of north-south relations cannot be completely divorced from Samarian-Judean relations in the writer's own social, historical, and religious setting. One inevitably affected the other.

I. *The Tale of the Good Samarians*

The unique story of the good graces afforded to captive Judahites by northern Israelites is placed in one of the worst periods of Judahite history—the reign of King Ahaz (ca. 743–728 BCE). The tumultuous tenure of Ahaz straddles a number of different developments in Syro-Palestinian history—the short reign of the Israelite king Pekah (734–731 BCE), the Syro-Ephraimite crisis, the western campaigns of the great Assyrian king Tiglath-pileser III (1 Chr 5:26), and the beginning of the reign of the last Israelite king, Hoshea (730–722 BCE).[8] But the situation with this potentate is even direr than a catalogue of such foreign interventions might suggest. Ahaz is arguably the worst of all Judah's monarchs (Ben Zvi 1993; Johnstone 1997: 174–87). The miserable estimation is tied to how poorly Ahaz fares in cultic matters, international diplomacy, and war. Both Judahites and their monarch practice idolatry (2 Chr 28:2, 10–16, 23; cf. 2 Chr 23:17; 24:7). The temple is shut down and the system of regular sacrifices ceases (2 Chr 28:24; 29:7, 18). In Chronicles, abandoning the Jerusalem temple is one of the most regressive actions a monarch can take (Japhet 1989; Dyck 1998).[9] Perhaps worst of all, Ahaz never reverses course and initiates positive reforms.[10] Far from it— he has a penchant for making matters worse for himself by embarking on one disastrous action after another.[11] Particularly noteworthy is the

---

8. In Chronicles the name Tiglath-pileser (תגלת־פלנאסר; so 2 Kgs 15:29; 16:10; Akkadian *Tukulti-apil-Ešarra*, "My help is the son of Esharra") is always spelled Tilgath-pilneser (תלגת־פלנאסר; 1 Chr 5:6; 2 Chr 28:20; or תלגת־פלנסר; 1 Chr 5:26). For the convenience of readers, I have followed the older and more familiar Hebrew version of the monarch's name.
9. Similarly, in later times Josephus (*AgAp* 193–98) lists the Temple cult as the first item in his tabulation of the essentials of Jewish worship.
10. In contrast, even Manasseh, the worst of all Judah's kings (as presented in 2 Kgs 21:1–18) repents, alters course, and implements reforms (2 Chr 33:1–20; Kelly 1996).
11. Although the Davidic dynasty (though threatened) is never at the brink of extinction (cf. 2 Chr 21:8–11, 16–17; 22:4–10; 23:18; 24:15).

tremendous loss of life, treasure, and territory.¹² The succession of setbacks may be summarized as follows.

- The Judahites suffer a "great deportation" (שביה גדולה) at the hands of the Aramean king to Damascus (2 Chr 28:5a).
- A "great slaughter" (מכה גדולה) of 120,000 Judahite warriors occurs at the hands of the Israelite king Pekah (2 Chr 28:5b–6).¹³
- The Judahite forces endure the deaths of the king's son, the commander of the palace, and the second (officer) to the king at the hands of Israelite warriors (2 Chr 28:7).
- The Israelites capture (שבה) 200,000 of their (Judahite) kinsmen, women, and children (2 Chr 28:8).
- The Israelites plunder Judah and take a great deal of booty to Samaria (2 Chr 28:8).
- The Edomites invade Judah and lead away (שבה) captives (שבי; 2 Chr 28:17).
- The Philistines tear away from Judah a number of towns in the Shephelah and in the Negev and subsequently settle (ישב) there (2 Chr 28:18).
- King Ahaz apportions (precious metals) from the temple and royal palace for the benefit of the Assyrian monarch Tiglath-pileser,¹⁴ but the Assyrian king comes to afflict Ahaz, rather than to function as a help (עזרה) to him (2 Chr 28:20–21).¹⁵

The only pause in this downward Judahite spiral comes from northern Israelites. The unusual kindness shown toward their southern kin occurs in the aftermath of a series of two separate invasions of Judah by Damascus (Syria) and Israel.¹⁶ Of the two, the writer's interests lie with the latter.

---

12. Sorting out all the troubles afflicting Ahaz chronologically (2 Chr 28:5, 6, 9) is difficult, because the text lacks precise temporal markers (De Vries 1989).
13. On the use of fabulous round numbers, see the note to 1 Chr 12:38 in my commentary (Knoppers 2004b: 569–71).
14. In summarily speaking of Ahaz raiding the temple and the royal treasuries, the Chronicler is alluding to the longer account in his principal source (2 Kgs 16:8), which accuses Ahaz of having removed the silver and gold from the temple and the royal treasuries to dispatch as a שחד (gift or bribe) to the Assyrian king.
15. In contrast, Chronicles often depicts God "helping" (עזר) faithful kings (e.g., 2 Chr 14:10; 18:31; 25:8; 26:7, 15; 32:8). Ironically, Ahaz's problem is not a lack of religiosity per se. After suffering a series of losses, he goes on to sacrifice to the gods of Damascus, reasoning that "because the gods of the kings of Damascus helped (עזר) them, they will help (עזר) me" (2 Chr 28:23).
16. According to 2 Kgs 16:5, King Pekah of Israel and King Rezin of Syria invaded Judah and advanced toward Jerusalem (Spieckermann 1982: 362–69; Schoors 1998). See also Isa

A New Beginning 77

Table 4.1 Judah's Decline and the Good Samarians

Introduction	2 Kgs 16:1–2a	2 Chr 28:1a
Regnal Evaluation	2 Kgs 16:2b–3a	2 Chr 28:1b–2a
Cultic Impropriety	2 Kgs 16:3b–4	2 Chr 28:2b–4
Syro(-Ephraimite) War	2 Kgs 16:5	2 Chr 28:5a
Israelite Invasion	—	2 Chr 28:5b
Edom Takes Elath[i]	2 Kgs 16:6	—
Casualties and Booty	—	2 Chr 28:6–8
Prophetic Censure	—	2 Chr 28:9–11
Positive Response	—	2 Chr 28:12–13
Release to Jericho	—	2 Chr 28:14–15

[i] Reading with many textual witnesses אדם and אדמים, and not ארם and ארמים in 2 Kgs 16:6 (*dālet/rēš* confusion). Note the appearance of the Edomites (אדומים) in 2 Chr 28:17 (Cogan and Tadmor 1988: 186–87).

It is not uncommon for Chronicles to mention the active involvement of national "leaders" (שרים) and "ancestral heads" (ראשי האבות) in the context of monarchical rule (e.g., 1 Chr 11:1–3; 13:1–4; 2 Chr 12:5, 6; 19:8; 21:4; 23:2), but it is relevant that the text does not mention any monarchical involvement. The story mentions Zichri the Ephraimite warrior, ancestral "heads of the Ephraimites" (ראשי בני-אפרים), some identified by name and patronymic, "the leaders" (השרים), and "the (Israelite) assembly" (הקהל), but the Israelite and Judahite kings do not play a role in either the prophetic confrontation or in the decision to release the captives, clothe them, feed them, and escort them to Jericho.[17]

When the victorious northern forces enter Samaria with their 200,000 Judahite captives, an otherwise unknown "Yahwistic prophet" (נביא ליהוה) appropriately named Oded (עדד), appears on the scene to deliver a stinging indictment of the Israelite army's conduct (2 Chr 28:9b–11).[18]

7:1–8:15. In 2 Kgs 16:5, the foreign invasions stem from Judah's reluctance to join the western anti-Assyrian coalition led by the kings of Israel and Damascus.

17. Hence, some think that Ahaz is dealing with postmonarchic Israel. The nonappearance of the king is puzzling, yet it is unlikely that the incident pertains to a time following the Assyrian conquests. First, Pekah (734–731 BCE) is the penultimate and not the last king of Israel. Pekah's successor, Hoshea, ruled the northern kingdom for most of its last decade (730–722 BCE). Second, the larger context of the narrative would also seem odd if the story were meant to depict a post-722 BCE phase of northern history. The tale assumes that the Israelites still have a functioning (and victorious) army. Third, there is no hint that Samaria is under duress or subject to Assyrian control.

18. The Hebrew root עוד in the *hip'il* means to warn or admonish. The personal name Oded (עדד) is usually derived from עוד.

A number of features in this speech and in the Ephraimite response are significant. First, Oded assumes that the Judahites enjoy a special relationship with the Israelites and does not treat the Judahites as aliens. Both groups—the Judahites and the Ephraimites—are subject to "Yhwh, the God of your fathers" (v. 9; cf. vv. 10, 13; Japhet 1993: 903). To be sure, Chronicles advances a Jerusalem-centered view of Israelite history. Oded does not cite northern fidelity as the reason for victory, but rather southern infidelity: "It was because Yhwh the God of your fathers was angry with Judah that he delivered them into your hand."[19] In acting as Yhwh's means to punish Judah, the Israelites have been excessive, putting their compatriots to death "with a rage that has reached up to heaven." God's wrath has been aroused and Israel is liable to punishment: "Is it not, however, you,[20] who have sins of your own against Yhwh your God (2 Chr 28:10)?" Nevertheless, the underlying relationship between the two groups remains, and for this reason, those Israelites residing in the north are obliged to respect their "kin" in the south (vv. 8, 11, 15).

Second, Israel, like Judah, is home to Yahwistic prophets who hold the people responsible for their actions. Oded is only one of a number of northern Israelite prophets whose ministries affect southern Israelite affairs (Knoppers 2010). Indeed, the text presents the northern prophet acting in a very similar way to that of southern prophets, confronting the people and holding them to account for their past behavior. One of the chief prophetic functions is to serve as Yhwh's "messengers" (2 Chr 36:15), mercifully warning the people of impending trouble, should their actions lead them astray (Japhet 1989; Kelly 1996). This is precisely the role Oded takes in this story. Third, the indictment of the northern army and its leaders assumes that they are subject to the same standards as Judahites are. The prophet plays on the alliteration among the terms שוב ("to turn, return"), שביה ("captivity, deportation"), and שבה ("to take captive, deport"), imploring the armed forces: "Return (השיבו; *hipʿil*) the captives (השביה), whom you have captured (שביתם) from your kinsmen" (2 Chr 28:11).

---

19. By treating the northern kingdom analogously to Judah's other adversaries, in this respect, the work denies to the northern regime any inherent legitimacy or sanctity in its victories over Judah (Knoppers 1996).

20. Thus the MT (*hălōʾ raq-ʾattem*). The LXX^Bab, the LXX^AN, the Armenian, and Theodotion read *ouk idou eimi*. The adverb *raq* has no equivalent in the LXX. We tentatively follow the MT as the *lectio difficilior* and interpret *raq* in a restrictive sense.

That Oded expressly prohibits the returning soldiers from indenturing (כבש) the captured Judahites raises, however, a question. Why was it so objectionable for the Israelites to enslave their prisoners of war? Such a practice (indenturing foreign captives as war booty) was quite widespread in ancient Near Eastern history. Indeed, subjugating foreigners enabled soldiers to profit from their participation in war. Oded's severe reprimand requires, therefore, some discussion. In biblical laws, a distinction is made between Israelite and non-Israelite slavery. Deuteronomy permits Israelites to obtain non-Israelite slaves in certain circumstances as a consequence of battle victory (Deut 20:10–14), while the Holiness Code allows Israelites to acquire foreign slaves (Lev 25:44–46). Hence, these legal collections do not oppose slavery per se. Nevertheless, the prospect of Israelites owning other Israelites presents another case altogether. In the Covenant Code (Exod 21:2–11) and in Deuteronomy (15:12–18), Israelites are allowed to acquire Hebrew male and female slaves, but the slavery can only be temporary (at least for males in Exodus and for both sexes in Deuteronomy), unless the slaves themselves wish to align permanently with their owners. Israelites are permitted to indenture themselves (or members of their families) to other Israelites on a temporary basis to pay off debts. The Holiness legislation of Lev 25:39–43 forbids, however, Israelite enslavement to other Israelites. None of these law collections contain stipulations allowing Israelites to enslave other Israelites forcibly in the context of war. Narrative accounts indicate that Israelite enslavement of other Israelites did occur, however, even in late times (e.g., Jer 34:8–16; Neh 5:5).[21]

This all-too-quick overview of Pentateuchal legislation elucidates the force of Oded's reprimand. Although the prophet does not directly cite earlier laws, his basic charge against the army leaders presupposes the values inherent in such laws. The intention to enslave Judahites subjects the northern Israelites to the probability of divine retribution. The northerners are already guilty before God (2 Chr 28:10), and such a forced subjugation of their kin would elicit divine retribution.[22] In other words, the text holds the northerners to the same standards to which the southerners are subject. If Oded did not think that the Judahites were Israelite

---

21. Such enslavement is also attested in the 4th-century Samaria papyri (chapter 5). Many of the names of the slaveholders and slaves have Yahwistic theophorics.
22. They stand guilty in the sense that their forefathers had abandoned the Davidic kingdom, the Jerusalem temple, the legitimate priesthood, and had introduced their own rival cultus (2 Chr 10:1–16; 11:13–14; 13:4–12; Knoppers 1990, 1993a).

in character (and therefore kin to the Ephraimites), he would have no basis to charge the soldiers with gross malfeasance. The very assertion of wrongdoing is predicated upon the assumption of shared bloodlines, values, and traditions.

Fourth, the Chronicler does not assume that religious declines in the southern monarchy are paralleled in the northern monarchy. Quite the contrary, in this case, the good Samarians seem to be more in touch with the traditions shared by all Israelites than the Judahite king is. As opposed to Ahaz and his people, who persist in a self-destructive pattern of behavior, the northern Israelites repent and deal compassionately with their vanquished foes. The Ephraimite reaction shows that they are perfectly capable of acknowledging their own culpability, heeding prophecy, and changing their ways. They implore the army officers not to bring the captives into the capital city of Samaria, lest they offend Yhwh and compound the people's guilt (2 Chr 28:13). Not only do the Israelites return the captives, as Oded demanded they should, but they also clothe the prisoners, feed them, release the captured booty, and escort their captives to Jericho (vv. 14–15). Such actions go above and beyond the call of duty.

Finally, the story reveals something else about Chronistic perceptions of the past—a tone of self-criticism. Judah itself fails to live up to the normative standards bequeathed to it and suffers defeat. The presence of formative institutions—the Davidic monarchy, the priests, the Levites, and the temple—does not in and of itself guarantee that Judah will escape calamity.[23] That a complete disaster was avoided on this occasion was not due to any Judahite action. A human tragedy was averted when northern Israelites responded appropriately to a prophetic rebuke. The depiction of this event thus reveals the author's abiding interest in northern Israel: the passage of centuries has not negated the possibility of northern Israelites responding positively to Yhwh, "the God of their fathers."[24]

Analysis of Kings and Chronicles reveals the distinctive traits of each work. In the Deuteronomistic writing, the Israelite monarchy comes to a dramatic and sorry end. The northern political experiment, although authorized by God (1 Kgs 11:1–13, 31–38; 12:15; Knoppers 1993b), comes

---

23. Indeed, the writer admits that the Yahwism he espouses, consisting of a centralized Yahwistic cultus in Jerusalem and the abolition of all other shrines in the country (Yahwistic or otherwise), was rarely realized in the preexilic period.

24. There is no clear evidence, however, that this admission of guilt and act of compassion signal a complete metamorphosis in the status of the north (Knoppers 1989).

to naught approximately two centuries after its founding (931–722 BCE). With the end of the kingdom, northern history stops. To be sure, the long and multilayered Deuteronomistic commentary on the aftermath of Israel's fall reveals, as we have seen, a more complicated situation, one involving the revival of the northern cultus under new sponsors, with new participants in new conditions (2 Kgs 17:23–34a).[25] But discussion of life in Samaria basically ends. In Chronicles the fundamental social structure shared by all Israelites endures through the centuries. Chronicles departs from the Deuteronomistic literary model, drawing a distinction between the people (along with their social institutions) and the monarchy. In Kings, Israel's demise is inextricably tied to the military disasters that attend the final years of its kingdom, but in Chronicles the Israelite people—along with their ancestral heads (ראשי האבות), leaders (שרים), prophets, and assembly (הקהל)—endure in spite of the long-term decline of their royal polity. Monarchs may come and go, but the people remain.

For an audience in the late Achaemenid or early Hellenistic era, the story of the good Samarians would have a special poignancy. The writers of Ezra-Nehemiah depict relations between Judeans and Samarians in the mid-5th century as marred by acrimony and Samarian interference in Judean affairs. Chronicles presents a different picture of northern identity and leadership. Although northerners and southerners have their important differences, they share a common heritage, types of social leadership, and Israelite identity. At a time in which Judahites found themselves in a dreadful state, Ephraimites reversed a negative course of action, obeyed a prophetic imperative, and acted compassionately toward their Judahite and Jerusalemite kin.[26] To the early readers of Chronicles, the good Samarians tale would thus rejoin the highly negative image of the Samarians found in Ezra-Nehemiah. The alterity promoted in Ezra-Nehemiah is countered by the affiliation promoted in Chronicles.

---

25. As we have seen (chapter 3), a dissident voice tacitly acknowledges that northern residents are descendants of Jacob, but takes issue with the assertion that they truly worship Yhwh (2 Kgs 17:34b–40).
26. For the argument that this story inspired the parable of the Good Samaritan (Luke 10:25–37), see Allen 1999: 601.

II. Renaissance and Reformation under Hezekiah

The remarkable story of Ephraimite kindness toward Judahite prisoners establishes a context for understanding the contours of later Judahite overtures toward their Israelite kin during the reign of Hezekiah, whose rule follows the decline and depopulation suffered under King Ahaz. Internationally, Hezekiah's tenure (727–699 BCE) straddles a series of far-reaching changes in the southern Levant: the campaign of the Assyrian king Shalmaneser V against Israel, resulting in the fall of the northern kingdom (722 BCE); the campaign of the Assyrian king Sargon II (720 BCE), evidently against a group of rebellious states (including Samaria); the establishment of the Assyrian provinces of Megiddo and Samaria (ca. 720 BCE onward); and the destructive invasion of Judah by the Assyrian king Sennacherib (701 BCE). If the Chronicler believed that Israelites survived the Assyrian onslaughts and the fate of these survivors was a topic of interest to him, one might expect to see some indication of this in his depiction of Hezekiah's tenure. The Chronicler does not disappoint. The work portrays a unique series of important contacts between northerners and southerners during Hezekiah's reforms. Indeed, the portrayal of this celebrated ruler differs remarkably from that found in Kings, even though the Chronicler borrows selectively from the earlier work to produce his own narrative. By means of omissions, additions, reworking, and recontextualization, the author creates his own distinctive presentation. If Ahaz is the worst Judahite monarch, Hezekiah may be the best.[27] More attention is devoted to Hezekiah (2 Chr 29:1–32:33) than to any other king except for David and Solomon. The Deuteronomistic work highlights Hezekiah's unwavering trust (בטח) during Sennacherib's devastating invasion (2 Kgs 18:13–19:37), but Chronicles highlights Hezekiah's reign as a time of tremendous national renewal. The striking divergences between the two works may be sketched as follows.

---

27. Hence Hezekiah's reign recalls those of both David and Solomon (Throntveit 2003).

Table 4.2 The Reign of Hezekiah in Kings and Chronicles

Introduction	2 Kgs 18:1–3	2 Chr 29:1–2
Cultic Reforms in Judah	2 Kgs 18:4	—
Incomparability	2 Kgs 18:5–6	—
Rebellion vs. Assyria	2 Kgs 18:7	—
Defeat of Philistines	2 Kgs 18:8	—
Exile of Israel	2 Kgs 18:9–12	—
Temple Repair and Purification	—	2 Chr 29:3–19
Sacrifices	—	2 Chr 29:20–36
Passover Summons	—	2 Chr 30:1–9
Mixed Response	—	2 Chr 30:10–12
Jerusalem Reforms	—	2 Chr 30:13–14
Passover	—	2 Chr 30:15–20
Unleavened Bread	—	2 Chr 30:21–23
Feast Extended	—	2 Chr 30:24–27
Intertribal Cultic Reforms	—	2 Chr 31:1
Priestly and Levitical Work	—	2 Chr 31:2–21
Public Infrastructure	—	2 Chr 32:1–8[i]
Sennacherib's Invasion	2 Kgs 18:13–19:37	2 Chr 32:9–23[ii]

[i] The Deuteronomistic account also contains a reference to Hezekiah's building (2 Kgs 20:20), but the record of his public works is much more extensive in Chronicles (Knoppers 1997).

[ii] There is another parallel to the account in 2 Kgs 18:13–20:19, namely, Isa 36:1–39:8 (Ackroyd 1974, 1982; Person 1997). Interestingly, the Isaianic story, like the Chronicles account, lacks any reference either to Hezekiah confessing his rebellion against the Assyrian king or to his plundering of the temple and palace treasuries to send tribute to Sennacherib (2 Kgs 18:14–16). On the progressive idealization of Hezekiah in late biblical and postbiblical literature, see Ackroyd 1982.

As can be seen from the outline, all of the material dealing with the temple renovation, Passover, Unleavened Bread, and pan-Israelite reforms is unique to Chronicles. Whereas Kings devotes only three verses to Hezekiah's reforms (2 Kgs 18:4, 16, 22), Chronicles devotes three chapters to the restoration of the temple (2 Chronicles 29), the national celebration of the Passover and Unleavened Bread (2 Chronicles 30), and other cultic reforms (2 Chronicles 31). Whereas Kings only mentions northern Israel to remind readers that the northern kingdom had been exiled

(2 Kgs 18:9–12), Chronicles devotes considerable coverage to Hezekiah's northern overtures.[28]

Hezekiah makes reclaiming the official Jerusalem cult the first order of business by beginning his reforms on the very first day of the first month of the first year of his reign (2 Chr 29:3, 17). The first stage of the reforms focuses on instructing the priests and Levites, purifying the temple, and reinstituting the temple's system of sacrifices.[29] A concern for the wider populace may be evident, however, when the king orders that the burnt offering and the sin offering be "for all Israel" (2 Chr 29:24). As the reforms progress, they involve more and more people. After the purification of the temple is complete (2 Chr 29:3–36), the action moves from removing illicit cult objects in Jerusalem (30:13–14) to abolishing idolatry in both Judah and Israel (31:1). My focus in what follows will be on the account of Hezekiah's national Passover and Feast of Unleavened Bread, which occur after the king has purified the temple and set its personnel in proper order.

Given that Hezekiah follows the dictates of Deuteronomy by holding a centralized paschal feast, it is instructive that the king goes to great lengths to include all Israelites "from Beersheba to Dan" in the celebrations (2 Chr 30:5).[30] Such efforts include sending around letters to Judahites and Israelites (Ephraim and Manasseh are specifically named) to journey to the Jerusalem temple to observe the Passover for "Yhwh the God of Israel" (2 Chr 30:1). To allow sufficient time for the priests to sanctify themselves and for travelers to arrive from afar, the king, the officials, and the entire Jerusalemite assembly agree to observe the feast in the second month, after the time of the restoration (2 Chr 30:2–3, 15).[31] Interestingly, the invitation to the national Passover (and Feast of Unleavened Bread) presupposes that both southerners and northerners were familiar with the

---

28. The reminder of the northern exile at the hands of the Assyrians (2 Kgs 18:9–12) is positioned to raise the question of whether Judah will be the next to fall to the Assyrians during Hezekiah's reign (Knoppers 1992).
29. On the possibility of various layers within this chapter, see Williamson 1982: 351–88; Steins 1995: 107–67, 208–10, and the references cited in these works.
30. The expression "from Beersheba to Dan" is a Chronistic merism for all Israel (1 Chr 21:2; 2 Chr 30:5). Compare 2 Chr 19:5, "from Beersheba to the hills of Ephraim."
31. It has been argued that the delay in the timing of the Passover celebration may represent a concession to the northern calendar (Talmon 1958). While this is theoretically possible, the reasons explicitly given in the text (2 Chr 30:3) have to do with the fact that not enough people had been able to assemble in Jerusalem and the priests had not yet consecrated themselves. The Passover legislation of Num 9:1–14 allows the scheduling of an alternate (or second) Passover to be held in the second month for persons, who are in a ritually impure state or on a long journey (cf. *m. Ḥul.* 4.11; *m. Pesaḥ.* 4.9; 9.1–2; *t. Pesaḥ.* 3.7; 8.4–5).

Deuteronomic (re)configuration of the Passover as a pilgrimage feast to be celebrated at the central sanctuary.³² The text assumes not only that the northern Israelites were aware of the Deuteronomic mandate, which revised older festal legislation, but also that they were acquainted with the claim that the Jerusalem temple was the central shrine alluded to in the Deuteronomic paschal laws. Of course, northern Israelites might disagree with southern Israelites about where such a sanctuary was to be located, but Hezekiah's pan-Israel invitation would make no sense at all if the recipients of the invitation did not possess any common traditions about a centralized paschal pilgrimage. The invitation's very formulation is predicated on the grounds that southern Israelites and northern Israelites shared important (Pentateuchal or proto-Pentateuchal) standards of cultic observance. I shall return to this point later.

Hezekiah's extraordinary proclamation (2 Chr 30:6–9)—filled with allusions to earlier biblical texts and replete with distinctive Chronistic terminology—seems to be particularly apt for the inhabitants of Samaria, even though he addresses a wide audience. His words openly acknowledge a continuing Israelite presence in the land, "the remnant that is left to you" (*hā-pĕlêṭâ hā-niš'eret lākem*; 2 Chr 30:6). The Judahite monarch addresses the remaining northerners as "the children of Israel" and invites them all to return to the God of their fathers, "the God of Abraham, Isaac, and Israel." Given the Assyrian creation of a province of "Samaria" (Akkadian *šāmĕrên*; Aramaic *šāmĕrayin*; Hebrew *šōmĕrōn*) in the late 8th century, it would be understandable if Hezekiah addressed northerners as Samarians.³³ But he does not do so. The devastating experiences of the past become a call to all Israelites to reunite, rally to the Jerusalem temple, and rededicate themselves to Yhwh. Life in the land has continued in spite of the Assyrian military campaigns. In this respect, it is amazing how much the Chronicler insists survived the Assyrian invasions. The very wording of the royal invitation reaffirms the Israelite character of those who reside in Samaria. There is no mention of foreign settlers in the land, much less a massive alien immigration (Japhet 1983; Cross 1998). In

---

32. In earlier legislation, the Passover is celebrated as a local, family affair, but in Deuteronomy it is combined with the Feast of Unleavened Bread and made into a centralized festival (Deut 16:1–8, 16; Levinson 1997: 53–97). On the combination of the two commemorations, see also Ezek 45:21 and 2 Chr 35:1–19. In other pieces of biblical legislation, the celebration of Passover and the Feast of Unleavened Bread are separate (Exod 12:1–27; 13:3–10; Lev 23:5–6; Num 9:1–14; 28:16–17; cf. Ezra 6:19–22).
33. They are described in Chronicles in tribal terms (e.g., Ephraimites) or more broadly in ethnic terms as Israelites, but never as Samarians (cf. 2 Kgs 17:29).

spite of foreign invasions, death, deportations, and international turmoil, Israel's tribal infrastructure remains intact (Myers 1965: 176; Coggins 1975: 19–22). In the narrative that follows, the sodalities of Ephraim, Manasseh, Issachar, Asher, and Zebulun are all specifically mentioned (2 Chr 30:11, 12, 18; Japhet 1989: 295–97). As Judah has its representative "assembly" (*qāhāl*; 2 Chr 30:2, 4, 25), so northern Israel retains its own "assembly" (*qāhāl*; 2 Chr 30:25). The Judahite monarch does not even allude to a new political arrangement—a system of Assyrian provinces—replacing the northern kingdom. The various tribes continue to be tied together by a shared ancestry, heritage, land, and deity—"the God of Abraham, Isaac, and Israel" (2 Chr 30:6).

The royal invitation strategically employs the experience of defeat and (partial) exile to argue for beginning a new chapter in Israelite history. The Assyrian conquests are construed as a divine judgment against the rebellious and obstinate ways of "your fathers and your kinsmen" (2 Chr 30:7). The repentance Hezekiah speaks of is therefore not simply an act of self-protection, because the divinely imposed penalty resulting from Yhwh's "fierce anger" is already in effect—"desolation (שמה) as you see" (2 Chr 30:7–8). The repentance called for is rehabilitative in nature.[34] The Judahite monarch presents a most unfortunate turn of events as an opportunity for the people to renew their relationship with God.

In a late Persian (or early Hellenistic) context, it is surely relevant that the missive associates returning to Yhwh with journeying to "his sanctuary, which he consecrated forever" (*lĕmiqdāšô 'ăšer hiqdîš lĕ'ôlām*; 30:8).[35] In depicting this incident, the Chronicler is likely encouraging participation by Yahwists from Samaria and other regions of the former northern kingdom in the Jerusalem cultus of his own time (Japhet 1993: 936–54; Williamson 1982: 360–70). It should be recalled that a Yahwistic sanctuary at Mt. Gerizim already existed in the time in which Chronicles was written. Hence, this Hezekian invitation to all Israel, unparalleled in Kings, in effect summons northern Israelites to a southern Israelite sanctuary. If so, it is important to pay attention to how the invitation is couched and what its premises, conditions, and promises are. One sees literary resonances

---

34. This kind of repentance is also evident in the later literature from Qumran (Nitzan 1999).
35. The terminology may be significant. The author refers to Yhwh's "sanctuary" (מקדש), not to his "temple" (בית). The Priestly writers often refer to the holy place in particular or to the tent of meeting as a whole as the מקדש (*HALOT* 2:625–26). Amos 7:13 speaks of Bethel as the "sanctuary of the king" (מקדש־מלך), the "royal palace" or "royal temple" (בית ממלכה; Paul 1991: 243). Hezekiah pointedly identifies Yhwh's מקדש as situated in Jerusalem.

with texts in Deuteronomy (4:25–31; 30:1–10) dealing with the prospect of exile, the wording of one of the petitions in Solomon's prayer (1 Kgs 8:46–52//2 Chr 6:36–40), the divine response to Solomon's prayer found in Chronicles (2 Chr 7:12b–16a), and the theophany to Moses at Mt. Sinai (Exod 34:6–7).[36] The offer both appropriates language from these earlier texts and ingeniously goes beyond them.

In describing the character of Yhwh Elohim as "gracious and compassionate" (*ḥannûn wĕraḥûm*), the invitation alludes to the foundational Sinaitic theophany of Exod 34:6 by means of inverted citation, "Yhwh, a God compassionate and gracious (*Yhwh 'ēl raḥûm wĕḥannûn*), slow to anger, and abounding in loyalty and truth."[37] Like Deuteronomy and Kings, Chronicles plays on the different nuances of the roots *šûb* ("to turn, return, repent") and *šābâ*, "to take captive, deport." The people's positive response, their returning (*šûb*) to God, may elicit divine compassion for their relatives before their captors (*šōbêhem*) in exile, because Yhwh may turn (*šûb*) from his fierce anger (2 Chr 30:6–9). As the gracious and compassionate deity revealed to Moses (Exod 34:6–7), Yhwh may respond to the people's repentance (*šûb*) by returning (*šûb*) their kin and their children to "this land" (2 Chr 30:8–9). Like Solomon, Hezekiah draws a correlation between returning to Yhwh and returning to the Jerusalem temple. Moreover, in speaking of Yhwh's consecrating (*hiqdîš*) this particular shrine (2 Chr 30:8), the king cites the second theophany to Solomon, as that theophany appears uniquely in Chronicles, "I have chosen (*bāḥartî*) and I have consecrated this temple (*wĕhiqdaštî 'et-hā-bayit hā-zeh*) so that my name will be there forever" (2 Chr 7:16).

But a contrast may also be drawn between Hezekiah and Solomon in addressing the plight of deportees in foreign lands. Solomon's seventh petition plays on the prospect of divine mercy toward those exiles who appeal to Yhwh in a far-off land, but it does not actually mention, much less promise, a return from captivity. Petitions directed toward the land, Jerusalem, and the temple are linked to divine compassion toward those

---

36. The text of 2 Chr 7:12–22 generally follows the account of the second theophany to Solomon (1 Kgs 9:2–9) but introduces additional divine promises and assurances (7:12b–15) with reference to Solomon's petitions at the temple dedication (1 Kgs 8:22–53//2 Chr 6:12–42).
37. Compare the elements cited in Exod 34:6, (1) *Yhwh 'ēl*; (2) *raḥûm*; and (3) *wĕḥannûn*, with the sequence found in 2 Chr 30:9: (1) *ḥannûn*; (2) *wĕraḥûm*; and (3) *Yhwh 'ĕlōhêkem*. The reuse of Exod 34 is not unique. The combinations *ḥannûn wĕraḥûm* and *raḥûm wĕḥannûn*, as applied to Yhwh, are common in late texts (Joel 2:13; Jon 4:2; Ps 86:15; 103:8; 111:4; 112:4; 145:8; Neh 9:17, 31).

who find themselves banished to another territory (1 Kgs 8:48–51//2 Chr 6:38–39). In offering addressees a clear hope of a return, Hezekiah departs from Solomon's prayer and appropriates one of the promises found in Deut 30:1–10. But lest one think that the Chronicler has simply exchanged Kings (and an earlier text in Chronicles) for Deuteronomy, there is also a contrast between Hezekiah's invitation and Deuteronomy in offering comfort to repentant exiles. Deuteronomy 30:1–10, which contains the strongest and clearest expression of hope for a return from exile in the Pentateuch, does not mention any particular sanctuary, much less a central sanctuary.[38] The author offers expatriates full repatriation, contingent upon repentance and keeping Yhwh's commandments (Deut 30:1–10), but Hezekiah implores native Israelites to repent and journey to Yhwh's "sanctuary." Hence, Chronicles selectively blends particular features of Deuteronomy and Kings with its own material. Torah and temple meet in the royal missive. He ingeniously ties a Mosaic revelation to a Solomonic revelation. The former verifies the latter. Hezekiah links the promise of repatriation to Jerusalem's centrality. Similarly, he pointedly links the divine attributes revealed to Moses at Mt. Sinai (Exod 34) to the divine consecration revealed to Solomon at Mt. Zion.

There is also one important contrast that may be drawn between all of these earlier texts and this text in Chronicles.[39] Both Deuteronomy and Kings address the plight of deportees by exhorting the exiles to repent. The promises Hezekiah makes are directed to survivors in the land, not to exiles outside the land. His address privileges autochthonous Israelites. Ezra-Nehemiah highlights the pivotal role played by expatriate Judeans in rebuilding and structuring the community in Yehud, but Chronicles highlights the pivotal role played by aboriginals. The people's repentance may lead to the restitution of their banished relatives to their ancestral

---

38. Deuteronomy 4:25–31 also deals with the plight of deportees, speaking of Yhwh scattering Israel among the peoples, with only a scant few surviving (*wĕniš'artem mĕtê mispār*). The text offers limited hope to those exiles who return (*šûb*) to Yhwh and obey him, namely, divine remembrance of his covenant, nonextinction, and divine compassion (*kî 'ēl raḥûm yhwh*). Unlike Deut 30:1–10, this pericope does not raise the possibility of repatriation should the exiles turn back (*šûb*) to Yhwh. The situation with Lev 26:42–45, part of the conclusion to the Holiness Code, is more complex. It speaks of Yhwh remembering his covenant with the ancestors and of his remembering the land. Yhwh will neither destroy his people nor reject them, but will remember his covenant with "the former ones" (those liberated from Egypt). The text does not speak explicitly of a return, but it may hint at this prospect, when it speaks of the land making up its Sabbaths, while the exiles pay for their iniquity (Lev 26:43; cf. 2 Chr 36:21).
39. Hence the relationship between Chronicles and earlier texts may be better characterized as one of dialogue than one of strict dependence (C. Mitchell 1999).

patrimonies. Looking at the contents of the letter from a late Persian or early Hellenistic perspective provides another lens through which to interpret the invitation. The literary setting of the Hezekian Passover is the end of the 8th century, but the historical setting of the Chronistic writing is almost four centuries later. The author lives at a time, perhaps the late 4th century BCE, in which the people of the southern Levant had already witnessed a series of returns to Judah from Babylon and other centers of the Persian empire (Knoppers 2004a).[40] To Jerusalem's inhabitants, the migrations from afar, however limited in number, confirmed the validity of God's promises to his people. In this context, it is surely relevant that Hezekiah does not specify precisely where the exiles are to return except to say that they may return "to this land" (*lāʾāreṣ hā-zōʾt*; 2 Chr 30:9). The king does not pray that the deportees might somehow all return to Judah. His broad declaration encompasses all regions of the country.

The Chronicler's audience could appreciate the tenability of the scenario sketched in the royal letter. Written in an age in which there was more than one Yahwistic sanctuary in the land, the letter offers northern Israelites the same hope as that afforded to southern Israelites. Yet it does so by associating returning to Yhwh not with any Samarian shrine or with no shrine at all but with journeying to the shrine that Yhwh "consecrated forever" (2 Chr 30:8), that is, the Jerusalem temple. The selection from, reworking of, and additions to earlier tradition have mutually enhancing benefits. Hezekiah's invitation draws upon the prestige of older texts, even as it redefines their terms. The national invitation promotes Jerusalem's centrality both to Yahwists throughout the land and to Yahwists scattered in other lands. The Jerusalem temple appears as an instrument of unity, rather than of division, in the life of the people.

---

40. One could dismiss the Chronistic account and others in the Hebrew Bible as propaganda, but such literary works and the historical scenarios they engage in Neo-Babylonian and Persian times seem to have made an impact even in later centuries. The medieval Samaritan chronicle *Abū ʾl Fatḥ* (77,92–79,95) portrays a return of northern Israelites, along with some southern Israelites (Judeans) after the pan-Israelite (not simply Judahite) exile of Nebuchadnezzar. Aside from 1 Chr 9:3, which alludes to a return of some Ephraimites and Manassites to Jerusalem, no historiographic account of such a northern restoration exists, to my knowledge, in the Hebrew scriptures. Interestingly, Chronicles does not claim that these Ephraimites and Manassites were exiled in the time of Nebuchadnezzar, only that they returned at the beginning of the Persian period. It is important to observe that *Abū ʾl Fatḥ* ((67,79–68,81) associates the return not with Yhwh's promises to Jerusalem but with Yhwh's favor to Mt. Gerizim/Beth El, following a terrible drought in the homeland. I hope to revisit this subject in a later essay.

To be sure, Hezekiah's appeal to the northern tribes is only partially successful. In Judah the response to the royal offer was overwhelmingly positive, but the reaction in the north was decidedly mixed. In the former northern kingdom, the royal couriers were "derided and mocked" (2 Chr 30:10). Nevertheless, "men from Asher, Manasseh, and Zebulun humbled (*nikně'û*) themselves and came to Jerusalem" (2 Chr 30:10). In this reaction, however mixed, one can discern an improvement from the situation in the early divided monarchy. Whereas the state of the disunion speech delivered by King Abijah to Jeroboam and all Israel (2 Chr 13:4–12) elicited no positive response from the northern tribes, Hezekiah's message generates some very positive responses. The Judahite leader shows his concern for northern participation in the Passover when he prays (*hitpallēl*) on behalf of those from Ephraim, Manasseh, Issachar, and Zebulun, "each one who set his heart to seek (*lidrôš*) Yhwh the God of his fathers," after many of them had failed to consecrate themselves before eating the paschal sacrifice (2 Chr 30:18–19). As a result, Yhwh "heeded Hezekiah and healed (*wayyirpā'*) the people" (2 Chr 30:20).[41] Yhwh thus honors the pledge he made to Solomon, following the temple dedication, namely, that if his people turn from their wicked ways, pray (*wěyitpallû*) to him, and seek (*wîbaqšû*) his face, he would heal (*wě'erpā'*) the land (2 Chr 7:14). The celebrations are, in fact, so successful that the participants agree to extend them an extra seven days (2 Chr 30:23–25). The people's unity recalls the heady days of Solomon's reign: "So there was great joy in Jerusalem, because there was nothing like this in Jerusalem since the days of Solomon, the son of David, the king of Israel" (2 Chr 30:26). Considering this unanimity, it is not surprising that Chronicles deploys the term Israel during Hezekiah's reign not only as a designation of the northern tribes (e.g., 2 Chr 30:1, 6, 25 [*bis*]; 31:6) but also to describe the larger unity encompassed by all of the tribes together (e.g., 2 Chr 29:10; 24, 27; 30:5, 21; 31:1 [*bis*], 5, 8).

The final movement of Hezekiah's reforms is the abolition of illicit cultic artifacts and shrines. The geographic scope of this popular effort is comprehensive, affecting cultic practices in the heart of Samaria, as well as in Judah and Benjamin: "Those present, all Israel, journeyed to the towns of Judah and smashed (שבר) the pillars, hacked down (גדע)

---

41. The assertion is all the more remarkable given the explicit directions in legal contexts as to how the paschal feast was to be observed (Exod 12:1–13, 21–27, 43–51; Lev 7:19–21; 23:5–8; Num 9:1–14; 28:16–25).

the asherahs, and tore down (נתץ) the high places and the altars from all of Judah and Benjamin, and in Ephraim and Manasseh, until they were finished. Then all the Israelites returned, each to his estate [and] to their towns" (2 Chr 31:1). Such claims are remarkable. To begin with, the work witnesses to a popular campaign, not an elite royal imposition on rural areas. Unlike most of the cultic reforms depicted in Kings and Chronicles, the reform is led by the people for the people. Second, the lay reformers included northern Israelites who devoted themselves to the Jerusalem temple as their central sanctuary. The story presupposes that the northern Israelites were committed to the Deuteronomic norms of cultic unity (Deut 12:4–7, 8–12, 26–27) and applied those norms to Jerusalem.

Third, the northern Israelites (together with Judahites) enforced the Deuteronomic stipulations of cultic purity, the mandate to abolish all non-Yahwistic shrines, artifacts, and cultic symbols (Deut 12:2–3, 29–31). To be sure, the changes made in the north do not seem to be as thorough as in the south. The text speaks of removing illicit objects "from all of Judah and Benjamin" (מכל־יהודה ובנימן), whereas the terminology is geographically more limited and vague with respect to northern tribal areas: "and in Ephraim and Manasseh" (ובאפרים ומנשה).[42] Nevertheless, the specialized terminology employed to depict the national crusade ("smashing the pillars," "hacking down the asherahs," and "tearing down the high places and the altars") underscores compliance with Deuteronomic norms.[43]

That some will dismiss the account of Hezekiah's reforms as postexilic Judean propaganda is perfectly understandable. There is no mistaking the pro-Jerusalem, pro-temple tenor of the text and its incredible claims. Yet, if this is somehow all propaganda, it is all the more important to analyze the nature of the propaganda and to apprehend what the text affirms (or concedes) about northern residents and what they share with their southern counterparts. Chronicles does not portray an empty (northern) land repopulated by foreigners. The treatment assumes that at least a minority of Israelites remained in their territories and that these Israelites clung to the traditions of their ancient forbearers. The social constitution of the northern tribes survived the Assyrian invasions and

---

42. In other words, the reforms reached areas to the north of Judah and Benjamin, but not more remote areas, such as Zebulun, Asher, and Naphtali.
43. On the use of such specialized Deuteronomistic terminology, see Weinfeld 1972: 320–24.

deportations largely intact.⁴⁴ Because Chronicles posits a partial unidirectional deportation, and not a total bidirectional deportation, it recasts the Assyrian exile as a single catastrophe in the ongoing story of the Israelite people.

It seems inconceivable that the Chronicler would take issue with one of the major tenets of the Deuteronomistic presentation, were this not an important issue. The king who espouses the most conciliatory view toward the survivors of the Assyrian catastrophe is none other than the king who is arguably the most celebrated in Judahite history.⁴⁵ Hezekiah's unstinting efforts to involve and accommodate northern Israelites would not be lost on the writer's audience in late Persian/early Hellenistic times. If Judah's best king went out of his way to unify all elements of his people, he set an example for others to follow. The constructive Hezekian approach, all the while upholding the centrality of Jerusalem's institutions, sets a positive precedent for Judeans to consider in dealing with the northern Israelites of their own time.

III. "Following in the Ways of David": Cultic Purity and Unity under Josiah

Chronicles dramatically departs from Kings in its portrayal of Josiah's northern reforms. Whereas in Kings Josiah's nationwide activity is confined to only one part of one year (2 Kgs 22:3; 23:3), in Chronicles the concern with the full array of Israelite sodalities is a sustained theme throughout Josiah's tenure. Both works compare Josiah (641–610 BCE) to David and laud his reign in extravagant terms: "He walked in the ways of David his ancestor and did not deviate to the right or to the left" (2 Chr 34:2//2 Kgs 22:2), but the evaluation takes on new connotations in Chronicles. Like the Chronistic David, whose ways he emulates, the Chronistic Josiah shows a consistent passion for the primacy of Jerusalem and for national unity from the very beginning of his reign (Knoppers 2004b). Moreover, like the Israel of David's time (1 Chr 11:1–12:41), the people of Josiah's time rally from all quarters to support their leader in consolidating their nation's worship.

---

44. In this, the work makes a fundamental distinction between the two and a half Transjordanian tribes—Reuben, Gad, and East Manasseh—and the rest of the northern tribes. The former are expelled by the Assyrians (1 Chr 5:25–26) and are never heard of again.
45. And the king who is associated with the divine deliverance of Jerusalem (2 Chr 32:1–23).

Table 4.3 Josiah's Reforms in Kings and Chronicles

Introduction	2 Kgs 22:1	2 Chr 34:1
Evaluation	2 Kgs 22:2	2 Chr 34:2
Cultic Reforms	—	2 Chr 34:3–7
Temple Restoration	2 Kgs 22:3–7	2 Chr 34:8–12a
Levitical Supervisors	—	2 Chr 34:12b–14
Discovery of Torah	2 Kgs 22:8–13	2 Chr 34:15–21
Huldah's Oracle	2 Kgs 22:14–20	2 Chr 34:22–28
Covenant Renewal	2 Kgs 23:1–3	2 Chr 34:29–32
Cultic Reforms	2 Kgs 23:4–20	2 Chr 34:33
Passover Celebration	2 Kgs 23:21–23	2 Chr 35:1–19

As the table indicates, Josiah's national reforms begin shortly after he begins to rule.[46] Both works depict Josiah acceding to the throne as a young eight-year-old (2 Kgs 22:1//34:1), but in Kings he does not begin refurbishing the temple until his eighteenth regnal year, more than halfway through his tenure (2 Kgs 22:3). In Chronicles Josiah, "while he was still a youth" in the eighth year of his reign, begins to seek (דרשׁ) Yhwh and in the twelfth year of his reign initiates national reforms (2 Chr 34:3). In his eighteenth regnal year, Josiah embarks on a campaign to restore the central sanctuary (2 Chr 34:8). The sequence underscores the king's long-term commitment to orthopraxis. To the Chronicler, it would be inconceivable that a pious king would not know what Yhwh required of his people. Josiah does not need a Torah scroll to be discovered and recited to him to know what is right and proper in cultic practice. Because Jerusalem's Davidic monarchs resided on the throne of Yhwh's kingdom (1 Chr 17:12–14; 2 Chr 13:5), they bore a special responsibility to their patron deity to implement his will. Accordingly, Josiah begins to "purge Judah and Jerusalem of the high places, asherahs, idols, and molten images" as a young adult (2 Chr 34:3). Indeed, Josiah's actions in the north correspond to those in the south, even though the latter are his primary focus. Josiah's campaign in Judah and Jerusalem includes tearing down the altars of the

---

46. The sequence also differs from that of Hezekiah (in Chronicles). Hezekiah moves from reinstating orthopraxis at the Jerusalem temple to encouraging wider reforms in Jerusalem, Judah, Ephraim, and Manasseh. The reverse sequence holds for Josiah. Josiah moves from stamping out heteropraxis throughout Judah and Israel to reinstating orthopraxis at the Jerusalem temple. Cultic purity precedes cultic unity.

Baals; hacking the incense stands; destroying the asherahs, the idols, and the molten images; and incinerating the bones of the (illegitimate) priests (2 Chr 34:4–5). But lest he give the impression that the king was playing favorites, the writer comments:

> And (he did likewise) in the towns of Manasseh, Ephraim, Simeon, and as far as Naphtali with their ruined sites all around.[47] He tore down the altars and the asherahs. As for the images, he ground (them) to dust and as for all the incense stands, he hacked (them) down throughout the land of Israel. Then he returned to Jerusalem. (2 Chr 34:6–7)

In their geographic scope, Josiah's campaigns outdo Hezekiah's earlier reforms, limited as they were to Judah, Benjamin, Ephraim, and Manasseh. The royal operation extirpates illicit cults not only in the north as far as Naphtali but also in the south as far as Simeon. Josiah's reforms are thus the most extensive of any monarch. The phrase "(the) land of Israel" occurs only four times in Chronicles, once each during the reigns of David (1 Chr 22:2), Solomon (2 Chr 2:16), Hezekiah (2 Chr 30:25), and Josiah (2 Chr 34:7).[48] In the case of Hezekiah, the expression refers to the widespread involvement of resident aliens in the national Passover, rather than to the geographic extent of his reforms. Hence, there is a resonance between the range of influence commanded by Josiah and that of David and Solomon. Josiah's campaign to refurbish the Jerusalem sanctuary is also distinguished by far-flung popular participation. For instance, when Josiah orders the repair and purification of the temple, the funds for this project do not stem simply from "the people" (2 Kgs 22:4), but rather "from Manasseh, Ephraim, and all the remnant of Israel (*ûmikkōl šĕ'ērît yiśrā'ēl*), and from all of Judah and Benjamin" (2 Chr 34:9). In other words, northern Israelites not only take an interest in Jerusalem but also contribute to the temple's restoration.

---

47. At the end of 2 Chr 34:6, I reconstruct בחרבותיהם, "with their ruined sites." The MT is corrupt: *ketiv* בהר בתיהם, "on the mount of their houses"; *qere* "with their swords" (בחרבתיהם). The term "ruined site" (חרבה) is common in late texts (Jer 7:34; 22:5; 25:11; Ezek 25:13; 36:10, 33; Mal 1:4; Dan 9:2; Ezra 9:9). Other possibilities include ברחובותיהם, "in their plazas" (cf. the LXX, Syriac), and בער בתיהם, "He torched their sanctuaries."
48. The expression ארץ ישראל is relatively rare (2 Sam 13:19; 1 Kgs 5:2, 4; 2 Kgs 6:23; Ezek 27:17; 40:2; 47:18; cf. 1 Chr 13:2 ארצי ישראל). Within Chronicles, the locution refers to the geographical habitat—whether real or ideal—of the Israelite people (Willi 1994).

Because Josiah effects comprehensive reforms throughout Israel early in his reign, the force of the Torah story takes on new meaning in Chronicles.[49] Whereas in Kings Huldah's oracles prompt Josiah to take drastic action in Judah and northern Israel, in Chronicles such royal initiatives have already occurred. Accordingly, Josiah's reaction to the scroll's discovery comports with the pan-Israelite sweep of his earlier reforms: "Go, seek Yhwh on account of me and on account of the remnant in Israel and Judah concerning the words of this book" (2 Chr 34:21). By contrast, in 2 Kgs 22:13, Josiah declares, "Go, seek Yhwh on account of me, on account of the people (העם), and on account of all Judah concerning the words of this book." Similarly, his chaste reaction to Huldah's oracles resonates with the terms for repentance set by Yhwh in his second theophany to Solomon (2 Chr 34:27; cf. 2 Chr 7:12–14). The consternation is readily understandable, given Huldah's doomsday interpretation of the Torah scroll. She informs the king that Yhwh is about to "bring disaster against this place (על־המקום הזה) and its inhabitants, all of the curses written in the scroll" (2 Chr 34:24). But Josiah is emphatically assured that he will "be gathered to his fathers and die in peace" and not see the calamity God will bring against "this place and its inhabitants" (2 Chr 34:28).

The distinction the prophetess makes between populace at large and the righteous king explains Josiah's subsequent actions, which focus entirely on the people. Huldah's bleak assessment suggests to the king that he underestimated his people's predicament. He has done well, but not well enough. Huldah's declamation spurs him to assemble the people to Jerusalem and renew the nation's covenant with God in which all those present recommit themselves to "follow Yhwh and to observe his commandments" (2 Chr 34:31). It is this royal resolve to be even more thorough in reforming popular piety that explains the unique claim that "Josiah removed every abominable object (כל־התועבות) from all the territories (מכל־הארצות) belonging to the Israelites, and he obliged all who were present in Israel (כל־הנמצא בישראל) to serve Yhwh their God" (2 Chr 34:33). The writer does not claim that Josiah's reforms were permanent, but he does claim that

---

49. In the Deuteronomistic work, it is following Josiah's covenant renewal (2 Kgs 23:1–3) that his reforms begin in Jerusalem (2 Kgs 23:4–7), extend into Judah (2 Kgs 23:8–9), and culminate in the former northern kingdom (2 Kgs 23:15–20).

they lasted his course: "Throughout his lifetime they did not desert Yhwh the God of their fathers" (2 Chr 34:33).⁵⁰

Josiah's efforts to rekindle and strengthen his people's worship culminate in an elaborate Passover. Kings also mentions a (Judahite) Passover, but Chronicles depicts the celebration in far greater detail than Kings does and underscores the involvement of all Israelites (2 Chr 35:1–19). Unlike Hezekiah's national Passover, Josiah's Passover is held according to the regular schedule (the 14th of the 1st month). Interestingly, the observance of the paschal feast is written not only with the demands of Deuteronomy in view but also with the stipulations found in other Pentateuchal legislation (Seeligmann 1978; Fishbane 1985; Japhet 1993; Levinson 1997). In this manner, the work attempts to reconcile disparate Deuteronomic and Priestly regulations. To complicate matters further, Chronicles meshes these different branches of Pentateuch legislation with Davidic decrees orchestrating the respective roles of the priests and Levites (Knoppers 2004b: 788–890).⁵¹ As David and the leaders of Israel were incredibly generous in their endowments of the future temple (1 Chr 29:1–9), so Josiah and the leaders of the Jerusalem temple are incredibly generous in their donations to the Passover preparations (2 Chr 35:7–9).

The result is a well-provisioned, carefully organized, and highly successful national celebration (2 Chr 35:10, 16; Jonker 2003). It should not be forgotten that the Passover, as presented in earlier biblical literature, commemorates foundational events in the constitution of Israel as a people. When the Pentateuchal statutes are considered together with the Davidic arrangements, the synthesis advances the paradigm of national identity promoted in the work. Accordingly, the festival contributes to the sense of shared identity among Israelites: "No Passover like it had been observed in Israel since the days of Samuel the prophet. Of all the kings of Israel, none observed a Passover like Josiah did with the priests and the Levites and all Judah and Israel present, as well as the inhabitants of Jerusalem" (2 Chr 35:17–18).⁵²

---

50. In this respect, both the Hezekian and the Josianic reforms, uniting elements of both north and south, amount only to a temporary semblance of the cultic unity that characterized the kingdom of David and Solomon (Knoppers 1989).
51. Following the *qere* (המבינים), rather than the *ketiv* (המבונים).
52. The base text of 2 Chr 35:18 basically follows 2 Kgs 23:22, with two major exceptions. The time span specifies the days of Samuel the prophet, who is a minor but revered figure in Chronicles (1 Chr 6:13, 18; 9:22; 11:3; 26:28; 29:29), rather than the more amorphous and inglorious time of the judges. Differently, McKenzie 1985: 166–67. The other difference resides in

It is telling that when the monarch reunifies elements of both north and south in his cultic reforms, this entity is designated "Israel."[53] The reign of Judah's last great reformer appears as a time in which every effort was made to reconsolidate the people's cultic unity. Aside from the rather inauspicious circumstances leading up to his death (2 Chr 35:20–24), there are no shortcomings in Josiah's reign.[54] The geographic reach of his forays achieves almost Davidic-Solomonic proportions.

Conclusions

At the end of this chapter, I would like to return to some of the issues raised at its beginning. We have seen that in Chronicles northern Israel retained its fundamental social fabric following the Assyrian conquests and deportations. Judah and Israel continued to be structured according to similar social configurations, such as a tribal organization, a group assembly (קהל), large kinship groups known as ancestral houses (בית־אבות), and Yahwistic prophets (נביאים). Unlike Kings, the work does not mention any major influx of imperially sponsored settlers from other lands into the vacated former northern kingdom. It does not stigmatize northern residents as the descendants of foreign settlers or as some sort of mongrel race. Chronicles inclusively acknowledges, even promotes, features shared by all Israelites over the centuries, whether such Israelites remain in the land or have been forcibly displaced from it. A common identity is affirmed for all people, who identify themselves as the descendants of Jacob (almost always called Israel in Chronicles). The victorious northern troops addressed by the prophet Oded were as Israelite as their Judahite captives were.[55]

With the end of the northern monarchy, a major obstacle to improving Israelite-Judahite relations was removed. In this storyline, relations between the northern and southern tribes progressed somewhat in the aftermath of the northern kingdom's demise. The reigns of

---

the specific assertion, consistent with the Chronicler's pan-Israel emphasis, that "the priests and the Levites and all Judah and Israel" were present and participated in the Passover celebration.
53. 2 Chr 34:7; 34:33; 35:3 (//1 Esd 1:3); 35:17 (//1 Esd 1:19); 35:18 (//1 Esd 1:20, 21); 35:25 (//1 Esd 1:32).
54. Josiah's death at the hands of Necho results from Josiah's failure to heed the warning issued by the Egyptian king, who avers that God (אלהים) is "with him" and reproves Josiah for interfering with his campaign (2 Chr 35:20–24; Ben Zvi 1999; C. Mitchell 2006).
55. Hence there is no hint of the later Hellenistic polemic in which the story of Genesis 34 (Shechem the son of Hamor) was cited to identify the residents of the north (the Samarians) as Sidonians/Canaanites (Pummer 1982).

Hezekiah and Josiah in particular witnessed a degree of northern support for centralization and Israelite solidarity not seen since the time of the united monarchy. The involvement of people from Ephraim, Manasseh, and other northern tribes in patronizing the refurbishment of the temple, instituting nation-wide reforms, and celebrating the centralized Passover bolstered, rather than diminished, the Jerusalem temple cultus. Particularly fascinating is the assertion that at least some northern Israelites were familiar with specific sections of Pentateuchal legislation and attempted consciously to abide by them. The narrative portrays the northern Israelites as conversant, to varying degrees, with ancient Israelite lore and a shared past. Indeed, the narratives about the Hezekian and Josianic Passovers presuppose that the northern Israelites accepted the Deuteronomic mandate for centralization. To be sure, only some northern Israelites interpreted this legislation as favoring Jerusalem's divine election. The work implicitly concedes that many northern Israelites either derided the southern overtures or applied the centralization mandate to a site other than Jerusalem. In this respect, the narrative, however idealized, does not feign complete Israelite unity. Many members of both communities may have embraced the principles of one God, one people, and one sanctuary, but still differed about where such unity was supposed to be centered. Such divisions are not surprising. The Zion-centered focus in Chronicles would be offensive to many traditionally minded Northerners.

The northern-southern interaction depicted during the late monarchy may have clear resonances for the writer's own context in the late Achaemenid or early Hellenistic period. His allusions to religious life in the former northern kingdom shed light on his own thinking about the conditions of the provinces of Yehud and Samaria in his own time. One would be hard-pressed to explain the adamant insistence on social, religious, and ethnic continuity in the former northern realm, if his presentation had no bearing on his era. Indeed, given the larger pattern of the Chronistic presentation, there is no reason to doubt that the post-610 BCE era in the north was definitively worse than previous eras. That is, there are no grounds for believing that after Josiah's reforms, the entire course of northern religious life somehow became dramatically worse than it had ever been before. Chronicles actually attributes, as we have seen, some improvement in Judahite-Israelite relations after the former northern kingdom's demise. There is no reason to think that things changed markedly in Samaria during the final decades of the Judahite monarchy.⁵⁶ The focus in narrating the last years of the Judahite kingdom's existence is solely on Judah and its decline. Hence, if the Israelites remained Israelite during the course of the united monarchy (ca. 1020–931 BCE), the divided monarchy (ca. 931–722 BCE), and over a century of the Judahite monarchy (722–610 BCE), it is unlikely that they somehow became un-Israelite in the 6th or 5th centuries BCE. It stands to reason that if the author thought that the Israelite tribal structure remained fundamentally intact from the tenth through the seventh centuries, with some northern Israelites actively supporting Josiah's reforms in the late 7th century, these Israelites remained Israelite in the centuries to follow. One of the paradoxes in the Chronistic presentation is that it posits an empty land in Judah at the very end of the monarchy (2 Chr 36:20–21), but not in Samaria. There, a remnant apparently survives within its ancestral territories.

For the writer's audience in the late 4th century, the stories about the good Samarians, the Passover of Hezekiah, and the pan-Israelite reforms of Josiah would have reinforced the larger message that a pan-Israelite perspective was not a lost cause. During a foreign occupation, striving for political unity between north and south was unrealistic, if not dangerous. But cultic unity was another matter. It may well be, of course, that the Chronistic depiction is anachronistic. The northern Israelites may not have embraced centralization at this early time in both of its two primary meanings (*Kultusreinheit* and *Kultuseinheit*); but, if so, it is all the more remarkable that the work depicts their doing so. If the writer projected the realities of his own time into the distant past, those realities included the acceptance of the Deuteronomic concept of centralization in both northern and southern Israel.⁵⁷ Based on such a shared acceptance of centralization in the present, the writer recast contacts between the two areas in the past.⁵⁸ Living in an age in which Yahwistic communities existed in Yehud, Samaria, Babylon, Egypt, Idoumea, and perhaps elsewhere, the

---

56. By comparison, there are no southern monarchs judged negatively in the regnal evaluations who expand Judah's territory or who reach out to northern Israelites.
57. As we shall see in the next chapter, the construction of a northern shrine at Mt. Gerizim in the mid-5th century provides some tantalizing hints that this may have been the case.
58. Or, to put matters differently, if the author merely projected his own idiosyncratic ideals onto the course of northern life (with no reflection of how things actually were in his own time), it is important that he did so, because he led his readers to consider northern Israelite society in a Deuteronomic vein. Such a literary project would be important in and of itself, because it suggests that at least some in Yehud considered life in the former northern kingdom to be comparable in important respects to circumstances in Judah.

author engaged in an inner-Israelite debate in defense of Jerusalem as the chosen place called for in Deuteronomy.[59]

Given the acknowledgment of a shared Israelite heritage, one can readily understand how many Judeans in the Achaemenid and Hellenistic periods could justify communicating, cooperating, conducting business, and even intermarrying with Yahwistic Samarians. From a Chronistic perspective, both groups descended from a common ancestor, the patriarch Israel. Indeed, granted the historical links between the two communities and the shared ancestry to a common progenitor, it would be incumbent upon southern Israelites to maintain and foster contacts with their northern kin. The gravity of such a felt responsibility would be enhanced by recollections of past acts of kindness (2 Chr 28:8–15) toward their Judahite kin.

A caution should be raised at this point. The nuanced point of view in Chronicles may not have been representative of its time. There is in any age a gap between elite opinion and actual reality. In some cases, the gap can be glaring. This was another of the mistakes made in earlier scholarship. The point of view of the Chronicler (understood to be the author of Chronicles-Ezra-Nehemiah) was taken as emblematic of the Judean community during the postexilic period. But as the ideological differences among works such as Chronicles, Ezra-Nehemiah, Ruth, Jonah, Second Isaiah, Third Isaiah, Ezekiel, Haggai, Malachi, and Zechariah attest, there was no unanimity in Yehud as to how to define Israelite identity, the leaders' chief priorities, and the people's relations to their neighbors. In the context of his own age, the Chronicler's voice may have been simply one among many. Moreover, because the Chronicler's case for group solidarity was partially predicated upon the argument that the rites, personnel, and sanctuary at Mt. Zion were vital to all Israelites, his work was probably more effective in shaping opinions among his compatriots in Jerusalem than it was in changing the opinions of the elite in Samaria. One of the most important things shared in common by Judeans and Samarians (according to Chronicles) would go unrecognized by many Samarians, namely, the exclusive status of Jerusalem and its temple.

Yet, in this case, one could raise a counterargument that the Chronicler's nuanced stance was more representative of elite opinion, at least for some

---

59. The recent publication of an unprovenanced 4th-century Aramaic ostracon from Edom may point to the existence of a small Yahwistic sanctuary (*byt yhw*) in the area between Hebron and Lachish (Lemaire 2004).

time, than was the isolationist stance of others within the Judean community. The pan-Israelite perspective affirmed in Chronicles echoes the similar, albeit not identical, pan-Israelite perspectives found within the books of the Pentateuch and most of the Latter Prophets. Many prophetic writings, such as Jeremiah, Ezekiel, and Zechariah, include restoration programs in which the various tribes of Israel are all reunified and recentered in the land.[60] This literary evidence suggests that, contrary to the reigning opinion of most scholars working in the late 19th and early 20th centuries, the peculiar stance promoted in Ezra-Nehemiah was only one opinion among others in postexilic Judah.

---

60. Although as John Harvey observes (personal communication), the nature, shape, and context of such restoration programs vary widely.

5

A Distinction without a Difference?

SAMARIAN AND JUDEAN CULTURES DURING
THE PERSIAN AND EARLY HELLENISTIC PERIODS

THE HISTORY OF the ancient Samarians has occasionally provoked a keen interest on the part of modern scholars. In the 19th and early 20th centuries, the existence of Samaritan-Jewish antagonism was considered to be a key factor, if not the key factor, in understanding the internal social and religious dynamics of both societies. Only such a partisan and acrimonious atmosphere, so it was thought, could explain the complaints about the "peoples of the land" and the interference of the Samarian governor Sanballat in Judean affairs as portrayed in Ezra-Nehemiah. Historically, this period was thought to be a time of schism between the two groups, although scholars avidly disagreed as to when such a rift occurred (Rothstein 1908; Rowley 1962; Purvis 1981; Coggins 1991; Knoppers 2007). Ideologically, the Samarian became the other used to define the Judean self.

Recent scholarship has rightly rejected understanding early Judean-Samarian relations in such binary terms.[1] There is no compelling evidence for positing a major schism at this time, whether in the 6th, 5th, or 4th centuries BCE (Crown 1991). Indeed, as we shall see, there is much positive evidence for positing sustained and meaningful contacts between the two adjacent provinces. An additional problem with dichotomizing the two communities is that such a negative characterization tells us little about the actual culture of Judah's northern neighbor—its history, population, and religious practices. Paradoxically, the older view—focusing as it did on Judean and Samarian animosities—neglected Samaria itself.

---

1. E.g., Cross 1966, 1998; Purvis 1968, 1986; Japhet 1983, 1989; Williamson 1977b, 1989; Willi 1995.

In what follows, I would like to concentrate on new archaeological and epigraphic evidence that pertains to historical and cultural matters. I shall begin by discussing some discoveries pertaining to the continuous existence of a significant Samarian population during the late Neo-Assyrian, Neo-Babylonian, Persian, and early Hellenistic periods. The long-term growth in the north is especially noteworthy, given that the community in Yehud was relatively small in the Achaemenid/early Hellenistic era. Second, I wish to point to some indications of a significant cultural overlap between the Samarian and Judean communities during the Persian period. The third section will examine the bearing of the recent archaeological discovery of a Samarian temple on Mt. Gerizim dating to Persian and Hellenistic times on our understanding of Samarian and Judean religious history. In the fourth part of this chapter, I shall pay particular attention to the many Samarian dedicatory inscriptions at Mt. Gerizim dating to the early Hellenistic period and what these texts may reveal about the population who worshiped there.

I. Samaria from the Late Neo-Assyrian Period to the Early Hellenistic Period

In dealing with Samarian history in the 7th–4th centuries BCE, one has to avoid projecting problems faced by Judah onto its neighbor to the north. The province seems to have passed from the Neo-Assyrian and Neo-Babylonian periods to the Persian period without encountering any of the major destructions that its southern neighbor experienced. From an archaeological perspective, one finds in the territory of Samaria basically one continuous period (Iron IIC or Iron III) from the late 8th century to the late 4th century.[2] The transitions from the Neo-Assyrian period to the relatively brief Neo-Babylonian period and then to the Achaemenid era are very gradual in the north. The decision to speak of a new Persian period in Samaria, as opposed to an older Neo-Assyrian or Neo-Babylonian period, is more of a historical judgment than one based on any sudden change in material culture.

---

2. I am following Zertal's distinction (2001) between an Iron II period and an Iron III period (late 8th century BCE onward). Similarly, Barkay (1992) argues that the Iron IIC culture in Judah (or Iron III) extends to the late 6th century (530–520 BCE). Barkay views the late 6th century as the end of "Israelite" material culture, because only at this time do some features of Achaemenid material culture emerge. Barkay also points to the survival of Iron Age culture in the Transjordan, the coastal strip, the northern regions, and the Negev.

The region suffered a tremendous demographic decline in the late 8th century, when the Assyrian armies conquered what was left of the northern kingdom and deported part of its population. From this decline, some areas rebounded more quickly than others. The southern region seems to have taken the longest to recover. In the southern Samarian Hills, the Persian period witnessed slightly less than half the number of sites of the relatively prosperous Iron II period (Finkelstein 1993a; 1993b: 1313–14; Finkelstein, Lederman, and Bunimovitz 1997).[3] Most sites in the Achaemenid era (538–332 BCE) were also smaller than their Iron II counterparts. According to Finkelstein, Ledermann, and Bunimovitz, a major recovery in southern Samaria only occurs in the Hellenistic era.[4] During this time, the population grew and prospered.

Of the various Samarian geographic zones, the northern and the western parts seem to have rebounded the most quickly from the Assyrian campaigns (Zertal 1990, 2001, 2003). The Achaemenid period witnessed an unprecedented number of sites in the northern region, suggesting considerable demographic expansion. The settlement was particularly heavy in the Dothan Valley and in the areas surrounding the city of Samaria. The Persian period represents the time in which the hills of Manasseh were the most densely populated of all periods, more than the Iron II period and the Hellenistic period, and considerably more than the Iron III period (722–586 BCE; Zertal 1993, 1999, 2004). It may be, as Zertal (1988) suggests, that this region was aided by its geography. In northern Samaria numerous springs can be found from north of Jenin to the foot of Mt. Gerizim in the south. Arable soil and broad interior valleys set the Mt. Manasseh region apart from the more rugged hill country to the south. The recovery may have also been aided by Assyrian investments in establishing regional centers, forts and garrisons, an increase in trade, and the absence of major political upheavals. Most sites in northern Samaria show continuity from the Iron III period (late 8th century) into the Persian period. The internal security and longevity of peace afforded by the Achaemenid era may have contributed to the greater utilization

---

3. I hesitate to attribute this decline to the destructions of both the Israelite and the Judahite kingdoms (so Finkelstein), because the latter should not have directly affected this area. If there was a continuing population decrease in the 7th–6th centuries, it may have been due to inner-population shifts (toward the west and the north) and economic factors. A distinction between Iron II and III is not observed in Finkelstein's study (cf. Zertal 2003, 2008).

4. Lipschits thinks, however, that a recovery began in the 7th century and continued through the 4th century (personal communication).

of available land (Zertal 1990: 13). A decline occurs, however, in the Hellenistic era, during which settlement was roughly cut in half, probably as a consequence of the 332 BCE revolt against the legions of Alexander the Great (Zertal 1999, 2004, 2008). Western Samaria was intensively settled during the Achaemenid era (Dar 1986, 1992; Applebaum 1986). Already during the latter part of the Iron Age, there was a significant increase of settlements and farmhouses. During the Persian period one finds a dense complex of settlements, although most are small and rarely exceed 2.5 hectares in area (Dar 1992). Aiding growth was the gradual development (or better utilization) of a system of major and minor roads (Dorsey 1991; Zertal 2008).

If recent studies have added much to our knowledge of demographic changes in various Samarian regions, much is still unknown about the city of Samaria during the Neo-Assyrian, Neo-Babylonian, and Persian periods. In Samaria, unlike in Jerusalem, one finds a fundamental continuity of settlement from the beginning of the Iron III period to the Achaemenid era. Some of the site's walls continue in use for a long period, and the city survives until the end of the Persian period (Reisner, Fisher, and Lyon 1924: 123; Crowfoot 1942, 1957a; Kenyon 1942). According to archaeological surveys, the areas around Samaria were thickly settled during the Achaemenid era, but much of the material evidence from the city itself stems from the Iron Age and the Hellenistic and Roman periods.

In the first part of the 20th century, two major excavations took place at Samaria, both of which dealt with the upper city of this large tell. Neither excavated the large lower city on the northern, western, and southern sides of the acropolis. The earlier of the two excavations (1908–10), an American expedition, discovered a variety of finds. Reflecting the early state of archaeology at the time, the excavators spoke broadly of a "Babylonio-Grecian period" that encompassed some four centuries (700–300 BCE).[5] A substantial portion of the building construction assigned to this period has been questioned, however, by later archaeologists. To be sure, the so-called Osorkon house, built over the ruins of an older Israelite monumental building (Franklin 2004), seems to date to the so-called post-Israelite period (Reisner, Fisher, and Lyon 1924: 58–60, 126–33). But the western gate complex, dated

---

5. Within this broadly defined period, the excavators identified at least two phases. In the excavators' estimation, the large round (Hellenistic) towers were built into an earlier post-Israelite stratum.

to the early post-Israelite period (commencing ca. 700 BCE), has been reassigned to the earlier Israelite period (Tappy 2001, 2007; Franklin 2004, 2005). The same holds true for the revetment walls (Building Period II). In early Hellenistic times, a series of impressive round towers were built to strengthen the walls of the older acropolis, dating to the Israelite monarchic period. Eventually, a new and much stronger outer wall was built, but this wall probably dates to the Hellenistic period (Avigad 1993). Small finds from the Harvard excavations relating to the Neo-Babylonian and Persian periods include a few early pre-Alexandrian coins (Reisner, Fisher, and Lyon 1924: 252–54 [pl. 60]), several fragmentary Aramaic inscriptions written on ostraca (Reisner, Fisher, and Lyon 1924: 247–48), and several pre-Alexandrian objects. Also stemming from the same broadly defined period is an assortment of early Greek pottery, now thought to date to the 6th–4th centuries BCE (Reisner, Fisher, and Lyon 1924: 281–83 [pls. 69–70]).[6]

During the later joint (1931–1933) and British excavations (1935), few building remains were discovered dating to the Neo-Babylonian and Persian periods (Stratum VIII). Small finds from this era include Persian-period pottery (Kenyon 1957: 98), a clay cup thought to be a direct Achaemenid import (Crowfoot 1957b: 216), several fragmentary ostraca in paleo-Hebrew script (Birnbaum 1957: 11–25), several Aramaic ostraca,[7] a large amount of Attic ware (Crowfoot 1957b: 213–16), some local coins, three Sidonian coins from reign of Straton I (ca. 370–358 BCE; Kirkman 1957: 43–70), a late Achaemenid coin that may stem from the reign of Darius III (Stern 2001: 425–26), and bronze parts of a throne probably belonging to a Samarian governor (M. Tadmor 1979). Also of interest was the discovery of a deposit of thick brown ("chocolate") soil, which covered an area of a 45 m x 50 m courtyard (Kenyon 1957). This garden, which presumably served the Samarian governor, resembles the carefully demarcated brown soil (gubernatorial) garden found in Persian-period Ramat Rachel near Jerusalem and similar constructions elsewhere in the Achaemenid empire (Lipschits et al. 2011).

Four major factors limit our knowledge of the city's history: the fact that only one part of the site was excavated; the shortcomings of older

---

6. Also to be acknowledged is the broad collection of "Babylonio-Grecian" pottery (Reisner, Fisher, and Lyon 1924: 283–299 [pl. 67]).

7. But the ostraca were unstratified. Birnbaum (1957: 25–32) dates them to the 4th century BCE.

excavations and archaeological methods; the series of destructions wrought by the forces of Alexander the Great in 331 BCE (Josephus *Ant.* 11.302, 331; Quintus Curtius Rufus *Hist. Alex.* 4.8.9–11; cf. 4.5.9), the Ptolemies in 312 BCE, Demetrius in 296 BCE, John Hyrcanus in 108 BCE, and Pompey in 63 BCE; and the phases of major rebuilding occurring at various times in the Hellenistic and Roman eras. The suppression of rebellion by Alexander's forces in 331 BCE was coupled with the displacement of native Samarians by Macedonian colonists, resulting in the site's transformation (Stern 2001: 424–27).[8]

Further reconstruction and expansion occurred during Herodian and Roman times (Reisner, Fisher, and Lyon 1924: 167–223). Estimates of the city's stature during the Achaemenid age are therefore inevitably speculative, being based on the city's size during the Iron III and Hellenistic periods, existing material remains from the Persian period, epigraphic finds, and the large cluster of towns and villages surrounding the site during the Persian period.[9] Over half of the Persian-period sites that have been found in the Samaria region have been found within a 10 km radius of the capital (Zertal 1990: 14). This evidence suggests that the city of Samaria prospered and grew during much of the Persian era. Employing the central place theory, Stern (2001: 424) thinks, in fact, that Samaria became one of the most important urban areas in all of Palestine during the Achaemenid era. Zertal (2003: 380) goes further in claiming that Samaria became the largest and most important city of Palestine. In sum, there is still much that is unknown about Samarian history, but archaeological studies suggest that the transition to the Persian period was not nearly as traumatic for the region as it was for certain cities along the Mediterranean coast and for parts of Judah. After suffering a tremendous

---

8. It is likely that many dislocated Samarians moved to Shechem (Campbell 2002) and Mt. Gerizim. No residential quarters at Mt. Gerizim were discovered dating to the Persian period, but a substantial town developed adjacent to the temple during Hellenistic times (Magen 2008b).

9. One indication of the city's prominence in the 4th century is the fact that it was allowed to mint coin issues stamped with the name Mazday (Mazaeus), abbreviated as מז (Meshorer and Qedar 1999: 17, 25–26, 97, 99, 101, 102 [nos. 74, 84, 96, 100]). On the obverse of one of these coins (Meshorer and Qedar 1999: 99, 101, 102 [no. 96]), the name of the province Samaria appears (שמרין), while on the obverse of another (Meshorer and Qedar 1999: 102 [no. 100]), the name of the province is abbreviated as שן. Mazday was the satrap of Transeuphrates from 345–331 BCE. The Samarian governor could not have minted such coins without satrapal permission (Mildenberg 1998: 49). Other Mazday issues are known from Tarsus, Sidon, and Babylon. The sharing of legends and iconographic motifs indicates that local workshops and mints did not work in total isolation from each other (Gitler and Tal 2006: 11). Indeed, some coinage specialists could have been employed in several workshops (Lemaire 1999).

demographic decline at the beginning of the Iron III period, most of the region recovered and grew.

In this context, some contrasts may be drawn between Samaria and postmonarchic Judah. Within the past few generations, population estimates for Yehud in the early Persian period have varied wildly. Albright (1963: 87) surmised that early postexilic Judah's population was scarcely more than 20,000 people, but others thought that the true number was five to ten times larger. Recent archaeological studies (e.g., Carter 1999) have veered back, however, toward Albright's low estimates. The Babylonian campaigns caused substantial destruction and depopulation in certain areas of the southern Levant. Some sites along the coast, such as Ashkelon, and sites inland, such as Jerusalem, Lachish, Tell Miqne, Tell Beit Mirsim, and Tel Batash, suffered major damage during the Neo-Babylonian era, with fateful consequences for their regional economies (Miller and Hayes 2006: 460–97; Finkelstein 2010; Faust 2001, 2003b). To be sure, there is also evidence for continuity of occupation at some sites (Lipschits 1998, 2001; Blenkinsopp 2002; Zorn 2003). Some areas north of Jerusalem in Benjamin were largely spared destruction (Lipschits 1999; Carter 2003). Accordingly, the most recent population estimates for peak population in Achaemenid Judah have been quite modest. Lipschits's appraisal (2003, 2005), for instance, posits about 30,000 in the Achaemenid era. Moreover, slow growth characterizes the Persian period and the beginning of the Hellenistic era (Lipschits and Tal 2007; Lipschits 2012).

By comparison, the region of Samaria seems to have escaped any large-scale damage from the Babylonian campaigns. Because Samaria's residents evidently did not participate in the rebellions against the Babylonians, they did not suffer any major deportations.[10] There are gradual changes in the material record from the late 8th century to the late 4th century, but no sudden breaks or sharp deviations. Site surveys indicate that the populations of northern and western Samaria actually grew substantially during the Persian period. The Achaemenid era witnessed a larger number of inhabited sites in northern Samaria than at any time during the Iron Age. Very few population estimates have been offered for the Samaria province during this time. In one of his early studies, Zertal (1990: 11–12) put the

---

10. Nehemiah may implicitly concede the point in his imprecations against Sanballat and his allies, "Hear our God, for we have become [the subject of] contempt. Return their taunts upon their heads! Deliver them up as plunder in a land of captivity!" (בארץ שביה; Neh 3:36).

number of residents in Persian-period Mt. Manasseh at about 42,000. Based both on Zertal's more recent archaeological work, in which new sites have been found, and the fact that his estimate only addressed one section of Samaria, albeit the most populous one, the figure for the province as a whole would have to be higher than this partial figure.[11]

The Jerusalem of the Achaemenid era has been described as a village with an administrative center. King and Stager (2001: 389) conclude that "postexilic Jerusalem was limited to the confines of the City of David (4.4 hectares excluding the Temple Mount) and was probably only half that size, with a few hundred inhabitants." In contrast, the Samaria of the Achaemenid era has been described as one of ancient Palestine's larger urban areas. If so, we are dealing not with a situation of comparability but with a situation of some disparity. One regional center was substantially larger and wealthier than the other. The difference between the two provinces and their two capitals cannot have but affected the intelligentsia of Jerusalem. During the Achaemenid era, members of the Judean elite were not dealing with a depopulated outback to the north. Quite the contrary, they were dealing with a province that was larger, better established, wealthier, and considerably more populous than Yehud.

II. Cultural Continuities

Recognition of Samaria's important status vis-à-vis Yehud compels us to inquire further as to the character of its culture(s) during the Persian period. Up to a few decades ago, this subject was completely foreboding due to the paucity of evidence. Recent discoveries have begun to change this picture. The topic may be approached by several different angles. It may be useful to begin by briefly discussing language and scripts. The long-awaited publication of the 4th-century Samaria papyri from the Wâdī ed-Dâlīyeh is helpful in this respect. Also helpful is the discovery over the past few decades of hundreds of Samarian coins and inscriptions dating to the late Persian and Hellenistic ages (Magen, Tsfania, and Misgav 2000; Magen, Misgav, and Tsfania 2004). Some of the coins have yet to be formally published.[12] But those inscriptions and coins that have

---

11. His surveys do not include the Mt. Ephraim region, an integral part of the northern kingdom. Admittedly, the population estimates garnered through site surveys are only educated guesses.
12. A sample of Persian period coins appears in Magen 2007.

been published provide important clues about linguistic usage and the employment of scripts in different historical contexts.

In his study of the language of the Samaria papyri, Gropp (1990: 170) shows that the language of the papyri is a conservative version of Official Aramaic. The language used is virtually identical to the language employed in the 5th-century Elephantine papyri and the Arsames correspondence. There is, in fact, little typological development from the 5th-century Elephantine texts to the 4th-century Samaria papyri. Despite their late provenience, the Samaria papyri show little or no Persian influence in either vocabulary or syntax (Gropp 1990: 170–71). Comparative study demonstrates, however, many differences in the composition of legal formulae, suggesting important divergences in legal traditions between the Samaria papyri and the Elephantine papyri (Gropp 1986: 130–39; 1990: 186–87). It is surely interesting, in the context of this discussion, that the Samaria papyri share a large number of isoglosses with the later Murabbaʿat and Naḥal Ḥever deeds (Gropp 2001: 5). Given the shared scribal conventions, these documents evidently belong to the same legal tradition. The fragmentary Samaria papyri thus provide useful evidence for reconstructing the history of early Judean and Samarian law.

The hundreds of fragmentary papyri and short inscriptions found in Samaria dating to the late Persian and Hellenistic periods suggest that the Samarians wrote and spoke the same language as the Judeans during this time. Aramaic evidently was employed, as it was in other provinces in western Asia, as the language of governance, everyday commerce, and international diplomacy. Hebrew was occasionally employed in (but not entirely restricted to) certain official or sacred contexts.[13] The scribes of both communities employed a similar system of scripts, an Aramaic script for diplomatic and commercial activities and a Hebrew script (called paleo-Hebrew) for certain religious or ideological purposes (Ephʿal 1998; cf. Lipiński 1990). Both the Judeans and the Samarians used the two scripts as late as the Hellenistic era. Naveh (1998: 91) comments: "No differentiation whatsoever is discernible in the scripts used in Judah and Samaria in the Persian period."

---

13. Lemaire (1995) discusses the complications in distinguishing between spoken Hebrew and written Hebrew in Yehud and in pinpointing the features of regional dialects. By contrast, Kottsieper (2007) contends that Hebrew was not spoken in Persian-period Judah, except by a specialized clientele (priests and perhaps some government officials). Since our focus is on Samaria, the issue need not detain us here.

One caveat should be offered, however. In the 5th–3rd centuries, the paleo-Hebrew script was used both on official seals and on coins in Yehud. Only a few coins with Aramaic legends are known from Yehud (Machinist 1994; Mildenberg 1996, 1998; Naveh 1998: 91–93). From the 3rd century onward, the early cursive Aramaic script developed in Yehud.[14] But in Persian-period Samaria, many coins were issued with Aramaic legends (e.g., Jeroboʻam, Ḥananiah, ʻAbdiʼel, Yehoʻanah). Coin legends with a Hebrew script comparable to the Yehud types (e.g., *Bdyh*) are relatively rare (Meshorer and Qedar 1999: 15, 84 [no. 7]). There is, however, one Samarian coin recently published, a pseudo-Athenian tetradrachm written in a paleo-Hebrew script with the Yahwistic name *Yoyišʻal* (Lemaire 2003–6). Samarian coins with mixed scripts are also attested. Finally, two Persian-period seal impressions from Samaria engraved in a paleo-Hebrew script (Cross 1971) warrant discussion, because these Hebrew inscriptions were impressed upon bullae sealing Aramaic legal documents written in an Aramaic script. One sealing (WD 23) among the Samaria papyri, perhaps reflecting a metal finger ring or an oval ring stone, bears the name of Yešuaʻ ([יֹ]שֻׁלִי; Leith 1997: 184–87 [Pl. xiv.2]; Dušek 2007a: 48–54, 321–31). If the name Yešuaʻ functions as a caritative (for Yešaʻyahu), it may refer to the same person mentioned in the longer paleo-Hebrew inscription (WD 22), "[Belonging to Yešaʻ]yahu, son of [San]ballaṭ, governor of Samaria" (Avigad and Sass 1997: 176 [no. 419]).[15] Both bullae belong to a centuries-old Israelite seal tradition. In this respect, the two seals (WD 22, 23) differ little from those used by Judahite officials during the late

---

14. Some issues of script nomenclature: what Cross (1961: 136–53) and others have called the paleo-Hebrew script, the imitation (or continuation) of the old Hebrew script, Magen, Misgav, and Tsfania (2004: 30–35) call the Neo-Hebrew script. We retain the older (and less confusing) designation. What Cross (1961: 136–53), Naveh (1971), and others have called the Proto-Hasmonean script, referring to the archaic (or archaizing) script that appears in approximately 250–150 BCE, the Mt. Gerizim epigraphers call Proto-Jewish. This script should be renamed, however, in light of the paleographic evidence found at Mt. Gerizim. Both designations (Proto-Jewish and Proto-Hasmonean) are inappropriate, because this script was once thought to be a distinctive local development from the standard Aramaic cursive of the late Persian empire. But the script is not only nondistinctive of Judah but also not unique to Yehud and Samaria. Following Dušek (2007b, 2012a), we label the script cursive Aramaic.
15. The Sanballat referred to may be Sanballat II, the grandson of Sanballat I, the contemporary of Nehemiah (Cross 1974). In the alternative reconstruction of Ḥ. Eshel (2007), Sanballat II of the mid-4th century is thrice removed (Delaiah, Shelemiah, Hananiah) from Sanballat I in the succession of Persian-period Samarian governors. Alternatively, Dušek (2007a: 261–63, 321–32; 2012b) casts doubt upon a papponymic succession of Sanballats in Persian-period Samaria.

monarchy (Cross 1974: 17–29 [pl. 61]).¹⁶ Hence, the more general point about the use of Aramaic and Hebrew scripts stands.

We have been discussing questions of language and script in ancient Samaria with special reference to possible contemporary Judean practices. One type of comparison that is useful in this context is the composition of personal names (PNs). To be sure, some caution must be exercised in dealing with onomastic evidence so as not to draw far-reaching and detailed conclusions about the history and culture of a particular area (M. C. A. Macdonald 1999; Becking 2002). There are limits to how much information about ethnicity or religious affiliation can be derived from the makeup of PNs. To take one example, the element בעל can function in a proper name as a theonym or as an appellative. In the former case, the term can refer to a particular deity, the Canaanite god Haddad or Haddu, but in the latter case, בעל can function as an epithet for a variety of ancient Near Eastern deities (Mulder 1975: 182–85), including Yhwh.¹⁷

To take a second example, in dealing with the onomastic evidence stemming from the Neo-Babylonian and Achaemenid eras, one has to account for the phenomenon of double (or second) names. Double names are cases in which a person may carry a second name with no relationship to that person's own ethnic background (Zadok 1988: 12–13; Dandamaev 2004). The use of double names may be subject to several different explanations within the larger international context of various ethnic groups coexisting during the Neo-Babylonian and Achaemenid eras. Indeed, the practice, even using different scripts, continued into Hellenistic times (Pearce 2010). But, in any case, the very phenomenon of second names augurs against assuming that those bearing foreign names had somehow abandoned their traditional gods or ethnic backgrounds. In short, the linguistic and religious features of PNs may be used in some cases to provide

---

16. Leith (1997: 16–24, 184–87 [pl. xiv.2]) observes that these seals are unusual both because of their archaizing tendencies and because they are inscribed. The two may be compared with a 4th-century seal, thought by Naveh to be Samarian, written in a similar Hebrew script, "Belonging to Ḥanan son of Škwy" (Avigad and Sass 1997: 99–100 [no. 162]). More broadly, the two Daliyeh sealings (WD 22–23) may be compared with the Ishmael bulla, written mostly in paleo-Aramaic script (Stern 2002), and WD 54, written in Phoenician script (Leith 1997: 78–79 [pl. v.2]).

17. E.g., b'lytwn, "Ba'l has given" (WDSP 12.4, 5). Compare איש בשת, "Ishbosheth" (MT 2 Sam 2:8) or אשבעל, "Ishbaal" (LXX 2 Sam 2:8; MT 1 Chr 8:33; McCarter 1984: 85–87). Cf. 1 Chr 12:6 בעליה, "Yhwh is (my) lord" (one of David's warriors). It is interesting that בעל appears as a PN and that the בעל element appears in a variety of PNs in Chronicles, by all accounts a postexilic work. Not all of these PNs are reproduced from the Chronicler's *Vorlagen* (Knoppers 2004b: 521, 562).

some indication of their bearers' identities (Tigay 1986, 1987; Layton 1990; Beaulieu 2011), but one must be careful to recognize the limitations of the evidence available to us. If the names appear with patronyms, affiliations, titles, or place-names, that information may be very useful as a control in contextualizing the possible significance of such anthroponyms.

In examining the PNs appearing in the 4th-century Samaria papyri, one may begin by observing the large number of names shared with those appearing in Judean literary sources. It has sometimes been maintained that many of the names in the Samaria papyri are non-Yahwistic in character or are foreign names. This is misleading, if not mistaken. Many are explicitly Yahwistic (Zsengellér 1996; H. Eshel 1997; Ephʻal 1998: 110–11; Gropp 2001). Cross's study (2006) delves into these matters in some detail, dividing the Samaria papyri anthroponyms into five separate categories. In this calculation, 41 percent of the PNs fall into an explicitly Yahwistic category. It has been occasionally claimed that the Yahwistic theophorics found within these documents (category no. 1) are largely restricted to the names of the sellers and buyers, but recent studies (e.g., Zsengellér 1996; Leith 1997, 2000; Dušek 2007a) demonstrate that many of the slave names are also Yahwistic in character.

A second category, comprising 23 percent of the total, consists of common Hebrew names lacking a theophoric element (most of which are hypocoristica). There is some ambiguity in this second category, because some PNs found in the Hebrew Bible and among the Samaria papyri are also found in other languages, such as Phoenician and Aramaic. The third category, comprising some 14 percent of the total, consists of theophorous names compounded with the names of foreign gods. The papyri indicate some diversity in the ethnic composition of Samaria in the 4th century (Cross 1974: 20–22). There are, for instance, two instances of PNs with the theophoric "Qos," *qwsdkr*, "Qos has remembered," and *qwsnhr*, "Qos is light" (Lemaire 2001: 105; Cross 2006: 84). One also finds an Egyptian-Phoenician name, *ʾīsīyātōn* (*ʾsytwn*), "Isis has given"; Aramaic theophoric names, such as *Barīkšāmeš* (*brykšmš*), "Blessed of Šameš"; and a couple of other interesting names, such as *Śahrnātan* (*śhrntn*), "Śahr (the moon god) has given."[18] There are a few instances of Babylonian and

---

18. The theonym Śhr is common in Arabic and North Arabic names, but the verbal element in this anthroponym is Northwest Semitic. It is possible that the bearer was an Aramean or an Aramaized Arab (Cross 2006: 85). The name שהרו (probably a hypocoristicon) is found on a Samarian coin (Meshorer and Qedar 1999: 27–28, 94 [no. 60]).

Iranian names. If Dušek's recent reconstruction (2007a) is sustained, a few more Babylonian names should be added to the list compiled by Cross.

One must raise, however, a few cautions. To begin with, a couple of the Iranian names pertain to Achaemenid kings: Artaxerxes (*'rtḫšs'*) and Darius (*dryhwš*). Second, legitimate questions may be raised about how representative the papyri are of the entire Samarian population (Ḥ Eshel 1997). The extant names pertain mostly to merchants, administrative figures, buyers and sellers of slaves, and the slaves themselves. If so, it is doubtful that all of the figures mentioned in these documents were Samarians. Third, one hesitates to read too much into the appearance of an Akkadian name, such as *Sin-'uballiṭ* ("Sin has called into life").[19] To begin with, the names attested for the sons of Sanballat (I)—Delaiah, and Shemaiah—are Yahwistic in nature, as is the name of the son of Sanballat II—[Yešaʿ]yahu—if there is such a person as Sanballat II.[20] There are also a variety of Akkadian names attested in the biblical literature from Yehud, such as "Shenazzar" (*šenʾaṣṣar*), "Sheshbazzar" (*šešbaṣṣar*), and Zerubbabel (*zĕrubbābel*; Zadok 1986).[21] But rarely, if ever, is the argument made that these names show that Shenazzar, Sheshbazzar, and Zerubbabel adhered to Babylonian cultic practices. It is usually assumed that these individuals were Judeans who happened to have Akkadian names. Similarly, the name of the Judean governor Bagohi (בגוהי) and the name of the Judean noble Ostanes (אוסתן) mentioned in the Elephantine Judean correspondence (AP 30.1, 18; 32:1), are Iranian in character, yet most scholars consider these officials to be ethnic Judeans.[22] Indeed, such an assumption seems justified, given that Ostanes had a brother called Anani (עננ<unk>; AP 30.19).

The fourth category of names resembles the second category. These are PNs lacking a theophoric element (most of which are hypocoristica), but which are neither common to Hebrew nor derived etymologically

---

19. Extrabiblical references to Sanballat(s) may be found in TAD 1 A4.7:29 (cf. TAD 1 A4.8:28); WDSP 11 recto 13; WD 22.2 (attached to WDSP 16) בלט[]; Avigad and Sass 1997: 176 [no. 419]); Josephus *Ant.* 11.302–3, 309–12, 315, 321–25, 342, 345; 13.256.
20. This holds true whether one follows the reconstruction of Cross (1974) and Mor (1989a, 2003, 2005) or that of Ḥ. Eshel (2007). But Dušek (2007a: 331) reads this figure as Delaiah (לדל[יהו]) and therefore a son of Sanballat (I).
21. In fact, the number of non-Yahwistic PNs in the repatriate lists of Ezra 2:1–70 (//Neh 7:5–72) is quite high (Becking 2011). This is especially true of the "Israelites," that is, the laypeople, (Ezra 2:3–35//Neh 7:8–38), the temple servants (נתנים; Ezra 2:43–54//Neh 7:46–56), and the children of Solomon's servants (Ezra 2:55–57//Neh 7:57–62), as opposed to the priests (Ezra 2:36–39//Neh 7:39–42) and the Levites (Ezra 2:40//Neh 7:43).
22. On the name, compare MT *Bigvay* (Ezra 2:2 [//Neh 7:7], 14 [//Neh 7:19]; 8:14; Neh 10:17). Cf. 1 Esd 5:14; 8:40 *Bagoi*; LXX (Esdras β) *Bagoua/Baogei/Bagoei*.

from within Hebrew. Again, as with the second classification, there is some inherent ambiguity within this fourth classification, because some names found either in other languages or in foreign geographic contexts may have been borrowed at one time or another into Hebrew. Moreover, there may have been some names that were employed in Judah but not in Samaria, or vice versa. In any case, this fourth category comprises some 9 percent of the total. Finally, a fifth miscellaneous category consists of unassigned and uncertain PNs, comprising 13 percent of the total (Cross 2006: 86). In sum, Yahwistic names and common Hebrew names (also attested in Judean inscriptions and literature) predominate in the Samaria papyri, comprising 64 percent of the total. By contrast, foreign theophoric names and names uncommon in Israelite and Judahite inscriptions and Judahite literature total only 26 percent of the total number of names found in the Samaria papyri. The largest category of appellatives attested within these documents—whether they be of owners, buyers, or slaves—are Yahwistic in character.

In addition to the Yahwistic nomenclature found within the onomasticon of the Samaria papyri, Yahwistic names have also been found on the legends of 4th-century Samarian coins (Meshorer and Qedar 1999: 20–28). These include "Ḥananyah" (ḥnnyh);[23] "Jehoʿanah" (yhwʿnh); "Bodyah" (bdyh), a name appearing on four different coin types;[24] dl, perhaps short for dlyh, "Delaiah"; šl, perhaps short for šlmyh, "Shelemiah"; and wny, perhaps short for wnyh.[25] Common Hebrew names include "Ḥayim" (ḥym), "Yadduʿa" (ydʿ), and "Jeroboam" (yrbʿm). In addition to Samarian coins bearing Yahwistic theophorics, there are some Samarian coins featuring non-Yahwistic theophorics.[26] Three Samarian coin types bear the letters mz, perhaps short for "Mazday," the satrap of the Persian province Abar-Nahara (Beyond the River; Mildenberg 1998: 43–53; Meshorer and Qedar 1999: 25–26, 97, 99, 102 [nos. 74, 84, 100]; Mor 2005: 49). One Samarian coin type appears with the divine name "Zeus"

---

23. Probably the same Hananiah, appearing as a governor in the Samaria papyri—*Ḥ*[*nnyh*] (WDSP 7.17); [*Ḥ*]*nnyh pḥt šmryn* (WDSP 9.14; Gropp 2001: 80–85, 93–96; H. Eshel 2007: 231–234). Alternatively, ʿ[*nnyh*] (Dušek 2007a: 211–212).
24. Cf. Ezra 10:35 *bĕdĕyāh*); WDSP 1.5 בְ[י]דאל (Cross 1985; Zadok 1998: 781; Dušek 2007a: 124).
25. MT Ezra 10:36: וני (Vg. *Vania*); cf. a few Heb. MSS זניה; LXX *Ouiechōa*; 1 Esd 9:34 καὶ Ανως. Among the Elephantine papyri one finds ונה, "Vanah" (AP 22.40). But the evidence is inconclusive. Note, e.g., the inscription engraved in the Jewish script of the Herodian era found at ʿIllar: "[The tomb] belonging to Manasseh son of Wannay" (Naveh 1998: 94).
26. There are also PNs with the divine element El, "Abdiel" (ʿ*bdʾl*; Meshorer and Qedar 1999: 27, 94 [nos. 57–59]).

(ΙΕΥΣ), along with an image of this deity (Meshorer and Qedar 1999: 29, 90 [no. 40]). On the reverse of this coin appears "Jehoʻanah" or, more historically accurate, "Yāhûʻānāh" (*yhwʻnh*), written in Aramaic script. On yet another coin, one finds the face and short form of the name of the deity "[Hera]cles," written in Greek script ([HPA]KΛEΣ; Meshorer and Qedar 1999: 29, 104 [no. 114]).[27] The appearance of Greek deities may indicate a stronger western cultural influence in Samaria than in contemporary Yehud (Lemaire 1990; 2001a: 107–9).

Zadok (1998) gathers all of the attested PNs from Samaria dating to the 5th–4th centuries BCE. His extensive study takes into account numismatic evidence, literary sources (Ezra-Nehemiah), archaeological evidence (Qadum, Yoqneam), and the onomastic evidence of the Wâdī ed-Dâlīyeh papyri. His classification of 92 different (complete) names distinguishes among Israelite names; common (North-)West Semitic names; Aramaic, Akkadian, and Aramaic-Akkadian names; Phoenician names; Iranian names; and Edomite (and other) names. In some respects, this system collapses a few distinctions made by Cross (e.g., separating Yahwistic names from common Hebrew names), yielding the following percentages:

1. Israelite names, minimally 50.0 percent and maximally 55.42 percent
2. Common (North-)West Semitic names, 10.86 percent
3. Aramaic, Akkadian, and Aramaic-Akkadian names, 15.2 percent
4. Phoenician names, 4.34 percent
5. Iranian names, minimally 4.34 percent and maximally 6.51 percent
6. Edomite (and other) names, 7.59 percent

Breaking down the percentage of names with theophoric elements (a total of 66 names), one finds that names with the divine element *Yhw* are by far the most common (57.57 percent). The other theophoric percentages are relatively small: El (*ʼl*) 4.54 percent, Sin (*sn*) 4.54 percent, Baal (*bʻl*) 3.03 percent, Shamash (*šmš*) 3.03 percent, Qos (*qws*) 3.03 percent, and so forth.[28] If PNs found on bullae, coins, and papyri are any reliable indication of religious affiliation, the extant evidence suggests that the majority of people in this province in the 4th century, or at least the majority of

---

27. The Σ is, however, somewhat indistinct (Meshorer and Qedar 1999: 104 [pl. 114])
28. One of the attestations of the Iranian god Mithra (*mtrʼ* on the upper wall of a Qadum jar) cited by Zadok is disputed by Naveh in his discussion of this 5th/4th century inscription (cited in Stern and Magen 1984: 11–12). Naveh argues that the drawings on the vessel, as well as the final *ʼālep*, are problematic for such an interpretation.

the elite, were Yahwistic. One may conclude, as Zadok (1998: 785) does, that "the late-Achaemenid Samarian theophorous onomasticon resembled that of post-exilic Judea: in both *Yhw* was predominant." Indeed, when looking at the larger history of epigraphic remains from northern Israel, the case has been made that the percentage of Yahwistic names attested from the 5th–4th centuries in epigraphic sources (Samaria papyri, Samarian coins) is much higher than the percentage of Yahwistic names attested from the 9th–8th centuries in epigraphic sources (the Samaria ostraca and various seal impressions; Lemaire 1977: 226–27; 2001; Zadok 1998: 785). Hence, Yahwism in Samaria was not a late arrival, that is, a Hellenistic development, but rather evolved from earlier times. If the use of personal names is any indication, the area of Samaria became more Yahwistic, not less so, in the Persian period than it had been in the Iron Age, the time of the Israelite monarchy.[29]

We have been discussing the deployment of bilingualism, the use of select scripts, and the predominance of Yahwistic names in the papyri, inscriptions, and coins from Samaria in the late Persian period. Such evidence points to a significant cultural overlap between the cultures of Samaria and Yehud in the Achaemenid era. But in examining the material cultures of the two adjacent provinces, one may also recognize distinctive features exhibited by each geopolitical entity. My argument is not that the material cultures of the two provinces were completely identical. There seem to be significant differences between the two in some respects. The range and number of coin types attested from Samaria, for example, dwarf those of coins from Yehud (Meshorer 1982, 2000, 2001; Mildenberg 1996). The study of Samarian coinage by Meshorer and Qedar (1999) lists some 224 different coin types. The issue of types is relevant, because the local mints of provinces and city-states in Palestine seem to have enjoyed considerable freedom in choosing iconographic schemes for the small silver coinage (mostly obols and fractions thereof) that they were allowed to produce (Barag 1986–87; Mildenberg 1997). Both the Judean coins and the Samarian coins bear witness to an eclectic range of influences and adaptations of older styles (Stern 1994b; Mildenberg 1998; Leith 1997, 2000). As with Judean coinage, Samarian coinage evinces a variety of Athenian prototypes, but the number and range of such prototypes

---

29. But it would be misleading to label this as an era of Judaizing (or "Yahweh-izing") in Samaria, as some have contended (most recently Meshorer and Qedar 2002), because the evidence indicates that Yahwism was not absent from Samaria in previous centuries.

are substantially greater. Various Sidonian and Tyrian motifs are also prominent. In contrast, the available Judean coins evince relatively little dependence upon Phoenician models. In addition to the Sidonian and Tyrian prototypes, some fifteen different Cilician designs are attested on Samarian coins (Meshorer and Qedar 1999: 32).

The analysis of recent Samarian numismatic finds has brought to light a range of new coin designs that were previously unattested among earlier or contemporary Palestinian coins. To be sure, some of these previously unattested designs are themselves based upon earlier Syrian, Babylonian, and Achaemenid seal types (or various combinations thereof). The prominence of Achaemenid iconographical patterns, in particular, on a range of Samarian coins is stressed by Uehlinger (1999), who points out that there are more "Persianisms" on Samarian coins than on coins from any other mint in the southern Levant. In contrast, Judean coins show only a few such Achaemenid motifs (e.g., coins that show the royal Persian head).[30] There are, of course, plausible historical explanations for these phenomena. Samaria was geographically closer to Cilicia and to the Phoenician city-states of Tyre and Sidon than Judah was. It seems likely that Samaria conducted a greater amount of trade with these particular areas than Judah did. Given that a significant Persian military presence in Samaria is attested (Neh 3:34; Uehlinger 1999: 178–79), some of the Samarian issues could have been minted (or authorized) by Persian officials stationed there.

The Samarians undoubtedly had their own distinctive traditions and customs in addition to whatever traditions and customs they shared with the Judeans. That among the numismatic evidence from Samaria one finds coins with the legend *yrbʿm*, "Jeroboam," suggests that at least some residents of Samaria felt an attachment to the traditions of the former northern kingdom. Five 4th-century coin types are attested with the name of this Samarian governor (or governors), the most for any personal name (Meshorer and Qedar 1991: 14–15; 1999: 24–25). By contrast, the name Jeroboam is unattested in Judean biblical literature and in Judean inscriptions, apart from its appearance as the nomenclature of these two northern kings.[31] In addition to its

---

30. By contrast, one may note the high number of Athenian and imitation Athenian designs on the coinage from Philistia, dating to the 5th/4th centuries (Gitler and Tal 2006). Athenian motifs (and their imitations) are also prominent in Judean coinage (Meshorer 1982, 2001), but the number and range of such motifs are considerably higher in the coinage from Ashdod, Ashkelon, and Gaza.
31. Jeroboam I: 1 Kgs 11:26–22:53; 2 Kgs 3:3–23:15; 2 Chr 9:29–13:20; Jeroboam II: 2 Kgs 13:13; 14:16, 23, 27, 29; 15:1, 8; Hos 1:1; Amos 1:1; 7:9–11; 1 Chr 5:17.

appearance on Samarian coins, the name Jeroboam is attested epigraphically in earlier centuries in the north. The name of one of the two monarchs, probably Jeroboam II, is attested on a seal from Megiddo (Avigad and Sass 1997: 49–50 [no. 2]). The name [ירבע[ם is also attested on an 8th-century jar fragment from Hazor (6.1), "Jeroboa[m], son of Elim[elek]."[32] Thus far, no attested figure from any of the southern tribes during either the monarchic or postmonarchic periods bears this particular name.

In sum, when acknowledging significant cultural continuities between Samaria and Yehud during the Persian period, one does not have to argue that the two adjacent provinces were indistinguishable from a material standpoint, much less indistinguishable in almost all respects. The point is not that the two formed a single, completely homogenous culture. Some distinctions can and should be made between the two. The selection of a largely dissimilar and much more varied repertoire of motifs on Samarian coins in comparison with Judean coins is an example of one such difference (Cornelius 2011).[33] On the whole, Samaria's elite seems to have been more cosmopolitan, connected to the Phoenician coast, and wealthier than its Judean counterpart, whose points of contact may have been oriented more toward the southwest (the cities of Philistia; Gitler and Tal 2006).

Hence the point is not that the two neighbors together comprised one society. Rather, the point is that the two provinces shared a number of striking and significant cultural and religious features in spite of their differences. Moreover, the distinctive traditions each society possessed did not hinder, for the most part, their ability to pursue common interests in a larger international context in which both provinces were but small parts of a much larger imperial regime. Some tantalizing pieces of evidence pertaining to the character of Samaria's relations to Yehud are found among the Elephantine papyri. When the Judeans at Elephantine wished to rebuild their temple in the late 5th century, they appealed to the authorities in both Jerusalem and Samaria for assistance (TAD 4.5–4.10; Vincent 1937: 253–55; Porten 1968: 278–98). Certainly the Elephantine

---

32. Dobbs-Allsopp et al. 2005: 188–89. Delavault and Lemaire (1979: 5–12) contend that the fragment is Phoenician rather than Hebrew. This is possible, given the shape of some letter forms, but the inscriptions were found in an Israelite archaeological context.

33. Of course, one expects the relevant numismatics of any province or state to differ somewhat from those of other provinces and states, because coin motifs and labels function as identity markers for the province or state in question. If there were no distinctive attributes, there would be no way to distinguish the coinage of one geopolitical entity from that of another.

colonists must have felt some affinity with the Samarian community or they would not have written them to ask for their help. Moreover, that Jedaniah and his priestly colleagues saw fit to mention their appeal to the Samaria authorities—Delaiah and Shelemiah, the sons of Sanballat, the governor of Samaria—in their correspondence with Bagavahya (Bagohi), the governor of Judah, suggests ongoing ties between the leaders of Yehud and Samaria (TAD 4.7:29; 4.8:28).

That the Jerusalem leadership shared normal diplomatic relations with the Samarian leadership is evidently confirmed by the joint communique written by Bagavahya, the governor of Judah, and Delaiah the son of Sanballat, the governor of Samaria, supporting the Elephantine community's bid to gain permission from Arsames, the satrap of Egypt, to rebuild the Elephantine Temple (literally, "the altar house," בית מדבחא; TAD 4.9:3).[34] One could argue the contrary point and maintain that this joint communique represented a unique or highly unusual instance of cooperation between the Jerusalem and Samaria authorities. But there is no hint of this within the draft of the missive itself. All the indications from the letters point to regular relations between the leadership in Jerusalem and Samaria.

III. New Evidence about Cultic Affairs in Persian/Hellenistic Period Samaria

If some scholars have been guilty of retrojecting the disputes of later literary sources into earlier times, what should one make of the state of religious affairs in Samaria during the Neo-Babylonian and Persian periods? Where did Yahwistic Samarians worship? At what point was a sanctuary constructed on Mt. Gerizim?[35] The following treatment is necessarily selective and focuses on positive evidence. One could add other criteria that are more negative, such as the relative absence of certain religious markers. One example is the absence of so-called pagan cults and cultic figurines during the Second Commonwealth. In Stern's view (1989; 2001: 479, 488; 2006), there is a complete absence of such artifacts in the material remains relating to Yehud and Samaria (cf. Keel and Uehlinger 1996: 385–91). Such a relative absence is all the more interesting, given

---

34. With the proviso that it only present cereal offerings (מנחה), drink offerings (נסך), and incense (לבונה; TAD 4.9:9; 4.10:11; Grelot 1972: 417–19). Sheep, oxen, and goats were not to be offered there as burnt sacrifice (TAD 4.10:11).

35. Earlier scholarly guesses ranged from the late 4th century to the early 2nd century.

the plentiful presence of such figurines at many sites in Iron Age Judah and Israel.

In any event, there are challenges in discerning the nature of Samarian cultic affairs, just as there are certain challenges in reconstructing the nature of Judean cultic affairs (Kratz 2006b). Some scholars have supposed that the Samarians, lacking any sanctuaries of their own, occasionally journeyed to Jerusalem to worship there.[36] In one variation of this theory, the very distinction between Samarians and Judeans was inherently political and not religious. The emergence of a distinct Yahwistic Samarian community did not occur until the 3rd century BCE or some time thereafter (e.g., Kippenberg 1971: 57–93).[37] Hence, the Yahwistic Samarian community was essentially a breakaway Jewish sect. Others (e.g., H. Eshel 1996) have disagreed, contending for the development of some sort of ongoing sacrificial cult(s) in the former northern kingdom.

Complicating the issue is the relative dearth of major excavations in Samaria during recent times. Hence, from a material standpoint, clear evidence is lacking, whether of a positive or a negative character. It must be said, though, that it is highly unlikely that the region of Samaria lacked any Yahwistic sanctuary (or sanctuaries) in the Iron III and Persian periods prior to the construction of a sanctuary at Mt. Gerizim. To begin with, literary sources indicate the existence of a major sanctuary at or near Bethel that survived the destruction of the northern kingdom (Koenen 2003; Knauf 2006; Köhlmoos 2006). To be sure, the Bethel sanctuary seems to have fallen into desuetude in the late Neo-Babylonian or early Persian period, but by this time it lay within the boundaries of Yehud (Stern 2001; Lipschits 1998, 2005; Na'aman 2010).

The theory assumes what it needs to prove, namely, that the Samarians and the Judeans were religiously united around one major sanctuary (Jerusalem) centuries before the Samarians split off to build their own sanctuary and formed their own separate religion. Such a scenario is historically implausible. As we have seen, Samaria as a whole did not suffer from the Babylonian invasions in the late 7th and early 6th centuries. As far as we know, Samaria did not participate in the rebellions against King Nebuchadnezzar, and as a consequence most of its towns did not

---

36. So, for instance, H. Tadmor 1994b: 261–96, who refers to Jer 41:5, Chronicles, Ezra (4:1, 12–14), and Nehemiah (3:33–34; 4:1–2; 13:28).
37. Kippenberg (1971) suggests that the separate cult was begun by priests (self-identified descendants of Eleazar). In this theory, Samaritanism began essentially as a new religious movement in the 3rd (or 2nd) century.

experience the serious losses that Jerusalem and other major Judean urban centers experienced in the early 6th century. Hence, there is no good reason to believe that its major sanctuaries all endured the kind of destruction that the Jerusalem temple suffered. In other words, it hardly seems likely that the district of Samaria was bereft of any Yahwistic sacred precincts before the construction of a sanctuary on Mt. Gerizim in the mid-5th century. Given the histories of various societies in the ancient Near East, it would have been truly extraordinary if an entire state or province lacked any substantial shrine dedicated to a principal deity of the land.

To be sure, it may be acknowledged that there were some northern patrons who supported the Jerusalem sanctuary (e.g., Jer 41:4–8), but such pilgrimages southward by some should not be taken as representative of the whole.[38] It may also be acknowledged that the questions of whether there was a temple in the city of Samaria itself, how long such a shrine survived, and where it was located remain unsettled. This is true both for the late 8th century (Sukenik 1942; Steiner 1997; cf. Timm 2002) and for the Persian period.[39] In short, there is little doubt that the erection of a Yahwistic temple on Mt. Gerizim in the Persian period was a highly significant historical development, but the literary and material evidence indicates that this was not the first time a Yahwistic temple had been built in the Samaria region.

Rather than thinking that a new sanctuary on Mt. Gerizim caused a precipitous and permanent split between Yahwistic Samarians and Yahwistic Judeans, it seems more plausible to recognize that cultic, historical, and political differences had divided the two areas (Israel and Judah) for many centuries. Even the Deuteronomistic and Chronistic writers, who uphold a pan-Israelite legacy of the united monarchy, concede that such an entity was short-lived and that most of Judahite history in the 10th–6th centuries was lived apart from northern Israel. To hold that constructing a Yahwistic shrine within Samaria during the Persian period

---

38. The "house of Yhwh" (*bêt Yhwh*) is not specified. Most think that the collocation refers to the remains of the Jerusalem temple, but Blenkinsopp (1998: 27–34) contends that it refers to Bethel.

39. So Ḥ Eshel 1996, with reference to *nskt'* in one of the Samaria papyri (WDSP 14; Gropp 2001 [pl. xvi]), but see Dušek 2007a: 290–300. Leith (1998, 2000) points to a 4th-century Samarian coin (Meshorer and Qedar 1991: 47–49 [no. 26]) with the name of "Jeroboam" (ירבעם) on the obverse and two female figures in what may be a shrine on the reverse. Given the Cilician prototype, which includes a fire altar, it is possible that the structure represents a Samarian shrine.

severed the unity of the Judean people (= Israel) falsely assumes that such a unified Judean people previously existed in Samaria and Judah.⁴⁰ It seems more historically plausible to acknowledge both similarities and differences between the Yahwists residing in northern Israel and those residing in southern Israel. The differences included where people worshiped.

As we have seen, there remains much uncertainty surrounding the status of many northern sites, but many seasons of archaeological excavations on Mt. Gerizim headed by Magen (1990, 2000, 2008b) have shed much light on the history of the site during the Persian, Hellenistic, Roman, and Byzantine periods. The excavations attest to the construction of an impressive city and sacred precinct on Mt. Gerizim in Hellenistic times. The large fortified town on Mt. Gerizim was approximately 30 dunams in size (40.5 hectares) during the time of Antiochus III (223–187 BCE). Most of the remains found during the many seasons of excavations at this large site date to the Hellenistic, Roman, and Byzantine periods. Eight different areas of the site were excavated. Hellenistic finds from Mt. Gerizim include sections of a city wall, towers, large domiciles, service buildings, courtyards, oil presses, storage jars, and various lamps.⁴¹ Also found were thousands of coins and hundreds of fragmentary inscriptions in Hebrew, Aramaic, and Greek (Naveh and Magen 1997; Magen, Misgav, and Tsfania 2004; Dušek 2012a).

Beneath the Hellenistic sacred precinct on Mt. Gerizim, Magen (2000) discovered an older layer, which he dates to the 5th century and identifies as the Samari(t)an Temple mentioned (but misdated) by Josephus.⁴² Of the various areas of the excavation on Mt. Gerizim, clear Persian-period remains have only been found in one, the sacred complex. The excavator suggests that the area occupied during the Persian occupation was at first relatively small, measuring some 96 m x 98 m in size, not including its gates. This Persian-period precinct was heavily rebuilt and expanded

---

40. So, e.g., Josephus (*Ant.* 11.323), who has Sanballat petition Alexander the Great for permission to build a Samarian temple on Mt. Gerizim on the grounds that Alexander's rule would be best served if the power of the Judeans were divided into two (εἰς δύο διῃρῆσθαι τὴν Ἰουδαίων δύναμιν) so that in the event of an insurrection, the people (τὸ ἔθνος) would not stand in solidarity against the rule of their (foreign) kings, as they had done in former times. Ironically, this statement presupposes that Judeans and Samarians were hitherto considered to be members of the same people. Kartveit (2009) and Pummer (2009) provide critical assessments of Josephus's work.

41. The city wall was found, however, only on the southern part of the site.

42. Josephus dated its construction to the time of Alexander the Great, *Ant.* 11.302–47; 13.254–56; *BJ* 1.62–65 (Kartveit 2009; Pummer 2009).

when it was replaced in the Hellenistic period (Magen 2000: 97). Both the Persian and the Hellenistic sacred areas were located on the mountain's summit.

Because of the heavy reuse and major expansion of the site in the Hellenistic and Byzantine periods, the Persian-period remains from the eastern and southern areas of the complex are quite limited.[43] But the western wall of the larger complex, extending some 84 m in length, is 1.3 m thick and seems to have been preserved to a height of 2 m (Magen 2007). This western wall lacks any gates.[44] But excavations have unearthed the remains of a multichambered (six or eight chambers) gate, measuring 14 m x 15 m on the north wall.[45] Excavations have also revealed fragments of interior courtyards, chambers, some enclosure walls, and stones that may have comprised part of an altar, all dating to the Persian period. The building construction was monumental in style. The enclosure walls were built of ashlar masonry. In contrast, the later and much larger Hellenistic precinct was constructed of smooth stones quarried at some depth.[46]

The Persian-period pottery dates to the 5th–4th centuries BCE.[47] Small finds from the Achaemenid era include silver jewelry, a copper snake, and metal implements (Magen 2000: 105–8). Of the 72 Persian-period coins found at the site, the earliest—a drachma minted at Cyprus—is said to date to 480 BCE (Magen 2007: 179 [fig. 27:1]). Particularly interesting was the discovery of many faunal remains. To the east of the area identified as the sacred precinct was a public building, approximately 11 m x 12 m in size, which contained thousands of burnt bones along with a great quantity of ashes. Magen (2007: 180–82) thinks that this was possibly the "House of Ashes" adjoining the altar upon which the burning of the

---

43. Due to the steep slope to the east, the eastern wall and gate of the Hellenistic precinct were constructed over the Persian-period wall, thoroughly demolishing the older construction. Given the numerous Persian- and early-Hellenistic-period finds discovered in the area, it seems likely that the eastern wall likely also had a Persian-period gate. In fact, Magen thinks that the Persian-period enclosure featured three chambered gates (northern, eastern, and southern).

44. The absence of gates in this wall may be due to the location of the Holy of Holies. It is possible that the Samaritan sacred site known as the "Twelve Stones" is located in the area of the Persian-period holy place (Magen 2008b).

45. The Persian-period gate was replaced by a smaller gate to the northwest, when the sacred precinct area was expanded in Hellenistic times.

46. Magen (2008b: 5) observes that in the Hellenistic phase, Greek construction techniques were employed. Similar building techniques are attested at Hellenistic Samaria (Crowfoot, Kenyon, and Sukenik 1942: 24–31).

47. Based on comparative data gleaned from ceramic finds from different archaeological sites with significant Persian-period remains in the hill country, the Sharon Plain, and the Judean Shephelah (Magen 2007: 178–79, 194–205).

sacrifices was carried out. The bones discovered were of principally four types: goats, sheep, cattle, and doves. The bones, scarred and burned, have been dated to the 5th century (Magen 2000: 111; 2007: 180–81).[48] Based on the ceramic evidence (found on the building floors), the carbon-14 dating of the faunal remains, the method of building construction, and the numismatic evidence, Magen argues that the Samarian Temple was established in the first half of the 5th century.[49]

To summarize, the excavations address the question of when a Yahwistic temple was constructed at Mt. Gerizim by providing multiple answers. There was a Yahwistic sanctuary at Mt. Gerizim, exhibiting monumental architecture and a sacrificial apparatus, at an earlier time than scholars previously thought. During the Hellenistic period, this sanctuary was massively rebuilt and expanded. This means that in addition to whatever Yahwistic shrines existed in the Diaspora, such as the Judean temple at Elephantine (Vincent 1937; Porten 1968; Bolin 1995; Kratz 2006b), there were at least two Yahwistic shrines within the land itself. A third Yahwistic shrine may have existed in Khirbet el-Qôm (4th century BCE), serving the small Judean community that existed in northern Idoumea (Lemaire 2004; 2006: 416–17).

IV. Archaizing, Piety, and Identity in the Mt. Gerizim Cult

Having discussed the two major stages in the history of the Gerizim sanctuary, it will be useful to discuss the cultic rituals and the people performing those rituals. In such an analysis, the approximately 400 fragmentary inscriptions from the site, published by Magen, Misgav, and Tsfania (2004) and recently reanalyzed by Dušek (2012a), are of considerable help. The inscriptions are written in paleo-Hebrew, lapidary (monumental) Aramaic, cursive Aramaic, and Samaritan scripts.[50] The discovery

---

48. Most of the bones were from animals less than three years old. Of these, a large group was less than one year old (Magen 2000: 111). The faunal remains need to be interpreted not only in the context of Pentateuchal stipulations about sacrifices but also in the context of a systematic analysis of the faunal remains, dating to different periods, found at other sites (e.g., Arad, Ashqelon, Dan, City of David, Mt. Ebal, Tel Halif, Hazor, Tel Hesi, Tel Jemmeh, Megiddo, Tel Michal, Tel Miqne, Ḥorvat Qitmit, Yoqneam).
49. On epigraphic grounds, Dušek (2012a: 3) favors the second half of the 5th century. The issue need not detain us here.
50. In employing this nomenclature, I am departing from the nomenclature advocated by the epigraphers working on the Mt. Gerizim inscriptions. See my earlier note (no. 14).

of a large number of inscriptions in cursive Aramaic script is especially notable. The texts inscribed in Samaritan script date to the late antique and medieval periods and need not be considered here. Unfortunately, most of the inscriptions, whatever their date, were not found in situ, but were found scattered in various areas around the site (Magen, Misgav, and Tsfania 2004: 14, 30, 271–72). Almost all of the inscriptions are of a votive or dedicatory character. A few inscriptions (nos. 382–85, 387), written in the Hebrew language and carefully engraved in paleo-Hebrew script, may have been designed as public inscriptions.[51] It should be noted that many of the texts written in Aramaic (lapidary Aramaic and cursive Aramaic) script and paleo-Hebrew (Neo-Hebrew) script were discovered in and around the area of the sacred precinct. Magen, Misgav, and Tsfania (2004: 13–14) hypothesize that the votives were inscribed on already extant stones embedded in walls surrounding or leading up to the temple. After the temple was destroyed, many of the stones on which the votive texts were inscribed were reused in later building phases. It would seem that most of the texts were written in the 3rd–2nd centuries BCE, with a view to the Hellenistic temple constructed to replace the older and smaller Persian-period temple.[52]

In what follows, I wish to discuss not only certain aspects of the inscriptions written in lapidary Aramaic, but also some of the cursive Aramaic and paleo-Hebrew inscriptions. It must be remembered that although these texts date to the Hellenistic era, they provide a glimpse into the *longue durée* of the Gerizim site. They either presuppose the existence of a Yahwistic temple or make explicit references to this shrine. As such, the inscriptions may provide us with insight into the developing Samarian community and its reception of the Gerizim sanctuary. Since epigraphic evidence from this general area dating to the 3rd–2nd centuries is not abundant, the texts provide welcome light on an obscure era.[53]

It may be appropriate to begin with a brief discussion of some PNs before we discuss inscriptions involving the temple and its religious affairs. As with the Samaria papyri and the Samarian numismatic remains, a

---

51. Observing their particular columnar style, Dušek (2012a: 62–63) suggests that these five inscriptions were part of one original monumental inscription.
52. Although the epigraphers believe that at least some of the texts—those written in lapidary (monumental) Aramaic script—may stem from the late Persian period (Magen, Misgav, and Tsfania 2004: 14, 41), Dušek (2012a) argues strongly that all of the texts date to the late 3rd and early 2nd centuries.
53. In what follows, my references will be to Magen, Misgav, and Tsfania 2004. The numbers are keyed to this primary publication.

variety of personal names of a Yahwistic character appear, such as Delaiah (דליה), Ḥananiah (חניה) and/or Ḥoniah (חני[ה]), Jehonathan (יהונתן), Jehoseph (יהוסף; cf. Ps 81:6), Joseph (יוסף), and Shemaiah (שמעיה), as well as common Hebrew names, such as Elnatan (אלנתן), Ephraim (אפרים), Zabdi (זבדי), Haggai (חגי), Jacob (יעקוב), Miriam (מרים), and Simeon (שמעון).⁵⁴ Less common names include Abishag (אבי[שג]) and Shobai (שבי; cf. שבי; Avigad and Sass 1997: 71 [no. 63]; Ezra 2:53). In a northern context, it is not surprising to find personal names such as Ephraim, Jacob, and Joseph. Yet one also finds הוד[י], Yehud (no. 43) and הודה[י], Judah (no. 49) among the anthroponyms. If there was a long history of intense rivalry and ongoing enmity between the Jerusalem and Gerizim communities, it would be less likely that one would find individuals named Judah and Yehud making dedications at the Mt. Gerizim shrine.⁵⁵ As with the Samaria papyri, there are also some foreign names among the Mt. Gerizim inscriptions.⁵⁶ Interestingly, but not too surprisingly given the long history of the Mt. Gerizim sacred precinct in the Persian, Hellenistic, Roman, and Byzantine eras, about one-fifth of the total proper names attested are Greek names.⁵⁷

Of particular interest is the appearance of several anthroponyms in the Mt. Gerizim onomasticon that recall the names given to famous figures in Israel's classical past. Names such as Miriam, Joseph, Jehoseph, Ephraim, Levi, and Phinehas are not simply traditional names. They occur rarely as personal names in Judean biblical literature, apart from their associations with the famous Israelites, mostly but not exclusively northern Israelites, they represent (Knoppers 2010). Some are reminiscent of ancestral times (e.g., Jacob, Joseph, Ephraim, Judah, Levi), while others are reminiscent of major figures associated with the times of Exodus, Sinai, and the emergence in the land (e.g., Amram, Eleazar, Miriam, Phinehas). The redeployment of particular ancestral names in Hellenistic times does not seem accidental. The archaizing tendencies in employing such names suggest

---

54. Perhaps the name *ṭabya* (no. 200) should be added to this list, although *ṭby'* normally means "deer" in Aramaic. The excavators believe, however, that the fragmentary *ṭby'* may be short for *ṭbyh* (or *ṭbyhw*). *Ṭabya* was a common Samaritan name in several periods.
55. Alternatively, it is possible that the dedicator was from Judah or Benjamin (e.g., Neh 11:9; cf. 1 Chr 9:7 Hodaviah [הודויה]; Knoppers 2000b; 2004a: 495). Judah could also have been the name of a Levite (e.g., Ezra 3:9; 10:23; Neh 12:8 [MT]) or a priest (e.g., Neh 12:34, 36).
56. One, בג[והי], "Bagohi" (no. 27), needs to be discounted, because the foreign element in the PN is entirely reconstructed (Dušek 2007a).
57. Given their number, along with the different scripts represented, these names deserve a separate study.

that at least some residents of Samaria identified with earlier figures in Israelite history. In summary, when surveying the Mt. Gerizim onomasticon with the early Hellenistic period in view, one is struck by three things: (1) the number of common Yahwistic names; (2) the number of archaizing names, that is, names that recall the anthroponyms of male and female figures associated with Israel's classical past; and (3) the number of common Hebrew names.

The names found in the Mt Gerizim inscriptions may be approached from another vantage point. It may be useful to pay some attention to the relevance of the inscriptions for our understanding of the temple and its religious context. To begin with, one inscription written in lapidary Aramaic mentions "bulls [פרין] in all... [sacrifi]ced in the house of sacrifice" (בית דבחא; no. 199; Becking 2007). The reference to a "house of sacrifice" is especially intriguing, because the same expression (in Hebrew) is used by the deity in Chronicles to refer to his election of the Jerusalem temple. In the Chronistic expansion of the theophany to Solomon (2 Chr 7:11–22; cf. 1 Kgs 9:1–9), following Solomon's ceremonial temple dedication, Yhwh specifically alludes to the petitions Solomon included in his public address: "I have heard your prayer and I have chosen (בחרתי) this place (במקום הזה) to be for me a house of sacrifice" (בית זבח; 2 Chr 7:12). The usage of the same expression in the Gerizim inscriptions and in Chronicles is striking.

Other inscriptions within the Mt. Gerizim corpus feature allusions to the sanctuary. Some contain formulae such as "before God/the Lord in this place," or simply "before God" or "before the Lord" (nos. 149–55). Based on biblical and extrabiblical parallels, such phraseology almost always suggests the context of a sacred precinct. One of the inscriptions written in paleo-Hebrew script contains the Tetragrammaton, apparently as part of the phrase "[the house of] Yhwh" (no. 383). The use of the Tetragrammaton is, however, relatively rare and is not found among the extant cursive Aramaic inscriptions (Magen, Misgav, and Tsfania 2004: 22–23). The common terms for the divine are Elaha, "God" (אלהא) and "the Lord" (אדני). For example, an inscription in cursive Aramaic script reads in part, "[that which] Joseph [son of...] offered [for] his [w]ife and for his sons before the L[ord in the temple]" (no. 150).

Some inscriptions contain the titles of a priest (כהן or כהנא) or priests (כהנים; כהניא), who served as cultic specialists at the site. Among the Levitical and priestly names found in the inscriptions is Levi (לוי), an appellative found on two different inscriptions (nos. 56; 156). It should be pointed out, however, that unlike the situation with the references to the priests as a group (כהנים; כהניא), there are no attested references to the Levites as a group (e.g., הלוים, לוים). Among the priestly names attested are Amram (עמרם), the name of the father of Moses in biblical tradition (no. 149), and Eleazar (אלעזר), the name of the son of Aaron, found on two separate inscriptions (nos. 1, 32), as well as on one square-shaped object, possibly a late seal (no. 390).[58] Another common priestly name found among the inscriptions is Phinehas (פינחס), the son of Eleazar in biblical tradition. The name Phinehas is found on five different inscriptions (no. 24; lapidary Aramaic script; no. 25; cursive Aramaic script; no. 61; cursive Aramaic script; no. 384; paleo-Hebrew script; no. 389; paleo-Hebrew script).[59] The repeated appearance of the name in paleo-Hebrew script may be important insofar as this script seems to have been favored (although not exclusively so) in sacerdotal dedications (Magen, Misgav, and Tsfania 2004: 257). Indeed, in one case, the adjective הגדול, "great" (line 3), occurs in a fragmentary inscription that also includes the name "Phinehas" (י[פ]נחס; line 1), raising the prospect that this particular individual was a high priest at Mt. Gerizim (Dušek 2012a: 58).[60] My argument is not that all of these figures with traditional Levitical and priestly names actually served as cultic functionaries or priests at Mt. Gerizim. The fragmentary evidence does not permit such a sweeping conclusion. Nevertheless, a few of the inscriptions do mention such sacerdotal personnel, along with their personal names, as the source of the relevant dedications.[61] In other words, it is clear that priests were among those who made dedications. It is also interesting that many of these priestly names replicate priestly names associated with Israel's classical past.

Given the traditionalism inherent in the Mt. Gerizim onomasticon, it might be tempting to draw a clear contrast between the names found in the 4th century Samaria papyri and coins and the names found in the 3rd–2nd century Gerizim inscriptions. Based on such a broad

---

58. A priest by the name of Eleazar son of Phinehas is attested in the times of Samuel (1 Sam 7:1) and Ezra (8:33; cf. Neh 12:42). But Eleazar is not exclusively a priestly name. Eleazar appears as the name of one of David's warriors (2 Sam 23:29//1 Chr 11:12; 27:24 [LXX]; Knoppers 2004b: 537, 548) and as the name of a layperson in Ezra's time (Ezra 10:25).
59. As to the priestly son of Eli, see 1 Sam 1:3; 2:34; 4:4, 11, 17, 19; 14:3.
60. The issue is relevant because of the appearance of הכהן הגדול in biblical literature (Lev 21:10; Num 35:25, 28; Josh 20:6; 2 Kgs 12:11; 22:4, 8; 23:4; Zech 3:1, 8; 6:11; Hag 1:1, 12, 14; 2:2, 4; Neh 3:1, 20; 2 Chr 34:9; cf. AP 30.18 כהנא רבא) to designate a high priest.
61. Magen, Misgav, and Tsfania 2004: 67–68 (no. 24; Phinehas); 68 (no. 25; [Phine]has); 258–59 (no. 389; son of Phinehas).

comparison, one could leap to the conclusion that the Samarian community generally became more conservative during the Hellenistic era. Such a conclusion about a major onomastic shift would be potentially misleading, however. The names available from the Persian period derive from commercial, administrative, and political contexts, whereas the names available from the Hellenistic period largely derive from a cultic setting at a different geographic location. It is not surprising that a good number of the appellations in the Mt. Gerizim inscriptions are priestly or Levitical in nature, whereas such appellations are rare, if not nonexistent, among the Samaria papyri and coins.[62] If one examines, for the sake of comparison, the anthroponyms found within the lists in Ezra-Nehemiah, one discovers that the lists of priests and Levites contain more Yahwistic names than those pertaining to other groups.[63] Similarly, the fact that the Samarian coins and papyri contain some Persian and Babylonian names is understandable, given the nature of the documentation and the larger imperial, diplomatic, and commercial setting within which the capital of Samaria functioned. Indeed, one cannot presume that all of the names in the Samaria papyri (mostly slave sales and slave dockets) are those of Samarians. One has to situate, as best one can, each onomasticon within its own particular geographic, social, and historical setting.

It may be more prudent to maintain that the Mt. Gerizim inscriptions provide evidence of continuity, even conservatism, within the 3rd–2nd century history of the Yahwistic community in Samaria. At least among the families whose members were making dedications at the sanctuary, archaizing in name giving was prominent. The elite was largely Yahwistic, as it was in Judah, and this elite, like the Judean elite, construed its identity, at least in part, by recourse to traditions about and figures drawn from Israel's classical past. Similarly, the avoidance of the use of the Tetragrammaton in the dedicatory inscriptions is striking. The preference for the use of "God" (אלהא) or the "Lord" (אדני) over the use of "Yhwh" (יהוה), is important, because the same inclination to protect the sanctity

---

62. A (Yahwistic) priestly name is attested on one 4th-century Judean coin, יוחנן הכוהן, "Johanan the priest" (Barag 1986–87; Meshorer 2001: 14 [no. 20]). At least some of the names appearing on Samarian coins could be those of priests (Mor 2005). The matter remains uncertain, because the coins do not label them as such.
63. Indeed, the number of Yahwistic personal names in the list is not large (Ezra 2:1–70//Neh 7:6–72). This is true of the Israelites, that is, the laity (Ezra 2:2–35//Neh. 7:7–38; cf. Ezra 2:59–60//Neh. 7:61–62), and even more so of the gatekeepers (Ezra 2:42//Neh 7:45), temple servants (נתינם; Ezra 2:43–54//Neh 7:46–56), and the sons of Solomon's servants (Ezra 2:55–57//Neh 7:57–59).

of the personal name of the God of Israel occurs in the development of early Judaism. In short, the recourse to traditional writings, the means to distinguish a particular heritage (e.g., through the reuse of particular names), and the means to honor the deity both groups worshiped were implemented in similar ways.[64] The epigraphic evidence from Mt. Gerizim shows that the religious overlap between the Samarians and the Judeans was as strong in the Hellenistic period, if not stronger than it was in the Persian period. From the vantage point of the material remains, there is no clear indication that the two Yahwistic communities were moving in two opposite directions or that the two communities were drifting far apart.

Conclusions

We have seen that the material remains from Samaria in the Persian and Hellenistic periods provide evidence for a striking series of cultural continuities between Samaria and Yehud. In the Persian era, the evidence includes the considered deployment of (Hebrew/Aramaic) bilingualism, the system of Hebrew and Aramaic scripts, the relative absence of so-called pagan cults and figurines, the predominance of Yahwistic names, and the large overlap in Hebrew names. In the early Hellenistic period, the evidence for an overlap in cultural tradition includes many common Yahwistic personal names, many common Hebrew names, an archaizing trend in name giving, the types and ages of sacrificial offerings (in conformity with Pentateuchal prescriptions), and the avoidance of employing the Tetragrammaton in dedicatory inscriptions.[65] Even the so-called proto-Hasmonean (cursive Aramaic) script, which was once thought to be a distinctive local development from the standard Aramaic cursive of the late Persian empire, turns out to be a common patrimony of a variety of societies in the southern Levant. When this material evidence is coupled with the literary evidence we have addressed in earlier chapters, it becomes clear that Yahwism in Samaria was not a late arrival and that Yahwistic Samarians were not a late-breakaway group from Judah, as

---

64. In particular, I am referring to the books that constitute the Pentateuch, but not to the Prophets or the Writings (Ben Zvi 1995; Pummer 2007). Indeed, in later tradition, the Samaritans viewed themselves as protectors of the Torah over against the beliefs found in the Prophetic writings (Mikolášek 1995).
65. When speaking of the types and ages of sacrificial offerings, I am assuming that the Jerusalem (second) temple would exhibit a roughly similar distribution in conformity with Pentateuchal statutes.

generations of older scholars have maintained. The Samarians have often been viewed as a schismatic Judean sect, but it would be more historically accurate to acknowledge, as we have seen, a continuous, albeit evolving and changing, Israelite presence in Samaria during postmonarchic times.

An overlap in cultural tradition with Yehud is not, however, tantamount to identity in cultural tradition. The Yahwistic Samarians had their own particular historical traits and traditions (Macchi 1994a; Hjelm 2000, 2004; Faü and Crown 2001; Cornelius 2011). Approaching Samarians as Judeans under a different name is too simplistic. The traditionally northern personal names, such as Ephraim, Joseph, and Jacob, found among the later (Hellenistic age) Mt. Gerizim inscriptions point in the same direction.[66] The prominence of such anthroponyms, which reproduce the anthroponyms of major figures associated with Israel's ancient past, suggests an ongoing process of identity formation in Hellenistic Samaria (Knoppers 2010). The Yahwistic Samarian community must be granted its own distinctive characteristics and historical integrity. For similar reasons, it is not particularly helpful to view the Yahwists in Judah as completely dominated by or particularly beholden to the Yahwistic Samarians, even though Samaria appears to have been larger and more populous than Yehud during the Neo-Babylonian and Persian periods.

Particularly important are the appearance of the anthroponym Jeroboam on five different 4th-century Samarian coin types (the most attested for any personal name), the use of 4th-century archaizing seal impressions in Samaria inscribed in paleo-Hebrew, and the range, selection, and number of iconographic motifs attested in the Samarian numismatic repertoire. Noteworthy is the revival of traditional northern anthroponyms, such as Jacob, Joseph, and Ephraim, in the Mt. Gerizim inscriptions. Each community also possessed its own major Yahwistic sanctuary. Additional evidence (chiefly literary; see chapters 4 and 6) suggests that some members of both communities advanced competing claims about upholding the heritage of Israel's ancient institutions. The importance of this consideration cannot be underestimated, because it affects not only our understanding of the nature of the Samarian cultic community but also indirectly our understanding of the development of the Pentateuch (chapter 7). However one dates the final editing of this work, it seems

---

66. Of these, some names, such as Joseph and Jacob, become very common in later Second Temple inscriptions found in Judean contexts both within the land and in the Diaspora (Ilan 2002: 150–68, 171–74; 2008: 111–27).

evident that both communities were drawing from an overlapping, albeit not entirely shared, reservoir of traditions during the late Achaemenid and Hellenistic eras. Moreover, given the early periods depicted in the Pentateuch, it would seem that northern Israelites, like southern Israelites, defined themselves, at least in part, by recourse to stories about figures and measures associated with a long bygone ancient Israel.

How best may one explain the strong cultural overlap between Samaria and Yehud? It does not seem possible to explain the lines of continuity between the two adjacent areas simply by recourse to historical explanations focusing on the common roots of these two communities. The projected time of origins would be far too distant in the past (the 10th century and before) to account for the overlapping cultural and religious traits in the Achaemenid and Hellenistic eras.[67] Moreover, to make such an explanation work, one would have to posit two parallel, but essentially unrelated, historical developments for several centuries in two geographically adjacent areas. This seems unlikely. Rather, one must assume contacts between these two neighboring areas during the late Iron, Neo-Babylonian, Achaemenid, and Hellenistic periods. In addition, the links must have been substantial and persistent, rather than simply superficial and sporadic. The existence of such ties makes a good deal of sense. The two contiguous communities both found themselves occupied by a succession of foreign regimes (Babylonian, Achaemenid, Macedonian, Ptolemaic, and Seleucid). The Persian and Hellenistic periods, in particular, were eras of cultures in contact. International trade and travel grew markedly. Not only would it be plausible for the elites of the two adjacent Yahwistic communities to make common cause on certain occasions, it would be advantageous for them to do so. Associations between the two communities undoubtedly took different forms: trade, travel, migrations (including migrations in time of crisis or war), sacerdotal cooperation, and scribal communications.[68] Each province had to deal with its own (or related) diaspora communities.

---

67. That is, even is one were to grant, for the sake of argument, the common origins of northern Israel and Judah in an erstwhile united monarchy or in an even earlier tribal confederation, the temporal gap between the time of pan-Israelite origins (12th–10th centuries BCE) and the Persian period is too great to explain the degree of cultural overlap between Samaria and Yehud in the Achaemenid-Hellenistic ages. There had to be significant contacts between the two adjacent areas during the intervening interlude. An interesting question is the point at which scribes in Judah began to employ the term Israel as the name for Judah itself (Williamson 1989; Kratz 2006a).
68. On the matter of sacerdotal coordination or cooperation, see chapter 7.

The discussion about cultural and religious continuities between Samaria and Yehud contrasts with the tense picture of Samarian-Judean relations one finds depicted in Ezra-Nehemiah. If the cultures of Samaria and Judah were fairly similar, how does one explain the heated conflicts between Nehemiah, the governor of Judah, and his counterpart, Sanballat of Samaria? Addressing this question will be the topic of the next chapter. The independent stance taken by Nehemiah in dealing with his local peers is a very important development in gaining a better understanding of long-term trends in Judean political history. Yet such gubernatorial actions undertaken in one particular period within a larger two-century-long Achaemenid occupation should not be allowed to obfuscate the common traits shared by the Yahwistic residents residing in the two neighboring regions. Even the authors of Ezra-Nehemiah acknowledge that Nehemiah's position was not shared by a good number of the Judean leaders within Jerusalem. One of the advantages to the study of the material evidence is that it provides a much-needed corrective to the literary evidence or, at least, that it places the literary remains in a better perspective.

6

Ethnicity, Communal Identity, and Imperial Authority

CONTEXTUALIZING THE CONFLICTS BETWEEN
SAMARIA AND JUDAH IN EZRA-NEHEMIAH

READING EZRA-NEHEMIAH, ONE cannot help but notice that its subject matter, scope, and ideological tendencies differ a great deal from those of another postexilic work we have discussed: the book of Chronicles. The two works do not simply differ in that Chronicles addresses the history of the Davidic monarchy, whereas Ezra-Nehemiah addresses the history of the Persian period. Nor do they diverge simply in the theme of external hostility, which features prominently in Ezra-Nehemiah, but not so much in Chronicles (C. Mitchell 2010). Rather, the two works differ in the very identity of the community discussed.[1] Although both speak of Israel, they mean two different things by this ethnicon. In Chronicles, Israel comprises twelve (or more) tribes tracing a common descent from an eponymous ancestor, Israel (Jacob). In this understanding, Israel is a broadly inclusive and internally complex somatic community. By contrast, the editors of Ezra-Nehemiah focus on the people of Judah, specifically the *běnê hā-gôlâ* ("the children of the exile") and their descendants from the eastern Diaspora (chiefly Babylon).[2]

The use of such specialized terminology is not accidental. The editors are referring to one specific elite, "the holy seed" (*zeraʿ hā-qōdeš*;

---

1. Japhet 1968, 1983; Williamson 1977, 1989; Ben Zvi 1995; Willi 1995; Dyck 1996, 1998; Knoppers 2004a, 2005, 2006; Scatolini Apóstolo 2006.
2. Ezra 4:1; 6:19–20; 8:35; 10:7, 16 (cf. *běnê gālûtâʾ* in Ezra 6:16). Similarly, *hā ʿōlîm miššěbî hā-gôlâ*, "the ones who came up from the captivity of the exile" (Ezra 2:1//Neh 7:6), or, more succinctly, *hā-gôlâ*, "the exile(s)" (Ezra 1:11; 9:4; 10:6; Neh 7:6).

Ezra 9:2).³ Those who have returned from the Babylonian captivity are presented as "Israel."⁴ When such repatriates congregate in a formal capacity, they appear as the "assembly of the exile" (*qĕhāl hā-gôlâ*; Ezra 10:8, 12–16) or as the "assembly of God" (*qĕhāl hā'ĕlōhîm*; Neh 13:1).⁵ One may speak of a specifically eastern Diaspora, because the communities of Judeans in Egypt (attested archaeologically and epigraphically) do not appear in Ezra-Nehemiah.⁶ The genealogical lists in Ezra-Nehemiah play, therefore, an important role in authenticating the pedigree of the returnees from Babylon (Ezra 2:1–70//Neh 7:6–72; Ezra 8:1–14; Neh 11:1–24; 12:1–26).⁷ To be sure, in the sources edited within the work, such as the so-called Nehemiah memoir (to be discussed later in this chapter), the terminology differs somewhat.⁸ Even so, Nehemiah projects a similar binary view of ethnicity, defining the Judeans over against all the surrounding nations.⁹

---

3. Cf. *zera' qōdeš* in MT Isa 6:13 (lacking in the LXX), referring to a holy remnant left in the land—"a tenth that is still left in it" (*wĕ'ôd bā 'ăśīrîyâ*)—following a succession of disasters. In Neh 9:2 the expression *zera' yiśrā'ēl*, "seed of Israel," refers to the returnees.
4. On the association of the "children of the exile" with Israel, see Ezra 2:1–2; 3:1; 4:3; 6:21; 7:28; 8:25, 35; 9:1, 4; 10:1, 2, 6, 8, 10; Neh 1:6–9; 8:1; 9:1–2; 10:34). In some instances, the term Israel is understood in a more restricted sense as referring to laity, as opposed to priests and Levites (e.g., Ezra 2:2,70 [//Neh 7:7,73]; 6:16; 7:7,10,13; 8:29; 9:5; 10:5, 25; Neh 2:10). The two meanings are not mutually exclusive, because the latter is a subset of the former.
5. The text quotes Deut 23:2–3, but the *qĕhāl Yhwh* there evidently refers to a more restrictive body than the general *qĕhāl yiśrā'ēl* (Deut 5:22; 31:30; cf. 33:4; Ezra 10:1). Hence, Neh 13:1 reinterprets the older lemma, broadening its application.
6. The best known of these is the Judean community in Elephantine in Upper Egypt (AP; BP; Porten 1968, 2001; Grelot 1972; Kratz 2006b; Lozachmeur 2006; Lemaire 2011), but a Judean community (or communities) in the Delta region may also be attested (J. S. Holladay 2004). Whether the Yahwistic names appearing on some 4th-century funerary stelae in Cyprus written in Phoenician are Judean (Hadjisavvas, Dupont-Sommer, and Lozachmeur 1984) or Samarian is unclear, because prosopographic and epigraphic analysis has not progressed to the point at which one can easily distinguish a Persian-period Judean anthroponym from a Samarian one.
7. Occasionally, glimpses of the larger Israel still come into view (e.g., Ezra 6:17, 21; 8:35).
8. The Nehemiah memoir is a modern source-critical construct, referring basically to the first-person narratives in Nehemiah (see section II of this chapter).
9. There is another exception within texts attributed to outsiders, namely, the letters incorporated in the Aramaic sections of Ezra (4:8–6:18; 7:12–26), in which the terminology refers to the people as *yĕhûdāyē'*, "Judeans" (Ezra 4:12, 23; 5:1, 5; 6:7, 8, 14). Such correspondence reflects a detached and formal viewpoint (Arnold 1996). Indeed, as Arnold (1996) and Berman (2006, 2007) observe, the third-person prose narration within the Aramaic section of Ezra 4:8–6:18 also seems to be formulated in accordance with an external narrative voice in referring to God, the temple, the law, and the people. Whether such passages reflect a specifically "Samarian

In tackling the difficult topic of communal identity, there is another issue on which Ezra-Nehemiah differs from many other works. Unlike Chronicles and most prophetic writings (e.g., Jeremiah and Ezekiel), Ezra-Nehemiah does not express an ongoing hope for the restoration of both northern Israel and southern Israel (i.e., Judah) under one leader. Such a pan-Israelite reunion is also a theme in some writings within the Deutero-Canon (or Apocrypha), Judean writings that were largely written in the Hellenistic and Maccabean eras (Fuller 2006; Goodblatt 2006). Ezra-Nehemiah occasionally refers to Judah and Benjamin (Ezra 1:5; 4:1; 10:9; Neh 11:4, 25, 35), but never to any of the northern tribes.[10] The focus is upon the struggles and achievements of the returned exiles in rebuilding the material and religious infrastructure of Jerusalem.

Others, who are neither repatriates nor their descendants, are referred to vaguely as "the people(s) of the land(s)."[11] Such peoples include the Samarians, Moabites, Ammonites, Arabians, Ashdodites, and so forth. To complicate matters further, it seems that those Judeans that left in the land in the wake of the Babylonian exiles (597 BCE; 586 BCE) and the Egyptian exile (ca. 582 BCE) are either excluded from discussion or are lumped together with the "people(s) of the land" (Japhet 1983; Bedford 2001). Equating the "children of the exile" with Israel, the editors do not directly address the fate of the Judeans who survived the Neo-Babylonian occupation (586–538 BCE).[12] Not all

---

perceptual point of view" (Berman 2006: 326) must be considered on a case-by-case basis. Most do not seem to do so. In any case, the Aramaic section within Ezra 1–6 reflects a bipolar view of ethnicity, pitting the Judeans against their neighbors in the southern Levant and even within the larger satrapy itself.

10. In Chronicles, by comparison, one finds references to members of the northern tribes, even in the history of the late Judahite monarchy (chapter 4). Israelites may reside in the north, in the south, or in exile. Jacob's descendants are composed of many tribes, each of which has its own particular genealogical profile, but they are nevertheless all Israelites. One also finds references to sojourners or resident aliens (*gērîm*), as well as foreigners who may be described as "peoples of the land(s)" (e.g., 1 Chr 5:25; 2 Chr 6:33; 13:9; 32:13, 19. For the *gērîm*, see 1 Chr 22:2; 2 Chr 2:16; 30:25. In 1 Chr 29:15 the term is used in King David's farewell address figuratively to apply to Israelites (Knoppers 2004b: 954, 961–66).

11. E.g., Ezra 3:3; 4:4; 9:1, 2, 11, 14; 10:2, 11; Neh 9:24, 30; 10:29, 31, 32. Cf. *gôyē-hā'āreṣ/kol-hā-gôyîm* in Ezra 6:21; Neh 6:16. Interestingly, the writers of Ezra-Nehemiah never refer to a possible intermediate status between the native citizen (*'ezrāḥ*) and the foreigner (*nokrî*), namely, the sojourner or resident alien (*gēr*).

12. In some studies, the "people(s) of the land" are equated with those Judeans left in the land of Judah during the Babylonian exile, but this calculation seems to be too simplistic to do justice to all of the evidence (Ben Zvi 2010a, 2010b; Kessler 2009).

foreigners are, however, cast negatively. Quite the contrary, the writers commend the Persian emperors and never openly criticize them.[13] Kings Cyrus the Great, Darius I, and Artaxerxes I allow the expatriates to return, repatriate the temple furnishings, make fiscal concessions, provide generous gifts, and support rebuilding Jerusalem's temple.[14] The old Davidic monarchy is no longer in charge of Judah, but the new imperial monarchy manages, for the most part, to aid the returnees in their quest to rebuild Jerusalem's infrastructure.[15] If there is an "other" against whom the returnee "self" is defined, it is, therefore, the "proximate other," that is, the "people(s) of the land."[16] In Ezra-Nehemiah, these foes basically comprise the locals (especially their leaders) with whom the repatriates have to contend.

The issue of Judean-Samarian relations in Ezra-Nehemiah may be best understood in the larger context of the editors' concentration on the ongoing reformation of the Judean community. Although some have contended that Ezra-Nehemiah furnishes clear evidence of a major schism between Samaria and Judah in the late 6th or mid-5th century, I shall argue that this is not the case. On the contrary, internal literary evidence from within Ezra-Nehemiah indicates that many contacts continued between the two areas, especially among their elites. In the highly segmented history presented in the work, the people or leaders of Samaria only come into view on certain occasions, usually in the context of opposing major building operations.

---

13. The poignant sentiment expressed in the so-called Levitical confession is exceptional: "Behold, as for us, we are today slaves, and as for the land which you gave to our ancestors to eat its produce and its bounty, behold we are slaves upon it" (Neh 9:36).
14. The writers thus uphold a royal polity for the governance of the community, but the king in charge is a foreigner. Conceptually and mythologically, this transformation is highly significant (Floyd 2006; Knoppers 2009).
15. In Ezra-Nehemiah, references to David are largely limited to cultic arrangements and precedents. The dynastic promises are not mentioned and Zerubbabel's Davidic pedigree is not stressed (Knoppers 2004a: 81–82). Although a few scholars have argued that the Davidic monarchy continued into the early postexilic age, their arguments are not strong (Na'aman 2005).
16. J. Z. Smith (1985: 15) discusses the nuances of such a distinction, arguing that "otherness is a matter of relative rather than absolute difference." The laws of warfare in Deut 20:10–18 serve as an example (Brett 1996: 10; 2008). There, near enemies are dealt with much more harshly than distant ones.

Table 6.1 Outline of Ezra-Nehemiah

First Return: The Temple Begun	Ezra 1:1–11 (538ff. BCE)
Second Return: The Temple Completed	Ezra 2:1–6:22 (520–515 BCE)
Ezra's Mission	Ezra 7:1–10:44; Neh 7:72b–8:18[i] (458 BCE)[ii]
Nehemiah's First Term	Neh 1:1–7:72a; 12:27–13:3 (445–433 BCE)
Confession, Covenant, Lists	Neh 9:1–12:26[iii]
Nehemiah's Second Term	Neh 13:4–31 (428–426 BCE?)[iv]

[i] The material in Neh 7:72b–8:18 relates to the time of Ezra, but has been placed in the present context by an editor intent on making Ezra and Nehemiah contemporaries.

[ii] This calculation changes if one dates Ezra after Nehemiah to 397 BCE, understanding the Artaxerxes of Ezra's time to be Artaxerxes II, who reigned from 404–358 BCE. The issue need not detain us here.

[iii] Within this section, the corporate covenant ('ămānâ; Neh 10:1–37) evidently relates to the time of Nehemiah (Neh 10:2), whereas the other materials relate to different times.

[iv] The dates of 428–426 BCE are only an approximation. Nehemiah returned to King Artaxerxes I in his thirty-second regnal year (433 BCE). Given the substantial problems with which Nehemiah had to contend upon his return to Jerusalem, one must allow some time to have elapsed in between his two terms as governor. How long Nehemiah may have remained as governor in his second term is unknown, but Artaxerxes died in 423 BCE.

As the outline indicates, Ezra-Nehemiah furnishes a very selective portrait of Persian-period history. It comprises not a continuous history but rather a series of particularly focused snapshots of postexilic life (Knoppers 2012). Significant segments of time (e.g., 515–458, 457–446, 444–428 BCE) are unaddressed, except through indirect commentary (e.g., Ezra 5:13–16; Neh 5:15). In short, the work presents select highlights from the postmonarchic period, rather than the period itself. Within this framework, Judean-Samarian relations are an issue at three points in time:

1. When the second group of returning exiles encounters external resistance in their quest to rebuild the Jerusalem temple (ca. 520–515 BCE);
2. When the Judean governor Nehemiah meets external opposition in his efforts to reconstruct Jerusalem's walls (ca. 445 BCE);

3. When the Jerusalem high priest's son is banished by Nehemiah after he weds the Samarian governor's daughter (ca. 428–426 BCE).

This chapter will focus on the latter two cases of strained Judean-Samarian relations. The suspicion shown toward outsiders is manifest in the story of the struggles to rebuild the temple, but specifically Samarian opposition is only a minor theme within the narratives dealing with the late 6th century.[17] The issue of Judean-Samarian relations is curiously absent in the major section devoted to Ezra's reforms. It may be that some early interpreters (e.g., Josephus), who took the liberty of specifying the generalized foes faced by the returned exiles, have unduly influenced modern interpretations.[18]

The fierce rivalry between Nehemiah and his counterpart in Samaria, Sanballat, during the mid-5th century BCE is a clear and prominent motif in the presentation of his governorship. The drive to rebuild Jerusalem's walls repeatedly meets resistance from Sanballat and his regional allies. The third case, the intermarriage among leading families in Judah and Samaria punished by Nehemiah upon his return from the service he had resumed at the Achaemenid royal court accentuates Nehemiah's dilemma as he struggles to decouple Judean internal affairs from any outside influence. Both the second case and the third case, I would argue, presuppose some significant contacts among Samarians and Judeans, particularly among the elites of the two neighboring provinces.

I. Samarian Opposition to Nehemiah's Building Campaign in the Mid-5th Century

Like the material elsewhere in Ezra-Nehemiah, the first-person narratives in Nehemiah, relating to Nehemiah's career in the mid-5th century as governor of *yĕhûd mĕdîntā'* (the province of Judah), project an oppositional frame of reference. To be sure, the Nehemiah first-person narrative differs in the terms it employs to frame its binary perspective. Yet, like the earlier narratives in Ezra, the Nehemiah memoir constructs a strong

---

17. Excepting Ezra 4:7–23, but this material self-evidently relates to the mid-5th century, not to the early 6th century. On this material in Ezra 1–6 relating to the "adversaries of Judah and Benjamin," see Knoppers forthcoming b.
18. Josephus "elaborates... so that the identity of the adversaries of the Jews is clearly established. They [the Samaritans] are singled out as the main opponents of the returnees from the Babylonian exile" (Pummer 2009: 101).

dichotomy between the in-group (the Judeans) and the out-group (the nations). Moreover, the Nehemiah first-person narratives display a dialectical literary structure that both embodies and advances such a polarized worldview. The leaders most often at the center of attack in this literary conceit are Sanballat of Samaria and his associate Tobiah of Ammon. On some occasions, Geshem (or Gashmu) the Arab also appears. Sanballat appears, therefore, as the ringleader of a local coalition, whose resources are repeatedly arrayed against Nehemiah as he seeks to rebuild Jerusalem's wall and secure a greater degree of Judean independence from its neighbors. Since Sanballat and Tobiah are often mentioned together, they will both be discussed. Ostensibly, the conflict simply involves only the question of fortifying Jerusalem, but Nehemiah construes rebuilding the city walls as the best means to defend the Judean people's integrity and secure their civic identity (Neh 1:3; 2:11–18; 3:1–4:17; 7:1–3). The issues, then, are not so much cultic and religious as ethnic and political. That Nehemiah's local rivals repeatedly object to his plan is construed as conclusive evidence of their ill will. The narratives portraying developments in the mid-5th century indicate, therefore, a serious deterioration in Samarian-Judean relations.

Both the charges and countercharges between Nehemiah and his local opponents deserve careful examination. The pivotal role played by Sanballat in opposing Nehemiah's fortification campaign is quite revealing. Yet I would argue that the profound tensions existing between these two leaders can only be properly understood by acknowledging close links between Samaria and Judah during earlier times in Judean history. If Nehemiah leads the charge against the status quo, the status quo must represent something quite different from the new reality Nehemiah wishes to introduce within Judean society. The very animosity that characterizes the relationship between the Judean governor and his Samarian counterpart presupposes a history of closer relations between the two societies in the past.[19]

As numerous scholars (e.g., Clines 1990; Grabbe 2004) have argued, the so-called Nehemiah memoir is a one-sided, propagandistic account that casts Nehemiah's words and actions quite positively and his opponents' words and actions quite negatively. If there are redeeming traits in

---

19. Indeed, Nehemiah himself distances his record as governor from that of all those preceding him (Neh 5:14–16). Considering that these predecessors included Sheshbazzar and Zerubbabel, Nehemiah's comments are revealing.

Nehemiah's adversaries, they have yet to be revealed. Yet, in spite of the highly selective and biased nature of the first-person accounts, it is nevertheless quite useful to analyze the nature of the propaganda. How does it characterize the governor's reforms and how does it polemicize against the Samarians and other Judean neighbors? What does Nehemiah's apologia reveal about the complexities of Judean society—its varied stakeholders (elders, nobles, priests, and prophets) and its internal pressures? What does it explicitly disclose and implicitly concede about his contemporaries both outside of Judah and within it?

I shall argue that Nehemiah's troubles with his near neighbors are related to his difficulties with prominent leaders within Yehud. In this, the Nehemiah story departs from the precedent set by the temple construction story. Nehemiah focuses on rebuilding Jerusalem's walls, not brooking any interference from Judah's external foes. Nevertheless, by his own admission, he regularly finds himself battling against important people within his own subprovince who do not share his views. At stake in Nehemiah's debate with nobles, priests, and even prophets, I would submit, are how best to define Israelite identity and how best Judeans might control commercial, diplomatic, and political contacts with non-Judeans, including non-Judean Yahwists, in neighboring regions. It may be appropriate to begin with definitions of insiders and outsiders and the animosity the Nehemiah first-person narrative projects about his frayed relations with his neighboring leaders, most notably Sanballat of Samaria and Tobiah of Ammon. Included within this study will be a close analysis of the self-incriminating statements attributed to Sanballat and Tobiah. I shall then complicate this binary picture of in-group versus out-group tensions by exploring the nature of Nehemiah's troubles with his own Judean elite and how these troubles relate to his troubles with Sanballat and Tobiah.

A. The Enemy Without

Within the so-called Nehemiah memoir, one finds a basic consistency in the expressions employed to describe the people with whom Nehemiah identifies. Most common are references to *hā-yĕhûdîm*, "the Judeans" (Neh 2:16; 3:33, 34; 4:6; 5:1, 8, 17; 6:6; 13:23) and to *hā'ām, kol-hā'ām, hā'ām hā-zeh*, "(all) the/this (Judean) people" (e.g., Neh 3:38; 4:7, 16; 5:1, 13, 15, 18, 19; 7:4, 5; cf. 13:1). The concentration on the territory of Judah, as opposed to a larger land of Israel, is telling. As might be expected, references to the people (or children) of *yĕhûdâ* (Neh 4:4; 13:12, 16) and the house of Judah (Neh 4:10) also appear. Apart from the allusions in the opening verses of Nehemiah (1:2, 3) to "the survivors who remained from the captivity" (*hā-pĕlêṭâ 'ăšer-niš'ărû min-hā-šĕbî*), references to the Judean exile do not appear in the Nehemiah memoir. In this respect, the vocabulary of the first-person Nehemiah narratives departs from that employed in other sections of the book. In the narratives and lists found elsewhere within Ezra-Nehemiah, one occasionally finds references to Judah and Benjamin as tribal entities with territorial associations (Ezra 1:5; 4:1; 10:9; Neh 11:1, 4, 7, 20, 25, 31, 36), but such references are not to be found in the Nehemiah memoir. This evidence suggests that when Nehemiah refers to the *yĕhûdîm*, he is almost always referring to the residents of Judah.[20] As with the narratives dealing with the early returns (Ezra 1–6), the Nehemiah narratives do not mention an intermediate class of people, the *gērîm*. The *gēr* is sometimes mentioned in biblical legislation as a sojourner or resident alien, who is afforded some limited protections as a vulnerable figure (Van Houten 1991).

If the first-person narratives clearly present Nehemiah and the Judeans as protagonists, they present equally clear antagonists, who strenuously resist Nehemiah's efforts. The major opposition to Nehemiah's initiatives does not stem from the Achaemenid king. Quite the contrary, Artaxerxes I (465–423 BCE) is portrayed rather positively. After Nehemiah's visiting kin deliver an alarming report about the dire condition of Jerusalem's infrastructure—"The wall of Jerusalem is breached and its gates are destroyed by fire" (Neh 1:3)—Nehemiah successfully secures a leave from his imperial employer. The Achaemenid monarch listens sympathetically as his cupbearer describes how the city housing the graves of his ancestors lies desolate, with its gates consumed by fire (Neh 2:3). The emperor sanctions Nehemiah's voluntary migration, providing him with letters of reference to ease his travel through various sub-provinces; supports his rebuilding of the city walls, requisitioning needed materiel for his use; and safeguards his travel, providing him with an armed escort on his

---

20. See also Josephus (e.g., *Ant.* 11.173; Cohen 1999). In a few cases, usage of the term may reflect a gradual shift from a purely territorial sense to an ethnic sense with religious overtones (Neh 4:6; 5:8; cf. Est 2:5 and passim; Blenkinsopp 1988: 223–25; 2009). Even so, the link with a specific territory remains. Among the relevant pieces of extrabiblical evidence, it is important to observe the use of the term *yĕhûdîn* to refer to the members of the Elephantine colony (e.g., AP 6.3–10; 8.2; 10.3; Lozachmeur 2006: nos. 135cv2; 182; XII; Lemaire 2011: 367–68) and the recently discovered cuneiform references to *āl-Yāhūdu*, "the town of Judah," in Babylonia (Joannès and Lemaire 1999; Vanderhooft 2003; Pearce 2006; Abraham 2005–6, 2007).

journey to the land of his ancestors (Neh 2:7–9). In later years, the same monarch permits Nehemiah to return to Judah for a second leave (Neh 13:6–7). In short, the Nehemiah materials project a flattering view of the Achaemenid emperor, similar to that found elsewhere in the book.

The main opposition to Nehemiah and the Judeans stems from locals, that is, from certain neighboring peoples and their leaders. A duo of local rulers stands out in the narratives—Sanballat of Samaria and Tobiah of Ammon (Neh 2:10; 3:33–35; 4:1; 6:12, 14). On some occasions, Geshem (or Gašmu) of the Arabs also appears (Neh 2:19; 6:1, 2, 6). Each of these leaders is the head of a neighboring polity or subprovince located to the north (Samaria), east (Ammon), and south (the so-called Qedarite tribal league or kingdom) of Judah, yet none of these figures is ever recognized formally as an actual governor.[21] Instead, the cupbearer to the king refers to them with derisive epithets—"Sanballat the Horonite," "Tobiah the Ammonite servant," and "Geshem the Arab." Among these select locals, Sanballat appears as the most powerful and seems to function, at least on some occasions, as a ringleader. In those cases in which Sanballat appears as part of either a duo (Neh 2:10; 4:1; 6:2, 6, 12, 14) or a trio (Neh 2:19; 6:1) of local leaders, he is almost always mentioned first. On one occasion in which Sanballat and Tobiah appear together (Neh 3:35), Tobiah is in Samaria, suggesting his less powerful status in relation to Sanballat.[22] Interestingly, Geshem never acts alone, but always as part of a duo or trio with Sanballat and Tobiah.[23] Moreover, Geshem never acts as part of a duo with Tobiah, but rather only with Sanballat.[24] These data point to the pivotal role played by Sanballat in the opposing camp. Given the size and prominence of Persian-period Samaria (chapter 5), the implicit importance conceded by Nehemiah to Sanballat is not surprising. From the indications provided in the Nehemiah memoir alone, one could surmise that Samaria was a major force in the southern Levant. Because of Samaria's size, status, and population, it may have posed special challenges

---

21. Geshem (Gašmu) was likely the king of the so-called Qedarite league. An inscription on one of the Tell el-Maskūṭah bowls, dating to ca. 400 BCE, mentions Qaynu the son of Gašmu (Dumbrell 1971).
22. Such a visit to Samaria need not imply that Tobiah was a subordinate Samarian official. On the likelihood that Tobiah was an actual governor (and not Sanballat's adjutant), see Knoppers 2007 and the references listed there.
23. By contrast, Tobiah acts on some occasions in his own right (Neh 6:17, 19; 13:4, 7, 8).
24. Given that Geshem's kingdom likely contained parts of what some scholars refer to as Edom, Geshem's interests in Jerusalem may well have been influenced by the fact that a minority of Judeans resided within his domain (Eshel and Zissu 2006).

for Jerusalem's elite. In the Persian period, the Judean leaders were faced with a bigger, more well-to-do, and more populous neighbor to the north.

But what of the population groups these communities governed? One regular expression found in the Nehemiah memoir involves the term *hā-gôyîm*, "the nations" (Neh 5:8, 9, 17; 6:6, 16; 13:26). What the repatriate leader usually means by this usage is *hā-gôyîm ʾăšer-sĕbîbōtênû*, "the nations roundabout us" (Neh 5:17; 6:6, 16), that is, the neighboring Samarians, Ashdodites, Arabians, Moabites, and Ammonites. On one occasion, Nehemiah speaks of the *ʿammîm*, "peoples," with similar connotations (Neh 13:24), but the expression "the people(s) of the land(s)" (*ʿam-hāʾāreṣ*; *ʿammê hāʾāreṣ*; *ʿammê hāʾărāṣôt*), which recurs frequently elsewhere in Ezra-Nehemiah, does not occur in the Nehemiah memoir.[25] Closely related to Nehemiah's use of "the nations" is his use of *ʾō/ôyēb*, "enemy" (Neh 4:9; 5:9; 6:1, 16; cf. 9:28), and *ṣār*, "adversary" (Neh 4:5; cf. Ezra 4:1; Neh 9:27), because he equates the nations with his foes. So, for example, during his campaign to implement social reforms among his fellow Judeans, he upbraids the nobles and prefects, saying, "The thing that you are doing is not right. Is it not better that you walk in the fear of our God than [elicit] the reproach of the nations (*ḥerpat hā-gôyîm*), our enemies (*ʾôyĕbênû*; Neh 5:9)?"[26] From Nehemiah's vantage point, Judah is surrounded by adversaries. Hence, if the Nehemiah first-person materials present clear protagonists, they also present clear antagonists who oppose each of the new initiatives Nehemiah advances. The governor's remarks reveal a vision of a Judah that is unencumbered by dependence upon any one of its neighbors.

Consistent with such a binary framework, Nehemiah's first introduction to Sanballat is negative: "When Sanballat the Horonite and Tobiah the Ammonite servant heard [of Nehemiah's arrival], it displeased them greatly that someone had come to seek the good of the children of Israel" (*bāʾ lĕbaqqēš ṭôbâ libnê yiśrāʾēl*; Neh 2:10). The comment is quite telling.

---

25. The reference to the peoples in Neh 1:8 occurs in the context of an allusion to earlier tradition (Deut 30:1–3). Other references in the book to the (foreign) people(s) appear in the so-called Levitical confession (Ezra 9:14) and in the prayer of Nehemiah (Neh 9:10, 22), generally considered to be an editorial creation (e.g., Blenkinsopp 1988; J. L. Wright 2004) or a source incorporated into the larger narrative (Boda 1999).

26. Yet, in this instance, he berates Judean senior-level leaders. The Samaria papyri mention the office of "prefect" (סגן) as a civil high official of that province (WDSP 7.17; 8.12; 10.10). In fact, the סגנים were likely the highest-ranked officials under the governor (Lemaire 2007). On the opposition within the Judean elite to Nehemiah's leadership, see further section I.B of this chapter.

First, it positions the theme of external hostility, well-known in the narration of the early postexilic period (Ezra 1–6), at the front and centre of Nehemiah's first term as governor. Such a suspicion typifies the presentation of Nehemiah's gubernatorial peers. From their perspective as government officials established in the land, Sanballat and Tobiah may have viewed Nehemiah as very much the newcomer and the outsider, especially since Nehemiah had traveled such a long distance from Susa in Persia to take up his Jerusalem position. Yet, from Nehemiah's perspective, Sanballat and Tobiah did not have the best interests of the people of Yehud at heart. Otherwise, they would not have been so upset that someone had come to "seek the good of the children of Israel." The same point is made in a different way in the pejorative epithet Nehemiah applies to Tobiah, "the Ammonite servant" (*hāʿebed hāʿammōnî*), which plays on one of Tobiah's probable official titles, such as the "servant of Ammon" or the "servant of the king of Persia."[27] Nehemiah disparages his contemporary by drawing attention to what he sees as Tobiah's divided loyalties. As Ammon's governor, Tobiah was obliged to pursue the best interests of his body politic within the larger context of his duties in the Achaemenid realm, but Tobiah also claimed to have interests in Judah and Jerusalem.

Second, the nomenclature excludes Sanballat and Tobiah from membership in Israel. Tobiah, for instance, may bear a Yahwistic name—"Yhwh is my good"—but Nehemiah classifies him as someone extraneous to the Israelites. Punning on the meaning of Tobiah's name, Nehemiah declares that he had come to Judah to advance the *ṭôbâ* of Israel, an Israel to whom *Ṭôbîyāh*, as an Ammonite, could never belong.[28] Hence, the Israelites are basically presented as synonymous with the Judeans, whom Nehemiah leads. In fact, Nehemiah rarely employs the term Israel except in referring to preexilic events in the nation's history (e.g., Neh 1:6; 13:26).[29] Nehemiah's fixation with the Judeans is quite important, because it effectively limits the range of the multiple group identities one might claim (family, clan, town, tribe, people, expatriate, repatriate, etc.). A member of one of Israel's northern tribes could reside in Persian-period Jerusalem, for instance, and still remain a member of the tribe of Ephraim or Manasseh

---

27. See Alt 1953b: 341–42; B. Mazar 1957: 144–45; Blenkinsopp 1988: 218. Hence *hāʿebed* is used with an adjective (*hāʿammōnî*), rather than in a construct state (cf. Kellermann 1967: 167–70; Rudolph 1949: 109).

28. Deut 23:4–7; cf. Neh 13:1, 4–7; Blenkinsopp 1988: 219. Interestingly, Tobiah's son also had a good Yahwistic name, Yôḥānan, "Yhwh has been compassionate" (Neh 6:18).

29. Nehemiah's prayer (1:5–11) is generally regarded as heavily edited, if not authored, by the book's editors (J. L. Wright 2004).

(1 Chr 9:3).³⁰ Tobiah may have viewed himself as a Yahwist who stemmed from a tribe other than Judah, Benjamin, and Levi. Naturally, he would have regarded himself as an Israelite, precisely because of his descent from an Israelite sodality.³¹ An exclusive focus on the Judeans would render, however, such a possibility irrelevant.

Third, the label Nehemiah applies to his Samarian peer is rather telling. Both the personal name and the soubriquet call for some discussion. Consistently referring to Sanballat as "the Horonite" (*hā-ḥōrōnî*) belittles Sanballat as someone who hailed from a small town, one of the Beth Horons in the Shephelah northwest of Jerusalem.³² Nehemiah never refers to Sanballat by his actual title as the governor of Samaria. Nehemiah could claim his long-term workplace to be the fortress (*bîrâ*) of Susa, the magnificent capital of the Achaemenid empire (Neh 1:1), but his opponent to the north hailed from a small town in a remote area. The first-person texts mention Samaria only in the context of its armed force (*ḥêl šōměrôn*; Neh 3:34).³³

Calling Sanballat "the Horonite" is also illuminating, because it signifies that Sanballat likely viewed himself as an Ephraimite.³⁴ This is not to address his ultimate ancestry—autochthonous, repatriated northern Israelite, Assyrian-sponsored immigrant, or repatriated Judean exile. The lack of a patronymic and the repetitious use of the same epithet occlude such information.³⁵ But whether one construes Sanballat's hometown as Lower Beth Horon or Upper Beth Horon, both sites are consistently listed as Ephraimite holdings (Josh 16:3, 5; 18:13; 21:22 [//1 Chr 6:53];

---

30. Consistent with the ideological concerns of the book's writers, the parallel in Neh 11:4 lacks any reference to Ephraim or Manasseh (Japhet 1989: 299–300).
31. Given Tobiah's location in the Transjordan (Ammon), Nehemiah may have thought it impossible that he could be an Israelite (or more specifically a Judean; cf. Ezra 2:60//Neh 7:62). If Nehemiah thought in Priestly terms, he may have regarded the Transjordan as lying beyond the land of Israel. Or, if Nehemiah held to a Deuteronomistic (or quasi-Deuteronomistic) view of Israel's past, he would have thought of the Transjordan tribes as having all been exiled from the land (2 Kgs 15:29). Similarly, along the same lines, Sanballat could not have been an Israelite, because the Cisjordan northern tribes were reportedly deported in the late 8th century (2 Kgs 17:5–6).
32. Less likely options are Haran in northern Mesopotamia (e.g., Galling 1954: 219); Hauran, a one-time Assyrian province in the northern Transjordan (e.g., BP: 107–8; Mittmann 2000: 15–17); and Horonaim in Moab (e.g., Kellermann 1967: 167; cf. Isa 15:5; Jer 48:3); see Rudolph 1949: 108 and, in much more detail, Zadok 1985: 657–72. If Sanballat hailed from Horonaim, one would expect the epithet to read החרנימי, rather than החרני (Zadok 1985: 570).
33. Elsewhere in Ezra-Nehemiah, see Ezra 4:10, 17 (Alt 1953b: 323; Mittmann 2000: 14).
34. The area to which he tries to lure Nehemiah in the Plain of Ono was therefore closer to his own hometown than Nehemiah was to Jerusalem (Neh 6:2; cf. Ezra 2:33//Neh 7:33; 11:34).
35. On the possibilities, see the detailed review in Knoppers 2007.

1 Chr 7:24; 2 Chr 25:13). Hence Sanballat is implicitly associated with one of the major northern tribes.³⁶ As an Ephraimite, he could and probably did claim the same Israelite nomenclature that Nehemiah claimed for himself. In the late-5th-century Elephantine papyri, the names attested for Sanballat's sons—"Delaiah" (דליה) and "Shelemiah" (שלמיה)—are Yahwistic in nature.³⁷ That Sanballat bears a foreign, non-Yahwistic name is not in conflict with his Ephraimite status.³⁸ Sanballat's parents may have given him such a Babylonian name (or he himself may have taken on such a name) in much the same fashion that one sees Akkadian names appear for prominent Judeans during this period (e.g., Zerubbabel, Esther, Mordecai, Bilshan, Shenazzar, Sheshbazzar).³⁹

To this may be added a related possibility. In Neo-Babylonian and Persian-period times, members of ethnic minorities sometimes bore Babylonian names or second names.⁴⁰ Perhaps the most famous biblical example of such a double name is Esther/Hadassah (אסתר/הדסה; Est 2:7). Hence, the many foreign names attributed to prominent Judeans and, in this case to a Samarian, may be simply a sign of the times. In any event, Sanballat's affiliation with (northern) Israel would not be enough for Nehemiah and his supporters. If, as seems probable, Sanballat regarded himself as a member of one of the northern tribes, Nehemiah could nevertheless dismiss him, because Nehemiah basically equated Judah with Israel.⁴¹ In sum, the Horonite label masks Sanballat's legitimacy as Nehemiah's true peer, a local leader who had understandable interests,

---

36. Chronicles construes Beth Horon as abutting the northern border of Judah during the dual monarchies (2 Chr 25:13). If this was still the case in postexilic times, it might partially explain why Sanballat, who stemmed from this border town, took such an interest in Judean affairs.
37. See, for example, TAD 1 A4.7:29; 1 A4.8:28; 1 A4.9; Josephus *Ant.* 11.302–303, 310–11, 315, 321–24, 342. In this context, the proper name "[Yešaʿ]yahu" (or "[Yadaʿ]yahu") appearing in the Wādī ed-Dālīyeh bullae and papyri is pertinent (WD 22). Even though the name is fragmentary, it points to the existence of another Samarian high official or governor with a Yahwistic name. Dušek (2007: 321–31) reconstructs this figure as Delaiah (לדל[יהו]), and therefore a son of Sanballat I. It should be remembered that the name of (apparently) another Samarian governor, (Ha)naniah or (ʾA)naniah (WDSP 7.17; 33 frg. 25), is also Yahwistic in nature.
38. His name is spelled *Sin-ʾuballaṭ* in one of the Elephantine papyri (AP 30.29) and in the Samaria papyri (WDSP 12.13).
39. In fact, many repatriate names of laity in the list of Ezra 2//Nehemiah 7 lack Yahwistic theophorics (Zadok 1986).
40. See in more detail our earlier discussion (chapter 5).
41. Similar restricted usage can be found in some Apocryphal or deuterocanonical works (e.g., Jdt 4:1; 1 Macc 1:11, 20, 25, 30, 36, 43; 2 Macc 1:26; 11:6; Sus 13:48, 57).

whether altruistic or not, in the standing, conduct, and fate of one of his neighbors.

This brings us to a fourth observation about the hermeneutic of suspicion that pervades Nehemiah's relationship with his peers. By consistently referring to his contemporaries with irreverent labels—Sanballat the Horonite, Tobiah the Ammonite, and Geshem the Arab—Nehemiah distances them from warranting consideration as local governors who might have genuine concerns about the fate of their adjoining province. When, for example, Sanballat repeatedly objects to the wall rebuilding, suggesting that Nehemiah was planning to rebel against the king, Nehemiah either ignores him or dismisses the claim. Historically, one may ask whether the question posed about Nehemiah's intentions was indeed preposterous. His arrival occurred when the tumultuous events of the 5th century were already well underway. In 486 BCE, after the Egyptians revolted against Persian rule (Herodotus 7.1, 3), the new king, Xerxes, launched a campaign to suppress the revolt (Herodotus 7.7). In 478 BCE a coalition (Greek) fleet conquered most of Crete (Briant 1996). By 470 BCE (and perhaps again in 466–465 BCE), the Persians reconquered the affected areas of the island. Yet a new insurrection broke out in Egypt in 460 BCE, and the Persians again were forced to intervene. Against this background of revolts and invasions during the early to mid-5th century, it would hardly be surprising if some of Judah's neighbors grew alarmed at the fortification campaign underway in Jerusalem.[42] These locals, who were also Persian officials, might have worried that during volatile times fortifying Jerusalem could be perceived as the first act in a long-term strategy to resist the Persian occupation (Rainey and Notley 2006: 291).[43] Nehemiah's dismissive reaction to such innuendo is thus revealing.

---

42. The all-too-common supposition that the fortification of Jerusalem was a unique phenomenon in Persian-period Levantine history is, however, mistaken. Persian-period fortifications are not limited to the coastal regions. As Stern (2001: 464) observes, fortifications have been uncovered not only at coastal sites, such as Akko, Tell Abū Huwâm, Gilʿam, Megiddo, Tel Megadim, Tel Mevoraḥ, Dor, Miḥmoret, Tell Abū Zeitun, Jaffa, Tell el-Ḥesi, and Ruqeish, but also at inland sites, such as Samaria, Tell en-Naṣbeh, Lachish, and Ḥeshbon (in the Transjordan). To his list should be added Ramat Raḥel (Lipschits et al. 2011). In short, the fortification of Jerusalem as an administrative centre would not be anomalous.

43. To this position, it could be objected that Yehud was geographically isolated from the Mediterranean coast along which the Persian armies marched to and from Egypt. Even though Judah was likely not a real concern to Persian authorities, this would not exempt it from having any geopolitical relevance. The very fact that Sanballat repeats the insurrection rumors in his Nehemiah correspondence indicates that the charge must have enjoyed some currency.

One strategy employed by Nehemiah to demonstrate his opponents' hostility is to quote both their comments and his responses. He declares that when Sanballat, Tobiah, and Geshem heard that the wall was to be rebuilt, "they mocked us and held us in contempt, saying, 'What are you doing? Are you rebelling against the king (Neh 2:19)?'" Later, when Sanballat repeats the charge of insurrection, Nehemiah's reply is telling: "Nothing has occurred along the lines of these reports you are alleging, for you are devising [these reports] from your imagination" (Neh 6:8). It is quite clear that Nehemiah views Sanballat's charge as absolutely without merit, a brazen attempt to make mischief and "to intimidate us, saying, 'Their hands will weaken (*yirpû yĕdêhem*) from the work so that it will not get done'" (Neh 6:9). Within the larger context of Ezra-Nehemiah, the comment alludes to the earlier success shown by the people of the lands in "weakening the hands of the people of Judah (*mĕrappîm yĕdê ʿam-yĕhûdâ*), making them afraid to build" during the early Persian period (Ezra 4:4). The citation of the opponents' intentions elicits, however, a diametrically different reaction from Nehemiah, who appeals, apparently to the deity, "Now, strengthen my hands!" (*wĕʿattâ ḥazzēq ʾet-yādāy*; Neh 6:9), and then presses forward undeterred.[44]

Citing quotes from the local leaders indicts them, suggesting that a higher level of boundary maintenance between Judeans and outsiders is needed. Nehemiah's quotation of his ripostes serves a similar purpose. His first direct address to Sanballat, Tobiah, and Geshem unambiguously responds to the scorn directed toward him:

> As for the God of heaven, he will make us prosper.
> As for us, his servants, we shall rise and rebuild.
> And as for you, you have no share (*ḥēleq*), claim (*ṣĕdāqâ*), or memorial (*zikkārôn*) in Jerusalem. (Neh 2:20)

The declaration of Judean independence is as blunt as it is unyielding. The comment would be especially stinging if Tobiah's family had a traditional memorial (*zikkārôn*) in Jerusalem. The writer of Zech 6:14 suggests that a person by the name of Tobiah did have such a *zikkārôn* in the temple, but it is not entirely clear that the Tobiah in Zechariah is

---

44. Or, reading with some Hebrew MSS, "And as for you (O God), strengthen my hands."

an ancestor of or a relation to the Tobiah of Nehemiah's time.⁴⁵ In any event, Nehemiah's blanket admonishment makes no attempt to distinguish between foreigners and those Israelites who are neither Judeans nor Benjaminites. Nor does Nehemiah distinguish between native Judeans and Yahwists from other lands. Indeed, it is quite possible that the Judean governor's rebuke alludes to the northern Israelite declaration of independence spoken to King Rehoboam at the assembly at Shechem many centuries before, following the death of Solomon (1 Kgs 12:1–18//2 Chr 10:1–17). There, the Israelites asked the rhetorical question, "What share (*ḥēleq*) have we in David?" and provided their own answer: "There is no inheritance (*naḥălâ*) in the son of Jesse" (1 Kgs 12:16//2 Chr 10:16). If Nehemiah is alluding to the northern declarations made at the Shechem convocation, he would be turning their own declaration of independence against them (Zakovitch 1999). The willful self-exclusion from Judah and Jerusalem in the late 10th century entails that northerners have no rights to exercise in Judah and Jerusalem in the mid-5th century.⁴⁶ In sum, the hard-line response allows for no accommodation of regional interests in Jerusalem. Nehemiah's opponents, whatever their self-professed identities and cultic allegiances, are to be excluded from serving the God of heaven in Jerusalem.

The citation of comments from one's adversaries has related uses, such as discrediting opponents and demonstrating their ineffectiveness against a determined Judean people. Thus, when Sanballat heard that the wall reconstruction had begun, "he became angry and very irritated (*wayyikʿas harbēh*) and heaped scorn upon the Judeans (*wayyalʿēg ʿal-hā-yĕhûdîm*), saying in the presence of his kin (*lipnê ʾeḥāyw*) and the force of Samaria, 'What are the feeble Judeans (*hā-yĕhûdîm haʾămēlālîm*) doing?⁴⁷ Will they abandon [it] to God?⁴⁸ Will they offer sacrifice?⁴⁹ Will they finish this day? Will they bring these stones back to life from the dustheaps, burned as they are?'" (Neh 3:33–34). It may well be that Sanballat's tirade

---

45. The case for such a connection is made by Mazar (1957: 137–45, 229–38) and more recently by Meyers and Meyers (1987: 340–43). On *zikkārôn*, compare Num 10:10; 31:54; Qoh 1:11; 2:16; Sir 45:9, 11 (DNWSI 330–31).
46. The resonance with the late-10th-century schism presumes, however, that the northerners are related to the northerners in Rehoboam's time. In other words, the allusion only works if Nehemiah implicitly acknowledges the northern Israelite identity of his opponents.
47. Perhaps insert *hāʾēlleh*, lost by haplography; cf. LXX^L (Rudolph 1949: 122).
48. Reading *hăyaʿazbû lēʾlōhîm* instead of *hăyaʿazbû lāhem* (so MT) in Neh 3:34 (cf. Williamson 1985: 213–14).
49. Perhaps in a self-protective sense (cf. Ezra 3:3).

was delivered for the benefit of a home audience (Williamson 1985: 216). He insults the Judeans in the presence of his own associates and military. The fact that the accompanying insult from Tobiah, "That which they are building—if a fox ascended it, it would breach their stone wall (ḥômat 'abnêhem)," was uttered while Tobiah was "alongside him" (Sanballat) supports such a view (Neh 3:35). The Samarian governor may have resorted to ridicule to save face with his own followers, because he had failed to impede the commencement of Jerusalem's fortification. But if Sanballat's intention was not so much to intimidate the Judeans as to reassure his own supporters, the quotation of his words in a new literary context indicted both him and Tobiah to a Judean audience.

We have been discussing the use of direct dialogue between Nehemiah and his foes as a literary device to impugn his contemporaries. The first-person Nehemiah narratives also model an appropriate Judean response to outside threats.[50] Nehemiah proceeds with the task at hand, even when the campaign of intimidation gives way to a campaign of obstruction: "When Sanballat and Tobiah, and the Arabians, and the Ammonites heard that healing had come to the walls of Jerusalem, because the breached parts had begun to be stopped, it angered them greatly and all of them conspired together to come fight against Jerusalem and to throw it into confusion" (Neh 4:1–2).[51] The prospect of physical force underscores the danger posed by neighboring groups. Yet, Nehemiah enjoys the advantage of having access to inside information about the planned conspiracy and implements defensive measures, such as arming the wall builders and stationing regular watches, while the construction continues (Neh 4:3, 7, 10, 11). Perhaps ignorant of the precautions undertaken by Nehemiah and his allies, the adversaries carry on: "And our foes (ṣārênû) were saying, 'They will neither know nor see until we enter their midst, kill them, and put an end to the work'" (Neh 4:5). Yet, having lost the element of surprise, Judah's neighbors are stymied: "When our enemies learned that it was known to us and that God had frustrated their plan, we all returned to the wall, each one to his work" (Neh 4:9). Eventually, the locals give up: "When word reached Sanballat, Tobiah, Geshem the Arab, and the rest of our enemies (yeter 'ôyĕbênû) that I had

---

50. The incorporation, shaping, and editing of the so-called wall-builders source (Neh 3:1–32) underline the involvement of many Judean families in the larger enterprise (Blenkinsopp 1988: 331–32; Eskenazi 1988: 186).
51. Reading in 4:1 with the LXX (*lectio brevior*). The MT adds "and the Ashdodites."

rebuilt the wall and not a breach remained in it…, they realized that this work had been accomplished with the help of our God" (Neh 6:1).

The campaign of obstruction having failed, Sanballat and Geshem launch a new strategy, inviting the Judean governor to a regional summit in the Ono Valley at which "they were reckoning to do me wrong" (Neh 6:2). Discerning his opponents' intentions, Nehemiah avoids putting himself in harm's way. Indeed, his response sent via messengers ironically underscores the importance of the very fortifications that so aggravated his antagonists: "I am engaged in a great work and I am unable to come down. Why should the work stop because I left it and came down to you?" (Neh 6:3). True, Nehemiah's message does not terminate the conflict. Yet his forging ahead with the fortifications yields the desired result: the completion of Jerusalem's walls and a Judah that stands independent of its neighbors. Having completed the project in a remarkably short period of time (52 days; Neh 6:15), Nehemiah appoints his brother to take charge of Jerusalem and stations gatekeepers, musicians, and Levites to stand watch and restrict traffic into the town (Neh 7:1–3). The community's dedication of the Jerusalem wall is a high point in the book (Neh 12:27–47). The work thus valorizes Nehemiah's bold direction in pursuing Jerusalem's fortification against consistent, albeit singularly ineffective, opposition. Persistent outside interference vindicates the hard-line stance taken by Judah's fearless leader. In short, the highly negative characterization of Sanballat, Tobiah, and Geshem is justified by the actions undertaken by these leaders to thwart the wall rebuilding, to undermine Nehemiah's authority and to harm, if not eliminate, Nehemiah himself. Consistent with a binary view of ethnic identity, the corporate self is defined sharply against the proximate other. Nevertheless, as we shall see, Nehemiah's own comments reveal that things are not nearly so simple.

B. The Enemy Within

The Nehemiah first-person narratives do not present an entirely harmonious and internally consistent record of gubernatorial success.[52] The portrayal of Nehemiah's foes is more complicated than the character

---

52. Nehemiah himself recognized a number of social, economic, and demographic problems that did not result from outside (regional) interference. These included: (1) the depopulation of Jerusalem, which required (in his estimation) a commitment from rural Judeans to move 10 percent of the population into the capital (Neh 7:4–5; 11:1–2); (2) high taxes during the

Nehemiah might wish it to be. Additionally, signs of internal Judean division appear in the Nehemiah story. Attempts to subvert the initiatives undertaken by the Judean leader do not originate simply with members of out-groups, but also with members of the in-group.[53] The indications of opposition within the community and their relationships to the opposition external to the community are particularly interesting, because they suggest that the issues of community solidarity and group boundaries were not as firm and fixed as Nehemiah would have liked them to be. The very struggle of Artaxerxes' cupbearer to enforce his view of Judean (and Israelite) identity suggests that this identity was itself a contested issue.

In what follows, I would like to look more closely at the portrayals of Sanballat and Tobiah and how these leaders relate to members of Nehemiah's own community. In this context, what Nehemiah concedes in his denunciations of those Judeans who cooperated with his enemies is telling. Nehemiah's own actions also warrant closer scrutiny. In some respects, his treatment of Sanballat and Tobiah comports with how he treats his other adversaries, but in other respects the treatment of these contemporaries is distinctive. At this point, the attempt to define clear boundaries between the self and the other begins to break down. Recognizing that the ethnic debates did not simply center on the definition of the Judeans as opposed to the nations but also involved Judah's relationship to Israel (and the definition of Israel itself) may elucidate the conflicts with Sanballat and Tobiah and illumine Nehemiah's appeals to God to vouchsafe his legacy.

To begin with, one should inquire as to why some of Judah's neighbors were arrayed against Nehemiah in his wall-building campaign, whereas others were not. Why do Sanballat of Samaria and Tobiah of Ammon, in particular, feature so prominently in the memoir?[54] Nehemiah's derogatory comments about this duo indicate that they enjoyed traditional interests

---

tenures of past Judean governors, which required some remediation and even forgiveness in his own time (Neh 5:14–18); and (3) a growing gap between smaller and larger landowners in Judah, occasioned by the negative consequences of debt slavery, which required a pledge on the part of the nobles (*hā-ḥōrîm*) and the prefects (*hā-sĕgānîm*) no longer to charge interest to their fellow Judeans and to restore properties exacted from negligent Judean debtors (Neh 5:1–13).

53. So, for instance, Neh 5:1–19; 6:10–14, 17–19; 13:4–5, 7, 17–18, 20–21, 23–28. Apart from the first-person narratives, see Neh 3:5.

54. As we have seen, Geshem occasionally appears in tandem with one or two of the others, but is much less prominent and never appears alone.

in Yehud that were jeopardized by the arrival of a new rival. It can be no accident that Sanballat and Tobiah (and less often Geshem) are repeatedly mentioned. These leaders would not object to the wall rebuilding unless they thought that they had something at stake in Jerusalem's internal affairs. Indeed, the very fact that they are accused of meddling is itself relevant. It is highly probable, for example, that other groups such as the Moabites and the Ashdodites who are elsewhere mentioned (Neh 13:23; cf. Ezra 9:1) also had their own leaders, but such leaders go unmentioned as resisting Nehemiah's reforms.[55] Hence, those particular governors with whom Sanballat clashed must have enjoyed some ties to Judean residents (or to their previous governors) and had something to lose in a more autonomous Yehud.[56]

Previously, we discussed Nehemiah's labels of and reactions to Sanballat, Tobiah, and Geshem. One should also try to determine, as far as possible, the identity, status, and functions of Sanballat and Tobiah as established local governors in the middle Persian period. As we have seen, Tobiah was invested in internal Judean affairs in part because he was a Yahwist, albeit one who resided in Ammon. The same is likely true of Sanballat. The status of Sanballat as a self-professed Israelite, rather than as a pagan, is hinted at in one passage. During the wall-building campaign, Sanballat repeatedly sent the same message to Nehemiah, the fifth time by his agent (*na'ărô*), who had an open letter with him (Neh 6:5). Written in this missive (*kātûb bâ*) was:

> Among the nations it is heard (*bā-gôyîm nišmā'*), and Gashmu also says, that you and the Judeans are planning to rebel. Therefore, you are rebuilding the wall and you are becoming their king, according to these reports. (Neh 6:6)

In this short message, Sanballat openly conveys what he has heard from unnamed sources. He presents himself as a confederate reporting allegations made by others about his counterpart in the south. The *gôyîm*

---

55. The Ashdodites also appear in MT Neh 4:1, but this lemma is lacking in the LXX.
56. The implied (earlier) domination of Judah by Samaria in the Nehemiah narrative has been a critical factor in the judgment of some (classically, Alt 1953b) that Yehud was a subdivision of the province of Samaria in the early Achaemenid period until Nehemiah secured Judah's own provincial status in the mid-5th century BCE. The epigraphic and literary (Ezra 1–6; Haggai; Zechariah) evidence does not support, however, such a supposition (Williamson 1985; Lemaire 1990; Grabbe 2004; Lipschits 2005, 2006).

appear as a collective third party exterior to Sanballat himself. In other words, Sanballat seems to be referring to the *gôyîm* in much the same way as Nehemiah does, as denoting other peoples. The implication seems to be that whatever differences separate the two leaders, they nevertheless stand within the same larger circle of Israelites. What Sanballat has heard from others is then confirmed by Geshem, who is willing to make the accusation directly. It is true that *gôy* can sometimes refer to Israel itself in some texts (Clements and Botterweck 1975: 429–31), but this is never the case in Ezra-Nehemiah.

In a related context, Nehemiah utters a series of complaints about and execrations against Sanballat and Tobiah, appealing to God to take action against his enemies (Neh 3:36–37). These implored actions include returning Sanballat and Tobiah's taunts upon their heads, sending them as plunder into a land of captivity (*bĕʾereṣ šibyâ*),[57] and neither covering up their iniquity (*wĕʾal-tĕkas ʿal-ʿănônām*)[58] nor letting their sin be blotted out before God (*wĕḥaṭṭātām millĕpānêkā ʾal-timmāḥeh*).[59] As commentators have pointed out, there are parallels between Nehemiah's prayer and the structure of some imprecatory psalms, including the address, the complaint, the petitions, and so forth, but this appeal has a very limited and specific set of enemies in view.[60] There are also parallels between the terms Nehemiah employs and those found both in the imprecatory psalms and in the lament psalms. But the imprecatory psalms, along with some of Jeremiah's laments, normally speak of the enemy or enemies in vague, general terms. Why would Nehemiah worry about God forgiving Sanballat and Tobiah and allowing their sins to be blotted out unless he implicitly recognized that his foes worshiped the same God as he did? His very imprecations seem to be predicated upon the assumption that his opponents were praying to the same deity that he was.[61] In such a context, Nehemiah entreats the deity to listen to the plaintiff (and not to his opponents).

We have seen that Nehemiah did his best to create a more distinct civic identity for his subprovince, shunning and rebuking his local

---

57. So the MT. A few Heb. MSS and the Syr read *šibyām* (cf. Jer 30:10; 46:27; 2 Chr 6:37, 38).
58. On the use of *kāsâ* in the sense of "to forgive" within a cultic setting, see also Ps 32:1; 85:3.
59. On the usage of *mḥh*, compare Gen 9:23; Exod 21:33; 26:13; 38:15; Num 4:9, 15; 22:5, 11; Deut 23:14; Josh 24:7; Judg 4:19; Ps 32:5; 40:11; 85:3; Job 9:24; 31:33; 36:30; Prov 10:18; 11:13; 17:9; 28:13 (*HALOT* 488a-b).
60. Williamson (1985: 217–18) calls attention to Psalms 35, 58, 59, 69, 109, 137 and Jer 18:23.
61. And therefore asking God to forgive their sins (e.g., Ps 32:5; 51:3).

contemporaries. Yet Nehemiah's Judah was not as isolated as he made it out to be. One may surmise from Nehemiah's first-person accounts that in spite of (or because of) Nehemiah's intense distrust of his peers, he must have had significant contacts in the regions they ruled. There would simply be no way that Nehemiah could speak authoritatively and confidently of his contemporaries' negative reactions within their own realms were it not for the existence of allies and informants who could apprize him of such facts. To be sure, he also enjoyed the benefit of timely information sent to him by Judeans who lived in Judean areas abutting the territories of neighboring provinces (Neh 4:6), and his "overheated imagination" (Grabbe 2004: 299) may well have led him to suspect conspiracies when none existed. But the existence of local Judean informants would not be enough to explain how Nehemiah had access to intimate information about the emotional states of local governors and the opinions they shared with their associates within their own lands. Indeed, the intelligence afforded to Nehemiah was of such timeliness and quality that he knew (or claimed to know) his enemies' intentions at every step in the wall-building process.[62] In brief, if one grants Nehemiah's account of the wall-building travails some historical credibility, one must also grant that he benefited from exceptional familiarity with the deliberations of his adversaries.

As Nehemiah sometimes concedes, his opponents enjoyed considerable support within the Judean community.[63] In fact, one of Nehemiah's complaints is that Sanballat and Tobiah enjoyed substantial Judean contacts, which they exploited to good effect. The existence of such allies belies, however, the impression of a Judean leadership that observed strict boundary maintenance. In one incident, a housebound Shemaiah ben Delaiah ben Mehetab'el (*Mĕhêṭab'ēl*) attempted to humiliate Nehemiah by luring him into the midst of the sanctuary (*tôk hā-hêkāl*) on the pretense that the Judean governor's life was in danger (Neh 6:10–11). Nehemiah accused the man, evidently a priest, of being a hireling, someone whom Tobiah and Sanballat bought off to utter a (false) prophecy about him (6:12–13).[64] In a related complaint, Nehemiah asks the deity to hold

---

62. Hence, if Nehemiah's goal was "no less than to create an isolated puritanical theocratic state" (Grabbe 2004: 307), it had to be one with a first-rate intelligence service.
63. This point is forcefully argued in Fried 2004: 156–212, which points to a variety of groups within Yehud who were at odds with Nehemiah. I do not believe, however, that Nehemiah was as completely isolated as Fried would have it. Grabbe (2004: 294–313) provides a general overview.
64. Shemaiah is a fairly common name in late texts (1 Chr 3:22; 4:37; 5:4; 2 Chr 11:2; 12:5,7,15; Ezra 8:13; 10:31), but it is particularly prevalent in Levitical (1 Chr 9:14, 16; 15:8; 26:4, 6,7;

to account "Noadiah the prophetess and the rest of the prophets who were attempting to frighten me" (Neh 6:14).⁶⁵ This is a striking admission on Nehemiah's part. Given that the prophets Haggai and Zechariah staunchly supported the temple rebuilding several decades earlier (Ezra 5:1–2), what made all the prophets of the mid-5th century sour on their political leader? Perhaps Nehemiah's headstrong character and prickly personality were factors, but one would think that more was going on than this to turn Judah's prophets *en masse* against their reformer ruler. Perhaps these prophets and this prophetess took issue with some elements of Nehemiah's reform program. Like earlier prophets, such as Jeremiah and Ezekiel, these prophets may have held to a comprehensive understanding of Israel. Such prophets inveighed against what they deemed to be infractions against God by individuals and groups, but they maintained an integral view of the people they served. If this remained the case, the prophetic figures of Nehemiah's time would have been uneasy with those aspects of Nehemiah's separatist program that seemed to pit Judeans against all others.

In a telling admission, Nehemiah observes that the nobles of Judah (*ḥōrê yĕhûdâ*) were keeping up a brisk correspondence with Tobiah and that "there were many in Judah who were his sworn allies" (*baʿălê šĕbûʿâ lô*; Neh 6:17–18). These associates would speak well of Tobiah to Nehemiah and relay Nehemiah's own words back to Tobiah (Neh 6:19).⁶⁶ This means that one of the leadership groups in Judah was arrayed, at least in part, against its own governor. Moreover, Nehemiah admits that Tobiah was the son-in-law (*ḥātān*) of Shecaniah the son of Araḥ.⁶⁷ Because Nehemiah repeatedly pronounces Tobiah to be an Ammonite, one might expect Nehemiah to construe this marriage as a case of intermarriage. Yet Nehemiah takes no action against Tobiah, against his spouse, or against Shecaniah (Neh 6:18). By the standards presented elsewhere in Ezra-Nehemiah, Tobiah's wife had an impeccable pedigree. The

---

2 Chr 17:8; 29:14; 31:15; 35:9; Ezra 8:16; Neh 11:15) and priestly contexts (1 Chr 15:11; 24:6; Ezra 10:21; Neh 3:29; 10:9; 12:6, 18, 34, 35, 36). Moreover, one has to ask what sort of person could meet Nehemiah in the sanctuary with impunity. Hence, if Shemaiah was a prophet (e.g., Grabbe 1998, 2004), he likely stemmed from a priestly lineage.

65. That Shemaiah's prophecy did not come true would be a reason not to fear him (Deut 18:22; Shepherd 2005).

66. Yet all the time this was going on, as Nehemiah relates it, Tobiah was sending letters (*'iggĕrôt*) to intimidate him (Neh 6:19). From Nehemiah's perspective, this showed that Tobiah was behaving in a duplicitous manner.

67. A few Hebrew MSS of Neh 6:18 read Shebaniah. The list of wall builders mentions a Shemaiah ben Shecaniah (Neh 3:29). Was he also part of this same family?

Arah family is mentioned as one of the more populous clans in the register of repatriates (Ezra 2:5//Neh 7:10).

In the same aside, Nehemiah reveals that Jehohanan, Tobiah's son, had married the daughter of Meshullam the son of Berechiah. In this manner, the family of Tobiah was linked to another of the major families in Judah. Meshullam the son of Berechiah the son of Meshezabel appears in the list of wall builders (Neh 3:4, 30).[68] Elsewhere, the names of both Meshullam and Meshezabel appear among those heads of the people who signed the covenant pledge (*ʾămānâ*; Neh 10:21–22). A later list, pertaining to the repopulation of Jerusalem, mentions a Petahiah son of Meshezabel, whose responsibility was no less than to serve "at the side of the king with respect to everything concerning the people" (Neh 11:24).[69] This catalog traces the genealogical roots of Petahiah the son of Meshezabel back to Zerah the son of the patriarch Judah.[70]

That Tobiah and his son Jehohanan married into such prominent Judean families suggests that not all Judeans who supported Nehemiah's building program also agreed with Nehemiah's views on other issues (Williamson 1985: 261). Even within the limited confines of the Judean community, one could be an ally of Nehemiah on one issue and an opponent of his on another issue. Nehemiah's failure to move against either Tobiah or the affected Judean families may be subject to a number of explanations. He may have been biding his time, recognizing that the enemy without enjoyed close ties to the kin within. Or perhaps he did not act because he realized that he was dealing with what others (although not he) would call an inner-Israelite dispute. If these Judean families, unlike Nehemiah, viewed Tobiah and his family as Israelite in character, they would not have seen any problem in arranging nuptials between members of their families. On the contrary, they might well have viewed such marital agreements as strengthening the ties among Israel's various sodalities. The matrimony arranged by ancestral heads from different regions would be construed as an act of piety, an attempt to build a larger sense of pan-Israelite solidarity in spite of the tribal and political affiliations of each family.

---

68. Berechiah is a fairly common personal name in Chronicles (1 Chr 3:20; 6:39; 9:16; 15:17, 23; 2 Chr 28:12), but it appears only twice in Ezra-Nehemiah, in each case referring to the same individual (Neh 3:4, 30).
69. Through these blood filiations, Tobiah was more deeply ensconced within the Judean community than Sanballat was.
70. Aside from these references (Neh 3:4; 10:22; 11:24), no other *Mĕšēzabʾēl* appears in the Hebrew Bible. On the Akkadian element in this personal name, see Zadok 1985: 389.

The serious opposition Nehemiah encountered within the Judean community explains several features of his highly selective autobiography. Nehemiah often quotes his opponents to indict them, precisely because these opponents had many supporters. Why would the Judean governor go to such lengths to discredit Sanballat and Tobiah, unless they enjoyed significant contacts in Jerusalem? By recording the self-incriminating comments made by his foes for the benefit of future generations, Nehemiah safeguards his legacy. If Samarians were to lose their regional dominance in centuries to come, history would show that some of their pain was self-inflicted. The autobiography thus becomes a literary testament to Nehemiah's efforts to establish a stronger and more independent Judah. Similarly, the shaping of the memoir in Ezra-Nehemiah advances the agenda of the larger work (Esler 2003; J. L. Wright 2004).

The issue remains, however, whether Nehemiah's exclusivist understanding of Judean identity was the norm or the exception. Did Nehemiah's actions represent a traditional or typical Judean stance in the Persian period, or did they represent an important new development? Although Nehemiah succeeded in rebuilding Jerusalem's wall, did his related campaign to push for a much more restrictive delimitation of Judean (Israelite) identity win the day in his own time? Or, alternatively, was Nehemiah's separatist agenda the exception that proved the rule of long-term cooperation with Judah's (Yahwistic) neighbors? A close examination of Nehemiah's second term will conclude that Nehemiah's opponents neither disappeared nor lost influence. His self-declared enemies continued to be found both within his self-defined out-group, notably Sanballat and Tobiah, and within his self-defined in-group, notably the priestly establishment in Jerusalem. To these matters we shall now turn.

II. "Déjà Vu All Over Again?": Nehemiah's Second Term

Nehemiah's second term (13:4–31) largely comprises a series of new reforms necessitated by substantial Judean regression during his extended absence from Judah.[71] Outsiders, including the governor of Samaria, continue to be very much involved in Judean affairs. Yet, unlike the major initiatives

---

71. Along with most commentators, I understand the collocation in Neh 13:4, "and before this" (*wĕlipnê mizzeh*), to refer to events that occurred (or began) during Nehemiah's absence, but which were confronted later, after his return to Jerusalem. The alternative argued by Mowinckel (1964a: 35–37) and Kellermann (1967: 48–51) is to understand the collocation as referring to events (including the additional reforms) all of which occurred before the initial

of his first term, which were mostly concerned with physical infrastructure (rebuilding the walls), the initiatives Nehemiah pushes in his second term (ca. 428–426 BCE) are primarily cultic in nature (temple purification, Sabbath enforcement, supporting the Levites, combating intermarriage). How long Nehemiah was away is unclear: "During all of this (*ûbĕkol-zeh*) I was not in Jerusalem, for in the 32nd year of Artaxerxes [433 BCE], king of Babylon, I went to the king and only after some time (*ûlĕqēṣ yāmîm*) did I request [leave] from the king" (Neh 13:6). Given the substantial problems that Nehemiah faced upon his return, one must allow at least a few years to have elapsed between his two terms as governor.[72] The intermarriage involving the grandson of the high priest Eliashib and the daughter of Sanballat, for example, presupposes the passage of some time. In what follows, my focus will be on the punitive actions taken against Sanballat and Tobiah.

That a priest named Eliashib, a relation of Tobiah (*qārôb lĕṭôbîyāh*), was appointed over the chamber(s) of the temple is an important indication that the Jerusalemite priesthood perpetuated, if not strengthened, its ties to Yahwists outside of Judah during Nehemiah's time in Susa (Neh 13:4). In accordance with Tobiah's status and Judean connections, this priest (probably not to be equated with the high priest of the same name) assigned Tobiah a large room, one in which the "temple servants had formerly placed the tribute, frankincense, utensils, and the tithe[s] of grain, wine, and oil" (Neh 13:5). The commercial concession granted to Tobiah was an important achievement for him, but the appointment of someone Nehemiah considered to be a foreigner to a large sanctuary chamber was totally unacceptable. When Nehemiah arrived in Jerusalem and learned of "the wrong that Eliashib committed on behalf of Tobiah," Nehemiah summarily evicted him (Neh 13:7–8). In a play on the furnishings (*hā-kēlîm*) of a household (*bayit*), Nehemiah recounts how he expelled Tobiah and "all of the furnishings of the house of Tobiah" (*kol-kĕlê bêt-Ṭôbîyāh*) to restore purity to this part of the sanctuary complex and to reinstall there "the furnishings of the house of God" (*kĕlê bêt hāʾĕlōhîm*; Neh 13:8–9).[73] The connection between purification and ethnic

---

wall construction. There is no second term in this theory. For a critique, see Williamson 1985: 380–94. A much more complex reconstruction that combines elements of both theories appears in J. L. Wright 2004: 189–269.

72. How long Nehemiah may have remained as governor in his second term is unknown, but Artaxerxes died in 423 BCE.

73. Yet even after this confrontation Nehemiah did not act against Tobiah's marriage. What happened to the priest Eliashib is not addressed.

alienage is especially striking. The forced removal of Tobiah was necessary, because his presence in the temple complex was viewed as ritually defiling. Indeed, Nehemiah's very command that the chambers be purified (*wayṭahărû hā-lĕšākôt*) presupposes the view that alienage was in and of itself ritually defiling (Albertz 2006). Certainly, there are no other factors mentioned, such as a possible failure of Tobiah to observe purity rules that would justify his eviction and the consequent purification of the room.

The problem Nehemiah encountered with his old nemesis Sanballat did not have to do with the sanctuary complex per se, but rather with its high priestly family. Upon his return, Nehemiah discovered that "one of the sons of Joiada the son of Eliashib the high priest was the son-in-law (*ḥātān*) of Sanballat" (Neh 13:28). This meant that the grandson of the high priest (or the son of the high priest, if Joiada had succeeded his father) had married the daughter of the Samarian governor.[74] Joiada's son stemmed from an impeccable lineage.[75] Eliashib was the descendant of Jeshua, the high priest in the time of Zerubbabel (Neh 12:10), while Jeshua was the son (or descendant) of the last high priest of the monarchic era—Jehozadak (Hag 1:1, 12, 14; 2:2, 4; Zech 6:11; Ezra 3:2, 8; 5:2; 10:18; 1 Chr 5:41), who was linked genealogically to the key priestly progenitor of the Sinaitic era—Aaron (1 Chr 5:29–41). The connection to Jeshua, and ultimately to Aaron, legitimated Joiada's (high) priesthood and that of his unnamed son. The connubium arranged by Joiada and Sanballat thus points to a highly important relationship cultivated (or affirmed) among the elite in Samaria and Jerusalem. That this marriage was contracted with a prestigious high priestly family in Jerusalem indicates cooperation among the highest levels of society in the two administrative centers.

If, as seems likely, Sanballat and Joiada both viewed themselves as Israelite, they would have seen no problem in arranging such a marriage. Joiada and Sanballat stemmed from distinct geopolitical entities within Transeuphratene, but shared some common religious traits and institutions. The two men belonged to different tribes, but each of these tribes claimed a common progenitor (Jacob). In this critical respect, the two ultimately shared common bloodlines. Given the historical ties

---

74. Grammatically, the title "high priest" can refer to either Joiada or Eliashib in Neh 13:28.
75. Josephus speaks of a succession of fifteen high priests (Joiada included), from Jeshua until the time of Antiochus Eupator at the beginning of the Hasmonean era (*Ant.* 20.234).

between the northern and southern tribes, the members of Jerusalem and Samaria's aristocratic families may well have viewed Nehemiah as the innovator, an interloper from afar who was calling for a radical break from past tradition. Indeed, Joaida and Sanballat may have seen themselves as recreating in a small and limited way the kind of northern-southern alliances that punctuated the earlier history of the northern and southern kingdoms.[76]

To Nehemiah, the nuptials were an intolerable case of exogamy at the highest religious level of his society, and hence he declares: "I drove him [the son of Joiada] away from me" (*wāʾabriḥû mēʿālāy*; Neh 13:29). In justifying the expulsion, Nehemiah draws upon and innovates beyond earlier moral and ritual traditions (Olyan 2000, 2004). That the Judean governor associates marriage to alien women (*nāšîm nokrîyôt*) with pollution is evident in his plea to the deity: "Remember them, O my God, on account of their defilement of the priesthood and the covenant of the priesthood and the Levites" (Neh 13:29).[77] Nehemiah's concluding remark, "I purified them from everything foreign" (*weṭihartîm mikkol-nēkār*; Neh 13:30), presupposes that the marriage of Joiada's son with Sanballat's daughter defiled the priestly bloodline, an act that, if not punished and atoned for, would have contaminated future generations of the priestly lineage. Yet it is not entirely clear what chasing him (and not her?) away entailed physically and legally.[78] If Nehemiah expelled Joiada's son from the province, as most assume, his actions went farther than Ezra's measures of divorce and dispossession did (Williamson 1985: 398–99; Blenkinsopp 1988: 365). The Judean governor does not reveal where Joiada went following his expulsion, but it seems reasonable to assume that he traveled to his wife's homeland. Her father was, after all, the governor.

The high-level union among elite families in Samaria and Jerusalem is not entirely unprecedented in the Persian period. So-called mixed marriages involving Judean priestly and Levitical families are also attested in the time of Ezra (Ezra 9:1–2). The priests involved in such connubiums

---

76. Such nuptials arranged between elite members of the northern and southern tribes seem to have continued even after the fall of the northern kingdom (2 Kgs 21:19; 23:36; chapter 3).
77. Reading with the MT (*lectio difficilior*). A few Hebrew MSS, LXX^L, and the Syr read "the priests" (*hā-kōhănîm*).
78. The lemma of LXX Neh 13:28, καὶ ἐξέβρασα αὐτὸν, "and I drove them," solves the puzzle as to what happened to the Samarian wife. The governor's strong rhetoric is tantalizingly ambiguous. Fried (2004: 208–12) stresses the negative economic complications of the campaign against elite exogamy.

included the family of the high priest Jeshua ben Jozadak and his kin (Ezra 10:18–23; cf. Ezra 2:2, 36).[79] To be sure, the text of Ezra does not specifically name the wives involved, and it is important to recall that neither Samaria nor the Samaritans are ever mentioned in the Ezra account.[80] Yet, whatever the wives' ethnicities, the claims made for priestly intermarriage are striking.[81] What Nehemiah attacked was not a new phenomenon. Exogamous unions involving priests of unquestionable pedigree were a fact of life in Persian-period Judah. What Nehemiah confronted and attempted to end was evidently a new version of an old practice.

One striking aspect of the (inter)marriage story is the tacit admission by the author of shared bloodlines in the Samarian and Judean priesthoods. Certainly, the Samarian governor would not have arranged for such a marriage unless he was comfortable with his prospective son-in-law and especially with his ancestral house. The story accounts, however obliquely and negatively, for the fact that both the province of Samaria and the province of Yehud claimed an Aaronide priesthood. The Nehemiah story hints that Samaria housed (or came to house) a family of priests tracing their ancestry all the way back to the original high priest Aaron.[82]

The lapses encountered by Nehemiah upon his return indicate that he did not enjoy widespread or long-standing community support for a number of his ideals. Members of the Judean elite attempted to subvert or reverse his initiatives. The campaign to strike a much more independent stance over against Judah's neighbors, including Samaria, continued

---

79. The list in 1 Esd 9:18–22 is somewhat shorter, but textual error is possible (Talshir 2001: 470–73). Josephus generally follows a version of 1 Esdras, but does not list the individual names (*Ant.* 11.151–52).
80. The list of foreign peoples in Ezra 9:1 with whom the exiles intermarried—the Canaanites, Hittites, Perizzites, Jebusites, Ammonites, Moabites, Egyptians, and Edomites (האדמי; LXX Ezra 9:1; 1 Esd 8:68; MT Amorites [האמרי])—expands the standard Pentateuchal roster of aboriginal peoples (e.g., Exod 34:11–16; Deut 7:1–4). Fishbane (1985: 116) insightfully argues that Ezra 9:1–2, 12 draws on both Deut 7:1–4 and Deut 23:4–9. The latter text, mentioning the Ammonites, Moabites, Egyptians, and Edomites in the context of (non)admission into the assembly, is reinterpreted to forbid exogamy with these additional peoples. One could argue that the expanded list is representative of a larger whole—note the generalized references to "foreign women" from "the peoples of the land" (Ezra 9:11; 10:2, 11, 17, 18, 44). It is striking, however, that the expanded roster of Ezra 9:1 includes surrounding peoples in postexilic times—Ammonites, Moabites, Egyptians, and Edomites—but does not mention the residents of Judah's northern neighbor—the Samarians. Given how prominent the struggle against Sanballat is in the Nehemiah narratives, the contrast between the Ezra and Nehemiah "memoirs" may be significant.
81. According to Josephus (*Ant.* 11.312), both priestly and lay intermarriage were common during the period.
82. We shall return to this matter in the next chapter.

to meet with both external and internal opposition. The Judean governor's repeated appeals to the deity to "remember" him (Neh 5:19; 6:14; 13:14, 22, 31) reflect a divided society. The fact that the book ends inconclusively with Nehemiah's final plea, "Remember [it] to my credit, O my God, for good" (Neh 13:31), indicates that the long-term outcome of his societal reforms was still in doubt.

Conclusions

We have seen that the stories about Nehemiah's struggles to rebuild Jerusalem's infrastructure in the mid- to late 5th century are punctuated by conflicts. While Samaria is one of a number of foes in the temple-reconstruction campaign (Ezra 3–6), Samaria (under the leadership of Sanballat) is the most prominent foe in the wall-reconstruction campaign. Nehemiah's efforts to distance Judah from its neighbors reveal, however, multiple connections between his constituents and their neighbors. Indeed, his reform account presupposes that he himself enjoyed access to privileged information from informants within the territories of his self-declared adversaries. To complicate matters further, Nehemiah's disparaging comments about and quotations of his opponents, coupled with extrabiblical evidence, suggest that at least some of his opponents, including Sanballat and Tobiah, were self-professing Yahwists who considered themselves to be of Israelite stock. It is, therefore, not surprising that Nehemiah repeatedly met with resistance from high-ranking members of his own elite. He and his supporters were trying not only to rebuild a physical wall but also to (re)create an ethnic wall and thus delimit the community itself.

In explaining the disputes and divisions evident in the narratives of Ezra-Nehemiah, some scholars have spoken of two contradictory perspectives operative in postmonarchic Judah. Those who advocated the first point of view, the assimilationist perspective, argued that Judeans needed to cooperate with their local neighbors in the southern Levant. Those who advocated the second point of view, the separatist perspective, argued that Judeans needed to safeguard their own distinctive identity and pursue a much more independent course. Neither of these parties advocated rebellion against their overlords, but each had its own way of dealing with the districts surrounding Judah. Both parties wished for the community's survival, but pursued different means to achieve it. One pushed for more integration, while the other pushed for more differentiation.

The distinction between assimilationists and antiassimilationists has its attractions, but examination of the Nehemiah memoir suggests that there was at least one other dispute operative within Yehud, one that involved the very identities of Judeans.[83] It may be helpful to speak of identities, rather than of a single ethnic identity, because there was more than one collective identity at stake in the struggles of Nehemiah with his opponents. The tensions between Nehemiah and Sanballat and Tobiah reveal that Yahwists in Judah, Samaria, and other regions had some different assumptions about their own ethnic identities, and just as importantly, about each other's identities. In this respect, the distinction between emic and etic classifications is helpful, because however arcane the debates may have appeared to outsiders, the insiders within the debates came to the issues with their own particular sets of assumptions, traditions, and commitments.

One group identity that Nehemiah takes as primary is that of the people of Judah. In this collective definition, the patriarch Judah functions as the eponymous ancestor of the Judeans, although Nehemiah himself does not put things exactly in these terms. The other collective identity at stake is a larger one involving the entire people of Israel. In this identity, a variety of sodalities trace their ancestry to a single eponymous ancestor, Israel (Jacob). The members of these tribes may have their individual histories and be originally associated with separate territories, but they all affirm a primordial unity in spite of their differences. By any definition, there was at least some overlap between the two collective identities, because the two societies were genetically linked in traditional lore.

In his work, Nehemiah all but collapses the distinction between the two identities. Inasmuch as he addresses the larger issue at all, he basically equates the Judeans with the Israelites. But there were others both outside his community and inside his community who clearly disagreed with his Judean nationalism. From the first-person accounts of Nehemiah battling his foes, one can see that he too sometimes had trouble defending the lines he drew between himself and his opponents. Those so-called adversaries of Nehemiah who held onto a broader concept of Israel either were reluctant to embrace Nehemiah's program or actively opposed it. They could agree about the importance of blood, language, cultic rites, ties to the land, and social customs but avidly disagree with the Judean governor about the relative importance of these attributes and how each

---

83. The question of Israelite/Judahite identity inevitably complicated the other debate about integrationist versus independent policies.

was to be construed and applied. Those who identified with the larger concept of Israel, such as the writers responsible for Chronicles, could affirm the need for exclusivity but debate Nehemiah about how exclusive exclusivity had to be. There were some in Yehud who viewed Tobiah and Sanballat as coreligionists, rather than as representatives of alien peoples. Indeed, it is quite conceivable that a good many of Nehemiah's own supporters balked at including self-professed Israelites in the general category of alien peoples. In other words, the debate within Nehemiah's Judah was not simply about Judean identity, but also about Israelite identity. The two were distinct but very much related projects.

The struggles depicted in Ezra-Nehemiah reflect, in part, ongoing Judean arguments about identity, ethnicity, and nationality in an age in which a number of Yahwistic communities existed both within the land and outside of it in far-flung places such as Babylon, Susa, and Egypt. The very definition of "Israel" becomes a contested topic in a world in which a number of groups claim to continue the legacy of Jacob's descendants. Hence, the tensions and conflicts depicted between the Jerusalemite authorities and the Samarian authorities in parts of Ezra-Nehemiah should not be privileged as representative of the entire Persian/early Hellenistic period.

That the Jerusalem leadership continued to share normal diplomatic relations with the Samarian leadership in the post-Nehemiah era may be seen in the missive coauthored by Bagavahya, the governor of Judah, and Delaiah the son of Sanballat, the governor of Samaria, in the late 5th century (TAD 4.9). The joint Samarian-Judean letter was written to sustain the Elephantine community's efforts to win permission from the satrap of Egypt (Arsames) to rebuild the Judean Elephantine temple (TAD 4.9:3). We have seen (chapter 5) that the existence of this joint communique points to regular relations between the leadership in Jerusalem and Samaria, at least for a period of time.[84] Historically speaking, the reforms of Nehemiah did not decisively end the matter with Tobiah's family either. The interests of the Tobiads proved to be enduring. In later centuries, the house of Tobiah would rival (and become connected by marriage to) the house of Onias for control of the Jerusalem high priesthood.[85]

---

84. A fragmentary text, dating to the 4th century BCE, from diaspora groups in ancient Egypt (Papyrus Amherst 63) points in a similar direction. In col. 16 (col. 17 in some other editions), the speaker declares that he hails from Judah, his brother hails from Samaria, and a man is bringing his sister from Jerusalem (Steiner 1997:321 [lines 1–6]). There is no hint of animosity in these assertions about fraternal Judean-Samarian relations.
85. See 2 Macc 3:1–12; Josephus *Ant.* 12.4; Grabbe 1992, 1:192–98; 2008: 75–78; VanderKam 2004: 177–81; Pummer 2009: 156–60.

Nevertheless, from a long-term historical perspective, it would be a mistake to underestimate the historical importance of the stress on a stronger and more independent Yehud that emerges in Ezra-Nehemiah. Rebuilding the temple and gradually rebuilding Jerusalem's infrastructure with imperial support were critical achievements, because it was by no means a foregone conclusion that such accomplishments would have naturally occurred, given the devastation, disorientation, and displacement caused by the Neo-Babylonian campaigns. There can be little doubt that the new directions set by Ezra and Nehemiah during the mid- to late 5th century were very significant developments in postmonarchic Judean history. Nehemiah's campaign to create a more independent Yehud by exercising aggressive political leadership set an important precedent for later Judean rulers, especially the Maccabees, who massively expanded the reach of the Judean state in the 2nd and 1st centuries BCE (Blenkinsopp 2009). The understanding of Israel in the Nehemiah memoir as Judah (or Judah as the embodiment of Israel) was a formative influence in the development of early Judaism.

Acknowledging such long-term trends, it is equally important to realize that those who disagreed with major components of his nationalist agenda did not disappear from the community. There was no major breach between Samaria and Judah at this time. The fact that Nehemiah felt compelled to justify his harsh treatment of outsiders indicates that there were other important viewpoints within the community. The very survival of disparate literary works, such as Ezra-Nehemiah, Chronicles, Ruth, Second and Third Isaiah, Jonah, Haggai, and Zechariah, testifies to the rich diversity of early Second Temple Judaism. Such writings not only offer a variety of perspectives on Israelite and non-Israelite identity but also provide fascinating perspectives on the ethnic variety inherent within Judean identity (Knoppers 2000a, 2001). In this respect, one must be careful not to draw sweeping historical conclusions about the state of Samarian-Judean relations in the Persian and early Hellenistic periods from portions of Ezra-Nehemiah. Nehemiah's reforms were important more for the influential precedent they established for later generations than they were for permanently altering Samarian-Judean affairs in his own time.

7

The Torah and "the Place[s] for Yhwh's Name"

SAMARIAN-JUDEAN RELATIONS IN HELLENISTIC AND MACCABEAN TIMES

THE HELLENISTIC PERIOD witnessed a series of events that marked a decline in the political fortunes of Samaria. In the late 4th century, the forces of Alexander the Great conquered much of the ancient Near East, including the Levant. In 331 BCE, Samarians murdered the Macedonian-appointed prefect of Syria (Andromachus) while Alexander the Great was extending his campaign into Egypt (Quintus Curtius Rufus *Hist. Alex.* 4.8, 9–10). This insurrection led to punitive reprisals by Alexander's forces against the guilty parties. The dozens of 4th-century private legal documents (mostly slave dockets) known as the Samaria papyri (Leith 1997; Gropp 2001; Dušek 2007a), hidden in the caves of the Wâdī ed-Dâlīyeh, most plausibly originate from elite Samarians fleeing from the forces of Alexander.[1] Hundreds of skeletons were found in those grottos.

According to Syncellus and one passage in Eusebius's *Chronicon* (Olympiad 112 [205F]), Alexander destroyed the town of Samaria and settled a colony of Macedonians at the site. Alternatively, according to another passage in the *Chronicon* and Jerome (Dušek 2011: 77), it was Perdikkas who settled the city with Macedonians. In any case, the capture and resettlement of Samaria meant that the province had lost its major population center and capital to foreigners. From at least this

---

1. Given the historical plausibility of this reconstruction, it seems improbable that the same imperial king would reverse course and sanction the construction of a new sanctuary in the province of Samaria (Josephus *Ant.* 11.322–24).

point forward, the area of Samaria had a mixed population.[2] A Greek inscription from Ptolemaic times found in the archaeological excavations at Samaria testifies to the existence of a temple to Serapis and Isis (Crowfoot, Crowfoot, and Kenyon 1957: 37 [no. 13]; Magness 2001). In the Seleucid period, Samaria seems to have become the home of a Seleucid army unit. The writer of 1 Maccabees speaks of Seleucid forces from Samaria (ἀπὸ Σαμρείας δύναμιν μέγαλην), in addition to the main Seleucid force commanded by Apollonius the Mysarch, as assembling in ca. 167 BCE "to fight against Israel," that is, the Judeans led by Judas Maccabeus (1 Macc 3:10).[3]

In many respects, the Hellenistic period was not kind to Judah either, because the Judeans, like the Samarians, found themselves sandwiched between the competing claims of the Ptolemies in Egypt and the Seleucids in Syria (Berlin 1997). Ptolemy I deported many captives from Jerusalem, Samaria, and Mt. Gerizim to Egypt (*Letter of Aristeas* 13; Josephus *Ant.* 12.7), while Demetrius I destroyed the city of Samaria in 296 BCE (Eusebius *Chronicon* Olympiad 121).[4] According to Zertal's archaeological surveys (2004, 2008), the eastern valleys and the Shechem syncline, especially the Dothan Valley, experienced population loss in the Hellenistic period.

While acknowledging these symptoms of decline, one should also recognize indications of growth and prosperity, at least in certain areas. The region of southern Samaria, for instance, increased in population and material wealth during the Hellenistic period (Finkelstein 1993b; Finkelstein, Lederman, and Bunimovitz 1997). If, as some (recently Dušek 2012a: 72–73, 154–55) contend, Antiochus III accorded the Mt. Gerizim temple the same fiscal privileges he reportedly accorded to the Jerusalem temple (Josephus *Ant.* 12.138–44), the Gerizim temple establishment would have benefited from such concessions.[5] In any event, the massive

---

2. There is an inherent ambiguity in Josephus's usage of the terms Σαμαρεῖται (Samaritans) and Σαμαρεῖς (Samarians). One might expect Josephus to use the former to designate the religious group and the latter to designate residents of Samaria, but Josephus is not consistent in his employment of these and other like terms (e.g., Σικιμῖται, "Shechemites"). See Kippenberg 1971; Egger 1986; Kartveit 2009; Pummer 2009. To complicate matters, the Seleucid province of Samaritis (Σαμαρῖτις) comes also into play, because the term Samaritan (Σαμαρίτης) would designate a resident of this administrative district (Dušek 2012a: 71).
3. These forces were roundly defeated (1 Macc 3:11–24).
4. Applebaum's assertion (1986) that significant parts of Samaria became royal domains is historically rather uncertain.
5. Abel (1967: 133–35), Avi-Yonah (1966: 45–50), and Dušek (2012a: 70–71) additionally contend that the eparchy of Samaritis included Galilee and Judea in the early 2nd century BCE (cf. 1 Macc 10:30–31).

expansion of the Mt. Gerizim sacred precinct and the construction of a new surrounding town would not have been possible if the Samarian cult lacked a large, well-to-do, and devoted group of followers. The quality of construction in the expanded temple complex is quite impressive. Finds dating to the 3rd to early 2nd century from Mt. Gerizim include sections of a city wall (on the southern edge of the site), towers, large domiciles, service buildings, courtyards, oil presses, storage jars, and various lamps (Magen 2008a, 2008b). Also found were some 14,000 coins and hundreds of inscriptions in Hebrew, Aramaic, and Greek (Magen, Misgav, and Tsfania 2004).

That the Mt. Gerizim temple was well received by Samarian Yahwists can be seen from another perspective. Like the Judeans, the Samarians had become in the Hellenistic period (if not before) an international phenomenon, with Samarians residing in a number of other lands (Crown 1974b; van der Horst 1990: 136–47; Pummer 1998c). Two Samarian inscriptions discovered on the Aegean island of Delos (one dating to the late 3rd/early 2nd century BCE and the other dating to the late 2nd/early 1st century BCE) mention Mt. Gerizim and employ the term "Israelites" to refer to Samarians (Bruneau 1982; White 1987; Pummer 2009).[6] The older inscription, honoring an otherwise unknown Menippos of Herakeion, speaks of "the Israelites who make offerings for the temple of holy Mt. Gerizim" (εἰς ἱερὸν ἅγιον Ἀργαριζεὶν; Noy, Panayotov, and Bloedhorn 2004, vol. 1: 228–33). The later inscription, which honors an otherwise unknown Serapion of Knossos, likewise upholds the sanctity of the site: "The Israelites in Delos, who make offerings for the temple of Mt. Gerizim" (ἱερὸν Ἀργαριζεὶν).[7] In each case, the expatriates responsible for the dedication identify themselves as Israelites who seek to honor the mountain and its sanctuary (εἰς ἱερὸν ἅγιον Ἀργαρζεὶν; Pummer 1987b: 20; Runesson, Binder, and Olsson 2008: 129–31) by donating offerings on its behalf. This epigraphic evidence from another part of the Mediterranean world testifies to the centrality of Mt. Gerizim in the affections of Yahwistic Samarians, even of those Samarians who resided in far-off places. Such inscriptions, dating to different times, presuppose a history. A publicly stated (re)dedication to

---

6. Paleographically, Kartveit (2009: 218–19) favors a date for the earlier inscription in the early 2nd century.

7. Dušek (2012a: 79) contends that the difference in titles appearing in the two inscriptions reflects a historical diminution in the sanctuary's status after 166 BCE, losing official recognition as a holy sanctuary, and concomitantly tax exemptions, by the Seleucid authorities (1 Macc 10:31; Josephus *Ant.* 12.142–44).

a holy place in one's ancestral land does not come about overnight, but rather assumes a long attachment to that site.

If the 3rd and early 2nd centuries present a mixed picture of Samarian fortunes, the mid- to late 2nd century does not. During much of the Maccabean era (167–37 BCE), a succession of Maccabean leaders directed their energies toward nation (re)building and gradually expanded the territory of their state into Samaria, Idoumea, Galilee, Gilead, Peraea, Moab, and beyond (Mor 1989a, 2003, 2011b). The ascent of Judah represented a major power shift among the peoples of the southern Levant. Whereas in the early Persian period Samaria enjoyed a relatively dominant regional position among the subprovinces in the region, in the Maccabean period Judah gradually came to dominate the southern Levant.[8] Some early stages in the process of territorial enlargement were justified as responses to external threats or to the mistreatment of Judeans residing within other lands (e.g., 1 Macc 5:1–68; 2 Macc 2:10); but, in any case, the Hasmonean era brought profound geopolitical changes to the southern Levant.[9] Such a major shift in the regional balance of powers could not help but leave its mark on the course of Samarian-Judean relations.

During the next decades, a series of Hasmonean rulers took advantage of divisions among the Seleucid authorities and ineptitude in Seleucid administration to expand the power of Judean state at the expense of Samaria and other neighboring districts.[10] The rule of Jonathan Maccabeus witnessed a series of political, religious, and military successes that affected the southern areas of Samaria. One claimant to the Seleucid throne, Alexander Balas, awarded Jonathan the critical post of high priest ca. 152 BCE (1 Macc 10:17–21; Josephus *Ant.* 13.45; VanderKam 2004). Several years later, a new Seleucid king, Demetrius II Nicator, awarded Jonathan three Samarian nomes—Aphairema (Ephraim), Lydda (Lod), and Ramathaim—to enlarge the territory of Judah (1 Macc 11:34–36; cf. 1 Macc 10:30, 38).[11] The gift of these territories was accompanied by a royal

---

8. Yet this dominance never really went uncontested in the larger region (S. Schwartz 1989, 2001).
9. Dušek (2012a: 115–16) believes that one early Maccabean action (ca. 167–164 BCE) was to exclude the Yahwistic Samarians from "common Israel."
10. That this expansion eventually involved various types of accommodation with the elites of the affected areas (S. Schwartz 1991) seems likely.
11. In Josephus's retelling (*Ant.* 13.49–50, 125; cf. 13.127), these nomes come to represent the toparchies of Samaria, Galilee, and Peraea (S. Schwartz 1989: 379–80). Another work of Josephus (*Ag. Ap.* 2.42–43) makes an even more audacious claim, namely, that Samaria was given to Judah by Alexander the Great.

promise of important tax exemptions for all those sacrificing in Jerusalem (1 Macc 11:34). This meant that those Samarians who continued to bring sacrifices to Mt. Gerizim were excluded from the exemptions (Goldstein 1976: 433).[12]

Several devastating blows to Samarian sovereignty occurred late in the rule of John Hyrcanus I (134–104 BCE). In 111–110 BCE, John Hyrcanus laid siege to Mt. Gerizim, destroyed the sanctuary, and laid it waste (Josephus *BJ* 1.63; *Ant.* 13.254–56, 275–79; Magen 2008b: 170–71). As for the surrounding town on Mt. Gerizim, this too was destroyed. The military campaign against the strongly fortified city of Samaria, in large part a military colony, was a more difficult prospect (110–108 BCE). Eventually, though, John Hyrcanus captured and destroyed Samaria, razing it to the ground and enslaving its citizens—likely composed mostly, albeit not entirely, of the descendants of original Macedonian settlers—in the process (Josephus *BJ* 1.64–65; *Ant.* 13.275–81).[13] The forces of John Hyrcanus also captured Shechem and reduced it to a village (E. F. Campbell 2002: 311). The entire area of Samaria was now under Maccabean control.

The deteriorating relations between the Judeans and Samarians in the last centuries BCE produced scattered literary reflexes in Judean literature dating to this period. For example, one of the postscripts to the book of Sirach (early 2nd century BCE) declares:

My soul detests two nations (שני גוים),
and the third is not a people (איננו עם);
The inhabitants of Seir and the Philistines,
and the foolish nation (גוי נבל) that lives in Shechem. (Sir 50:25–26)[14]

---

12. The earlier letter of Demetrius I to Jonathan assures that the residents of the three nomes would recognize no other authority than that of the (new) high priest Jonathan (1 Macc 10:38). The extravagant promises proffered to Jonathan by Demetrius I (1 Macc 10:24–45) were given no credence (1 Macc 10:46), yet in the expansive reinterpretation of Josephus (*Ant.* 13.54), the imposition of ancestral laws by the Judean high priest entails that the residents of these three nomes (understood as Samaria, Galilee, and Peraea), as *Ioudaioi*, would be subject to the Judean high priest and observe the ancestral laws of the *Ioudaioi* (S. Schwartz 1989: 382).

13. The site was clearly not devoid of Yahwists. Among those bringing offerings to the Yahwistic temple at Mt. Gerizim in Hellenistic times were pilgrims from Samaria ([ן]שמרי; Magen, Misgav, and Tsfania 2004: 59 [no. 14.2]; 60 [no. 15.2]. A third fragmentary inscription (Magen, Misgav, and Tsfania 2004: 74 [no. 34.2]) is more ambiguous, possibly emanating from either Shechem or Samaria.

14. The Greek (LXX) translation (late 2nd century BCE) reads a little differently, speaking of those who settled on Mt. Samaria, the Philistines, and the foolish people who live in Shechem (Pummer 2009: 11–12).

The precise force of the complaint is debated, but most agree that "the foolish nation" living in Shechem is written with the Samarians in view.[15] Other examples of such antagonism could be given (van der Horst 2006). In sum, there can be little doubt that the Hasmonean era witnessed a serious degradation in Samarian-Judean relations. While such a marked deterioration did not constitute a complete schism, since some contacts continued in later decades (Pummer 2007), there can be little doubt that the events of the 2nd century soured relations between the two communities for centuries to come.

Given such developments, it may seem strange to speak of periodic cooperation among members of the Yahwistic elites of Samaria and Judah in the late Persian and early Hellenistic period. On the contrary, it might be tempting to mark a straight line from the conflicts of Nehemiah with Sanballat in the 5th century to the estrangement between the Judeans and Samarians in the 2nd century. Starting from the tensions arising from the intermarriage between the Judean high priest's brother and the Samarian governor's daughter in the late 4th century, one might then draw a direct line to the conflicts between the Hasmoneans and the Samarians. This chapter argues, however, against such a simplistic historical reconstruction. While it is important to acknowledge the 2nd century as a time of increasing estrangement, the 4th and early 3rd centuries present a much more complex situation. The traditional model construes relations between Samarians and Judeans too much in a binary fashion and ignores contrary evidence. There were likely more high-level contacts and occasions of cooperation between the two elites than many have acknowledged.

It is important to begin by observing that the literary evidence about this era is not univocal. Josephus's account about how the Samarians came to construct their own temple under Sanballat's governorship posits Judean emigrations northward to Samaria, many Judean priestly defections to Mt. Gerizim, and the appointment of a Judean high priest in Samaria

---

15. Zangenberg (1994: 42) contends that the text alludes to the Song of Moses (Deut 32:21): "As for them [Israel], they made me jealous with what is no god (לא-אל) and they provoked me with their futilities; therefore, I shall make them jealous with what is no people (לא-עם), with a foolish nation (גוי נבל) I shall provoke them." If so, the Judean writer cleverly employed an authoritative text accepted by both groups to assert that the behavior of the Samaritans fulfilled a prophetic pronouncement uttered by Moses concerning Israel (=Judah). Aspects of the Ben Sira polemic may be picked up in the fragmentary "Text about Joseph" (4Q371; 4Q372) at Qumran (Schuller 1990, 1992). The Samaritans consider themselves, as we have seen, to be the descendants of Joseph (and Levi).

from the elite high priestly family of Jerusalem (*Ant.* 11.297–347).¹⁶ The very narrative about how the Samarian governor (Sanballat) persuaded Alexander the Great that his rule would be best served if the power of the Judeans were divided in two (εἰς δύο διῃρῆσθαι τὴν Ἰουδαίων δύναμιν) so that in the event of an insurrection the people (τὸ ἔθνος) would not stand in solidarity against the rule of their (foreign) kings, as they had done in former times (*Ant.* 11.323) presupposes that Samarians and Judeans belonged to the same people.¹⁷ In this critical passage, the Judeans are construed as historic Israel, encompassing both north and nouth, one people (*ethnos*).¹⁸ Moreover, Josephus provocatively claims that Shechem, the Samarians' "mother city" (μητρόπολις) of that time, was inhabited by renegade Judeans (ἀποστατῶν τοῦ Ἰουδαίων ἔθνους; *Ant.* 11.340).¹⁹ In another context, Josephus avows that whenever a Jerusalemite committed a sin, such as violating the Sabbath or consuming unclean food, he would take flight to the Shechemites, claiming that he had been unfairly banished (ἀδίκως ἐκβεβλῆσθαι; *Ant.* 11.346–47).²⁰ If Shechem did indeed have a mixed population, this was partly because it proved to be a magnet for dissident Judeans (Nodet 1997: 137).

The dispute(s) among Judean and Samarian expatriates residing in Egypt during the 3rd century BCE about whether their offerings should be sent to the Jerusalem temple or to the Mt. Gerizim temple (Josephus

---

16. See the excellent recent treatments of Kartveit 2009 and Pummer 2009. I hope to return to these matters in a future study.
17. Alternatively, one could argue that Josephus is portraying Sanballat's voice as deceptively deployed in opportunistic international diplomacy, rather than projecting his own view. Yet, assuming that this may be so, Josephus does not correct or qualify the assertion. On Josephus's problematic statements about the origins of the Samarian temple at Mt. Gerizim and Judeans residing in the community surrounding it, see further Knoppers (2012c).
18. The usage of *Ioudaioi* in this comprehensive sense is by no means unique (S. Schwartz 1989: 381–88; cf. D. R. Schwartz 2007). Yet, more often than not, Josephus speaks of Samarians as a separate ethnos from that of the Judeans (e.g., *Ant.* 10.184; 17.20; 18.85; Feldman 1996: 117–26). In Nehemiah, as we saw in the last chapter, things are diametrically different. He never speaks of the Samarians and Judeans as comprising one people (*'am*), although some of his actions indicate that the ethnographic, social, and religious realities of his time were more complicated than he was willing to allow.
19. On the translation and its significance, see Pummer 2009: 124–25 (cf. Egger 1986: 78). The settlement in Shechem was thought to have ended ca. 475 BCE (G. E. Wright 1965: 167; Lapp 2008: 5–6, 19–39), but recent analysis indicates that it probably continued to the 4th century (Stern 2001: 427–28). Samarian refugees likely resettled Shechem, following the establishment of a Macedonian settlement in the capital of Samaria (G. E. Wright 1965: 180–91). Sites in the Shechem vale grew and prospered in Hellenistic times (E. F. Campbell 1991; G. R. H. Wright 2002), and Shechem itself was evidently fortified in the Ptolemaic period (E. F. Campbell 2002: 311–16).
20. Or (textual variant): ἐκκεκλῆσθαι, "accused."

Ant. 12.7–10; 13.74–79) presupposes that the two groups were part of one community (S. Schwartz 1989: 386; Pummer 2009: 179–96). Similarly, the writer of 2 Maccabees (5:22–23) considers the Judeans and the Samarians to belong to the same people or nation (γένος; D. R. Schwartz 2008: 264). Accordingly, the persecution of Antiochus IV (Epiphanes) against the Judeans (τοὺς Ιουδαίους) was initially directed against both the Jerusalem temple cultus and the Mt. Gerizim temple cultus (2 Macc 6:1–6; Goldstein 1983: 270–73; D. R. Schwartz 2008: 270–78, 537–40; Pummer 2009: 161–78).[21] Antiochus IV applied similar policies in his treatment of Mt. Zion and Mt. Gerizim, pushing for the (re)dedication of the Jerusalem sanctuary to Ζεύς Ὀλύμπιος (Olympian Zeus) and the (re)dedication of the Mt. Gerizim sanctuary to Ζεύς ξένιος (Hospitable Zeus).[22] The treatment implies that each of these two cultic precincts were viewed as important and legitimate (2 Macc 5:22–23; 6:2). According to Josephus (*Ant.* 12.257, 261), this foreign oppression led to strains between the Judeans and Samarians, because the Samarians (Σαμαρεῖται) successfully petitioned Antiochus, claiming that they were not responsible for the unrest and were not kin to the Judeans.[23]

In short, some of the evidence for strains among Judeans and Samarians during this time paradoxically underscores how similar the two groups had become over the centuries. If Yahwists in the two neighboring regions had long drifted apart or were perpetually at loggerheads with one another, it is unlikely the two groups would exhibit so many common traits. Clearly, there must have been serious and sustained interaction between at least some members of the two Yahwistic communities. In this

---

21. This raises the question of whether some Samarians had been working in tandem with the Judeans, who rebelled against Antiochus IV (Mor 1989a: 11–15; Daise 1998: 35–39).
22. In Josephus (*Ant.* 12.261, 264), the name of the temple is ἱερὸν Διὸς Ἑλληνίου (sanctuary of Zeus Hellenios).
23. In the actual correspondence cited by Josephus (*Ant.* 12.258–61), the authors of the missive to Antiochus IV claim to be Sidonians in Shechem (Σικίμοις Σιδωνίων). In an earlier appeal to Alexander the Great, the Shechemites claimed to be Hebrews (Ἑβραῖοι), but ones who were called the Sidonians in Shechem (οἱ ἐν Σικίμοις Σιδώνιοι; *Ant.* 11.343–44). The precise import of the nomenclature is unclear. Whether these Sidonians of Shechem were a group of Sidonian colonists residing in Shechem (Magen 2008c: 23–24; Dušek 2012a: 101–4), Hellenized Sidonian settlers (Alt 1953b: 398; Kippenberg 1971: 79–80), Hellenized Samarians (Mor 1989a: 15), a group of indigenous northern Israelites (Nodet 1997: 141–42; 2011), or something else is disputed. What does seem clear in Josephus's narration is that the claimants are Samarians (Σαμαρεῖται; *Ant.* 12.257, 261) who deny that they are Judeans (*Ant.* 11.342, 344; 12.260). Rappaport (1995: 283–87), followed by D. R. Schwartz (2008: 539), argues that the correspondence cited by Josephus represents an early Jewish forgery. Pummer (2009: 172–74) is also doubtful. Dušek (2012a: 81–85) vigorously disagrees.

chapter, I wish to turn to evidence pointing to just such a complicated set of relationships.

In the past several decades, the publication of the Dead Sea Scrolls (DSS) has afforded new insights into the editing and transmission of the Pentateuch in the last centuries BCE. One result of this important research is that scholars no longer view the genesis of the Samaritan Pentateuch with its distinctive set of theological readings as dating to early postmonarchic times. Rather, it is generally recognized that the rise of the SP occurred sometime in the 2nd–1st centuries BCE. In what follows, I shall argue that such an important historical process presupposes that the Samarians previously held a version of the Pentateuch into which changes were introduced. The appearance of a distinctive SP points back to the existence of an older forbearer in earlier Hellenistic times.

One task of this chapter will thus be to examine the text-critical evidence available from the DSS, the (Jewish) Masoretic text (MT), the Septuagint (LXX), and the SP to argue that both Judah and Samaria possessed versions of the Pentateuch in the Hellenistic age, although the text of the Pentateuch was not yet set in all of its details. The pluriformity characterizing biblical texts in this era indicates that the transmission of the Pentateuch continued to be accompanied by occasional scribal interventions within its text. That Yahwistic Samarians and Judeans cherished a basic set of common sacred writings points to a history of intermittent cooperation between Judean and Samarian scribes over a considerable period of time prior to the Maccabean expansion.

The question then is: How did this happen? What did both Judeans and Samarians see in the Pentateuch? What social and historical forces led these Yahwistic communities to embrace a common set of foundational scriptures? Given that the Pentateuch itself mandates centralization—the elimination of all illicit sanctuaries in the land and the focus of Israelite worship at only one divinely chosen sanctuary—how did each society reconcile these exclusive demands? While Judeans thought of Jerusalem as God's chosen place, Samarians thought of Mt. Gerizim in the same terms. If each group accepted the text's authority, how did each interpreted that text differently to justify their own beliefs and practices? A second task of this chapter will be thus to demonstrate how each people read basically the same scriptures with their own institutions in view.

Samarian-Judean relations were not bereft of strains in the late Persian and early Hellenistic periods; rivalries and tensions certainly existed. Yet this chapter will argue that elements of both societies regularly found common cause to cooperate on several levels. The Maccabean period is a critical one in Samarian-Judean history not because it rendered permanent a downward spiral of bitter antagonism between the two groups but because it marked an important break away from a long-established precedent of periodic cooperation between the two ancestral communities.

I. The Rise of the Pentateuch and Judean-Samarian Relations in the Late Persian–Early Hellenistic Period

One of the most obvious features shared by the Samaritans and Jews is a common collection of prestigious scriptures—the Pentateuch. In both religions, the five books of Moses hold a special place as a holy and authoritative set of stories and laws revealing God's will for Israel. In Samaritanism, the Pentateuch is basically the extent of the canon, but in Judaism the Pentateuch is accompanied by other collections—the Prophets and the Writings—to form a larger set of scriptures called the Bible (or Tanakh). Nevertheless, these two other collections of ancient scrolls—the Nevi'im and the Ketuvim—are not considered as authoritative as the Torah is. Rather, the Prophets and Writings are regarded as commentaries and reflections on Israelite history in light of the Pentateuch's injunctions. If there is a canon within the canon, it is the Pentateuch. Hence, in both communities the Pentateuch enjoys a unique status as sacred instruction.

Given that the five books involved (Genesis, Exodus, Leviticus, Numbers, and Deuteronomy) address a wide range of subjects—the beginning of the world, the creation of humanity, the age of the ancestors, the formation of the people of Israel, the exodus from Egypt, the gift of divine instruction at Mt. Sinai, the wilderness wanderings, and the covenant on the Steppes of Moab—the substantial literary corpus represents a major point of commonality between the two communities. The fact that the laws in the Pentateuch contain hundreds of ritual, moral, familial, political, economic, and administrative stipulations meant that Judeans and Samarians shared a foundational constitution that each group considered normative for their societies. How the Samaritans and the Jews came to share the same basic set of holy scriptures, why they did so, and when this sharing occurred are thorny issues that have occupied scholars for centuries. Did one simply borrow the written Torah from the other, or is the Pentateuch itself, in the end, the result of a prolonged collaboration between the two communities? The latter option seems much more likely than the former, given historical considerations and the analysis of manuscript evidence from the DSS.[24]

Close study of the wide array of Pentateuchal texts found among the fragmentary Qumran texts has been of tremendous importance in gaining a better understanding of the formation, editorial history, and early transmission of the Pentateuch in the last centuries BCE. Whereas a century ago, many thought of only three basic witnesses to the text of the Pentateuch (MT, SP, and LXX), most now speak of a pluriformity of witnesses (Ulrich 1999; Tov 2012). The gradual publication of the DSS has shown that the variations in length, order, and content that one finds among the MT, LXX, and SP reflect fluidity in the composition and growth of biblical texts in the Persian and Hellenistic eras. It is also now apparent that the Pentateuch was not a sudden or late arrival in Samaria in the 2nd and 1st centuries, but rather developed, at least in its final stages, in tandem with the forms of the Pentateuch circulating in Judah. It will be useful to sketch why this is so and why such textual analysis sheds a better light on Judean-Samarian contacts, especially among their religious elites, during late Persian and Hellenistic times. In so doing, it will be necessary to say a few things about the nature of the SP and its textual affiliations.

Of the three major textual witnesses to the Pentateuch—the Masoretic text (of the Jewish Pentateuch—the MT), the Septuagint (the Greek translation of the Pentateuch begun in the 3rd century BCE in Egypt (the LXX), and the Samaritan Pentateuch (SP)—the MT and the SP are close to one another in many respects. This fact is obscured in many modern treatments of the SP, which speak of some 6,000 textual variants between them.[25] The very large number implies that there are a great number of important differences between the two textual traditions. As a result, the MT and the SP have been regarded by some as representing two significantly distinct literary enterprises. But the 6,000 figure is quite misleading, because most of the variants are rather minor in nature.

Another common mistake has been to view the SP and the LXX as closer textual affiliates than they actually may be. The usual figures involve some 1,900 or 2,000 common readings that these two witnesses share

---

24. Whatever answer one gives to the question, it involves accounting for some serious interaction between the Judeans and the Samarians in the Hellenistic period. For more detail, see Knoppers 2011c.
25. In Tov's view (2012: 79), the total is closer to 7,000.

over against the MT (e.g., Eissfeldt 1965: 695; cf. Eshel and Eshel 2003: 216–19). The many common readings of the LXX and the SP are important and certainly deserve sustained study, yet a rather detailed analysis by Kim (1994) indicates that the actual number of cases in which the SP and the LXX share a common text over against the MT may be only half (964) the traditional number appearing in handbooks.[26] Hence, there may be many more cases in which the MT and the SP line up together against the LXX than cases in which the SP and the LXX line up together against the MT.

A few examples may suffice to make the larger point. In Gen 31:46–52 the *Vorlage* of the LXX evinces a different sequence from that of the MT, but the sequence in the SP matches that of the MT.[27] In a number of intriguing cases, the LXX* differs substantially from the MT in Exodus 35–40, but the SP largely agrees with the MT (Tov 2012: 316–17). In Num 9:22–23 the LXX* preserves a shorter and probably earlier text than that of the MT, which includes material from Num 9:21–22, 13:33, and 15:35 (cf. Wevers 1998: 143–45). Again, the SP aligns with the MT, over against the LXX*. In Num 10:34–36, the LXX presents a different sequence from the MT, reading vv. 35, 36, 34, in that order (Tov 2001: 339–40). Here, too, the MT and the SP agree over against the LXX.

Generally, the SP is a longer and fuller text than the MT in that the SP contains linguistic corrections, adds conflations based on parallel texts, replaces unusual forms (e.g., irregular spellings of names) with usual forms, includes minor alterations and rearrangements, provides sources for quotations, and establishes correlations between commands and their fulfillment.[28] Only rarely does the SP evince a minus over against the MT. In spite of such important differences between them, the MT and the SP are quite similar in both sequence and content. From the above list, it will be pertinent for our purposes to focus on three sets of dissimilarities between the MT and the SP: chronological systems, textual expansions,

---

26. Unfortunately, Kim does not address the diversity of textual witnesses to the LXX itself. This important matter deserves close scrutiny.
27. In referring to the LXX* I am speaking of the original Old Greek translation. In the course of its transmission, the LXX* was subject to a series of revisions, often toward the developing Hebrew (protorabbinic or proto-Masoretic) text. On the complicated issues of the LXX's origins and development within antiquity, see Trebolle 1998; Tov 2012: 127–49.
28. Such changes may have begun in the 2nd century BCE, but the textual interventions and updates were not a one-off phenomenon. Rather, the text-critical evidence indicates that they continued for some time (Zahn 2011; Tov 2012).

and sectarian readings.²⁹ It may be helpful to outline each before exploring the significance of these variants.

In presenting the genealogical development of humanity in the primeval prologue of Genesis 1–11, each of the three major witnesses (MT, LXX, SP) exhibits its own chronological system (Gen 5:19–31; 8:1–22; 11:10–26). In this case, the SP differs not only from the MT but also from the LXX (Hendel 1998: 61–80). There is, however, some overlap between the SP and the LXX in secondary features. The second category of conflations is quite important, both because of the number of such instances in the SP and because the parallel passages sourced to create such conflations appear elsewhere in the Pentateuch. These harmonizing additions were thought in the past to constitute one of the distinguishing marks of the Samaritan tradition over against the Jewish tradition of the Pentateuch. The promulgation of such a blanket thesis is mistaken. Many of the harmonizing additions found in the SP are paralleled in certain Pentateuchal witnesses found among the DSS and occasionally among witnesses to the LXX as well.³⁰ To take one example, the recollection of the golden calf episode in Deut 9:20 has Moses declare, "Yhwh was so incensed with Aaron that he was ready to destroy him and thus I interceded with him." This Deuteronomic assertion is lacking in the source text of (MT) Exod 32:10, but a nearly identical declaration to the one in Deut 9:20 has been interpolated into the text of Exod 32:10 in some witnesses to the LXX and into 4QpaleoExodusᵐ as well.³¹ The same insertion appears in SP Exod 32:10.³² The fact that this plus, as well as many others, are found within some witnesses to the LXX and in some of the DSS is quite significant. One is inevitably confronted with long-range developments within the growth of the Pentateuch during the last centuries BCE. The text of the Pentateuch was not yet a static entity, impervious to change. A process of selective growth through supplementation, based on other texts within the Pentateuch, began before such texts were translated into Greek and continued afterward.

---

29. On the linguistic updates, adaptations, and corrections, see Schorch 1997, 1999, 2004. Zahn (2011) thoroughly analyzes small-scale rearrangements, minor alterations, replacements, and conflations.
30. Tov (2012: 136) contends, in fact, that the LXX contains perhaps two to three times more small-scale harmonizations than the SP does in the Torah.
31. But 4QpaleoExodusᵐ (4Q22) maintains the third-person narration (ו[י]תפלל משה).
32. Such harmonizing additions are consistent with the early Jewish view that Deuteronomy is a "copy of the Torah" (משנה תורה; Tov 2001: 86–87).

To take a second example, illustrating the phenomenon of textual conflation, 4QDeutⁿ adds the text of Exod 20:11 after Deut 5:15, effectively harmonizing the second version of the Sabbath commandment in Deuteronomy with the earlier version in Exodus (E. Eshel 1991; Crawford 1995; 2008: 30–35). The same textual addition occurs in the SP. Illustrating the same tendency is the insertion of texts from Deuteronomy into parallel sections of earlier books. A particularly striking instance of this exegetical procedure in the Sinai pericope involves inserting a Deuteronomic oracle of reassurance (5:28b–29) into the conclusion of the Exodus account (20:21) in 4Q158.[33] In line with the unambiguous request by the people to Moses (דבר־אתה עמנו ונשמעה) delivered earlier that God speak to them indirectly through Moses (Exod 20:19), rather than to them directly (ואל־ידבר עמנו אלהים), the Deuteronomic authorization of prophecy (Deut 18:18–19) is interpolated into Exodus following the insertion of the Deuteronomic oracle of reassurance (5:28b–29) in the same text (4Q158 Exod 20:21). The sequence Deut 5:28–29, 18:18–19 is also found in 4QTestimonia (4Q175). A similar series of interpolations appears in the SP. There, Deut 5:28b–29 appears as part of Exod 20:18 (= MT Exod 20:21) immediately followed by Deut 18:18–22. The insertion of Deut 5:28b–29, 18:18–22 into some traditions of Exodus thus predates the formation of the SP.

In analyzing such instances of conflation, the variety of textual witnesses attested among the DSS is enormously important, because a small but significant number of Qumran Torah fragments (about 5–6 percent of the total) are close to the SP in plusses they share with the SP over against the MT. This vital discovery has led scholars to question the initial categorization of these texts as "proto-Samaritan," because the relevant textual fragments do not include the sectarian additions normally associated with the SP.[34] The conflations serve exegetical and literary functions, but generally do not advance a particular theological point. The presence of such texts at Qumran reveals that we are not dealing with Samaritan texts as opposed to Judean texts, but rather with a more complex phenomenon within the late development of the Pentateuch that is attested in Judah, Samaria, and the Egyptian Diaspora. One effect of the carefully

---

33. The fragments classified as 4Q158 are thoroughly reexamined and analyzed in forthcoming edition by M. J. Bernstein and M. M. Zahn (Discoveries in the Judaean Desert 5).
34. The nomenclature "pre-Samaritan," rather than "proto-Samaritan," for these MSS was chosen "on the assumption that one of them [the harmonistic Pentateuchal texts] was adapted to form the special text of the Samaritans" (Tov 2001: 97).

selected and carefully formulated additions present in the so-called pre-Samaritan texts is to create a more integrated and internally coherent literary work (Tigay 1985). Some harmonizing additions were borrowed from elsewhere within a given book, but others were interpolated into one book (e.g., Exodus) on the basis of a reading found in another book (e.g., Deuteronomy).

Because the additions within a given scroll (e.g., Exodus) do not vary in form or kind from the additions that have been inserted into one book (e.g., Exodus) on the basis of another (e.g., Deuteronomy), it seems clear that the scribes responsible for such additions conceived of the Pentateuch as a single literary whole. The result of their interventions is a slightly expanded Pentateuch that exhibits greater internal literary coherence.[35] Technically speaking, the scribes responsible for these expansionary plusses did not create new texts ex nihilo but borrowed passages from one context to address perceived lacunae in another. But the presumption behind such scribal interventions is that the Torah is an integrated, self-consistent, and seamless work (Kugel 2001). The five books in the Pentateuch are but individual parts of a cohesive whole. What the scribes created at the paradoxical cost of altering the text they knew and revered was a longer text that more accurately reflected the text they thought the Pentateuch should be.

It should be pointed out that that the so-called pre-Samaritan texts are not all identical to the base of the SP. Some contain fewer harmonistic readings than the SP does, while others (e.g., 4QNum^b) contain more (Jastram 1998; Tov and White 1994). Moreover, the pre-Samaritan fragments do not display an entirely uniform character. There are some manuscripts (4Q158; 4Q364; 4Q365) that move beyond other texts in the pre-Samaritan tradition by creating new material (inserting interpretive explanations or theological comments that are unparalleled elsewhere in the Pentateuch).[36] In any case, the larger point remains. Certain texts found at Qumran are exceedingly close to the SP in a number of important respects. That these manuscripts were found among the DSS means

---

35. Such attempts to create greater harmony are in evidence elsewhere within the MT and the Versions (the ancient translations and paraphrases of the Hebrew text)(Aejmelaeus 1993; Levinson 2001; Zahn 2011).
36. Crawford terms these texts "hyperexpansive" (2008: 53). Whether these texts should be considered as rewritten scripture or simply as expanded scripture is a legitimate question, because the texts in question do not identify themselves by means of content, perspective, or voice as anything other than Pentateuchal MSS (Segal 2000; Bernstein 2005; Tov 2010; Zahn 2011).

that some of the specific features that were formerly thought to be distinguishing marks of the SP turn out to be nonexclusive to the Samaritans. Rather, these particular texts belong to the common legacy of Samaria and Judah in the last centuries BCE. The textual evidence suggests that the peculiarly Samaritan layer in the SP is, therefore, rather slender (Tov 2001: 81–100).

What particularly distinguishes the SP from the Jewish Pentateuch are some limited but highly significant sectarian additions in the SP that are unparalleled either in the MT or in the witnesses to the Pentateuch found among the DSS. One of the critical additions involves the Samaritan version of the Tenth Commandment, which includes Exod 13:11a and Deut 11:29b, 27:2b–3a, 4a, 5–7, and 11:30 in this order.[37] Again, the practice does not involve inventing new phrases or dicta but rather borrowing passages from literary contexts elsewhere within the Pentateuch to generate a new text in an older context. In particular, the inclusion of material from Deut 11:29–30 in both versions of the Decalogue (cf. MT Exod 20:17; Deut 5:18) underscores the point that Yhwh wished to make his favor upon Mt. Gerizim evident to his people already at Mt. Sinai.[38] The insertion of this material is critical, because the laws given in Exod 20:1–17 carry a special status in the Sinaitic legislation as the only statutes communicated directly by Yhwh to the people of Israel.[39] Hence, the "ten words" take on a particularly localized significance in Samaritan tradition.[40]

The best known discrepancy between the MT and the SP may be the variant of the Deuteronomic expression "the place that Yhwh your God will choose (יבחר)" as "the place that Yhwh your God has chosen (בחר)" in each and every relevant context within Deuteronomy.[41] The variation in the SP is quite commonly taken as a late sectarian change, in part

---

37. Dexinger 1977; Sanderson 1986: 235–37, 317–20; Ben-Ḥayyim 1995: 487–92; Himbaza 2004: 63–66, 183–219; Kartveit 2009; Pummer 2009.
38. Separating Deut 11:29a from 11:30 not only creates a bracketing frame for the interpolation of additional material from another literary context (Deut 27:2b–3a, 4–7) but also geographically specifies the interpretation of all this material as pertaining to Mt. Gerizim.
39. Among the relevant texts, see especially Exod 19:10–14, 21–25; 20:18–21 (cf. Deut 5:19–28; 18:15–19).
40. On Exod 20:2–17 (//Deut 5:1–18) as the "ten words" (עשרת הדברים), see already Exod 34:28; Deut 4:13; 10:4; "the ten words" is a literal translation of the Hebrew phrase that is popularly translated as the "Ten Commandments."
41. The relevant texts are: Deut 12:5, 11, 14, 18, 21, 26; 14:23, 24, 25; 15:20; 16:2, 6, 7, 11, 15, 16; 17:8, 10; 18:6; 26:2; 31:11 (cf. Josh 9:27 [יבחר]; Weinfeld 1972: 324 [no. 1a]; Pummer 2007: 244–45).

because all of the major LXX witnesses support the MT reading.[42] Yet the text-critical situation is not so straightforward and requires some discussion. Schenker (2008, 2010) has recently observed that there are witnesses to the LXX, the Old Latin (OL), the Bohairic, and the Coptic that support the SP lemma. He contends that the major LXX witnesses were all corrected at some point toward the emerging MT text.[43] By contrast, it is unlikely that the SP influenced the readings of the minor witnesses to the LXX, OL, Bohairic, and Coptic versions, because the SP would not have been known (in all probability) by these translators. Hence, the standard SP lemma (בחר) may not necessarily be a sectarian reading.[44]

Schenker's argument for the priority of the SP reading is, however, not as strong. He points out that the Deuteronomistic references to the Deuteronomic central place formula, "the city/Jerusalem that Yhwh has chosen" (e.g., 1 Kgs 8:16, 44, 48; 11:13, 32, 36; 14:21; 2 Kgs 21:7; 23:27), are phrased consistently in the perfect (בחר).[45] Reasoning that later biblical writers are quoting prestigious older texts, Schenker contends that the *Vorlage* used by these writers likely read בחר. In Schenker's view, the

---

42. The major LXX witnesses read consistently the first aorist middle subjunctive of *eklegō* (*eklexētai* = יבחר of the MT) in all of the above cases in Deuteronomy. Among the DSS witnesses to Deuteronomy, there are two (4QpaleoDeutʳ to Deut 12:5; 1QDeutᵃ to Deut 14:25) that might support the MT, yet both of those lemmata are fragmentary: [יב]חר and must be reconstructed (Ulrich 2010).
43. It is also possible that the variegated textual evidence of the Versions points toward more fluidity in the use of בחר and יבחר in the textual witnesses to Deuteronomy prior to the formation of the MT, the LXX, and the SP. Were the pre-MT, pre-LXX, and pre-SP witnesses to Deuteronomy internally consistent in the use of יבחר or בחר? For instance, does the appearance of שם שמו את לשכן בחרתי אשר המקום, "the place which I have chosen to make my name dwell there," in the citation of Deut 30:1–4 and Deut 12:5 in Neh 1:9 (Williamson 1985: 172; Blenkinsopp 1988: 210) indicate that the authors were using a pre-SP version of Deuteronomy (Schenker 2010: 113–15), or does the appearance of this terminology indicate that the *Vorlage* of Deuteronomy employed by the authors of Nehemiah was not as completely self-consistent as both the MT and the SP are? To complicate matters, biblical scholars are accustomed to think in terms of three main classifications of Pentateuchal textual witnesses (MT, LXX, and SP), but no small number of biblical manuscripts at Qumran fall into the so-called nonaligned category. In Tov's calculation (2012: 107–10, 158–60), of the 46 Torah texts, the nonaligned texts represent 39 percent of the total. It may well be that the complete consistency one finds both in the MT and in the SP masks a more complex textual situation in the centuries prior to the conflicts of the Hasmonean era.
44. To complicate matters further, the question of whether the Samareitikon represents a Samaritan version (or adaptation) of the LXX (Joosten 2010; forthcoming) comes into play. But, in any case, there is no evidence of early contamination from Samareitikon readings that would have affected the Old Latin, the Bohairic, and the Coptic Versions.
45. On the formula המקום אשר בחר / יבחר לשכן שמו שם, found in Deut 12:11; 14:23; 16:2, 6, 11; 26:2, see Weinfeld 1972: 325 (no. 3); Richter 2002.

MT lemma in Deuteronomy (יבחר) represents a late Judean (sectarian) alteration.[46]

Yet if one looks at the context and distribution of the Deuteronomistic citations, a different picture emerges. The first occurrence of the election formula appears in the Joshua conquest accounts. There, one responsibility of the subjugated Gibeonites will be to serve as "hewers of wood and drawers of water" at "the place He [Yhwh] will choose (יבחר; Josh 9:27). The use of the imperfect is important, indicating that the divine choice still lies in the future. The next usage of the election formula occurs in the elaborate Solomonic dedication of the Jerusalem temple (Knoppers 1993b). On that festive pan-Israelite occasion, Solomon offered thousands of sacrifices and the priests ushered the ark into the temple. Because of an impressive theophany, "the priests were unable to stand to serve on account of the cloud, the glory of Yhwh [in] the house of Yhwh" (1 Kgs 8:11).[47] Quoting the deity at this festive pan-Israelite celebration, Solomon construes the manifestation of Yhwh's glory as public proof of Jerusalem's divine election:

> From the day I brought my people Israel out from Egypt I never chose (בחרתי) any city from any of the tribes of Israel (בעיר מכל שבטי ישראל) to build a house for the presence of my name[48] and I never chose (בחרתי) any man to be ruler over my people Israel, but I chose (ואבחר) Jerusalem for the presence of my name and I chose (בחרתי) David to be in charge of my people Israel. (1 Kgs 8:16)

The double play on Deuteronomic election theology and Nathan's dynastic oracle (2 Sam 7:7–16) in this public blessing is no accident. Simultaneously citing and recasting the divine pledges made to his father, Solomon pronounces the Deuteronomic centralization mandate to be successfully completed. If the place Yhwh will choose (יבחר) to place his name was unknown in previous centuries, it is known now. Solomon interprets the Davidic promises (or at least one of them) as divinely fulfilled (2 Sam 7:10–13).

---

46. Dušek (2012a: 115–16) agrees and hypothesizes that the earlier lemma of יבחר was systematically changed to בחר in the early Maccabean era (167–164 BCE).
47. Cf. Exod 33:7–11; 40:33–38 (Haran 1978: 194–204).
48. Reading with the parallel in 2 Chr 6:5–6 and 4QKgs^a. MT 1 Kgs 8:16 omits through whole-phrase haplography (homoioteleuton) *welōʾ bāḥartî bĕʾîš lihyôt nāgîd ʿal-ʿammî yiśrāʾēl wāʾebḥar bîrûšālayim lihyôt šĕmî šām* (*lihyôt šĕmî šām* to *lihyôt šĕmî šām*). See also the LXX^B of Kgs 8:16. MT 1 Kgs 8:16 is incoherent in that Yhwh responds to his previous history of never choosing a city by choosing David.

In the Deuteronomistic reappropriation and extension of Deuteronomic theology, chosen city and chosen dynasty become paired in the dual election of Jerusalem and of David. Accordingly, the later appearances of the Deuteronomic election formula in explaining the (mis)fortunes of national history always refer to the divine election (בחר) of Jerusalem (1 Kgs 8:44, 48; 11:13, 32, 36; 14:21; 2 Kgs 21:7; 23:27; Nihan 2012). The appearance of the election formula in Solomon's speech represents, therefore, a deliberate turn in the Deuteronomistic formulation of the past.

In short, the text-critical evidence in Deuteronomy is complex. It is no longer self-evident that the consistent appearance of בחר ("He has chosen") in the SP, over against יבחר ("He will choose") in the MT, represents a late sectarian correction.[49] In any event, it is not necessary for our purposes to determine which is earlier. The matter may be put somewhat differently. It is not the case that that one reading (SP) is somehow ideological while the other (the MT) is not. Each formulation expresses an election theology.[50] Moreover, one can make the case that each lemma makes a certain amount of sense within its larger literary context (יבחר in

---

49. Whether the repeated use of the perfect (בחר) in the halachic text 4QMMT (4Q394 3–7 ii.19; 8 iv.9–11; 4Q396 1–3 iii.1; Qimron and Strugnell 1994: 10, 12, 19) found at Qumran reflects a Deuteronomic *Vorlage* with בחר (Schorch 2011: 33–34) is uncertain. To be sure, the use of the pronoun אשר ("which") in 4Q394 3–7 ii.19 suggests a quote from a biblical text (Qimron and Strugnell 1994: 50). Yet the 4QMMT text, in speaking of Jerusalem as "the place" (המקום) and the "holy camp" (מחנה הקדש), is not simply quoting Deuteronomy, because Jerusalem is nowhere mentioned in Deuteronomy. The writers are making a larger statement about the special sanctity of Jerusalem that draws from a variety of earlier sources (e.g., Lev 17:3–4; 1 Kgs 8:16). The authors make two related claims. The first is that Jerusalem enjoys a special status as the "head of the camps of Israel" ([היא ראש מ]חנה ישראל) over against the "camps of Israel," that is, the other towns of Israel (4Q394 8 iv.11–12; Qimron and Strugnell 1994: 12, 143–44). The second claim is that Jerusalem (and not simply the Jerusalem temple; 2 Chr 7:12, 16) "is the place which He has chosen from all of the tribes of Israel" ([היא המקום שבחר בו מכל שבטי י]שראל; 4Q394 8 iv.10–11; 4Q396 1–2 iii.1[= B 61]; Qimron and Strugnell 1994: 12, 19, 52). The sanctity of all Jerusalem was a major concern of the Qumran sectarians, because such a determination had important implications for the scope of purity regulations (Kratz 2008: *61–*62). The second claim eruditely echoes a standard refrain in Deuteronomistic (e.g., 1 Kgs 8:16; 11:32; 2 Kgs 21:7) and Chronistic (2 Chr 6:5–6; 12:13; 33:7) commentary on the travails of the Judahite monarchy. Thus, Yhwh explains the survival of the Davidic monarchy, despite Solomon's sins (1 Kgs 11:1–10), as occurring for the sake of David and for the sake of "Jerusalem, the city which I have chosen from all of the tribes of Israel" (ירושלם העיר אשר בחרתי בה מכל שבטי ישראל; 1 Kgs 11:32). The Deuteronomistic locution adapts, in turn, one of the Deuteronomic election formulae, "the place which Yhwh your God will choose [SP has chosen] from all your tribes" (המקום אשר־יבחר יהוה אלהיכם מכל־שבטיכם; Deut 12:5; cf. 18:5) and applies it to Jerusalem. Given the Deuteronomistic, Chronistic (see also 1 Chr 28:3–8), and Psalmic (e.g., Ps 78:68; 132:12–13) reuse of the lemma found in Deuteronomy, it seems likely that the authors of 4QMMT allude to and extend a well-established Judean line of interpretation.

50. It should be recalled that the prefix (nonperfective) conjugation has a broad range of meanings, including denoting preterite action, at least in some cases (Waltke and O'Connor

the MT; בחר in the SP). I wish to return to this matter later (section II of this chapter).

We have seen that the SP differs from the Jewish Pentateuch in the addition of a series of small but critical sectarian changes.[51] These sectarian additions were introduced fairly late in the 2nd century or 1st century BCE, probably during Maccabean times, when the relations between the Samarians and Judeans took a decidedly negative turn. The growing divide between Samaritans and Jews during the second and first centuries BCE coincides with the rise of a distinctive Samaritan reading tradition (Schorch 1997, 1999, 2004, 2007). Interestingly, the fact that sectarian expansions were added to the SP tells us something about the status of the Pentateuch at that time in Samaria. For such theological additions to be envisioned by the relevant scribes, carefully interpolated into the Pentateuch, and received as legitimate, the Samaritan community must have previously been accustomed to the Pentateuch (Sanderson 1986: 317). The selective editing of certain passages in the Pentateuch could only occur if the community both possessed and valued the Pentateuch in the first place. The very creation of a distinctive new edition of the Torah in Samaria is predicated on the availability and acceptance of that Torah in the earlier history of the community.

Significantly, the sectarian additions in the SP go beyond the textual variants shared by the SP and fragments found within the so-called "pre-Samaritan" Pentateuchal manuscripts found at Qumran (Purvis 1968: 80; Tov 1989, 1990, 2012). If, as seems likely, the SP was developed with its distinctive sectarian readings out of one particular family of Pentateuchal texts at a relatively late date, this has significant implications for our understanding of the editing and transmission of the Pentateuch (or proto-Pentateuch) in the late Persian and early Hellenistic periods. The Pentateuch has to be regarded as a common patrimony from the time before the relations between the Judeans and the Samarians became seriously aggravated in the last two centuries BCE.

The shift from the view of the Pentateuch as a collection of well-regarded classics to the view of the Pentateuch as a self-contained, coherent unity must have occurred over a substantial period of time.

1990: 497–502 [§31.1d–h]). The point is not to deny that the prefix conjugation, e.g., יבחר, can also be used to represent future time, but rather to show that the prefix conjugation can be put to an impressive variety of uses (Waltke and O'Connor 1990: 502–4 [§32.a–c]).

51. We have also seen, of course, with reference to Deut 27:4 that the textual witnesses to the Judean Pentateuch were not impervious to sectarian changes.

That this is so can also be discerned from systematic examination of the text-critical evidence (MT, LXX, SP, DSS), which indicates that the conflationary expansions in the pre-Samaritan manuscripts were made over the course of centuries and did not occur as the result of a systematic recension at one particular time. Many expansions are found only in the pre-Samaritan manuscripts and the SP, while some others are shared by the SP and the LXX (over against the MT). A few harmonistic expansions are shared by the MT and the SP (over against the LXX), while yet others are peculiar to one of the major traditions (MT, SP, LXX). To this consideration another must be added. One must allow sufficient time for each of the major witnesses—MT, LXX, and SP—to develop its own peculiar features, for example, the three different chronological systems relating to the primeval era that we discussed earlier. Hence, one is inevitably dealing with a series of historical developments, rather than with one sudden event (Cross 1961, 1966; Purvis 1968; Tov 1989; Crawford 2008). Precisely how long a process may be involved to account for all the textual divergences to accumulate is unclear, but from a chronological vantage point, the shared traits of the pre-Samaritan tradition and the *Vorlage* of the LXX that are arguably secondary must have taken some time to develop prior to the translation of the Pentateuch into Greek, beginning sometime in the 3rd century BCE (Hendel 1998: 93–103).

Ironically, the late date for the emergence of a distinctive edition of the SP undermines the view that the early transmission of the Pentateuch should be viewed as either simply a Judean enterprise or simply a Samarian enterprise. How long these two communities possessed the Pentateuch as a common literary corpus before the sectarian additions were added to what later became known as the SP is unclear. We do not know precisely how many centuries elapsed before the rise of a distinctive SP, because the date at which the Pentateuch was completed in the postmonarchic period is disputed.[52] Also unclear is why the Samaritans evidently chose one of the harmonistic texts of the Pentateuch, whereas one of the more common, less harmonistic, texts of the Pentateuch eventually prevailed in Jewish circles.[53] One has to admit, of course, that to speak of the Torah

---

52. See, e.g., recently, Blum 1990, 2011; Schmid 1999, 2011; Römer 2002, 2011; Achenbach 2003; Schaper 2007; Otto 2009.
53. Tov (2001: 100) hypothesizes that the proto-Masoretic text was associated with the Jerusalem temple establishment; but, if so, it would be helpful historically to have ancient documentation verifying such an association.

as the common legacy of the Judean and Samarian communities does not address the ultimate origins of the Pentateuch itself. On this issue, one should allow for a variety of different possibilities.[54] Nevertheless, it is very significant that both groups affirmed the Pentateuch (and not a Tetrateuch or a Hexateuch) as a (or the) foundational corpus of religious literature for their communities.

That both Yahwistic groups came to affirm the same collection of scriptures as authoritative for their communities can hardly be accidental. Moreover, assuming that both populations possessed a basically common Pentateuch (or proto-Pentateuch) for some time, how did the two arrange for the maintenance and transmission of the body of literature that they both shared? What social mechanisms may have facilitated such a process of scribal communications? Not much is known about the interactions between the political and religious leadership of the two provinces, but it is important to recognize the existence of one vital social and religious institution shared by the two: the Aaronide priesthood. The temple priesthoods at Mt. Gerizim and Mt. Zion both claimed a common priestly pedigree rooted in the classical past. Each sought to legitimate its sacerdotal leadership by tracing its origins to Aaron, the authoritative high priest of the Sinaitic period.

At least as importantly, each tradition acknowledges that the priests serving at the other group's temple were also ultimately of an Aaronide pedigree. Hence, the clerical staffs of both sanctuaries were Aaronide in character. To be sure, each tradition views the Aaronide priesthood officiating at the other's sacred site as derivative of one's own. In the case of early Judaism, Josephus relates a story about how the brother (named Manasseh) of the Aaronide high priest (named Jaddua) in Jerusalem in the late 4th century defected to Samaria to oversee the construction and management of a new temple at Mt. Gerizim (*Ant.* 11.301ff.). That Aaronide had earlier married the daughter of the Samarian governor (Sanballat) and had shared the high priesthood with his brother (τοῦ ἀρχιερέως ἀδελφὸν ἀλλοφύλῳ συνοικοῦντα μετέχειν; *Ant.* 11.306) before he was barred from serving in this post any longer (*Ant.* 11.308–9). Resenting his dismissal and not wishing to divorce his wife, Manasseh complained to his father-in-law, who not only pledged to him the position of high priest but also, with the eventual consent of Alexander the Great, built

---

54. Carr (forthcoming) provides a convenient overview of recent criticism.

Manasseh his own sanctuary (*Ant.* 11.310–24).⁵⁵ The construction of a new sanctuary was rooted, therefore, in a spirit of competitive emulation, rather than in compliance with any divine norm or command.⁵⁶ Nevertheless, the Josephus tale acknowledges that the Mt. Gerizim high priest stemmed from an impeccable pedigree.

Samaritan tradition also acknowledges the Aaronide character of the breakaway faction that established a rival sanctuary, but locates this rupture in premonarchic times. The Samaritan chronicles, dating to medieval times, are a complex subject in their own right and must be approached critically (Stenhouse 1985, 1989; Crown 1994; Florentin 1999; Hjelm 2000). The relevant works for our consideration are the oldest chronicles (or parts thereof): the *Tulida*, the earliest section (‏1ב–23ב2‏) of which dates to the mid-12th century CE,⁵⁷ the so-called *Chronicon Samaritanum* or (Arabic) Samaritan Book of Joshua (Sam Josh), whose base dates to the 13th century CE,⁵⁸ and the *Kitāb al-Tarīkh of Abū 'l Fatḥ* (abbreviated as *Abū 'l Fatḥ*), whose base dates to the second half of the 14th century CE.⁵⁹ According to the *Chronicon Samaritanum*, Israel's cultic unity was shattered when an overweening priest named Eli led a dissident faction of Israelites in seceding from worship at the central sanctuary of Mt. Gerizim to build a rival sanctuary at Shiloh (Sam Josh 43).⁶⁰ Being a descendant of Ithamar, Eli belonged to the right tribe (Levi) and even to the right phratry (Aaron) within the tribe, but to the wrong lineage within that phratry (Ithamar, not Phinehas).⁶¹ Eli should have deferred to Uzzi, the

---

55. The Samaritan high priestly list (within the *Tulida*) lacks a high priest named Manasseh in the relevant period. There is a high priest in the larger succession named Manasseh (*Tulida* 8ב‏ﬡ‏105), but he is removed from the time of Alexander the Great by several generations to the late 2nd century BCE (Florentin 1999: 85; Pummer 2009: 116–17).
56. The stress on Mt Gerizim's dependence upon an older and long-established exemplar is also found in *Ant.* 13.256.
57. Florentin (1999:vi–xiv) observes that the *Tulida*, as its name implies ("Chronicles"), is a composite work, compiled by a series of Samaritan scribes over the centuries and written in different dialects (Hebrew, hybrid Samaritan Hebrew, Samaritan Aramaic). The latest section (1ב18–10ב18) continues into the 19th century.
58. See Juynboll 1848; Crane 1890; Stenhouse 1985, 1989. The author(s) of this chronicle may have known the work of Josephus indirectly through *Josippon* (Pummer 2012).
59. The work of *Abū 'l Fatḥ* differs from Samaritan Joshua on some significant details, but not on the early high priestly succession. On this chronicle and its selective reuse of Sam Josh, see Vilmar 1865; Stenhouse 1985, 1989.
60. Similarly, *Abū 'l Fatḥ* 40,47–48,56; Adler-Séligsohn 1.205–6 [25 3054].
61. *Tulida* 6ב36; Sam Josh 40; *Abū 'l Fatḥ* 39,45–40,47. Similarly, Adler-Séligsohn 1.205–6 [25 3054]. Josephus repeatedly claims that the high priesthood passed for a time from the family of Phinehas to the Ithamaride family of Eli (*Ant.* 5.361–62; 8.12), but this is not the belief in Samaritan tradition.

much younger, but legitimate, Aaronide heir in the line of Eleazar and Phinehas (cf. 1 Chr 5:31; Ezra 7:4). It was Phinehas, after all, to whom the deity awarded an eternal covenant of priesthood (Num 25:12–13), a point stressed in the *Tulida* (1ב1–2, 4–5).

To sum up, there is important agreement among Jewish and Samaritan traditions on the Aaronide management of both the main temple and the dissident temple. Each places an emphasis on the Aaronide priesthood as the only legitimate priesthood in ancient Israel. All of the tribe of Levi has a special cultic role to play in Israel, but only Aaron and his descendants enjoy priestly prerogatives (Watts 2007). Both traditions posit a priestly expulsion or desertion from an authoritative and well-established centralized cultus. Each sees the other's central cult centre as relatively late, lacking divine sanction, and modeled after the original within its own domain. Nevertheless, the two converge in recognizing the breakaway priestly faction as authentically Aaronide. This fundamental agreement between the two major traditions, when they disagree on so much else, is significant, because it sheds light on the inherent overlap between them. The fact that the Aaronide priesthood controlled both Mt. Zion and Mt. Gerizim undoubtedly facilitated contacts between the two communities. The acknowledgment of priesthoods related one to another by reference to ultimate origins in a common eponymous ancestor illumines not only similar sacrifices, rites, and feasts, but also the phenomenon of scribal communications between the two temple staffs.

If, as some Pentateuchal scholars hold, certain editorial changes and expansions were made to the Pentateuch in the fourth and early 3rd century BCE, one should consider the possibility that such editorial changes and expansions were made virtually identically in the Pentateuchal manuscripts held within both Judah and Samaria.[62] Given such a set of circumstances, considerable cooperation between at least some elite members of each group has to be assumed. After all, one has to account for the issues of maintenance and transmission, if not also of editing and small additions. The probability of some contacts and periodic cooperation between the scribes of the two communities may help to explain why the MT and SP share many readings over against the LXX. The proposition that precisely the same changes arose spontaneously and independently in both communities so that both Pentateuchs remained virtually identical over

---

[62]. But one has also to account historically for the fact that the process of translating the Pentateuch into Greek evidently began in the 3rd century BCE (van der Kooij 2007).

a considerable period of time strains historical credulity.[63] It makes much more sense to view the Pentateuch, at least for a time, as a common literary enterprise.[64]

In this context, the pan-Israelite point of view contained within the Pentateuch is critically important, because it affirms a larger corporate entity greater than any one tribe, city, or region. The Israel upheld in the books of the Pentateuch embraces a wide variety of different sodalities in northern and southern Israel. Such a comprehensive perspective, which acknowledges social, tribal, and regional differentiation, but ultimately subordinates such diversity to a larger ethnic unity (Israel), could easily have appealed to and been accepted by both Yahwistic Samarians and Yahwistic Judeans. Important political differences (e.g., the northern kingdom of Israel and the southern kingdom of Judah, the province of Samerina and the province of Yehud) could be implicitly accommodated in this ethnographic schema. Yahwistic Samarians and Yahwistic Judeans could readily attest, for instance, to significant points of divergence in political history extending beyond the classical era of Moses, but construe those differences as affecting tribal relations within the larger history of Jacob's descendants. The larger unity of Israel could be affirmed in spite of political, religious, and social differences among the sundry sodalities constituting that greater entity.

In an age in which both Judah and Samaria were occupied by the same foreign regime and subject to its administrative, military, and economic policies, the Pentateuch provided each group with a larger social and religious identity. The "scroll of Moses" justified each group's claims of great antiquity in a world that valued all things antiquarian. Given that both Samarians and Judeans could be found both within the land and outside of it in the Diaspora, the Pentateuch as a portable corpus of prestigious texts bound the homeland and diasporic communities together.[65] Northern and southern Israelites could affirm that the land

---

63. In the local texts theory of Cross (1964), followed by Purvis (1968: 84–85), the period (or periods) of such influence was the Hasmonean or Herodian age, when a number of Judeans returned from Babylon. Whatever the case, as Trebolle Barrera points out (1998: 297), some mixing of textual families must have occurred before the sectarian additions were interpolated into the SP. Such a partial merging of text-types presupposes cooperation among the scribes editing and copying texts within the two (or more) traditions.
64. So also Albertz 1994: 523–33; Macchi 1994a, 1999; Knauf 1994: 173; Nihan 2007b; Pummer 2007; Magen 2008c; Dušek 2012a.
65. The enduring notion of a larger Israel is evident in the pseudepigraphic *Letter of Aristeas*, which depicts the creation of the Septuagint as involving six elders from each of the twelve tribes (lines 32, 39, 45–50). The 2nd century BCE *Letter of Aristeas* is widely regarded as a

was integral to Israelite identity but recognize that the Pentateuchal laws governing Israelite communal life were valid before the Israelites ever set foot in that land. Members of the two communities could disagree on many things, of course, including the very understanding and application of key texts within the Torah. But the Pentateuch validated the claims of each group to be descendants of the eponymous ancestor Jacob/Israel and provided each community with foundational stories and legal precepts to structure societal life. Fulfilling this corporate function, the Torah was a foundational source of social unity, historical identity, and religious praxis.

II. Location, Location, Location: Different Ways of Reading the Same Book

Acknowledging the potential attraction of the Pentateuch as an esteemed set of texts in both Judah and Samaria does not resolve the seemingly contradictory demands that the work imposes on those communities. It is one thing to accept that the ancestors Abraham, Jacob, and Isaac visited a variety of northern and southern sites, such as Shechem (Gen 12:6–8; 33:18–20), Hebron/Qiryath-'arba' (Gen 12:9; 23:2, 19; 33:18; 35:27; 37:14), Beersheba (Gen 21:14, 25–34; 22:19; 26:23–33; 28:10; 30:23–24; 46:1, 5), and Bethel/Luz (Gen 12:8; 13:3; 28:10–22; 31:13; 35:1–15; 48:3), during their scattered travels, because residents of communities in Samaria and Judah could readily identify with the honor associated with such ancient stories.[66] Yahwists in each province could affirm the value of the Pentateuch as in some sense constituitive of their identity, whether as members of individual societies separate from one another or as part of a greater entity named Israel.

It is, however, another thing to deal with demands in the Torah that make exclusive claims about the creation of institutions at one particular site within the context of a much larger tribal federation. Inasmuch as Judeans and Samarians accepted the concept of centralization enshrined

---

pious fiction, but it is nevertheless interesting to acknowledge the manner in which it defends the translation of the Pentateuch. In a diasporic setting, the *Letter of Aristeas* perpetuates the ancient ideal of a pantribal Israelite federation, albeit one that is securely headquartered in the Jerusalem temple.

66. This is a large subject that cannot be adequately explored here. Some of the southern sites at which the ancestors stayed (e.g., Beersheba and Hebron) were situated outside the boundaries of Yehud in the Persian and early Hellenistic periods. Yet this does not mean that these towns and surrounding areas were bereft of any Yahwists. There is some textual and epigraphic evidence to suggest otherwise (Lemaire 2004, 2006; Fulton 2011).

within the Deuteronomic legislative program, how could each group simultaneously embrace the exceptional cultic demands that this program placed on their societies? The Deuteronomic laws of centralization mandate both cultic unity, involving only one sacred site, and cultic purity throughout the entire land (Deut 12:1–13:1). To be clear, such regulations entail the elimination of all non-Yahwistic sanctuaries and all rival Yahwistic sanctuaries to the central sanctuary.

Related legislation transforms traditional festivals, such as Pesaḥ (Passover), Shavuʿot (Weeks), and Sukkot (Booths; Deut 16:1–17; Levinson 1997), in light of the centralization mandate, while other legislation reorders the duties of societal leaders, such as prophets, priests, judges, and kings, to accommodate Deuteronomic principles of professionalization, distribution of powers, and centralization (Deut 16:18–18:22). How could one such collection of ancestral laws be shared by the citizens of two separate provinces and their diaspora communities? Is it possible that the two populations valued basically the same set of scriptures and yet understood them differently? We have seen that each major witness—the MT and the SP—is internally consistent in speaking of the place that "Yhwh will choose" or "has chosen," but there was obviously much more at stake than this divergence in verbiage.[67] There must be something about the internal makeup of Deuteronomy that could have given rise to (or allowed) such conflicting interpretations. Are there clues within Deuteronomy itself that might help us gain a better understanding of what the relevant gaps and hermeneutical fault lines were?

In what follows, I would like to argue that each community construed the centralization legislation in its own way and developed its own interpretive traditions in dealing with the specifics of the Deuteronomic program. To concentrate on the centralization decrees is necessary, because the understanding of these decrees lies at the heart of the disagreements between Jews and Samaritans about whether Jerusalem or Mt. Gerizim is the chosen place alluded to in Deuteronomy. The purpose of this exercise is not to contend for one tradition or another, but rather to explore the particular interpretive traits of each tradition. Special attention will be paid to the larger literary context, because the two communities construed the relevance of this differently. Since Jews and Samaritans embrace

---

67. The consistent difference between יבחר and בחר is certainly relevant and important, but the issue of which reading precedes the other historically is only one part of a larger picture. That is, deciding upon the priority of one reading is insufficient by itself to prove the validity of one sanctuary over against the other.

a Pentateuch (and not a Hexateuch) as Torah, the discussion will make only scattered references to Joshua.⁶⁸

At the outset, it is important to underscore that ambiguity exists in both Pentateuchs. This imprecision is extremely important and too pervasive to be accidental. In each case, the precise location of the site in Deuteronomy 12 is not revealed. Whether "the place" (המקום) is already chosen (SP) or is yet to be chosen (MT), the site repeatedly goes unnamed (Deut 12:5, 11, 14, 18, 21, 26). Precisely because of this vagueness, one can better appreciate how both the Judean and the Samarian communities accepted basically the same five books of Moses as authoritative scripture. Each community could (and did, and does) read the Pentateuch in its own way. Indeed, the imprecise language is itself a sign that the Pentateuch is fundamentally a compromise document.⁶⁹ To be sure, the sectarian additions interpolated into the SP at a late stage (in the 2nd–1st centuries BCE) resolve the ambiguity to a large extent, because Yhwh's preference for Mt. Gerizim becomes an integral part of "the ten words." Yet setting aside, for the time being, the late sectarian additions in the SP and a few in the MT, one can make the case that both lemmata—the "Yhwh will choose" (יבחר) refrain of the MT (and most witnesses to the LXX) and the "Yhwh has chosen" (בחר) refrain of the SP (and a few witnesses to the LXX)—fit within their larger literary contexts—the Pentateuch alone (so the SP) and the Pentateuch and the Former Prophets (so the MT).⁷⁰

In what follows, I shall explore how Samarians likely construed the centralization legislation within its literary context in Deuteronomy and

---

68. Joshua is part of the Hebrew Bible, but is not considered canonical by the Samaritans. Versions of Joshua (or parts thereof) are found among the Samaritan chronicles (Stenhouse 1989; Hjelm 2000). The possible reconstruction of a separate (shorter and variant) Hebrew Joshua in Samaritan tradition is much debated (Crown 1974a, 1994, 1998).

69. Nihan (2007b: 215–16) contends that Deut 27:4–8, 11–13 was written as a compromise text (supplementing an earlier layer, consisting of vv. 1–3, 9–10), designed to win the support of Samarians for adopting the Pentateuch as a common literary work shared with the Judean community:

> This suggests that for the author of Deut 27:4–8 the altar on Mount Gerizim *is* legitimate, *but only in the sense that the Torah preserves a law authorizing multiple sanctuaries* that coexists with the centralization law of Deuteronomy 12. In this regard, the tension created by the *de facto* existence of *two* conflicting altar laws inside the Torah, in Exodus 20 and Deuteronomy 12, was brilliantly used by the Judean redactor who inserted Deut 27:4–8 to legitimate the co-existence, in his own time, of two major sanctuaries, which both claimed to be the unique sanctuary prescribed by Deuteronomy 12.

70. The importance of this consideration (Pentateuch vs. Enneateuch) was underscored to me by R. G. Wooden (personal communication).

the larger Pentateuch during late Persian and early Hellenistic times. This Samarian approach will then be compared with how Judeans interpreted the same material. So that one may attempt to grasp how Samarians and Judeans understood Deuteronomy, reference will not be made to the later sectarian additions to the Pentateuch (as best these can be reconstructed), except on a secondary level. To be sure, the sectarian readings are important to highlight salient issues in early Jewish-Samaritan hermeneutical debates.[71] The sectarian changes and the comments made by the early interpreters are invaluable in understanding how Pentateuchal statutes were construed in antiquity. Nevertheless, it is critical to begin by reconstructing, as best one is able, an earlier stage (or stages) in the formation of the Pentateuch before such sectarian changes were made, whether from Samarian or Judean sources. Samarian hermeneutics may thus be contrasted with Judean hermeneutics in dealing with the same textual material.

From a Samarian vantage point, the proximity of the centralization demand (Deuteronomy 12) to what immediately precedes it (Deut 11:26–32) was important to grasping the force of the centralization command.[72] The matter of context was, of course, also important for Judeans, but Samarians employed the immediate literary context of the so-called law code of Deuteronomy (12:1–26:15), the central legal section of the book, which contains a variety of ritual, moral, festal, political, administrative, and familial stipulations concerning life in the land of Israel, as a hermeneutical key to construing the centralization legislation.[73] In fact, both sets of instructions preceding (11:26–30) and

---

71. Admittedly, how far back the diverse Jewish and Samaritan interpretations extend is not altogether clear. Each case must be judged, as far as it is historically possible, on its own merits.
72. Brewer (1992: 20) and Kalimi (1995: 18–34) discuss arguments based on order (of words and phrases) and literary proximity in biblical and rabbinic exegesis.
73. When Deut 11:29–30 was composed is itself an interesting question (note the sing. used for the addressee(s) in these verses, compared with the pl. both in vv. 26–28 and in vv. 31–32), because it evidently does not belong to the oldest layer of the work (recently, Nihan 2007b). From a literary perspective, one can progress from the conclusion of v. 28 to the beginning of v. 31 quite easily without the intervening material in vv. 29–30. Nevertheless, it is doubtful that the text belongs to a very late time, because it seems unlikely that Judean authorities would have consented to the insertion of the demand for a Gerizim blessing if they knew that contemporary Samarians would interpret the injunction as relating to their temple. It seems at least equally (or more) likely that the insertion predated the Gerizim temple construction in the 5th century BCE. The addition of Deut 11:29–30 to the "ten words" in SP Exodus 20 and Deuteronomy 5 was made later to bolster the warrant for the Samaritan reading of the conjunction between the divine instructions to Israel about Mt. Gerizim (Deut 11:29–30) and the divine instructions about establishing a central sanctuary (Deuteronomy 12). That such a textual intervention was thought necessary indicates that the בחר lemma (as opposed to יבחר) did not settle the hermeneutical issue.

concluding (27:1–26) the main collection of laws (12:1–26:15), have to do with public ceremonies Israel is mandated to conduct at Mt. Gerizim and Mt. Ebal.[74] That adherence (or nonadherence) to the Torah has consequences is spelled out before the Israelites hear the injunctions themselves: "See, as for me, I am setting before you this day a blessing and a curse" (Deut 11:26).

As the chiastic schema suggests, the directions about public liturgies

Public Ceremonies and Public Laws
A   Blessings and Curses at Gerizim zand Ebal (11:26–30)
B   Introduction to the Law Collection (11:31–12:1)
C   Laws of the Covenant (12:2–26:15)
B' Conclusion to the Law Collection (26:16–19)
A' Ceremonies at Gerizim and Ebal (27:1–26)

(11:26–30; 27:1–26) contextualize the centralization legislation. The first set of instructions (11:26–30) consists of public pronouncements of blessings and curses validating God's covenant with Israel, while the second (27:1–26) consists of a series of instructions, including the erection of large stones upon which the Torah is to be written, the construction of an altar upon which sacrifices are to be offered, the pantribal proclamation of blessings and curses upon Mt. Gerizim and Mt. Ebal, and the Levitical proclamation of twelve execrations.[75]

Such a corporate ritual (or rituals) inside the land may have been deemed necessary, because the Israelites in Deuteronomy are outside the land, encamped upon the Steppes of Moab, listening to a series of sermons by their leader Moses (1:1–4:43; 4:44–28:69; 29:1–30:20). In this respect, the Deuteronomic discourse about benedictions and maledictions pertains not only to the formal collection of laws (Deut 12:1–26:15)

---

74. In the SP, Deut 11:31–32 introduces the legal material mandating centralization that follows (the *qiṣṣa* appears at the end v. 30). The SP reading tradition thus interprets the initial conjunction *kî* in v. 31 as temporal: "When you cross the Jordan to enter to possess the land… be careful to practice all of the statutes and judgments which I, I am delivering before you this day" (Deut 11:31–32). Weinfeld (1991: 453) comments that Deut 11:31–32 links the prologue of Deuteronomy 1–11 to the laws of Deuteronomy 12–26, functioning both as a conclusion to the material that precedes it and as an introduction to the material that follows.

75. The placement and content of the material in Deut 27 are unusual; some modern commentators regard the entire chapter as an interruption between the laws (12:1–26:15) and the

guiding Israel's life in the land, but also to a formal ceremony (or sequence of ceremonies) Israel is to enact upon entering the land: "You will pronounce the blessing upon Mt. Gerizim (*wĕnātattâ 'et-hā-bĕrākâ 'al-har gĕrizîm*) and the curse upon Mt. Ebal (*wĕ'et-hā-qĕlālâ 'al-har 'ēbāl*; Deut 11:29). One effect of such an all-Israelite ceremony will be to formally ratify the Israelites' commitment to observe the statutes delivered to them through Moses. If the land represents God's gracious gift to the people of Israel, the people's formal participation in ceremonies within the land represents Israel's public embrace of the gift of the Torah through a corporate "act of foundation" (Weinfeld 1991: 10). Hence, both Israel's successful entrance into the land and life within the land are intimately tied to Torah observance.

We have seen that the preliminary instructions provided by Moses about a national recitation of the blessing on Gerizim and the curse on Ebal (Deut 11:29–30) anticipate the much more detailed instructions about this national ceremony (27:1–26), which follow the formal delivery of the laws (12:1–26:15). The question is: Do these instructions about ritual ceremonies to be conducted upon Mt. Gerizim and Mt. Ebal suggest that this area is divinely favored as the future site of the centralized sanctuary? What textual evidence might explain why Samarians and Judeans could reach diametrically opposed answers to such a question?

To begin with, the detailed instructions about the corporate ceremonies inside the land in Deut 11:29–30 and 27:1–26 are not easy to follow. There is real ambiguity in the long "topographical gloss" (Weinfeld 1991: 452) of Deut 11:30, identifying the relevant sites at which the national commemoration is to take place. Referring to Mt. Gerizim and Mt. Ebal from the perspective of someone who is east of the Jordan, the text speaks of the two sites as "across the Jordan beyond the westward road in the land of the Canaanites who reside in the Arabah opposite Gilgal (הישב בערבה מול הגלגל), next to the oaks of

---

blessings and curses (Deut 28:1–68). Verse 1 speaks of Moses in the third person and anomalously introduces the elders as his partners, while v. 9 anomalously speaks of Moses and the Levitical priests as acting in consort to instruct the Israelites. Alternatively, Rofé (2002: 100) regards 11:26–30; 27:4–8, 11–13 as remnants of an older Shechemite tradition incorporated into Deuteronomy. Because we are focusing on a penultimate form of Deuteronomy (not the earliest layers of composition), such questions need not be dealt with here. Nihan (2007b) provides a judicious analysis of past discussions.

Moreh" (אצל אלוני מרה; Deut 11:30).⁷⁶ Although the geographic instructions seem quite specific, they are actually quite confusing.

Based on other appearances of the expression "the oak(s) of Moreh" (Gen 12:6; cf. Gen 35:4; Josh 24:26; Judg 9:37), the reference here is most naturally taken as a location by Shechem.⁷⁷ But the inclusion and identification of Gilgal are puzzling. Is the locution "opposite Gilgal" (מול הגלגל) merely intended to define the location of the particular Canaanites living in the Arabah (cf. Num 13:29; Josh 11:23), or is it intended to identify the location at which the Israelites are to stop once they cross the Jordan?⁷⁸ In the first instance, the mention of Gilgal is incidental to the main point, namely, the Israelites' journey to Mt. Gerizim and Mt. Ebal. In the second instance, the mention of Gilgal is critical to pinpointing the first destination of the Israelites within the land.

To complicate matters, there is more than one Gilgal attested in ancient Israelite literature (Sellin 1917). Is the Gilgal of Deut 11:30 the Gilgal located in the Jordan Valley (e.g., Josh 4:19–20; 5:9–10; 9:6; 10:6–9, 15, 43; 14:6; Judg 3:19; 2 Sam 19:16, 41)? Such a location makes some sense, because it lies close to the Jordan River. Yet this interpretation is not without difficulties, because the site of ancient Gilgal in the Jordan Valley is some thirty miles from the other mentioned sites—Mt. Gerizim and Mt. Ebal. Hence, some have looked for a site closer to Mt. Gerizim and Mt. Ebal, such as Kh. Ǧilǧiliye (G. A. Smith 1897: 253–54; Cogan and Tadmor 1988: 31; Tigay 1996: 116–17, 419), south of Tel el-Balaṭah (ancient Shechem), or Tel el-ʿUnuq (Zertal 1991),

---

76. So the MT (*lectio difficilior*). The LXX and SP read the singular ("oak") in conformity with Gen 12:6.
77. Some have contended that SP Gen 22:2 (the *Aqedah*) should be added to this list: "Go to the land of Mūra (ארץ המורה) and offer him [Isaac] as a burnt offering on one of the mountains I shall point out to you." By writing המורה, Mūra, and not Moriah (המריה; so the MT), the editors responsible for the SP purportedly allude to their version of Deut 11:30 אצל אלון מורא, "next to the oak of Mūra," מול שכם "opposite Shechem." There may be a connection, yet the situation is complex. Almost all SP MSS read המוראה, not המורה. In this respect, the lemma (המורה) of Shechem MS 6 (the base text of Tal 1994) is quite unusual. Moreover, the Samaritan reading tradition pronounces the term Ammūriyya (not Mora, as is often assumed) in Gen 22:2 and Mūra (not Mora, as is often assumed) in Deut 11:30. Thus, the most obvious and direct connections are among SP Gen 12:6 (מורא; pronounced Mūra); Exod 20:13ī (מורא; Mūra); Deut 5:17ī (מורא; Mūra); and Deut 11:30 (מורא; Mūra). For Samaritan midrashes, commenting on the possible textual interrelationships, see Kalimi (2002: 48–51).
78. The phrase is sometimes regarded as a gloss, but it appears in the MT, the LXX, and the SP and thus must be explained.

approximately 6 km east of Mt. Gerizim and Mt. Ebal.[79] It would seem quite possible that one of these lesser-known sites is in view, most probably Ğilğiliye, which preserves the ancient name and which some of the northern prophets presume to be located north of Bethel and south of Shechem (2 Kgs 2:1, 18; 4:38; Hos 4:15; Amos 4:4; 5:5; 9:15; 12:12; Wagenaar 2007).

Another option to explain the text's puzzling features is to revisit the locations of Mt. Gerizim and Mt. Ebal. If Gilgal is somewhere in the Jordan Valley, might Gerizim and Ebal actually be somewhere nearby? Such a proposition may seem far-fetched, given the topography of the Jordan Rift, but it was embraced by some early Jewish and Christian interpreters.[80] That the issue was debated already within the last centuries BCE can be seen in the localization of "the oak(s) of Moreh" in the addition of SP Deut 11:30 as "opposite Shechem" (מול שכם). Such an expansion of specification would not have occurred unless there was avid disagreement about the sites' locations.[81] The same sectarian plus (מול שכם) appears in both occurrences of the Samaritan version of the tenth commandment (SP Exod 20:13; Deut 5:17).

It would seem a radical move to relocate Gerizim and Ebal, but some early interpreters came to this conclusion based not only on the ambiguous evidence of Deut 11:30 but also on the specific instructions given to the Israelites in Deuteronomy 27. To that evidence we now turn. Following their presentation of the central collection of laws (Deut 12:2–26:19), the writers return to the topic of pan-Israelite ceremonies. The instructions are, however, much more elaborate and diverse than those given earlier (Deut 11:26–30), which consist primarily of the ritual

---

79. E. F. Campbell (2002: 43–46) argues that the site may be Kh. Ibn Nâṣir southwest of Gerizim.
80. See the discussions in *m.* 7:5; *t. Soṭah* 8:1–11; *b. Soṭah* 33b–34a; 35b–36a; *b. Sanh.* 44a; *y. Soṭah* 7:3; 21c; 29a–b. Eusebius (*On.* 64) and Jerome (*Liber locorum* 65–66) locate both sites (Mt. Gerizim and Mt. Ebal) in the Jordan Valley, but acknowledge that the Samaritans believe otherwise. See also Epiphanius *De xii gemmis* 184.9 (88); *Adv. haer.* 9.2.4; Procopius of Gaza *Comm. in Deuteronom. PG* 87.905, 908; Pummer 2002. The composers of the 6th-century CE Madaba map have it both ways, situating Mt. Gerizim and Mt. Ebal near Jericho and near Neapolis (Shechem). Donner (1992) argues that a slight preference for the latter location may be discerned in the larger letters used to designate these sites, but such a designation may simply mark the well-known locations. If so, the smaller letters used for the sites near Jericho would point viewers to the area visited by the Israelites after they crossed the Jordan.
81. Reading with the MT and the LXX (*lectio brevior*). The addition in the SP, attested neither in LXX nor in MT Deut 11:30, was later labeled by some rabbis as an unnecessary forgery (*y. Soṭah* 7.3; *b. Soṭah* 33b; *Sifre* Deut §56).

citations of blessings and curses on Mt. Gerizim and Mt. Ebal. The new directions may be summarized as follows:

1. On the day the Israelites cross the Jordan (והיה ביום אשר תעברו את־הירדן), they are to erect large stones, coat them with plaster, and write upon them "all the words of this Torah" (Deut 27:1–3).
2. When the Israelites cross the Jordan (והיה בעברכם את־הירדן), they are to "erect these stones about which I am commanding you this day" on Mt. Gerizim,[82] coat them with plaster, and "write very distinctly upon them all of the words of this Torah" (Deut 27:4, 8).
3. The Israelites are to build there an altar to Yhwh their God, an altar of unhewn stones (מזבח אבנים לא־תניף עליהם ברזל) upon which to present burnt offerings and offerings of well-being (Deut 27:5–7).
4. Having become "this day" the people of Yhwh, the Israelites are to heed the voice of Yhwh and follow all his commands and decrees (Deut 27:9–10).
5. Upon crossing the Jordan River (בעברכם את־הירדן), the tribes of Simeon, Levi, Judah, Issachar, Joseph, and Benjamin are to stand upon Mt. Gerizim to bless the people, while the tribes of Reuben, Gad, Asher, Zebulun, Dan, and Naphtali are to stand on Mt. Ebal to pronounce the curse (Deut 27:11–13).
6. The Levites are to proclaim loudly a series of twelve anathemas, which the people are to affirm (Deut 27:14–26).

First, a word about textual criticism. In Deut 27:4, I have read הרגריזים with the SP, Papyrus Giessen 19 (argar[i]zim; Tov 2001: 95), the Samareitikon (argarizim), and the OL in monte Garzin. The same reading, written in scriptio continua, בהרגרזים, has been found on a late-2nd- or 1st-century BCE DSS fragment of Deut 27:4b–6 (Charlesworth 2009). The MT (הר עיבל) and the LXX (orei Gaibal) read Mt. Ebal. That SP, a DSS witness, Papyrus Giessen, and OL agree in Deut 27:4 indicates that "Mt. Gerizim" is not a sectarian reading. The OL is clearly not a Samaritan-type textual tradition. Note that all traditions agree that the blessing is to be spoken on Mt. Gerizim (11:29; 27:11). As Nihan (2007b: 213) observes, "it

---

82. The name הרגרזי[ם], written in scriptio continua, is also attested at Masada in a late-1st-century BCE or early-1st-century CE papyrus fragment (Talmon 1999). Because the scriptio continua of Mt. Gerizim—הרגרז(י)ים—is found in a diversity of textual traditions, it does not automatically indicate Samari(t)an authorship (Pummer 1987a).

is entirely unlikely that Mount Ebal, which stands as the place for *curses* in v. 13, should be chosen for the erection of stones engraved with the Torah and the building of an altar as commanded in vv. 4–8." The MT reading of Mt. Ebal in Deut 27:4 probably represents a later Judean correction, perhaps in light of Josh 8:30–35 (McCarthy 2004; 2007: 122*–23*).[83]

As the above summary indicates, the text does not speak with one voice about where exactly the pan-Israelite ceremonies are to occur. Gilgal does not appear at all in this second set of instructions. Indeed, the initial instructions of Moses and the elders of Israel (27:1) are even more imprecise than those found earlier (11:29–30). Since Gerizim and Ebal are a significant distance inland from the Israelite camp on the other side of the Jordan River, it would pose a real challenge for travelers to reach the area of Shechem in a single day. The issue is not simply distance (about 30 miles by foot) but also the vertical climb (Jericho in the Cisjordan is approximately 161 ft above sea level, while Mt. Gerizim is 2,889 ft above sea level). To complicate matters, the instructions of v. 3 enjoin the Israelites to "inscribe all of the words of this Torah when you have crossed over (בעברך) to enter the land Yhwh is giving to you," suggesting that the Israelites are to act summarily after passing through the Jordan River.[84] Yet the text immediately goes on to mandate setting up the stones (את־האבנים האלה) on Mt. Gerizim and inscribing them there (v. 4). Hence one can understand why some early interpreters were inclined to relocate both Gerizim and Ebal to the Jordan Valley. In short, Deuteronomy presents variant injunctions about what the Israelites are to do upon crossing the Jordan River.

Most commentators have been inclined to think that our passages preserve vestiges of two different claims about where the ceremony is to occur, one in the Jordan Valley and one in the central hill country (e.g., Weinfeld 1991: 452–53). In this theory, Deuteronomy preserves different sources and hence competing claims about where the Israelites are to congregate. The occurrence of discrepant demands in close proximity

---

83. See also Dexinger 1977: 127–28; Kartveit 2009: 300–9; Dušek 2012a: 88–89. Ulrich (1994; 2012) plausibly argues on the basis of 4QJosh^a that both Gerizim and Ebal are secondary readings added to an originally briefer text (Deut 27:4), which left the site unnamed. In a later redaction, the site was specified as Mt. Gerizim (preserved in some MSS and the SP) and in a yet later redaction this site was changed to Mt. Ebal (preserved in the MT and most LXX witnesses).
84. The directions (27:3, 8, 26) presuppose the existence of Deuteronomy (or at least an earlier version thereof) as a preexisting entity. Cf. Deut 1:5; 4:8, 44; 17:18; 28:58, 61; 29:20; 28; 30:10; 31:9, 11, 12; 32:46.

generates, however, its own possibilities of interpretation. Already within antiquity, most readers interpreted the mention of different sites as indicating a succession of stops the Israelites were commanded to make on their journey inland. Such a two-stage implementation of the Deuteronomic instructions is reflected in MT and LXX Joshua. There, one ceremony is enacted at Gilgal, near Jericho, shortly after the Israelites cross the Jordan (Josh 4:19; 5:9–10), while another involving the construction of an altar occurs later as the Israelites suddenly appear in the central hill country (MT Josh 8:30–35).[85] The second account presupposes many, if not all, elements of the instructions in Deut 27:2–26 (van der Meer 2004: 504).

The second episode seems to have been incorporated, however, into Joshua at a late stage in the work's compositional history, as the ceremony's literary placement within the textual witnesses varies.[86] The LXX provides a variant textual location for the second ceremony (LXX Josh 9:2a–f), while in the fragmentary text of 4QJosh^a (Ulrich 1994, 1995), Joshua and the Israelite leaders conduct a commemorative rite earlier (at the end of Joshua 4) than that depicted in the MT (8:30–35) and the LXX (9:2a–f).[87] The witness of Josephus presents yet another scenario, positing a ceremony near Jericho immediately after the crossing of the Jordan involving the establishment of twelve stones from the twelve tribal leaders, the construction of an altar with sacrifices offered to God, and the celebration of Passover (*Ant.* 5.20–34). A later ceremony occurs at Shechem, involving the erection of the altar mandated by Moses (*Ant.* 4.305), the positioning of half the Israelite army on Gerizim (*Garizein*) and the other half on Ebal (*Hēbēl*), the offering of sacrifices, and the inscription of the curses upon the altar (*Ant.* 5.69–70; cf. *Ant.* 4.308).[88] The all-Israelite convocation only occurs, however, after the Israelites have subjugated the Gibeonites (*Ant.* 5.49–57; cf. Josh 9:1–27) and defeated a series of royal adversaries (*Ant.* 5.62–67; cf. Josh 10:1–12:24). In other words, the national celebration postdates the complete conquest

---

85. That the Israelites suddenly congregate in the area of Shechem (Josh 8:30–35) is puzzling, because Shechem was not yet conquered. In the narratives that follow, Gilgal remains the Israelite base of operations (9:6, 10:6–9; 14:6).
86. The sequence in 4QJosh^a may find a reflex in the testimony of Josephus (*Ant.* 5.16–20; Ulrich 1994), although Josephus's work also includes a later episode, situated at Shechem (*Ant.* 5.68–70), that self-reflectively refers back to Deut 27 (*Ant.* 4.305–8).
87. Although not necessarily including the building of an altar (van der Meer 2004: 511–14).
88. In contrast, Joshua writes a copy of the Torah (or Deuteronomy—so the LXX) on the altar stones (MT Josh 8:32; LXX Josh 9:2c).

of the land and predates the division of the land (*Ant.* 5.71–92; cf. Josh 13:1–21:40).

Because the Samaritan canon is limited to the five books of Moses, the Samaritans lack the book of Joshua in their scriptures. Nevertheless, it is interesting that one of the Samaritan Chronicles, the *Chronicon Samaritanum*, follows a modified outline of Josephus in portraying Israel's arrival in the land.[89] This chronicle speaks of the erection of twelve stones (but not an altar) at Ğalīl (Sam Josh 15) in conjunction with the communal singing of a celebratory hymn (Sam Josh 16) that recalls the Song of the Sea (Exod 15:1–18). Subsequent to the conquest of the entire land in a single year, a pan-Israelite feast occurs at "the blessed mountain" (Sam Josh 21).[90] There, Joshua offers sacrifices for the people before the land apportionment begins (Sam Josh 22).

Another medieval Samaritan chronicle, *Abū 'l Fatḥ*, follows, with some important variations, the broad outline found in MT Joshua. Having defeated the enemy at Hūta (*Abū 'l Fatḥ* 13,14–14,16; cf. Ai in Josh 8:1–29), Joshua builds an altar of stones at Mt. Gerizim, sacrifices there, and reads the Torah in its entirety with half the people facing Mt. Gerizim and the other half facing Mt. Ebal (*Abū 'l Fatḥ* 14,16). These two chronicles differ on numerous details, but they each depict two-stage ritual itineraries in the land, lack any sacrifices in the celebration at Gilgal, and highlight the offering of sacrifices on the altar Joshua constructed at Mt. Gerizim.[91] In this respect, medieval Samaritan interpreters follow the basic pattern advanced by their Jewish counterparts, but adjust certain important details to accommodate their own distinctive traditions, the most important of which is the unrivalled sanctity and status of Mt. Gerizim.

This discussion of the various early Jewish and medieval Samaritan explanations of Joshua's fulfillment of Deuteronomy's stipulations brings us back to Deuteronomy itself. Early interpreters could read basically the same texts and reach different conclusions about their significance. The textual evidence from MT and LXX Joshua, the DSS, and Josephus

---

89. Indeed, the *Chronicon Samaritanum* is also known to modern scholarship as the (Arabic) book of Joshua (Juynbol 1848; Crane 1890; Stenhouse 1989). It should be pointed out, however, that the work does not identify itself as the writing(s) of Joshua (Sam Josh 1).

90. Hence not a five-year conquest as in Josephus (*Ant.* 5.68; cf. Josh 14:7–10), and a sacrificial ceremony at Mt. Gerizim, not at Mt. Ebal (MT Josh 8:30; LXX Josh 9:2a; cf. Deut 27:4).

91. Whether these medieval works recall late antique Samaritan interpretations is unclear, because many early Samaritan literary works were evidently destroyed during the reign(s) of Hadrian and Commodus.

indicates that the implications and fulfillment of the relevant instructions in Deuteronomy were debated already within antiquity. The issue was not simply the location of the site of God's choosing, as critical a question as that might be, but also the locations and significance of the sacrificial rites the Israelites were commanded to conduct upon entering the land.

From an early Samarian perspective, the placement of the centralization instructions immediately following the instruction to pronounce the blessing on Mt. Gerizim and the curse on Mt. Ebal (11:29) was critical to grasping the force of the centralization injunctions. By comparison, Jerusalem is not explicitly mentioned in the Pentateuch.[92] The divine command to concentrate all legitimate sacrifice at a single central sanctuary of Yhwh's own choosing was intimately tied to Yhwh's command to invoke the divine blessing on Mt. Gerizim. The mention of Mt. Gerizim in Deut 11:29, just prior to the introduction of the centralization commands, reinforces by association the position of Mt. Gerizim as the divinely mandated central sanctuary. From such a northern perspective, literary proximity was a key to understanding the force of the centralization mandate. One statute is interpreted in the light of the other. The claim that Yhwh elected (בחר) the central sanctuary (SP) comported with the earlier set of commands given in Deut 11:29–30 indicating divine favor upon Mt. Gerizim. Both the instructions about journeying to a central location, involving sacrifices on a mandated altar, and the instructions about centralization, involving sacrifices on a mandated altar, were portrayed as national affairs, incumbent on the entire people. Both were sanctioned by the spoken (and written) word and not by an epiphany or angelophany (Rofé 2002: 100).[93]

---

92. The most likely referent for *šālēm* (Salem) in Gen 14:18 may be Jerusalem (if one construes *šālēm* as a hypocoristic; *HALOT* 1539b), but Jerusalem is not itself explicitly named. Cf. SP and *Sam. Tg.* Gen 14:18 (מלך שלם). In Ps 76:3 Salem appears parallel to *Zion* (see also *Tg. Ps.* 76:3), but LXX Ps 76:3 interprets *šālēm* as an adjective. The identity of Salem becomes an issue among the early interpreters. *ApGen* 22:13, Josephus (*Ant.* 1.180; *BJ* 6.438), and *Tg. Onq.*, *Tg. Neof.*, and *Tg. Ps.-J.* Gen 14:18 identify it with Jerusalem, but some early Christian interpreters speak of a place named Sālim (*HALOT* 1539b). LXX Gen 33:18 depicts Jacob traveling to "Salem, a city of Shechem" (*Salēm polin Sikimon*)—similarly, the presentation of SP (שלום עיר שכם) and Sam Tg. Gen 33:18 (שלם קרית שכם). The lemma of the MT *šālēm 'îr šekem* can be interpreted either as "safe [to] the city of Shechem" or "[to] Salem, the city of Shechem." Jubilees 30:1 reflects the former option: "Salem, which is east of Shechem" (cf. modern Sâlim on the flanks of Jebel el-Kebîr; E. F. Campbell 1991: 28–32, 112). Drawing on, yet going beyond, the traditions of the SP and LXX, Pseudo-Eupolemus asserts that Melchizedek was received by Abraham at the temple of Mt. Gerizim (Eusebius *Praep. Evang.* 9.17).

93. The best manner of divine communication was already debated in biblical times. Responding to Aaron and Miriam's questioning whether Yhwh speaks (*dibbēr*) through them

The supporters of the Jerusalem sanctuary could legitimately counter the pro-Mt. Gerizim arguments with formidable arguments of their own. To begin with, their shrine was much older than the shrine constructed on Mt. Gerizim in the mid-Persian period. Moreover, they could claim that the very wording of the altar command in Deut 27:5–7 was written in such a way as to correspond with the altar of unhewn stones legislation in Exod 20:24–26.[94] Given that the Deuteronomic legislation reuses, revises, and rewrites the legislation in Exodus within its own far-reaching reformation program (Ginsberg 1982; Levinson 1997), Judeans could understand the legislation in Deut 27:5–7 very differently. The altar mandated on Gerizim was the type of altar mandated in an earlier dispensation of divine law (Nihan 2007b; Schorch 2011).[95] At Mt. Sinai (MT Exod 20:24), Yhwh commanded the people to build an earthen altar (מזבח אדמה) "in every place (בכל המקום) at which I shall cause (אזכיר) my name to be remembered, I shall come to you and bless you." If Israelites decide to build an altar of stones, they must not do so with hewn stones (אתהן גזית), because "if you wield your chisel [literally, "sword"] upon it, you will profane it" (כי חרבך הנפת עליה ותחללה; Exod 20:25).

Because this earlier legislation allowed for multiple legitimate altars, it may be contrasted with the centralization legislation, which categorically allows for only one legitimate altar: "Be careful lest you present your burnt offerings at any place (בכל־מקום) that you happen to see, but rather at the place (כי אם־במקום) Yhwh will choose in one of your tribes—there you will present your burnt offerings and there you will

---

or only through Moses (Num 12:2), Yhwh pointedly declares that he speaks with his servant Moses "mouth to mouth" (*peh ʾel peh ʾădabbēr-bô*) and not through prophetic visions or dreams (Num 12:6–7; Achenbach 2003). One may compare how Gad's command to David to build an altar at the threshing floor of Araunah the Jebusite (2 Sam 24:18–25) to arrest the divinely imposed plague on Israel becomes in Chronicles an explicit warrant for the construction of the central sanctuary in Jerusalem (1 Chr 21:1–22:1; Knoppers 2004a: 742–69). The dispatch of fire from heaven to consume David's burnt offering (unique to 1 Chr 21:26) recalls the dispatch of fire from on high on the Tabernacle altar (Lev 9:24). David construes the miracle as a divine warrant for the creation of a permanent institution at that very spot (1 Chr 22:1). David presents burnt offerings and offerings of well-being; 2 Sam 24:26//1 Chr 21:26), the same offerings that appear in the altar injunctions of Exod 20:24 and Deut 27:6–7.

94. Or, as Nihan (2007b: 216) observes, "referring the Gerizim sanctuary to the altar law of Exodus 20 actually leaves entirely open the issue of the identity and location of the unique altar commanded by Deuteronomy 12, which could thus legitimately be claimed by both communities simultaneously."

95. Admittedly, the issue of altar construction and timing is a large one. See further Knoppers forthcoming a.

do all that I am commanding you" (Deut 12:13–14b).⁹⁶ In other words, Judeans could read the legislation of Deut 27:1–26 and conclude that this material manifestly applied to Israel's conduct upon entering the land and not to centralized worship at Yhwh's chosen site. Because the instructions pertained to Israelite behavior upon entering the land, they amounted to a unique set of injunctions pertaining to a single historic Israelite convocation. That the Israelites were to adhere to Covenant Code legislative precedent in building the Mt. Gerizim altar meant that (from a Judean point of view) the Mt. Gerizim altar was explicitly not the single altar called for in Deuteronomy's centralization mandate. The literary proximity between the injunction presented before the centralization legislation (11:29) and the centralization legislation itself (12:1–13:1) suggested a disjunction between the two. Hence, Judeans could read the same legislation as Samarians did and arrive at diametrically different conclusions about what the legislation meant.

The Judean interpretation is made explicit in the later work of Josephus. When explaining Moses's instructions in Deut 27:5–7, Josephus (*Ant.* 4.307) stresses that recording the blessings and curses was meant to ensure that "their lesson might never be lost through time" (ὡς μηδέποτε ἐκλιπεῖν τὴν μάθησιν αὐτῶν ὑπὸ τοῦ Χρόνου). Yet the presentation of burnt offerings and other sacrifices on the altar was to be an exceptional event, not to be repeated, "for that would not be lawful" (οὐ γὰρ εἶναι νόμιμον; *Ant.* 4.308). That Josephus felt compelled, however, to offer such a qualification indicates that he recognized an ambiguity in the text.

The Samarians could respond to the Judean counterarguments with counterarguments of their own. The relationships among the Exodus altar legislation (Exod 20:24–25), the central altar legislation (Deut 12:13–14), and the Mt. Gerizim altar legislation (Deut 27:5–7) could be understood differently. The relevant centralization decrees (Deut 12:5–7, 11–14, 18–19, 26–27) do not address precisely how "the altar of Yhwh your God" (12:27) is to be constructed. The authors speak of various sacrifices, but they do not specify the altar's mode of construction. The Samarians could thus read the altar of unhewn stones legislation of Exod 20:24–26 as setting an authoritative precedent for how one should construe the centralized altar legislation of Deuteronomy 12. The latter should be interpreted in light of the former. Indeed, the later legislation (27:5–7), inasmuch as

---

96. So the MT. Some MSS, witnesses to the SP, and a marginal gloss to *Tg. Neof.* reflect בכל־המקום, "in every place."

it specifies an altar of unhewn stones, could be understood as an explicit reaffirmation of the Exodus regulations.

Nevertheless, it cannot be denied that the centralization legislation of Deuteronomy 12 both cites and carefully rewrites the older altar legislation in the Covenant Code (Levinson 1997). Even if one allowed that the central altar (Deut 12:27) could be constructed of unhewn stones (Exod 20:24), the issue of the multiple altars allowed in the Exodus legislation remained. To maintain that the Mt. Gerizim altar (Deut 27:5–7) did not conflict with the legislation authorizing a centralized Israelite altar does not entail that the Mt. Gerizim altar was the centralized Israelite altar called for earlier in Deuteronomy. On the contrary, the altar of Deut 27:5–7 could be understood simply as one instantiation of the altar legislation presented in Exodus.

That Samarian scribes realized this ambiguity and disagreed with Judean interpretations may be seen in the later sectarian changes made in the Exodus altar law (20:24) within the SP. Whereas the MT reads: "In every place (בכל המקום) at which I shall cause (אזכיר) my name to be remembered, I shall come to you and bless you," the SP reads: "In the place (במקום) at which I have caused (אזכרתי) my name to be remembered, there (שמה) I shall come to you and bless you."[97] The SP formulation in Exodus effectively presupposes centralization. In so doing, it all but collapses a critical distinction between the two laws. In both cases, the SP version allows for only one altar "at the place" (במקום; Exod 20:24; Deut 12:5, 11, 14, 18, 21, 26). Given this correlation, the Deuteronomic altar replicates the Exodus altar. That continuity allows in turn for the Mt. Gerizim altar of Deuteronomy 27 to be understood as consistent with both earlier pieces of legislation. In the end, all three point to the same reality.

The slight but highly significant SP reworking of Exod 20:24 is even more far-reaching in that it points the reader back to Abram's construction of an altar at Shechem upon his arrival in the land of Canaan. The SP indicates by allusion to Abram's altar at the "place of Shechem" (מקום שכם), following his arrival in the land of Canaan (Gen 12:6–8), that Gerizim had been favored by the deity from ancestral times (Tov 2001: 95; Levinson 2008). In the context of the SP, there is, therefore, a

---

97. The syntax of the SP *Vorlage* likely resembled that of the LXX in this case (ἐν παντὶ τόπῳ οὗ ἐὰν ἐπονομάσω τὸ ὄνομά μου ἐκεῖ καὶ ἥξω πρὸς σὲ καὶ εὐλογήσω σε) and thus varied slightly from the MT (Wevers 1990: 319). Nevertheless, the general point stands.

line of clear continuity from Abram's altar at Shechem (Gen 12:6) and the altar legislation given at Mt. Sinai (Exod 20:24) to the centralization legislation pronounced upon the Steppes of Moab (Deuteronomy 12) and the Gerizim altar called for in the convocation legislation of Deuteronomy 27. With each instance, a stronger case is built for the centrality of Mt. Gerizim in Israelite law and lore. Nevertheless, the changes made to SP Exod 20:24 would not have been deemed advisable, much less necessary, had not the issues of interpretation and application been acutely debated within antiquity. The very fact that Exod 20:24 was modestly, but effectively, rewritten strongly suggests that the Pentateuchal altar laws had become a highly contentious issue in Judean-Samarian relations.

The same controversy illumines the Judean textual change manifest in Deut 27:4. The textual alteration, however slight, had major ramifications for interpretation and practical application. By reading Mt. Ebal (and not Mt. Gerizim), Judean scribes effectively eliminated a linchpin in the Samarian line of argumentation. The altar the Israelites were to construct upon entering the land was located on the mountain on the northern side of the Shechem valley opposite the mountain on the southern side of the Shechem valley, where the Samarians thought it was supposed to be located. To be sure, the blessing was still to be pronounced on Mt. Gerizim and the curse was still to be pronounced on Mt. Ebal (Deut 11:29–30). But from the perspective of the revised text of Deut 27:4 (MT, followed by most LXX witnesses), the Samarians had constructed their altar (and temple) at the wrong place.

We have seen that the Samarian and Judean communities could (and did) interpret the ambiguities in the Deuteronomic centralization legislation to the advantage of their own cultic centers. In Samarian circles, the literary proximity of the instructions given about Mt. Gerizim to the centralization legislation was deemed to be no accident. Given that the divine mandate for cultic centralization followed the divine mandate to profess blessings on Mt. Gerizim and preceded the divine mandate to inscribe the Torah on large stones at Mt. Gerizim, Mt. Gerizim enjoyed pride of place in Samarian interpretation. The construction of a temple on Mt. Gerizim was thus understood to be congruent with the divine demand for cultic purity and cultic unity. If Israelites were to "heed the voice of Yhwh and follow all his commands and decrees" (Deut 27:9–10), they were obliged to accord Gerizim a pivotal status in their national life. From this perspective, the Deuteronomic legislation conferred a stamp of divine authority upon the sacred mount. Because the repeated mention of Mt. Gerizim within Deuteronomy was considered to be a hermeneutical key to understanding Deuteronomy, the centralization legislation could be construed as consistent with earlier cultic legislation within the Pentateuch. Reading Deuteronomy in this manner confirmed the Samarian belief that the Pentateuch was more than a collection of books. The Torah was, rather, a self-contained, self-consistent, and unified entity.

By contrast, one can readily understand how Judeans could attend to the same centralization command and reach different conclusions. Because the altar called for in the Gerizim instructions (Deut 27:5–7) was consistent with the type of altar called for in the multiple-altar legislation of the Covenant Code (Exod 20:25–26), it was deemed not to be the single altar demanded in the centralization legislation. However important the corporate foundation ceremonies were to Israel's initial life in the land, the national ceremonies did not mark either of the sites associated with these ceremonies as "the site" to be chosen by Yhwh.

Interpreting the Pentateuch within the context of a larger Enneateuch, Judeans understood the Pentateuch to be a fundamental part of Israel's ancient story from the time of its beginnings to its existence in the land. From this vantage point, they naturally moved from the stories about Israel on the Steppes of Moab (Deuteronomy), the ritual crossing of the Jordan, the encampment and erection of twelve stones at Gilgal (Josh 5:19), and the establishment of Israel in the land (Joshua-Judges) to the stories about the consolidation of the united kingdom under David and Solomon (Samuel-Kings). From this vantage point, the very vagueness of the centralization formula—"the place Yhwh will choose"—from within one of Israel's tribal territories (MT Deut 12:14) is a clue that the precise location of the central sanctuary is not to be found within Deuteronomy. Rather, the legislation points forward to a time when Israel will finally enter its allotted rest (אל־המנוחה ואל־הנחלה; Deut 12:9). Attaining that state is predicated on Yhwh granting Israel rest from all of its surrounding enemies (והניח לכם מכל־איביכם מסביב) with the result that the people will reside securely (וישבתם־בטח) within the land (Deut 12:10). Not just entry into the land but also peace in the land is at stake.

Admittedly, the text does not specify a time frame when all of Israel's enemies will be vanquished and the people will enjoy security within their allotted inheritance. But the legislation's implication seems to be that the achievement of this condition is a precursor to the revelation of the chosen sanctuary itself.[98] Only with the establishment of such a sanctuary does the centralization legislation become fully operational and, as a result, the Israelites are obliged to bring all of their burnt offerings, sacrifices, contributions, and votive offerings to the place for Yhwh's name (Deut 12:11). Judeans could read virtually the same Pentateuch as the Samarians did and reach markedly different conclusions about the meaning of the centralization legislation.

Conclusions

The textual and literary evidence from within the Pentateuch shared by Judeans and Samarians indicates that the Pentateuch was ultimately a compromise document, a work that could (and did, and does) function as scripture for both communities. It would not have been difficult for the framers of Deuteronomy (or the editors of the Pentateuch) to clarify Yhwh's choice if they wanted to do so. The ambiguous phraseology in the centralization legislation in which the site of Yhwh's own choosing goes unnamed was a critical component of the Judean-Samarian compromise. Such imprecise language could be (and was, and is) interpreted differently by each group. The lack of definition in this critical edict allowed for multiple readings and sustained the notion that both Samarians and Judeans belonged to a larger people called Israel. Both societies were bound by the same authoritative scriptures, even if they understood some key texts in these common writings differently.

Ironically, a critical factor in the demise of the myth of common identity was the eventual realization of the cultic unity and cultic purity commanded in Deuteronomy.[99] When John Hyrcanus destroyed the Mt. Gerizim temple in 112–111 BCE, he ended the existence of the chief Yahwistic competitor to the Jerusalem sanctuary within the land.[100] In so

---

98. This is a point of contention within the Deuteronomistic work itself. Did Israel achieve this peace in the time of Joshua (Josh 11:23; 21:43–45; Josephus *Ant.* 7.342; cf. Josh 13:1b–6; 23) or in the time of Solomon (1 Kgs 5:18; 6:1)? The latter interpretation dominates the Deuteronomistic depiction of Solomon's reign, while the former interpretation becomes a major point of emphasis in the Samaritan chronicles (Knoppers 2012b).
99. The scriptural precedent for this corporate violence was likely the centralization legislation in Deuteronomy and the northern cultic campaigns found in Kings and Chronicles (see chapters 3–4 in this book), rather than Deut 13:13–17 (Magen 2008c: 25–29), because the latter punishes seditious agitation involving worshiping other gods. There is no evidence that I know of indicating that the Yahwistic Samarians at Mt. Gerizim worshiped foreign deities.
100. The Aaronides were not above officiating at more than one Judean temple even in late times. After the Maccabees claimed the supreme priestly office in Judah, an Aaronide priest

doing, he enforced one important understanding of cultic centralization. Given the paradox of cultic diversity that characterized previous centuries, his actions were probably hailed by his supporters.[101] Indeed, the archaeological remains attesting to the extensive incineration of the temple site suggest that there was no intent to resettle the site or to rebuild it (Magen 2008c: 25–28). Remnants of a large public building built at the site, probably the fortress alluded to by Josephus (*Ant.* 14.100), have been excavated on the northern face of Mt. Gerizim underneath the steps leading up to the (later) Roman temple (Magen 2009: 257–60 [Figs. 6.26, 6.29–6.30]).[102] On the basis of stratigraphy, pottery, numismatic finds, and glyptics, Magen (2009: 260–61 [pl. 54]) dates this fortress to the 1st century BCE. A Hasmonean garrison remained at the site until the time of Alexander Jannaeus or some time thereafter (Magen 2008c: 29). Similarly, in later Herodian times, the Samaritans were evidently still forbidden from reconstructing their central sanctuary. It may be that John Hyrcanus and his successors thought that the Samarians as Israelites would become Judean (religiously) in the absence of the Mt. Gerizim shrine (S. Schwartz 2001: 17–18), and probably some did.[103]

The pendulum had thus swung entirely toward Judah. Any sort of balance of power between the two units was gone. If Samaria was the dominant power in relationship to Judah during the Neo-Babylonian and part of the Persian period, the opposite was now true. With a Maccabean leader in charge of a greater Judah whose size was beginning to approach the legendary dimensions of the Davidic-Solomonic kingdom, there was no longer any need to contemplate points of strategic cooperation with Judah's northern neighbor. Given that a succession of Maccabean leaders, such as Jonathan (152 BCE) and Simon (143 BCE), laid claim to the office of high priest (1 Macc 14:41), the relationship between the cultic

---

(probably Onias IV), a legitimate claimant to the high priestly line, founded and led a Judean temple in Leontopolis, Egypt. The statements of Josephus about this temple are not entirely clear or self-consistent (*Ant.* 12.387–88, 397; 13.62–73, 285; 20.36; *BJ* 1.33; 7.420–36; VanderKam 2004: 214–22; Capponi 2007).

101. In later rabbinic times, the anniversary of the Mt. Gerizim temple's destruction was still considered to be a day during which mourning was forbidden (*b. Yoma* 7).

102. Another garrison may have later been stationed at Ma'abarta at the foot of the mountain (Magen 2009: 29–30, 355).

103. The two groups still shared much in common, and if Josephus's assertions (*Ant.* 11.302–3, 340, 346–47) about interrelated priesthoods, interrelated families, and (former) Judeans residing in Shechem are well-founded, it is plausible that at least some eventually resorted to the Jerusalem temple. The two sanctuaries were, after all, similar (Josephus *Ant.* 11.321–24; 13.256).

authorities in Jerusalem and the Aaronide priests in Samaria undoubtedly also changed.[104] For John Hyrcanus, exterminating the Mt. Gerizim temple not only fulfilled the centralization mandate (Deut 12:1–13:1) but also consolidated political, sacerdotal, and economic power in Jerusalem. The reduction in size of some Samaritan settlements and the absence of settlement at others (e.g., Qedumim, Kh. Samara, El-Ḥirbe) in the 1st century BCE has been tied to the negative effects of the Maccabean conquest (Magen 2008c: 57).

Yet the cultic, political, and economic achievement of an unrivalled, single Yahwistic shrine within the land of Israel came at a significant cost. The actions of Hyrcanus designed to realize a certain Judean understanding of cultic unity and cultic purity exacerbated divisions among the populace he ruled. The military and religious victory won by Hyrcanus resulted in tremendous Samaritan resentment of and alienation from their Judean neighbors. Having lost the "place for the name of Yhwh" they revered, Samaritan scribes sought to enshrine its unrivalled status in the very Pentateuch they shared with Judeans. The Samaritan sectarian additions, although they represent only a thin layer of small changes, new readings, and new texts, based, as we have seen, on texts appearing elsewhere in the Pentateuch, effectively created a new edition of the Pentateuch that differed from the Jewish Pentateuch in a number of critical respects. By including Mt. Gerizim in a revised version of the "ten words," Samarian scribes ensured that their recently destroyed central shrine was indelibly and perpetually enshrined within the scriptures they held dear.

This literary achievement also came at a cost. By intervening in the texts they revered, Samaritan scribes effectively changed the very texts they considered sacred. In their own conception, they may have been removing ambiguities and rendering explicit what they thought that the Pentateuch meant in the first place. Indeed, the practice of introducing alterations and conflations within the text was, as we have seen, nothing new. Nevertheless, the distinctively Samarian additions to the books of Moses effectively distanced these texts from those of their Judean counterparts. The thin stratum added to the Torah may have been designed, in part, to expose, if not disallow, the pro-Jerusalem interpretations of

---

104. The Maccabees claimed Aaronic descent through Jehoiarib (יהויריב), who enjoyed a privileged place in the Chronistic system of twenty-four priestly courses (1 Chr 24:7; 1 Macc 2:1; Knoppers 2004a). By contrast, "Joiarib" (יויריב) appears near the end of the list in Neh 12:12–21 (v. 19).

their Judean peers, but the result was that Samarians and Judeans no longer shared a common set of virtually identical scriptures. The creation of a unique SP thus created its own set of social, historical, and religious problems among Samarians and Judeans.

By the same token, the small Judean textual change of Mt. Gerizim to Mt. Ebal (Deut 27:4) effectively removed a major source of the Samarian authentication of their central sanctuary. The Samarians could still argue, of course, that Mt. Gerizim was "the place" (המקום) repeatedly alluded to in the central sanctuary formulae found in Deuteronomy, but they would have to do so (if they resorted to the Judean Pentateuch) without drawing a direct link between the centralization commands (Deuteronomy 12) and the altar commands (Deuteronomy 27), directing Israelite conduct in the land. The basis of "mutual respect and fraternal interchange" (Purvis 1986) between Judeans and Samarians was thus now gone. Paradoxically, the texts of what became the Jewish and Samaritan Pentateuchs became mutually distinct documents. The two works still shared a tremendous amount of material in common, but on the critical question of the central sanctuary mandated in Deuteronomy the two no longer shared a common text. The very Pentateuch that formerly united the two communities now came to divide them.

If one of the marks of what distinguishes a Samaritan from a Yahwistic Samarian, on the one hand, and from a Yahwistic Judean, on the other hand, is a distinctive set of scriptures, then the rise of the Samaritan Pentateuch with its thin layer of unique theological readings is a pivotal event in the history of Samaritan-Jewish relations. But there are, of course, a number of other distinguishing characteristics that come to define the "Guardians" (= שומרים) of the Torah, as the Samaritans prefer to be called.[105] These include the delimitation of the canon to the five books of Moses, the belief in the exalted status and uniqueness of Moses as a prophet (and the concomitant rejection of the prophets and the prophetic books in the Jewish Tanakh), the belief in the unity of God (monotheism, transcendence, self-sufficiency, constancy, eternity, power, justice, mercy, etc.), the practice of their own calendar, and the belief in a day of divine vengeance and recompense (J. Macdonald 1964). Hence, one should not think of Samaritanism and Judaism as two separate but

---

105. This interpretation of שומרים is already attested in the time of Origen (*Comm. in Joh.* 20.35.312; *Hom. in Ez.* 9.1) and was known by Epiphanius ("Φύλακες"; *Panarion* 9.1; Pummer 2002: 7–8, 123; 2009: 4–7).

related religions defined simply by their variant Pentateuchs. Such a stance would be anachronistic and reductive, effectively defining each group by the scripture it does or does not hold. There are many important developments in the course of each community in later centuries that affected their formative beliefs and practices. Indeed, some of these developments demonstrate, as we shall see in the next chapter, continued links between the two. But the emergence of two distinctive Pentateuchs is definitely an integral part of the larger picture.

The brief discussion about acute estrangement in Maccabean times brings us back to our analysis of earlier times. Only by appreciating the close ties that grew between the two communities during previous eras can one explain how they became so similar in belief and practice. To put it somewhat differently, accounting for how two such similar groups as the Samaritans and Jews became alienated from one another during the Maccabean and Roman periods involves explaining how the two were so closely related in the first place. The solution to this puzzle is to be found in the Assyrian, Neo-Babylonian, Persian, and Hellenistic periods.

8

An Absolute Breach?

"JEWS DO NOT share things in common with Samaritans" (John 4:9). This comment by the author (or more likely by a later editor) illumines the Samaritan woman's quizzical response to Jesus's personal request: "Why do you, a Jew, ask a drink from me, a woman of Samaria?"[1] At the beginning of this book, we discussed how the story of Jesus's encounter with the Samaritan woman near the historic location of Jacob's Well near Shechem plays on the highly fraught relations between Jews and Samaritans in the 1st century CE. Although both groups claimed the patriarch Jacob (Israel) as their ancestor, the two did not necessarily view Jacob/Israel as the eponymous ancestor of the other group. Paradoxically, the relationship to Jacob was (or became) an exclusive one, at least from a Jewish perspective.[2] From such a vantage point, the Jews and the Samaritans were neither fellow Israelites nor coreligionists. This meant that the two peoples had now become keen competitors, laying claim to the same heritage in ancient Israel.

Yet, as we have seen in previous chapters, the mutual animosity marking relations at the turn of the era had not always characterized interactions between the two groups. There was, in fact, much that Yahwistic Judeans and Yahwistic Samarians shared in common during earlier periods of Israelite and Judean history in spite of some important differences between them. Their languages were nearly identical and their material

---

1. The comment is not found in some important textual witnesses (chapter 1, n. 1).
2. There is an important difference in the categorization of the other between the two groups. Samaritans regard Jews as bona fide Israelites (descendants of the patriarch Judah) and thus neither as foreigners nor as converts (Knoppers 2012b). From a Samaritan perspective, the differences between the two groups have to do with other things (scriptures, central sanctuary, etc.).

cultures, beliefs, and religious rites were quite similar.[3] Both communities had cooperated to some extent in composing and editing a common corpus of foundational religious literatures (the Pentateuch). Both groups acknowledged, albeit in different ways, that their priesthoods shared a common progenitor (Aaron). Both had come to embrace the Deuteronomic doctrine of cultic centralization—the abolition of all non-Yahwistic sanctuaries in the land and the localization of Yahwistic sacrifice at only one divinely designated cultic site—even if they strongly differed as to precisely where that centralized system of sacrifices was to occur (Mt. Gerizim vs. Mt. Zion). Both groups became international in nature, with diasporic communities in other lands. To serve the needs of Jews and Samaritans during Hellenistic times, in particular those expatriates residing in the Egyptian diaspora, the Pentateuch was translated into Greek (Joosten forthcoming).[4] Both neighboring areas in Palestine were forced to endure foreign occupation over the course of several centuries by the same international empires. In facing the challenges of working with alien authorities, it sometimes made sense for leaders in the two subprovinces to find common cause with one another. In late Hellenistic and Roman times, both groups had to come to terms with a new set of challenges, namely, how best to deal with large groups of non-Jews and non-Samaritans residing within their ancestral territories.

This historical pattern of strategic interaction and elite cooperation was increasingly tested, however, in the 2nd century BCE, when the power dynamics obtaining in earlier times became increasingly obsolete. After the Maccabees gained power, gradually expanded their holdings to cover much of the southern Levant, took over the Jerusalem high priesthood, and eliminated the northern Israelite sanctuary at Mt. Gerizim, relations between the two groups soured considerably. In other words, it was not the circumstances surrounding the construction of the

---

3. On the dialectal differences between northern Israelite Hebrew and Judean Hebrew, see recently Rendsburg 1990, 1991a, 1991b, 2002.

4. The pan-Israelite identity of the Septuagint is evident in the 2nd century BCE pseudepigraphic *Letter of Aristeas*, which depicts the work's creation as stemming from the labors of six elders from each of the twelve tribes (lines 32, 39, 45–50; Bartlett 1985: 11–34). As previously noted (chapter 7), the *Letter of Aristeas* is not generally regarded as genuine, but it is important to recognize the manner in which authors of this literary fiction defend the translation of the Pentateuch in a diasporic setting. As Joosten (forthcoming) observes, the fragments of the *Samareitikon* attest to how the Septuagintal translation employed by Samaritan writers was later adapted to conform to the particular features of the Samaritan Pentateuch. For a somewhat different view, see Pummer (1998b).

Mt. Gerizim temple but rather its destruction centuries later that embittered the Samaritans against their Judean neighbors. Given that the Samaritans were not allowed to rebuild their central sanctuary under either the Hasmoneans or their successors (whether Jewish or Roman), the demise of their temple remained a divisive issue for many generations to come.

The rise of a distinctive Samaritan Pentateuch, with its thin layer of unique theological readings, created a further divide between Samaritans and Jews, because the two communities no longer shared a virtually identical set of common scriptures. Within both versions of the "ten words" in the Samaritan Pentateuch, the final commandment explicitly mandates honoring Mt. Gerizim (SP Exod 20:13[א–י]; Deut 5:17[א–ח]). Given the importance of the "ten words" in both early Jewish and Samaritan tradition, as a brief summation or representation of the Torah, such a discrepancy between the two Pentateuchs could hardly be ignored. The promulgation of distinctive Jewish and Samaritan Torahs thus became an additional point of conflict between the two rival communities.

It would be tempting, then, to conclude this book by pointing to a complete breakdown of relations between Samaritans and Jews during the first few centuries CE, resulting in self-enforced isolation, deep-seated hatred, and open conflict. Such a conclusion would not be totally unfounded, because it finds some literary support in Roman, Jewish, and Judeo-Christian sources dating to the 1st and 2nd centuries CE. Indeed, we shall look, albeit briefly, at some examples to illustrate this history of worsening relations. Yet it would be misleading, I would argue, to conclude from this increasing alienation that the two communities followed wholly divergent paths in the centuries that followed. Having summarized some evidence for mounting polarization in early Roman times, I shall complicate this general picture by pointing to long-range material evidence for ongoing engagement between some members of the two groups. Such evidence hardly negates the basic supposition of mutual distrust and hostility, but it does caution against characterizing this era as reflecting simply a historical process of self-enforced isolation and religious dissimilation. The widely held view of an absolute breach between members of the two communities during Roman and Byzantine times goes beyond the available evidence by presuming what it needs to prove, namely, that the two groups were self-contained and unitary entities, which each went their separate ways.

I. Catalysts toward Deteriorating Relations in Early Roman Times

There are some fascinating indications of ill-will in Samaritan-Jewish history during Roman times. Space constraints do not permit my providing a full history, but the following examples derived from literary sources should suffice to make the larger point.[5] Josephus relates an episode in the early 1st century CE, demonstrating antagonism between the neighboring Jewish and Samaritan communities in Palestine. During the administration of the prefect Coponius (6–9 CE; Josephus *BJ* 2.117), certain Samaritans entered Jerusalem surreptitiously (ἄνδρες Σαμαρεῖται κρύφα εἰς Ἱεροσόλυμα ἐλθόντες διάρριψιν), gained access to the temple before the start of the Passover festival, and scattered human bones along the colonnade of the sanctuary (Josephus *Ant.* 18.29–30). Thereafter, the priests took measures to protect the sanctuary precincts and banned everyone from the temple. It is not clear what this interdiction exactly meant (cf. *m. Tamid* 1.1).[6] Presumably, security measures at the Jerusalem temple were tightened.[7] In any event, the episode points to the animosity felt toward Judaism's central shrine by Samaritans at a time when their central shrine no longer stood.

A clearly negative sentiment stemming from the party opposite appears in the Gospel of Matthew. The commission Jesus delivers to his twelve disciples explicitly commands them to travel no "path among the Gentiles" (εἰς ὁδὸν ἐθνῶν) and not to enter any "town of the Samaritans" (εἰς πόλιν Σαμαριτῶν; Matt 10:5).[8] Rather, the disciples are enjoined by their master to go to "the lost sheep of the house of Israel" (πρὸς τὰ πρόβατα τὰ ἀπολωλότα οἴκου Ἰσραήλ; Matt 10:6). In this mandate, the Samaritans are unambiguously excluded from membership in Israel.

---

5. One major question, for instance, concerns Samaritan (non)participation in the Second Jewish War, the Bar Kochba revolt (132–35 CE). The literary evidence is not nearly as abundant as one would like, and the issues are complex (Hall 1989; Mendels 1992; S. Schwartz 2001; Goodman 2008; Magen 2009).
6. There may be a disturbance in the text (Feldman 1965: 27). A similar type of story appears in the medieval *Chronicon Samaritanum* (Sam Josh 47). Similarly, *Abū 'l Fatḥ* 122,154–123,156.
7. The ban might suggest that Yahwistic Samarians were not hitherto forbidden from approaching the temple precincts (Montgomery 1907: 85), but, given the fact that the Samaritans entered Jerusalem by stealth, such access cannot be assumed (Crown 1991: 40).
8. The statement is unparalleled in the other New Testament Gospels. Each of the New Testament Gospels that mention the Samaritans (Mark does not) approaches them in a distinctive way. The topic goes beyond the scope of this chapter.

Jesus has come to proclaim good news to his fellow Jews. Indeed, Jesus prohibits the disciples from journeying to any Samaritan settlement.[9] Nevertheless, in addressing the ethnic diversity of his day, Jesus does not unreservedly equate the Samaritans with the Gentiles. In the Matthean categorization of the other, the Samaritans are a *tertium quid*—neither Jews nor Gentiles, but rather something in between.

Josephus relates another incident during the procuratorship of Ventidius Cumanus (ca. 48–52 CE) that further kindled hatred between Samaritans and Jews. This particular conflict initially involved Samaritans and Galilean Jews. Late in Cumanus's tenure, some Samaritans attacked and killed a festal pilgrim from Galilee at Gēma (biblical ʿēn-gannîm; Josh 19:21; modern Jenin).[10] Incited by what Josephus derisively calls "the brigands" (οἱ λῃσταί), some Judeans retaliated by raiding a series of villages in the border area of Akrabatene (modern Aqraba), massacring their inhabitants, and setting the villages on fire (Josephus *BJ* 2.234–35; *Ant.* 20.118).[11] With Cumanus slow to respond, Jerusalemite leaders intervened on their own, donning sackcloth and ashes, counseling self-discipline, and urging restraint, lest the situation degenerate into outright civil war (Josephus *BJ* 2.236–38).[12] That they felt it necessary to resort to such extraordinary measures provides one indication of how concerned they were about the political troubles afflicting their land.

The narration of Josephus indicates that the Judean populace was itself very divided, with some elements fomenting rebellion against the Roman authorities and others warning against the destructive consequences of insurrection. Nevertheless, by this point conditions had deteriorated

---

9. So also when a Canaanite woman from the district of Tyre and Sidon begs him for help, Jesus responds by insisting that he has come only to save the lost sheep of Israel (Matt 15:21–24). Only in the so-called "great commission," delivered during Jesus's last postresurrection appearance, is the disciples' mandate extended to apply to "all the nations" (πάντα τὰ ἔθνη; Matt 28:19).

10. So Josephus (*BJ* 2.231–33; cf. *Ant.* 20.118 Γιναῆς). The later account of Josephus inflates the scale of the incident at the Samaritans' expense and accuses the Samaritans of bribing Cumanus (*Ant.* 20.118–19). But the same account also accuses Cumanus of marching with the *Sebastenoi* or *cohors Augusta Sebastenorum* (a cavalry unit stationed at Caesarea and Jerusalem, who originally were Herod's troops; *Ant.* 19.365; cf. σπείρης Σεβαστῆς in Acts 27:1) against the Jews, killing many (*Ant.* 20.122). Josephus's *Antiquitates judaicae* is generally more negative toward the Samaritans than is his earlier *Bellum judaicum* (Cohen 1979).

11. The statement of Tacitus (*Ann.* 12.54) that Marcus Antonius Felix was already procurator of Samaria at this time is probably an error. Felix was procurator of Judea, including Samaria, 52/53–55 (Josephus *BJ* 2.247; *Ant.* 20.137–38). He succeeded Ventidius Cumanus, who had governed Judea (and Samaria and the Galilee) in 48–52.

12. In the later account (*Ant.* 20.123), the mediation by the Jerusalemite leaders occurs after Cumanus's slaughter of some Jews.

considerably, negatively affecting relations between the Jews (or segments thereof) and their close neighbors. Intermittent hostilities between the Jews and the Samaritans continued in the years to come (Josephus *BJ* 2.238; *Ant.* 20.120–24). The Roman historian Tacitus (*Ann.* 12.54) comments that the two long-feuding peoples—the Jews and the Samaritans—were now less restrained than ever in acting upon their enmity, because of the common contempt they felt for their foreign rulers. Indeed, for a time local Roman authorities found it convenient to play the two groups off against one another, all the while profiting from the material proceeds of the internecine Jewish and Samaritan raids (Tacitus *Ann.* 12.54).

We have been discussing some examples of Jewish-Samaritan tensions in the Roman period. A major issue in understanding the failing state of Jewish-Samaritan relations involves Samaritan participation, or lack thereof, in the two Jewish Wars (66–73 CE and 132–35 CE).[13] One might initially think that the Great Revolt of 66 CE would leave Samaria relatively unscathed, because the hostilities involved a Jewish uprising against the Roman authorities. Yet things are rarely that simple. The province of Judea covered an area that included Judea proper, Samaria, and Idoumea (Josephus *Ant.* 17.317–20).[14] As such, the province encompassed a good part of the former Maccabean and Herodian kingdoms. This is an important point, because no matter how hostile elements of the two groups became toward one another, they remained part of the same geopolitical entity for over a century.[15] This meant that whether the Samaritans and Jews liked it or not, their fates were to some extent intertwined. Considering that the Samaritans were part of the larger Roman province of Judea, shared many beliefs with the Jews, and adhered to many rites that paralleled Jewish practices, did the Romans carefully distinguish between Samaritans and Jews? Could they do so? Historically, it may be unwise to draw an unqualified distinction between the two.[16]

---

13. The latter is especially difficult to reconstruct in Samaritan-Jewish relations (Hall 1989; Mendels 1992; S. Schwartz 1993).
14. Prior to the time of Herod, Samaria was for a time evidently part of the larger province of Syria.
15. The province lasted until the end of the Second Jewish War (135 CE). At the conclusion of this conflict, the Romans created a new province, named Syria Palaestina (135–390 CE), combining Roman Judea with Roman Syria.
16. Before the time of Constantine and with the exception of reports such as that of Origen about the Roman ban on bodily mutilation (= circumcision) being lifted for Jews in the reign of Antoninus Pius (138–61 CE), but not for Samaritans (*Cels.* 2.13; Pummer 2002: 56–57), Roman officialdom seems largely to have taken no note of Jewish-Samaritan distinctions

In any event, one may surmise that the two Jewish Wars were not only disastrous for the Jewish people but also caused new strains in Jewish-Samaritan relations. Various occasions of conflict arose, a few of which may be mentioned here. In a Jewish reprisal for a mass slaughter of Jews in the mixed city of Caesarea in 66 CE (Josephus *BJ* 2.457), parties of Jews raided a wide range of mixed cities in the southern Levant—Philadelphia, Heshbon, Pella, Gerasa (Jerash), Scythopolis (Bet Shean), Gadara, Hippos, Gaulantis, Kedasa, Ptolemais, Gaba, Ascalon (Ashkelon), and Sebaste (Josephus *BJ* 2.458–60). In many of the Hellenistic cities of Palestine, reprisals were then taken against Jewish inhabitants (Josephus *BJ* 2.461–65). To complicate matters, inner-political conflicts among the Jews punctuated this urban turmoil (Mendels 1992: 360–62). It is doubtful that all of these disturbances left the Samaritans somehow unscathed. Samaritans were, after all, among the population groups residing within at least some of the affected cities (Dar 2011).

There is, moreover, evidence that during the First Jewish War some Samaritans were suspected of seditious agitation. In 67 CE, the renowned Fifth Legion of Macedonia (*Legio quinta Macedonica*), led by Sextus Vettulenus Cerealis, found it necessary to journey to Mt. Gerizim, probably in response to an anticipated Samaritan insurrection (Crown 1991).[17] Surrounding the Samaritans, who occupied the summit, Cerealis waited for an indeterminate time, while the Samaritans suffered from lack of supplies and a deficiency of water during a summer heat wave (Josephus *BJ* 3.307–13). Although the Samaritans were repeatedly urged by the Romans to surrender, they refused to do so and Cerealis's troops stormed the summit. The result was a slaughter, a Roman massacre of 11,600 Samaritans at this time (Josephus *BJ* 3.313–15).

Whatever one makes of the high numbers cited by Josephus (Mendels 1992: 365–66), it seems clear that this rout constituted a disaster for the Samaritan community. The Great Revolt was waged against the Roman

---

(Linder 2006: 136–62). The situation clearly changes in the late 4th and 5th centuries. Thus, e.g., Codex Theodosianus 16.8.6 (404 CE) forbids Jews and Samaritans from holding public office. Novella 3 (438 CE), a pronouncement extending or clarifying the previous law, prohibits Jews and Samaritans from municipal offices, though they still owe vaguely defined public service. In Codex Iustinianus 1.7.5 (438 CE), Jews and Samaritans are sects to be distinguished from Christianity. By 531 CE (Codex Justinianus 1.5.21), Jews are distinguished from Samaritans. The latter are now treated as if they were heretics or Manichaeans (cf. Codex Justinianus 1.7.6 [455 CE]).

17. Their presence at Samaria is attested in an epitaph to a soldier found during the Harvard excavations of 1908–10 (Reisner, Fisher, and Lyon 1924: 251 [no. 1]).

authorities in Judea, but Samaritans were not immune to its effects. The incident recounted by Josephus is telling in another respect. It shows that in the 1st century CE, Samaritans still very much valued Mt. Gerizim as their cultural and religious epicenter (cf. Josephus *Ant.* 13.256; John 4:20). The Hasmonean campaign of Judaizing Idoumea and Galilee eventually met with considerable success (Josephus *Ant.* 13.257–58; 15.245; S. Schwartz 2001: 45–52, 61), but many pious Samaritans persisted in maintaining their traditional allegiances. In discussing the Samaritans of his time, Josephus acknowledges (*Ant.* 18.85) that Mt. Gerizim was "regarded by them as the most holy of mountains" (ἁγνότατον αὐτοῖς ὀρῶν ὑπείληπται). The comment is telling, because it shows that the Samaritans did not view only the site of their destroyed sanctuary as hallowed ground but also the entire mountain upon which it was located. Later rabbinic tradition attests to Samaritan religious practices of praying while facing Mt. Gerizim and pronouncing blessings in its name (*b. 'Abod. Zar.* 26b–27a).[18]

The Jewish Mishnah, a compilation of oral law dating to the early 3rd century CE, recounts another occasion of Jewish-Samaritan tensions, probably dating to a time in the late 2nd century CE. To explain the introduction of a new (or complementary) system to announce the arrival of new moons, consisting of the deployment of messengers, the Mishnah recalls an earlier Jewish system of employing a series of signal fires on mountaintops (*m. Roš. Haš.* 1.3; 2.2, 4). The work accuses the Samaritans of being responsible for the demise of the older system, because they purportedly played havoc with the signal fires (*m. Roš. Haš.* 2.2). To be sure, the historical situation is not entirely clear.[19] Given that the Samaritans employed a comparable, but not identical, lunisolar calendar to that employed by the Jews, the Samaritans may have had their own system of signal torches. In that case, the interference may have been inadvertent, rather than intentional. Yet, in any event, the fact that the Samaritans were accused of deliberately interfering with the established arrangement of beacons is itself revealing, because it underscores Jewish suspicions of Samaritan ill-will and subversive behavior.

---

18. Similarly, Solomon's temple dedicatory prayer repeatedly speaks of prayers directed toward Jerusalem and the temple within it (1 Kgs 8:22–53//2 Chr 6:12–42; cf. 2 Chr 20:5–12; 32:20; Dan 6:10).

19. A point acknowledged by Schiffman (1985: 345–46) et al.

Confirmation of deepening mutual mistrust and aversion appears in Jewish religious sources. Schiffman (1985) points to a notable shift in the attitudes of Jewish sages toward the Samaritans between the time of the Tannaim (early sages) of the early 2nd century and the times of the later Tannaim (mid-to-late 2nd century) and the Amoraim (later sages; 3rd–5th centuries CE). The former (the early Tannaim) are fairly accepting of the Samaritans, regarding them as if they were Jews or semi-Jews. The latter speak of the Samaritans as having become corrupted or as non-Jews.[20] The distinction is illustrated by the diametrically opposed views of Rabban ben Gamaliel, who taught that a Samaritan is like a Jew in all respects, and Rabbi Judah the Prince (הנשיא), who taught that a Samaritan is like a non-Jew (*t. Ter.* 4:12, 14). Considering that Simeon II ben Gamaliel II was the father of Rabbi Judah the Prince, who became prominent in the post-Hadrianic period, one cannot help but notice an important shift in opinion. In the later Babylonian Talmud, an additional step may be discerned in that Samaritans could be considered unquestionably as Gentiles (*b. Ḥul.* 6a; Kippenberg 1971: 94–98).

The views cited in these literary sources are quite revealing, because they indicate that even during the 1st century and the early 2nd century, the time during which most of the incidents reviewed above occurred, the Samaritans were (still) considered by at least some rabbis as Jews. Yet over time the Samaritans were deemed to have been corrupted. The Samaritans went from being Jews and semi-Jews to being considered as non-Jews. In sum, one can make the argument that Samaritan-Jewish relations generally worsened during the early centuries of Roman rule, including the time of the two Jewish Wars (66–73 and 132–35 CE). To be sure, the circumstances leading up to the two wars are not well-documented in Samaria. If and when further archaeological excavations occur in the region of Samaria, more precise information about the material history of the first two centuries of the Common Era will allow scholars to be more definitive regarding how much the two wars affected the future course of the native Samaritan population. In any event, one can say, based on the available literary and material remains, that the two Jewish revolts

---

20. The reasons for this negative determination are not entirely clear. Schiffman (1985: 349–50) supposes that the criticism stems from the alleged refusal of the Samaritans to aid the Jews in the Bar Kochba revolt. Montgomery (1907: 82–98), followed by Magen (2008c), contends that the criticism has to do with the purported Hellenization of Samaritans in later Roman times. But see the nuanced comments of van der Horst 1990, 2006; Grabbe 1992, 2008; and Pummer 2000.

increased the strains on both the Jews and the Samaritans. Just as importantly, this time of adversity, upheaval, and humiliation did not bring the two groups closer together against a common enemy. Quite the contrary, it drove the two groups further apart.

Even so, the supposition of a complete breach between the two communities may push the available evidence too far. The literary evidence, which admittedly we have only partially reviewed, largely concerns particular incidents, governmental interventions, and individual conflagrations. It does not engage the daily lives of individual families, the issue of local geography, or the social, commercial, and demographic conditions of the larger province. To Samaritans and Jews residing in mixed cities within the southern Levant, for example, the issues may have differed considerably from those faced by Samaritans and Jews residing in Samaria and Judea proper.

In dealing with the early Roman period, it is important to recall that neither of the two groups (the Samaritans and the Jews) comprised homogenous, tightly knit social unities. Neither was completely dominated religiously, as far as we know, by any one central hierarchical authority. That a large number of Jews and Samaritans resided in diasporic communities in Syria, Egypt, and elsewhere made life difficult for anyone who desired to impose any standard of uniformity upon the whole. There were serious differences of class, social standing, and political orientation (Goodman 2008). Religiously, some Jews and Samaritans were clearly much more traditional and conservative than others. To what degree attitudes differed among urban elites and rural villagers is also at issue.

Practically speaking, Jews and Samaritans in Palestine had to deal with a number of common challenges. The lives of both groups were complicated by the large numbers of non-Jews and non-Samaritans that had come to reside within both Judea and Samaria. Some Jews and Samaritans were much more accepting of Hellenization than others were. Politically, there was tremendous diversity of opinion as to how best to deal with a series of ill-prepared and ill-disposed Roman rulers in the province of Judea. Because Samaria was part of this larger province, Samaritans and Jews were inevitably dealing with the same authorities.

In discussing the Judaism of his day, Josephus (*BJ* 2.119–66; *Ant.* 13.171–73; 18.11–25) mentions three major groups: the Sadducees, the Pharisees, and the Essenes, as well as the Fourth Philosophy (freedom fighters or extremists, depending on one's point of view).[21] Even though Josephus's typology does not seem to be exhaustive (Goodman 2008), it provides a basic sense of the diversity inherent within 1st-century Judaism. By comparison, the internal social, cultural, and religious differences among Samaritans at this time are much less well-understood (Fossum 1989). Yet it may not be too much of a leap to assume that significant social, economic, and religious diversity also characterized the Samaritan population.

In brief, one cannot suppose that there was one single Samaritan stance toward the Jews any more than one can suppose that there was one single Jewish stance toward the Samaritans. Diversity was the order of the day. Moreover, given that Judea and Samaria were geographically contiguous areas, one has to allow for some variations among the number and degree of contacts between elements of the population. In border areas, one would expect, for example, more Jewish-Samaritan interactions than in isolated areas. Similarly, in mixed cities, there were undoubtedly more contacts among different population groups. Given that Jews and Samaritans practiced similar rites and rituals, there were inevitable issues of (inter)marriage, trade, and exchange of agricultural produce.[22]

How much Jews and Samaritans distinguished between holding strictly to their theological tenets and dealing practically with the realities of ordinary life also varied. A Samaritan could express hostility toward the Jerusalem temple and yet have practical dealings with contemporary Jews. Similarly, a Jew might firmly hold to the notion that Jerusalem was elect of God and still do business with his Samaritan neighbors. The story of the encounter between the Samaritan woman and Jesus in the Gospel of John that we have previously discussed is a case in point. Jesus shows no hesitation in traveling through Samaria on his way to Galilee. It is this journey that forms the backdrop to Jesus's lengthy exchange with the Samaritan woman near Jacob's Well (John 4:1–43). The narrative presupposes deep-seated convictions, as well as an acknowledgement that the Samaritans and the Jews share some common beliefs and traditions. From

---

21. The composition of the groups to be categorized as belonging to the Fourth Philosophy continues to occasion much debate (Goodman 2008). Other ancient sources commenting on the factionalism of Jewish life during this period include the New Testament Gospels and the Palestinian and Babylonian Talmuds.
22. There would not be debates registered in the Mishnah, the Tosefta, and in the Palestinian and Babylonian Talmuds (including within the minor rabbinic tractate *Masseket Kutim*) about these issues if this were not the case.

Jesus's perspective, the Jewish people enjoy a privileged place in the divine economy. In conversation, he affirms to the Samaritan woman that "salvation is from the Jews" (ἡ σωτηρία ἐκ τῶν Ἰουδαίων ἐστίν; John 4:22), yet this exclusive declaration hardly precludes dialogue or day-to-day business. Jesus's disciples show no compunction in entering the Samaritan city of Sychar to buy food (John 4:8). Moreover, following the very positive reception accorded to him by the Samaritan woman and her neighbors, Jesus decides to stay with the Samaritans for two days before setting out to resume his travels to Galilee (John 4:43).

The Gospel of John as a Jewish-Christian writing is, of course, hardly representative of the full panoply of Jewish beliefs and practices in Roman times. Nevertheless, it provides one example of the diversity of Jewish (and Jewish-Christian) positions in early Roman times. Rather than think that a single attitude and a single set of prescriptions prevailed in governing Jewish-Samaritan relations, it makes more sense to recognize that different views and actions coexisted.

II. Religious Development and Cultural Exchange

In addition to the evidence for heightened tensions between members of the Jewish and Samaritan communities during the first centuries of the Common Era, there are also, paradoxically, some indications of significant cultural exchange in the religious evolution of the two groups. During Roman and Byzantine times, the Jews and the Samaritans developed similar religious symbols, cultural institutions, and literary genres. Some of these developments may be explained by a process of competitive emulation, as each community laid claim to the heritage of ancient Israel and adjusted to the realities of life under Roman subjugation, but I would argue that such a process presupposes a studied knowledge of the symbols and institutions being imitated. The few case studies to be discussed here are: Samaritan synagogues, synagogue mosaics, mezuzot, and ritual baths (miqva'ot).[23] Rather than attempt to provide a comprehensive and systematic analysis, my study will be limited to touching on some basic points of comparison.

---

23. A mezuzah is a select Pentateuchal text (or texts) attached to doorposts or to an entryway or main room within one's house. The definition varies, as we shall see, among the two groups in question.

In what follows, my argument is not that the Samaritan institutions and symbols were identical to their Jewish counterparts. Far from it; the Samaritans adapted their customs, traditions, and institutions to suit their own distinctive purposes. But the very fact, as we shall see, that the Samaritans shared such symbols and types of religious structures with the Jews in the homeland indicates that the two communities were not moving in diametrically opposite directions. Both the parallel developments and the particular lines of differentiation provide important clues that at least certain members of the two groups were cognizant of what the proponents of the other religion believed and practiced. Such a process of parallel development and selective dissimilation assumes continuing contacts between the two neighboring communities. In other words, the available material and literary evidence in the first centuries CE militates against positing an absolute breach between the Jews and the Samaritans.[24]

For both Jews and Samaritans, the rise of the synagogue is a formative social, historical, and religious development.[25] The institution's origins and history are much contested, but Jewish synagogues are attested earlier and are much more numerous than Samaritan synagogues.[26] Examination of Samaritan synagogues from Roman and Byzantine times reveals that they are in many respects indistinguishable from Jewish synagogues (Pummer 1998a, 1999; Magen 2008c). This is not to say that Jewish and Samaritan synagogues all share a similar building design or structure. Synagogue architecture evinces much variety in the Roman and Byzantine ages in both Jewish and Samaritan settings (Strange 2003). Significant regional variation must also be taken into consideration (Levine 2000).

In this context, it may be observed that names and epithets attributed to various Samaritan synagogues vary: *euktērion*, "prayer house" (Tod 1951: 27–28); *proseuchē*, "place of prayer";[27] (*byt*) *knwšy'*, "gathering house"

---

24. Similarly, Pummer (1999: 139) speaks of "continued mutual cross-fertilization" in reference to the development of Jewish and Samaritan synagogues.
25. Binder 1999; Levine 2000, 2003; Olsson 2003; Richardson 2003; Runesson 2003; Strange 2003; Runesson, Binder, and Olsson 2008.
26. This fact has led some scholars (e.g., Magen 2008c) to say that the Samaritans borrowed the institution from the Jews, but others (e.g., Pummer 1999: 139; Strange 2003: 46–58) argue that the synagogue emerged historically from a common Jewish-Samaritan matrix.
27. Epiphanius *Panarion*, 80.1.6. Historically, it is unclear when this term was first used for a Palestinian synagogue (whether Jewish or Samaritan). Binder (1999: 111–18) provides a helpful survey.

(e.g., Adler-Séligsohn, 2.89 [32 4632], 3.232 [24 4758]), "house of God,"[28] "place" (*topos*) or perhaps "holy place" (Di Segni 1993: 232; Magen 2008c: 139 [no. 3; fig. 36]), ΤΟΑΓΙΟΝ, "the holy place,"[29] and "the temple" ([]ΥΤΩΝΟΝΕΩΝ).[30] Similar variation is attested in the nomenclature given to ancient Jewish synagogues (Binder 1999: 91–154). To be sure, the usage of "temple" (*neōn* [*naōs*]) in a recently discovered mosaic in a Samaritan synagogue in the Bet Shean region is most unusual, if not unique.[31] Even so, there are some broad parallels in early Jewish usage (e.g., *hieron*, "temple"; Binder 1999: 122–30).

Samaritan synagogues are attested (whether in literary sources, epigraphy, or archaeology) in the Diaspora at sites such as Rome, Syracuse, Tarsus, and Thessalonica;[32] in the larger homeland at sites such as Bet Shean,[33] Shaʿalvim (Salbit), and Tell Qasile; and in Samaria at Mt. Gerizim,[34] Neapolis(Ḥuzn Yaʿqub), Kafr Fahma, Ḥorvat Migdal (Ṣur Natan), Kh. Samara (Deir Sarur), El-Ḥirbe, and Qedumim.[35] Mosaics

---

28. A title given to the synagogue built by the high priest ʿAqbūn VII (V) (*Abū 'l Fath* 178,233).
29. In reference, in all likelihood, to the Samaritan synagogue situated on the summit of Mt. Gerizim in the 4th–5th centuries (Di Segni 1990; Magen 2008c: 122 [no. 7.5]).
30. The last inscription concerns a late-5th-century Samaritan synagogue recently discovered by the Israel Antiquities Authority (IAA) in the agricultural hinterland of Bet Shean. The inscription, which appears in a geometric mosaic situated on the floor of the building, is yet to be fully analyzed and published., but a convenient photo appears on the IAA website.
31. The preliminary transcription of the text (see previous note) helpfully provided by the excavators (W. Atrash and Y. Harel) is: Τ[]ΟΥΤΟΝΝΕΩΝ. The reading of ΝΕΩΝ is clear from the photo, but what precedes it is not. As my colleague Paul B. Harvey points out (personal communication), a more accurate transcription and reconstruction might be: ΤΟ]ΥΤΩΝΟΝΕΩΝ, "The temple of these" (reading ΝΕΩΝ as a nominative singular with the definite article Ο). The lexicon of Liddell and Scott (1996: 1160) provides a helpful list of attested nominative forms of ναός.
32. Some of these are disputed by Magen 2008c, because their existence is postulated on the basis of literary, as opposed to archaeological, remains. The evidence for their existence is well-summarized by Pummer 1998a, 1999.
33. Up to three different synagogue structures in the Bet Shean area have been identified as Samaritan, but there is no unanimity of scholarly opinion on this matter (Levine 2000).
34. Magen (2008c: 118–24; 2009: 261–69 [figs. 6.31–48]) argues archaeologically for the presence of two synagogues on Mt. Gerizim, one located on the summit (above the site of the earlier temple precinct) and the other on the northern face (by the stairs leading to the Roman temple). The identification in the second case is not absolute, because said building was evidently a Roman structure in secondary reuse.
35. In Samaritan tradition, Baba Rabba is said to have rebuilt or constructed synagogues at several sites, including Qiryat ʿAmrata (עמרתה), Qiryat Ḥagga (חגא), Qiryat Bet Namra (בית נמארה), Qiryat Ṭira (טירה), Qiryat Ṣabrin (צברין), Qiryat Šalem (שלם), Qiryat Bet-Dagan (בית דגן), and ʾAvnata (אבנתא; Adler-Séligsohn, 2.90–91 [32 4632]). The list in *Abū 'l Fath* 143,182–83 varies slightly. Archaeological exploration in Samaria has been quite limited, however, and material confirmation for the existence of these synagogues in the particular period in question is

An Absolute Breach? 231

found at Jewish and Samaritan synagogues in the homeland share many symbols, such as the temple façade, the menorah (seven-branched candelabra), the table of the bread of the presence (*leḥem pānîm*), various vessels, and the incense shovel (*maḥtâ*).[36] Both types of buildings are so similar that one has to look for the possible presence of other markers to label the structure as Samaritan, rather than as Jewish (Pummer 1998a, 1999). These indicators include the geographical location (whether in Judah or in Samaria), the orientation (whether the façade or apse of the synagogue is pointed toward Mt. Gerizim or toward Mt. Zion,[37] the employment of paleo-Hebrew script,[38] the employment of Samaritan script,[39] the presence of inscriptions quoting telltale passages in the Samaritan Pentateuch, the possible avoidance of the lulav symbol (an unopened palm frond; cf. *kappōt těmārîm*; Lev 23:40) and the etrog symbol (citron; cf. *pěrî ʿēṣ hādār*; Lev 23:40) in mosaics,[40] the lack of figural art, and the use of an empty bird cage in mosaics. Samaritan synagogues also tended to be located on the outskirts, rather than in the centers, of towns and villages (Levine 2000: 292–94).

The presence of a vacant cage may strike readers as a rather obscure criterion for identifying a mosaic as distinctively Samaritan, but it is tied

---

lacking. The Samaritan account may reflect medieval, not late-antique, realities. Additionally, the synagogue remains at Qedumim are quite fragmentary (Magen 2008c: 170–71).

36. Magen (2008c: 174) prefers to speak of two trumpets (*ḥaṣôṣěrôt*), rather than of ram's horns (shofrot), in referring to the wind instruments appearing on Samaritan mosaics (cf. Num 10:1–10; Josephus *Ant*. 3.291). In this, he discerns a difference with Jewish mosaics, depicting a shofar. The point may be valid, but the instruments appear to be similar in appearance. For an example from El-Ḥirbe, see Magen 2008c: 134–37 (figs. 28–33). See also the dust jacket of this book. On the variety of shofrot, see Hachlili 2001: 214–15 (figs. V.3–4). In distinguishing between the two, Milgrom (1990: 372–73) stresses the point of users (priests vs. laypeople). Interestingly, a clear example of two *ḥaṣôṣěrôt*, accompanied by a menorah and showbread table, from the Second Temple appears on the Arch of Titus (Hachlili 2001: 266 [pl. II.2]).

37. Although there is no uniform orientation of synagogues in antiquity.

38. This is not a guarantee of Samaritan identity, because Jewish congregations could also employ paleo-Hebrew script if they so wished.

39. An example appears on one of the mosaics found in the Shaʿalvim synagogue (located outside Samaria proper). The text in Samaritan script quotes SP Exod 15:18, "The LORD will reign forever and ever" (Sukenik 1949).

40. Reflecting a particular interpretation of the four-species list of Lev 23:40. Whereas in Jewish tradition the four species constitute separate items (*Tg. Onq*. Lev 23:40; *b. Sukkah* 3; Maimonides *Mishneh Torah* 7:1–8:11), in Samaritan tradition the four are all parts of the sukkah (Pummer 1987b: 23 [pls. xxxix–xli]. Hachlili (2009: 223) avers that traces of the lulav and ʾetrôg symbols may be found on the right side of the El-Ḥirbe mosaic, but this claim cannot be verified based on the photos available to me. Assuming, for the sake of argument, that they do appear, the questions are whether they are depicted in the same manner and have the same function as their Jewish counterparts (Pummer 1999: 147).

to the common Samaritan interpretation of the Decalogue's proscription of images as inclusive of human and animal images.[41] The force of Yhwh's prohibiting Israelites from making for themselves "any sculpted image (*pesel*), or any likeness (*těmûnâ*) of anything that is in heavens above, or that is in the earth beneath, or that is in the waters underneath the earth" (MT Exod 20:4; Deut 5:6; SP Exod 20:4; Deut 5:7) was debated by the early interpreters.[42] For most Samaritans, the divine command meant that they could not tolerate artistic renderings of any living creatures. By comparison, bird cages with birds appear in a variety of late-antique Jewish and Christian mosaics (Hachlili 2001, 2009).

The Torah shrine façades appearing in the two Samaritan synagogue mosaics at Kh. Samara and El-Ḥirbe are particularly fascinating, because they differ somewhat both from their Jewish counterparts and from the synagogue mosaic found in Bet Shean Synagogue A, thought by some, but not by all, scholars to be Samaritan in character.[43] The depiction of a four-columned front, a swirling *pārōket* (curtain), partially drawn to reveal part of the shrine's door (Exod 26:31–35), two tongs (Exod 25:38), and almond-blossom-shaped cups on the menorah branches (Exod 25:33–37) recall particular iconographic features of the ancient wilderness tabernacle.[44] Such artistic traits are simultaneously conservative and innovative.[45] The mosaics are conservative because they uphold the heritage of the wilderness tabernacle in Samaritan tradition and avoid incorporating new iconographic

---

41. Examples appear in the mosaics from Bet Shean A (Levine 2000: 199–200); Mt. Gerizim (Magen 2008c: 122–24 [figs. 13–14], El-Ḥirbe (Magen 2008c: 127–42 [figs. 28–40]), Kh. Samara (Magen 2008c: 142–67; figs. 56, 59, 67–80) and Ṣur Natan (Ḥorvat Migdal; Magen 2008c: 167–68; fig. 83).

42. Because figural representation is occasionally lacking in ancient Jewish synagogues, the criterion is not absolute. Indeed, reading Josephus (*Ant.* 17.149–63; 18.55–59, 262–88), one might conclude that the same aversion was characteristic of early Judaism, but archaeological finds tell a different, more complex story (Levine 2000: 206–19; Hachlili 2001, 2009).

43. Or a synagogue shared by Jews and Samaritans, as some have suggested. Levine (2000: 199–200) provides a helpful overview of the issues. That the later Bet Shean mosaics (6th century) evince different patterns from the earlier El-Ḥirbe and Kh. Samara synagogue mosaics (4th century) does not automatically disqualify them from being Samaritan in character (*pace* Magen 2008c). One has to accept regional variation, historical development, individual congregational (or donor) preference, and social diversity within the Samaritan population of this period (Fossum 1989; van der Horst 1990).

44. Magen 2008c: 136–39, 157–65 (figs. 28–33, 36, 68–70, 80). Cf. the ornate menorah arms on the 'Eshtemoa' lintel and on the menorah appearing on the mosaic floor at Ḥammat-Tiberias (Hachlili 2001: 149). Tongs (Exod 37:23; Lev 24:1–4; Num 4:9) on mosaics are relatively rare (Hachlili 2001: 233).

45. There are also some small-scale differences between the Kh. Samara and El-Ḥirbe synagogue mosaic designs (Hachlili 2009: 25–33).

trends, such as the zodiac panel appearing in a variety of Jewish and Christian mosaics (Hachlili 2009: 35–56), but they are innovative in that they deviate from older iconographic patterns to blend features of the Samaritan shrine with those of the tent shrine constructed by Moses.[46] If so, the particular artistic conventions underscore Samaritan claims of historic ties with Sinaitic Israel. At a time in which not only Jews and Samaritans but also ascendant Christians professed to represent historic Israel, these mosaics projected a particular Samaritan vision of Israel's classical past.

In spite of these and other intriguing differences between Samaritan mosaics and Jewish mosaics, it is important to keep in mind that the variations appear within set parameters. The material culture of the early Samaritans is largely indistinguishable from that of the Jews. Both groups may have drawn from some of the same guilds of specialized artisans (Hachlili 2009: 243–80). The process of religious differentiation evident in the usage of certain symbols (e.g., the vacant bird cage), the lack of figurative art, the geographical orientation of the building, the archaizing tendencies in some Samaritan mosaics, and the employment of Samaritan script distinguishes certain symbols and particular institutions as peculiarly Samaritan. Nevertheless, the institution of which the mosaics are but one part—the synagogue—becomes a defining feature of both Jewish and Samaritan identity. For both groups the Torah shrine, the menorah, the showbread table, and various ritual objects are highly prominent symbols. The individual deviations are certainly important, but occur within the context of a broader, shared cultural paradigm.

The mezuzot (literally, "doorposts") offer another case in point. Deuteronomic legislation enjoins Israelites: "You are to write these words which I [Yhwh] am commanding you...on your houses and on your gates" (Deut 6:6, 9; 11:20).[47] From the context in Deuteronomy, it is not entirely clear which particular words are to be inscribed. Do "these words" refer to the Decalogue previously recited in Deut 5:6–22? Or do they refer to the text within which the injunction occurs, namely, the Shema (Deut 6:4–9;

---

46. As Runesson observes (2001), it may be more accurate to speak of Torah shrine façades than of temple façades (*pace* Magen 2008c). Of course, the Torah shrine designs were themselves inspired by temple designs (in this case, with reference to Mt. Gerizim). The conscious conflation of tabernacle and temple characteristics occurred already during the Second Temple period (e.g., 1 Chr 9:23–34; Knoppers 2004a: 506–14). For *aediculae* fragments found within the synagogue remains at Ostia, Sardis, Nabratein, and other sites, see Runesson 2001 and Hachlili 2009: 220–23.

47. In Deut 6:9, I am reading the plural with the LXX and the SP. MT Deut 6:9 and 11:20 read the singular "house." The "gates" refer to town or city gates.

11:13–21)? Or do they refer to Deuteronomy itself (Tigay 1996: 78)? Within biblical tradition, no mezuzot are attested, but this picture changes in postbiblical times.

Among both the Jews and the Samaritans, the divine injunction found in Deuteronomy has been construed as involving affixing Pentateuch portions within the domain of one's house.[48] Yet the form of the mezuzot varies between the two groups. In Jewish tradition, the mezuzot take the form of small boxes with inscribed parchments that are attached to door frames. In Samaritan contexts, the mezuzot take the form of small stone inscriptions that were hung on or mounted on walls in private houses, either in the entrance or in the largest room.[49] Inasmuch as the Samaritan mezuzot reflect a more literal interpretation of Deuteronomy than do the Jewish mezuzot, they may bear witness to the older of the two practices (Tigay 1996: 444).

In late antiquity, the Samaritan mezuzot usually featured select Pentateuchal texts, such as the Priestly Blessing (Num 6:24–26), Deut 6:4–9 (the Shema), and the Decalogue. The choice of particular texts, especially the Shema and the Decalogue, corresponds to antique Jewish practice, as attested by the Nash Papyrus (Albright 1937; Greenberg 2007), the *Letter of Aristeas* (line 158), the Qumran finds (Mezuzah A–G; 4Q149–55; Mezuzah; 8Q4), Josephus (*Ant.* 4.213), and Philo (*Spec.* 4.142). At Qumran, the mezuzot always include the Shema, as well as additional texts, such as the "ten words" and other selections from Deuteronomy 6. It is possible that some of the Samaritan Decalogue inscriptions, dating to various times, originally functioned as mezuzot in private homes or in synagogues.[50] As in some streams of early Jewish tradition (*m. Tamid* 5.1; *Mek.* 1; *y. Ber* 1.8 [3c]; *b. Ber* 12a), the Decalogue enjoyed a special significance in early Samaritan tradition.[51] In liturgical settings, its text was reproduced

---

48. But no ancient phylacteries or tefillin (Philo *Spec.* 4.142; Matt 23:5) are attested from ancient Samaritan remains. Some phylacteries were found, however, at Qumran (Phylactery A–U; 4Q128–48; Schiffman 2000). There is diversity of opinion within ancient Jewish sources (including some LXX witnesses) whether the demand for tefillin is to be taken literally (Tigay 1996: 442–43). A negative answer is also found in Samaritan tradition.
49. As is still the case today (Pummer 1987a, pl. xxivb). Perhaps some texts were written on papyrus or cloth, but these did not survive antiquity.
50. See Kippenberg 1971; Dexinger 1977; Ben-Ḥayyim 1995. The dates of the Samaritan stone inscriptions appearing in Samaritan script are disputed by Magen (2008c: 234–40), who wishes to date most of them, especially those containing quotes from the Pentateuch and the Ten Commandments, to the Crusader and Ottoman periods. For arguments favoring much earlier dates (2nd century CE and later), see also Purvis 1968.
51. The comment in *Sipre Deut* §313 is telling. God demonstrated his care for Israel (Deut 32:10) by revealing the "ten words" to Israel. The Decalogue also enjoyed a special status in

as a representation or summary of the Torah (SL). In sum, both communities developed mezuzot to comply with an important Pentateuchal command, but the material form such mezuzot took varied between the groups in question. Again, one can discern differentiation within a broader cultural pattern. Both groups contributed to a common religious development, but took different paths to reach basically the same goal.

One last example from the world of material culture may suffice to establish the point about cultural exchange. The material remains from ancient Judea and Samaria bear witness to the construction of ritual baths (miqva'ot) in certain settings. Samaritan chronicles relate the building of a ritual bath (miqveh) near Mt. Gerizim by the famous Samaritan leader and reformer Baba Rabba, probably in the late 3rd century CE.[52] The ritual bath was located close to the synagogue he purportedly (re)established at the foot of Mt. Gerizim (Adler-Séligsohn, 2.90 [32 4632]). He may have also built a large miqveh in front of the Samaritan synagogue at 'Avnata, but he is not said to have done likewise at the other synagogues he (re)established.[53] Actual examples of miqva'ot near Samaritan synagogues are attested in the archaeological record at a number of sites: Qedumim (Magen 2008c: 187–90; figs. 1–9), El-Ḥirbe (Magen 2008c: 190–93; figs. 10–18), Kh. Samara (Magen 2008c: 194; fig. 19), and Ṣur Natan (Ḥorvat Migdal; Magen 2008c: 194; fig. 19). Ritual baths have also been located at a variety of Samaritan locations with olive oil installations, including Qedumim and Ṣur Natan (Magen 2008c: 186, 194).[54] It should be pointed out that most of these sites have more than one miqveh attested.

---

some early Christian churches. The *Didascalia Apostolorum*, an early Christian treatise likely originating in northern Syria, presents itself as stemming from the Twelve Apostles at the time of the Jerusalem Council (Acts 15; cf. Gal 2), but actually dates to the 3rd/4th centuries. In chapter 26 (vi.16), the *Didascalia Apostolorum* accepts the authority of the law, but distinguishes between the divine revelation given at Mt. Sinai before the incident of the Golden Calf and that which follows. Only the former is authoritative. Such distinctions may have led the rabbis to deemphasize the unique status of the Decalogue in favor of the entire Torah (however one defines it). I am thankful to Karin Zetterholm for this reference.

52. So *Abū 'l Fatḥ* 143,182–44,184; Adler-Séligsohn 2.90 [32 4632], 3.235–37 [34 4876]). Cf. SL 2:xx–xxii; *Tulida* 9א121.

53. Hence, one cannot assume that all early Samaritan synagogues had stepped-stone water cisterns nearby. As in Jewish settings, one has to allow for regional variation, group preferences, and historical evolution.

54. For early commentary on the importance of such considerations, see Josephus *BJ* 2.21–22; 5.5–6; *Ant.* 12.120; *Ag. Ap.* 2.23; *Vita* 13; m. *Ṭoh.* 10.1–3; m. *Ḥag.* 2.7; m. *Mid.* 1.6; m. *Neg.* 14.8; m. *'Ed.* 1.11; m. *'Abod. Zar.* 2.6; m. *Šeqal.* 3.40b; m. *Yoma* 3.2–3; y. *'Abod. Zar.* 5.44c.

From a material standpoint, the architecture and structure of these miqva'ot are virtually identical to those found adjacent to some early Jewish synagogues (Reich 1988; 1995: 290–92; Magen 2008c). All of the stepped-stone cisterns are rock-cut, and none are fed by sedimentation pools. Indeed, the purity of the Samaritan version of ritual baths is affirmed in the Tosefta (*t. Miqw.* 6.1). A somewhat different view appears in the later Jerusalem Talmud. There, the fact that Samaritan miqva'ot could be filled with a minimum of 40 *seah* of water (approximately 800–1000 liters) is disputed (*y. 'Abod. Zar.* 4.34d).[55] The dimensions of the ritual baths unearthed at Samaritan sites indicate, however, that they all could easily hold the required amount of nondrawn water required in Jewish law (Magen 2008c: 186).

Interestingly, the practice of constructing miqva'ot near Samaritan synagogues persists into Byzantine times, whereas the tendency by some Jews to situate miqva'ot near synagogues decreases drastically in post-Temple times, the era of the Mishnah and the Talmud (Reich 1995: 295).[56] Both the Mishnah and the Tosefta have tractates devoted to the miqveh, but neither the Palestinian Talmud nor the Babylonian Talmud do.[57] The original Samaritan practice of constructing ritual baths near their synagogues may have been influenced by the practice of certain Jewish groups, but it seems unlikely that the practice of building miqva'ot was simply imposed on the Yahwistic Samarians under the rigors of Hasmonean rule (Magen 2008c: 186), because the earliest attested Jewish synagogues in Palestine date to the second half of the 1st century BCE, a time that postdates Hasmonean hegemony (Grabbe 1995; Reich 1995: 289).[58] The Samaritan ritual baths that have been excavated all date to later (Roman and Byzantine) times.

It may be that certain Samaritans borrowed the institution from Jewish practice but adapted it for their own purposes and particular needs. It should be recalled that, as far as we know, the Samaritan

---

55. Yet *b. Giṭ.* 10a avers that the Samaritans could be trusted in matters of ritual purity. Unsurprisingly, other rabbis demurred (*b. Ḥag.* 25a; *Rab. Deut* 2.33).
56. The Jewish ritual baths appear near the synagogues at Gamla, Masada, Herodium, and Jerusalem (the so-called Theodotus synagogue). Given the locations, Reich (1995) hypothesizes that the practice of locating ritual baths by synagogues was particularly favored by the Zealots.
57. Except for the Ostia synagogue, few ritual baths are found near Diaspora synagogues (Levine 2000: 281).
58. If one adds the so-called Jericho synagogue to this list, one may have to push back the date a little, but the reservations of Levine (2000: 42–43, 68–69) should be borne in mind.

priesthood never lost leadership of or control over the Samaritan population in the land, whereas the rabbis increasingly gained influence and power among the Jewish population in the wake of the two Jewish wars.[59] To be sure, our major Samaritan sources date to the medieval period (or later), so it is difficult to know for certain. The great Samaritan reformer Baba Rabba was himself the son of a high priest (Sam Josh 49; *Abū 'l Fatḥ*, 135,171–72). There may well have been challenges and qualifications to sacerdotal authority over the centuries.[60] Nevertheless, the leadership of homeland Samaritan synagogues remained, in all likelihood, linked to the tribe of Levi, and the Samaritan priesthood never lost its intercessory functions (*Tulida* 8ב117–10א48; Crown 1989a).[61] The Samaritan chronicles even contain an assertion that a later Samaritan high priest, ʿAqbūn V, anointed the foundations of a synagogue he was (re)constructing in Shechem (*Abū 'l Fatḥ* 178,232–33). In short, priestly involvement may help to explain why certain Samaritan synagogues continued to have miqvaʾot located adjacent to them in late Roman and Byzantine times.

Conclusions

We have been discussing some examples of cultural exchange in the religious evolution of the early Samaritans and Jews in Palestine. The brief case studies involving synagogues, synagogue mosaics, mezuzot, and ritual baths point to continuing Jewish and Samaritan interaction during the Roman and early Byzantine periods. To be sure, we have also

---

59. This can also be seen in negative fashion. The reign of the Emperor Commodus (176–92 CE) is known in Samaritan tradition as one of the worst in history, a time of severe persecution (*Abū 'l Fatḥ* 128,162–131,168). What were his offenses? Among his crimes, he interdicted Samaritans from reading the Torah, offering formal instruction, and employing the synagogues for prayer and reading (the Torah). Unfortunately, there is nothing in the Roman legal (or literary) tradition about his animosity.

60. Reference is sometimes made to Baba Rabba's leadership reforms (*Abū 'l Fatḥ* 139,177–142,182), which led to the appointment of seven *ḥukamāʾ*, "sages," as a council consisting of three priests and four laymen, but this reform circumscribed priestly authority, rather than terminated it. Moreover, there does not seem to be a late antique Samaritan counterpart to the Jewish/Rabbinic office of *nāśīʾ*/*comes* ("patriarch").

61. In his substantial study of *Abū 'l Fatḥ*, Stenhouse (1985: lii) observes that the sequence of actions in the medieval account of Baba Rabba's reopening of old synagogues is telling. *Abū 'l Fatḥ* (138,177) declares that Baba Rabba "and his brothers first of all assembled in them and then read out the Scroll of the Torah in the hearing of all the people. They multiplied their praises and glorified God with all their might." In this narrative, pride of place is given to the priests (and Levites). They assemble first and perhaps also (re)consecrate the building (so Stenhouse) before making it accessible to the Samaritan populace. Similarly, Adler-Séligsohn 2.89 (32 4632).

seen examples of cultural dissimilation. Yet, inasmuch as religious or cultural differentiation involves a conscious decision to mark a particular text, symbol, or physical structure as Samaritan as opposed to Jewish or Christian, it presupposes some awareness of what may constitute the identifying marks of the texts, symbols, or physical structures of what it is not. In other words, the self is defined, in many respects, by the self's perceptions of the other. In cases in which the identity of the self is set against that the proximate other, as with Samaritan-Jewish relations, this process of self-definition is especially critical (J. Z. Smith 1985). From an etic (outsider) standpoint, the differences between the near neighbors may seem to be relatively minor in comparison to what they all share in common. But from an emic (insider) standpoint, the differences are crucially important to identifying the distinctive features of the two groups and maintaining an appropriate degree of boundary maintenance between them (Headland, Pike, and Harris 1990).

Such a reconstruction does not deny an increase in mutual acrimony during this broad era. There is, as we have seen earlier, evidence of a marked deterioration in Samaritan-Jewish relations during the Hasmonean and Roman periods. Yet this decline did not amount to a total rupture. Bad relations between groups are still relations. Indeed, the scathing polemic appearing in some literary sources masks the degree to which members of the two groups were still in contact with one another. Each of the cases we have reviewed presumes considerable Samaritan knowledge of the symbols and institutions shared with Jews. Similarly, the detailed comments in rabbinic sources about the Samaritans reveal some rather detailed knowledge of and engagement with Samaritan beliefs, rituals, and behaviors on the part of the rabbis, even if their intention is only to address specific points of issue (Pummer 2000: 200–201).

The case studies in this chapter have focused on select items of material culture, but similar case studies exhibiting parallels between Samaritans and Jews could be conducted involving written remains. Each group developed similar exegetical techniques and similar ways of expanding upon foundational literature.[62] As in early Judaism, Samaritan scholars prepared an Aramaic translation (Targum) of the Hebrew text of the Pentateuch, dating to the 3rd/4th centuries (Tal 1980–83, 1988).[63]

---

62. An outstanding example is the midrashic literary work *Tībāt Mārqe* (Ben-Ḥayyim 1988).
63. The work is sparing in its paraphrase, largely lacking midrashic explanations and interpretations (Tal 1988).

As in classical Judaism, Hebrew is referred to as the "holy language" (לשון הקודש) in medieval Samaritan prayers and poetry (Tal 2011). From medieval times literary influences from Jewish writings on Samaritan works range from the list of 613 precepts (*miṣwôt*; *b. Mak.* 23b–24a; Noja 1967; Baillet 1988; Florentin 2005: 50–56) to the Arabic translation of the Pentateuch (Pummer 1998b: 307–9).[64] In other words, as the Samaritan community continued to evolve, it did so, at least in part, in relation to the other. The increased polarization of Samaritans and Jews did not lead to an absolute breach or to an end to contacts between them. Even as each group continued to develop its own beliefs, leadership, and traditions, the two communities did not move in diametrically opposite directions. One of the enduring paradoxes in the early history of the Samaritans and the Jews is that in pursuing their different paths, the Samaritans and Jews often did so in remarkably similar fashion.

---

64. Unfortunately, a complete critical edition of this work is lacking, although Shehadeh (1977) demonstrates some five major text-types.

Bibliography

Abbreviations for works in biblical and ancient Near Eastern studies follow those used in *The SBL Handbook of Style for Ancient Near Eastern, Biblical, and Early Christian Studies*, ed. P. H. Alexander, J. F. Kutsko, S. Decker-Lucke, J. D. Ernest, and D. L. Petersen (Peabody, MA: Hendrickson, 1999) and *Old Testament Abstracts* 24. Abbreviations for additional works in classics follow those used in *The Oxford Classical Dictionary*, ed. S. Hornblower and A. Spawforth (3rd ed.; Oxford: Oxford University Press, 1996). Other abbreviations included within the work follow below.

Abū 'l Fath E. Vilmar, *Abulfathi Annales Samaritani: Quos Arabice edidit cum prolegomenis*. Gotha: Perthes, 1865. Translated by P. L. Stenhouse as *The Kitāb al-tarīkh of Abū 'l Fath*, Studies in Judaica 1 (Sydney: Mandelbaum, 1985).
Adler-Séligsohn E. N. Adler and M. Séligsohn, Une nouvelle Chronique Samaritaine. *Revue des Études Juives* 44 (1902) 188–22; 45 (1902) 70–98, 223–54; 46 (1903) 123–46.
AP A. E. Cowley, ed., *Aramaic Papyri of the Fifth Century B.C.* Oxford: Clarendon, 1923.
BP E. G. Kraeling, ed., *The Brooklyn Museum Aramaic Papyri: New Documents of the Fifth Century B.C. from the Jewish Colony at Elephantine*. New Haven, CT: Yale University Press, 1953.
CAD A. L. Oppenheim et al., eds., *The Assyrian Dictionary of the Oriental Institute of the University of Chicago*. Chicago: Oriental Institute of the University of Chicago, 1956–
DNWSI J. Hoftijzer and K. Jongeling, *Dictionary of North-West Semitic Inscriptions*. 2 vols. Leiden, the Netherlands: Brill, 1995.
DSS The Dead Sea Scrolls

GKC *Gesenius' Hebrew Grammar*. Edited and enlarged by E. Kautzsch, 2nd English ed. revised in accordance with the twenty-eighth German edition (1909) by A. E. Cowley. Oxford: Clarendon, 1910.

GN Geographic Name

HALOT Ludwig Koehler and Walter Baumgartner, *The Hebrew and Aramaic Lexicon of the Old Testament*; subsequently revised by Walter Baumgartner and Johann Jakob Stamm. 5 vols. Leiden, the Netherlands: Brill, 1994–2000.

LXX The Septuagint

Macdonald II J. Macdonald, ed., *The Samaritan Chronicle no. II, or Sepher Ha-Yamim: From Joshua to Nebuchadnezzar*. Beihefte zur *Zeitschrift für die Alttestamentliche Wissenschaft* 107. Berlin: de Gruyter, 1969.

MT The Masoretic Text

OL Old Latin

PG Procopius of Gaza

PN Personal Name

Sam Josh T. W. J. Juynboll, ed., *Chronicon Samaritanum: Arabice conscriptum, cui titulus est Liber Josuae*. Leiden, the Netherlands: Luchtmans, 1848. Translated by O. T. Crane as *The Samaritan Chronicle, or The Book of Joshua the Son of Nun* (New York: Alden, 1890).

SL A. E. Cowley, ed., *The Samaritan Liturgy*. 2 vols. Oxford: Clarendon, 1909.

SP A. Tal, *The Samaritan Pentateuch Edited According to MS 6 [C] of the Shekhem Synagogue*. Texts and Studies in the Hebrew Language and Related Subjects 8. Tel Aviv University: Rosenberg School, 1994 (Hebrew).

TAD B. Porten and A. Yardeni, eds. and trans., *Textbook of Aramaic Documents from Ancient Egypt*. 4 vols. Winona Lake, IN: Eisenbrauns.

Tulida M. Florentin, *The Tulida—A Samaritan Chronicle: Text, Translation, Commentary*. Jerusalem: Ben Zvi, 1999 (Hebrew).

WD Wâdī ed-Dâlīyeh

WDSP Wâdī ed-Dâlīyeh Samaria Papyri

Abel, F.-M.
1967 *Géographie de la Palestine*. Vol. 2, *Géographie politique; Les villes*. 3rd ed. Paris: Gabalda.

Abraham, K.
2005–6 West Semitic and Judean Brides in Cuneiform Sources from the Sixth Century BCE: New Evidence from a Marriage Contract from Āl-Yahudu. *Archiv für Orientforschung* 51: 198–219.
2007 An Inheritance Division among Judeans in Babylonia from the Early Persian Period. Pp. 148–82 in *New Seals and Inscriptions: Hebrew, Idumean, and Cuneiform*, ed. M. Lubetski. Hebrew Bible Monographs 8. Sheffield, UK: Sheffield Phoenix.

Achenbach, R.
2003 *Die Vollendung der Tora: Studien zur Redaktionsgeschichte des Numeribuches im Kontext von Hexateuch und Pentateuch*. Beihefte zur *Zeitschrift für Altorientalische und Biblische Rechtsgeschichte* 3. Wiesbaden, Germany: Harrassowitz.

Ackroyd, P. R.
1974 An Interpretation of the Babylonian Exile: A Study of 2 Kings 20, Isaiah 38–39. *Scottish Journal of Theology* 27: 329–52.
1982 Isaiah 36–39: Structure and Function. Pp. 3–21 in *Von Kanaan bis Kerala: Festschrift für J. P. M. van der Ploeg*, ed. W. C. Delsman et al. Alter Orient und Altes Testament 211. Kevelaer, Germany: Butzon & Bercker.

Aejmelaeus, A.
1993 Septuagintal Translation Techniques: A Solution to the Problem of the Tabernacle Account? Pp. 107–21 in *On the Trail of Septuagint Translators: Collected Essays*. Kampen, the Netherlands: Kok Pharos.

Aharoni, Y.
1979 *The Land of the Bible: A Historical Geography*. 2nd ed. Philadelphia: Westminster.

Ahlström, G. W.
1993 *The History of Ancient Palestine*. Journal for the Study of the Old Testament Supplement 146. Sheffield, UK: JSOT.

Albertz, R.
1994 *A History of Religion in the Old Testament Period*. Vol. 2, *From the Exile to the Maccabees*. Old Testament Library. Louisville, KY: Westminster John Knox.
2003 *Israel in Exile: The History and Literature of the Sixth Century B.C.E.* Atlanta, GA: Society of Biblical Literature.
2006 Purity Strategies and Political Interests in the Policy of Nehemiah. Pp. 199–206 in *Confronting the Past: Archaeological and Historical Essays on Ancient Israel in Honor of William G. Dever*, ed. S. Gitin, J. E. Wright, and J. P. Dessel. Winona Lake, IN: Eisenbrauns.

Albright, W. F.
1937 A Biblical Fragment from the Maccabean Age: The Nash Papyrus. *Journal of Biblical Literature* 56: 145–76.
1939 Review of *Géographie de la Palestine*, by F.-M. Abel. *Journal of Biblical Literature* 58: 177–87.
1963 *The Biblical Period from Abraham to Ezra*. New York: Harper.

Allen, L. C.
1999 "For He Is Good...": Worship in Ezra-Nehemiah. Pp. 15–34 in *Worship and the Hebrew Bible: Essays in Honour of John T. Willis*, ed. M. P. Graham, R. R. Marrs, and S. L. McKenzie. Journal for the Study of the Old Testament Supplement 284. Sheffield, UK: JSOT.

Alt, A.

1953a *Kleine Schriften zur Geschichte des Volkes Israel.* Vol. 1. Munich: Beck.
1953b *Kleine Schriften zur Geschichte des Volkes Israel.* Vol. 2. Munich: Beck.
1959 *Kleine Schriften zur Geschichte des Volkes Israel.* Vol. 3. Edited by M. Noth. Munich: Beck.

Amiran, R.
1970 *Ancient Pottery of the Holy Land: From Its Beginnings in the Neolithic Period to the End of the Iron Age.* New Brunswick, NJ: Rutgers University Press.

Applebaum, A.
1986 Historical Commentary. Pp. 257–70 in Dar 1986.

Arav, R.
1999 Bethsaida Excavations, 1994–96. Pp. 1–110 in *Bethsaida: A City by the North Shore of the Sea of Galilee,* vol. 2, ed. R. Arav and R. A. Freund. Kirksville, MO: Truman State University Press.
2008 Bethsaida (Et-Tell). *New Encyclopaedia of Archaeological Excavations in the Holy Land* 5: 1611–15.

Arnold, W.
1996 The Use of Aramaic in the Hebrew Bible: Another Look at the. Bilingualism in Ezra and Nehemiah. *Journal of Northwest Semitic Languages* 22: 1–16.

Asa-El, A.
2004 *The Diaspora and the Lost Tribes of Israel.* Berkeley, CA: Publishers Group West.

Astour, M. C.
1988 The Origin of the Samaritans. Pp. 9–53 in *Studies in the History and Archaeology of Palestine,* vol. 3. Aleppo, Syria: Palestine Archaeological Centre.

Auld, A. G.
1994 *Kings without Privilege: David and Moses in the Story of the Bible's Kings.* Edinburgh: Clark.

Avigad, N.
1993 Samaria. *New Encyclopaedia of Archaeological Excavations in the Holy Land* 4: 1300–10.

Avigad, N., and B. Sass
1997 *Corpus of West Semitic Stamp Seals.* Jerusalem: Israel Academy of Sciences.

Avi-Yonah, M.
1966 *The Holy Land from the Persian to the Arab Conquests (536 B.C. to A.D. 640): A Historical Geography.* Grand Rapids, MI: Baker.

Baillet, M.
1988 Commandements et lois (*Farâ'id et Tûrot*) dans quatre manuscrits samaritains. Pp. 259–70 in *Études samaritaines: Pentateuque et Targum, exégèse et philologie, chroniques,* ed. J.-P. Rothschild and G. D. Sixdenier. Leuven, Belgium: Peeters.

Barag, D.
1986–87 A Silver Coin of Yoḥanan the High Priest and the Coinage of Judea in the Fourth Century B.C. *Israel Numismatic Journal* 9: 4–21.

Barkay, G.
1992 The Iron Age II–III. Pp. 302–73 in *The Archaeology of Ancient Israel*, ed. A. Ben-Tor, trans. R. Greenberg. New Haven, CT: Yale University Press.
1993 The Redefining of Archaeological Periods. Pp. 106–12 in *Biblical Archaeology Today, 1990*, ed. A. Biran and J. Aviram. Jerusalem: Israel Exploration Society.

Barrick, W. B.
2000 Dynastic Politics, Priestly Succession, and Josiah's Eighth Year. *Zeitschrift für die Alttestamentliche Wissenschaft* 112: 564–82.
2002 *The King and the Cemeteries: Toward a New Understanding of Josiah's Reform*. Vetus Testamentum Supplement 88. Leiden, the Netherlands: Brill.

Barstad, H. M.
1996 *The Myth of the Empty Land: A Study in the History and Archaeology of Judah during the "Exilic" Period*. Symbolae Osloenses Fasc. Suppl., 28. Oslo: Scandinavian University Press.
2003 After the "Myth of the Empty Land": Major Challenges in the Study of Neo-Babylonian Judah. Pp. 3–20 in Lipschits and Blenkinsopp 2003.

Bartlett, J. R.
1985 *Jews in the Hellenistic World: Josephus, Aristeas, the Sibylline Oracles, Eupolemus*. Cambridge, UK: Cambridge University Press.

Beaulieu, P.-.A.
2011 Yahwistic Names in Light of Late Babylonian Onomastics. Pp. 245–66 in Lipschits, Knoppers, and Oeming 2011.

Becking, B.
1992 *The Fall of Samaria: An Historical and Archaeological Study*. Studies in the History of the Ancient Near East 2. Leiden, the Netherlands: Brill.
1997 From Apostasy to Destruction: A Josianic View on the Fall of Samaria. Pp. 279–97 in Vervenne and Lust 1997.
2002 West Semites at Tell Šēḥ Ḥamad: Evidence for the Israelite Exile? Pp. 153–66 in *Kein Land für sich allein*, ed. U. Hübner and E. A. Knauf. Orbis Biblicus et Orientalis 186. Fribourg, Switzerland: Universitätsverlag.
2007 Do the Earliest Samaritan Inscriptions Already Indicate a Parting of the Ways? Pp. 213–22 in *Judah and the Judeans in the Fourth Century*, ed. O. Lipschits, G. N. Knoppers, and R. Albertz. Winona Lake, IN: Eisenbrauns.
2011 *Ezra, Nehemiah, and the Construction of Early Jewish Identity*. Forschungen zum Alten Testament 80. Tübingen, Germany: Mohr Siebeck.

Bedford, P. R.
2001 *Temple Restoration in Early Achaemenid Judah*. Supplements to the *Journal for the Study of Judaism* 65. Leiden, the Netherlands: Brill.

Beentjes, P. C.
1982 Inverted Quotations in the Bible: A Neglected Stylistic Pattern. *Biblica* 63: 506–23.

Beit-Arieh, I.

2008 Tel Ḥadid. *New Encyclopaedia of Archaeological Excavations in the Holy Land* 5: 1757–58.

Ben-Ḥayyim, Z.

1988 *Tibåt Mårqe: A Collection of Samaritan Midrashim*. Jerusalem: Israel Academy of Sciences and Humanities.

1995 The Tenth Commandment in Samaritan Research. Pp. 487–92 in *Essays in Honour of G. D. Sixdenier: New Samaritan Studies of the Société d'Études Samaritaines*, ed. A. D. Crown and L. Davey. Studies in Judaica 5. Sydney: Mandelbaum.

Benjamin, J. M.

2001 *The Mystery of Israel's Ten Lost Tribes and the Legend of Jesus in India*. New Delhi: Mosaic.

Ben-Tor, A.

1987 *Tell Qiri, a Village in the Jezreel Valley: Report of the Archaeological Excavations, 1975–1977*. Qedem 24. Jerusalem: Institute of Archaeology.

1997 Tel Qiri. *Oxford Encyclopedia of Archaeology in the Near East* 4: 387–89.

2008 Hazor. *New Encyclopaedia of Archaeological Excavations in the Holy Land* 5: 1769–76.

Ben Zvi, E.

1993 A Gateway to the Chronicler's Teaching: The Account of the Reign of Ahaz in 2 Chr 28,1–27. *Scandinavian Journal of the Old Testament* 7: 216–49.

1995 Inclusion and Exclusion from Israel as Conveyed by the Use of the Term "Israel" in Post-Monarchic Biblical Texts. Pp. 95–149 in *The Pitcher Is Broken: Memorial Essays for Gösta W. Ahlström*, ed. S. W. Holloway and L. K. Handy. *Journal for the Study of the Old Testament* Supplement 190. Sheffield, UK: Sheffield Academic Press.

1999 When a Foreign Monarch Speaks. Pp. 209–28 in *The Chronicler as Author: Studies in Text and Texture*, ed. M. P. Graham and S. L. McKenzie. *Journal for the Study of the Old Testament* Supplement 263. Sheffield, UK: Sheffield Academic Press.

2003 The Secession of the Northern Kingdom in Chronicles. Pp. 61–88 in *The Chronicler as Theologian*, ed. M. P. Graham, S. L. McKenzie, and G. N. Knoppers. *Journal for the Study of the Old Testament* Supplement 371. London: Clark.

2010a Reconstructing the Intellectual Discourse of Ancient Yehud. *Studies in Religion/Sciences Religieuses* 39: 7–23.

2010b Total Exile, Empty Land and the General Intellectual Discourse in Yehud. Pp. 155–68 in *The Concept of Exile in Ancient Israel and Its Historical Contexts*, ed. E. Ben Zvi and C. Levin. Beihefte zur *Zeitschrift für die Alttestamentliche Wissenschaft* 404. Berlin: de Gruyter.

Berlejung, A.

2012 The Assyrians in the West: Assyrianization, Colonialism, Indifference, or Development Policy? Pp. 21–60 in Nissinen 2012.

Berlin, A. M.
1997 Between Large Forces: Palestine in the Hellenistic Period. *Biblical Archaeologist* 60: 2–51.

Berman, J. A.
2006 The Narratorial Voice of the Scribes of Samaria: Ezra IV 8–VI 18 Reconsidered. *Vetus Testamentum* 56: 313–26.
2007 The Narratological Purpose of Aramaic Prose in Ezra 4.8–6.18. *Aramaic Studies* 7: 1–27.

Bernstein, M. J.
2005 "Rewritten Bible": A Generic Category Which Has Outlived Its Usefulness? *Textus* 22: 169–96.

Betlyon, J. W.
1982 *The Coinage and Mints of Phoenicia*. Harvard Semitic Monographs 26. Chico, CA: Scholars Press.

Bewer, J. A.
1933 *The Literature of the Old Testament*. Rev. ed. New York: Columbia University Press.

Binder, D. D.
1999 *Into the Temple Courts: The Place of the Synagogues in the Second Temple Period*. Society of Biblical Literature Dissertation Series 169. Atlanta, GA: Society of Biblical Literature.

Birnbaum, S. A.
1957 Inscriptions: Ostraca. Pp. 9–32 in Crowfoot, Crowfoot, and Kenyon 1957.

Blenkinsopp, J.
1988 *Ezra-Nehemiah: A Commentary*. Old Testament Library. Philadelphia: Westminster.
1998 The Judaean Priesthood during the Neo-Babylonian and Achaemenid Periods: A Hypothetical Reconstruction. *Catholic Biblical Quarterly* 60: 25–43.
2002 The Bible, Archaeology and Politics, or The Empty Land Revisited. *Journal for the Study of the Old Testament* 27: 169–87.
2003 Bethel in the Neo-Babylonian Period. Pp. 93–107 in Lipschits and Blenkinsopp 2003.
2009 *Judaism, the First Phase: The Place of Ezra and Nehemiah in the Origins of Judaism*. Grand Rapids, MI: Eerdmans.

Bloch-Smith, E.
2009 Assyrians Abet Israelite Cultic Reforms. Pp. 35–44 in *Exploring the Longue Durée: Essays in Honor of Lawrence E. Stager*, ed. J. D. Schloen. Winona Lake, IN: Eisenbrauns.

Blum, E.
1990 *Studien zur Komposition des Pentateuch*. Beihefte zur Zeitschrift für die Alttestamentliche Wissenschaft 189. Berlin: de Gruyter.
2011 Pentateuch-Hexateuch-Enneateuch? Or: How Can One Recognize a Literary Work in the Hebrew Bible? Pp. 43–71 in Dozeman, Römer, and Schmid 2011.

Boda, M. J.
1999 *Praying the Tradition: The Origin and Use of Tradition in Nehemiah 9*. Beihefte zur *Zeitschrift für die Alttestamentliche Wissenschaft* 277. Berlin: de Gruyter.

Bolin, T. M.
1995 The Temple of *Yahu* at Elephantine and Persian Religious Policy. Pp. 127–42 in *The Triumph of Elohim: From Yahwisms to Judaisms*, ed. D. V. Edelman. Contributions to Biblical Exegesis and Theology 13. Kampen, the Netherlands: Kok Pharos.

Brett, M. G.
1996 Interpreting Ethnicity: Method, Hermeneutics, Ethics. Pp. 3–22 in *Ethnicity and the Bible*, ed. M. G. Brett. Leiden, the Netherlands: Brill.
2008 *Decolonizing God: The Bible in the Tides of Empire*. Bible in the Modern World 16. Sheffield, UK: Sheffield Phoenix.
2010 National Identity as Commentary and as Metacommentary. Pp. 29–40 in *Historiography and Identity(Re)formulation in Second Temple Historiographical Literature*, ed. L. C. Jonker. Library of Hebrew Bible/Old Testament Studies 534. New York: Clark.

Brettler, M. Z.
1995 *The Creation of History in Ancient Israel*. London: Routledge.
2002 *The Book of Judges*. London: Routledge.

Brewer, D. I.
1992 *Techniques and Assumptions in Jewish Exegesis before 70 CE*. Texte und Studien zum Antiken Judentum 30. Tübingen, Germany: Mohr Siebeck.

Briant, P.
1996 *Histoire de l'empire perse: De Cyrus à Alexandre*. Achaemenid History 10. Paris: Fayard.

Bright, J.
1981 *A History of Israel*. 3rd ed. Philadelphia: Westminster.

Broshi, M.
1974 The Expansion of Jerusalem in the Reigns of Hezekiah and Manasseh. *Israel Exploration Journal* 24: 21–26.

Broshi, M., and I. Finkelstein
1992 The Population of Palestine in Iron Age II. *Bulletin of the American Schools of Oriental Research* 287: 45–60.

Bruneau, P.
1982 Les Israélites de Délos et la juivierie délienne. *Bulletin de Correspondance Hellénique* 106: 465–504.

Bull, R. J.
1968 The Excavation of Tell er-Râs on Mt. Gerizim. *Bulletin of the American Schools of Oriental Research* 190: 58–72.

Burney, C. F.
1903 *Notes on the Hebrew Text of the Books of Kings*. Oxford: Clarendon.

1918 *The Book of Judges: With Introduction and Notes*. London: Rivingtons.

Campbell, A. F., and M. A. O'Brien

2000 *Unfolding the Deuteronomistic History: Origins, Upgrades, Present Text*. Minneapolis: Fortress.

Campbell, E. F.

1991 *Shechem II: Portrait of a Hill Country Vale—The Shechem Regional Survey*. Atlanta, GA: Scholars Press.

2002 *Shechem III: The Stratigraphy and Architecture of Shechem/Tell Balâṭah*. Vol. 1, *Text*. American Schools of Oriental Research Archaeological Reports 6. Boston: American Schools of Oriental Research.

Capponi, L.

2007 *Il tempio di Leontopoli in Egitto: Identità politica e religiosa dei giudei di Onia, c. 150 a.C.–73 d.C.*. Pisa, Italy: ETS.

Carr, D. M.

2005 *Writing on the Tablet of the Heart: Origins of Scripture and Literature*. New York: Oxford University Press.

(Forthcoming) Changes in Pentateuchal Criticism, in *The Hebrew Bible/Old Testament: The History of Its Interpretation*, vol. 3, *From Modernism to Post-Modernism*, pt. 2, ed. Magne Sæbø. Göttingen, Germany: Vandenhoeck & Ruprecht.

Carroll, R. P.

1992 The Myth of the Empty Land. *Semeia* 59: 79–93.

2001 Exile! What Exile? Deportation and the Discourses of Diaspora. Pp. 63–79 in *Leading Captivity Captive: "The Exile" as History and Ideology*, ed. L. L. Grabbe. Journal for the Study of the Old Testament Supplement 278. Sheffield, UK: Sheffield Academic Press.

Carter, C. E.

1999 *The Emergence of Yehud in the Persian Period: A Social and Demographic Study*. Journal for the Study of the Old Testament Supplement 294. Sheffield, UK: Sheffield Academic Press.

2003 Ideology and Archaeology in the Neo-Babylonian Period. Pp. 301–22 in Lipschits and Blenkinsopp.

Chambon, A.

1984 *Tell el-Fârʿah*. Vol. 1, *L'âge du fer*. Paris: Éditions Recherche sur les Civilisations.

Charlesworth, J. H.

2009 What Is a Variant? Announcing a Dead Sea Scroll Fragment of Deuteronomy. *Maarav* 16: 201–12, 273–74 (pls. ix–x).

Clements, R. E., and G. J. Botterweck

1975 גוֹי; gôy. *Theological Dictionary of the Old Testament* 2: 426–33.

Clines, D. J. A.

1990 *What Does Eve Do to Help? And Other Readerly Questions to the Old Testament*. Journal for the Study of the Old Testament Supplement 94. Sheffield, UK: JSOT.

Cogan, M.

1974 *Imperialism and Religion: Assyria, Judah, and Israel in the Eighth and Seventh Centuries B.C.E.* Society of Biblical Literature Monograph Series 19. Missoula, MT: Scholars Press.

1978 Israel in Exile: The View of a Josianic Historian. *Journal of Biblical Literature* 97: 40–44.

1988 For We, Like You, Worship Your God: Three Biblical Portrayals of Samaritan Origins. *Vetus Testamentum* 38: 286–92.

1993 Judah under Assyrian Hegemony: A Reexamination of Imperialism and Religion. *Journal of Biblical Literature* 112: 403–14.

2004 A Slip of the Pen? On Josiah's Actions in Samaria (2 Kgs 23:15–20). Pp. 3–8 in *Sefer Moshe: The Moshe Weinfeld Jubilee Volume—Studies in the Bible and the Ancient Near East, Qumran, and Post-Biblical Judaism*, ed. C. Cohen, A. Hurvitz, and S. M. Paul. Winona Lake, IN: Eisenbrauns.

Cogan, M., and H. Tadmor

1988 *II Kings: A New Translation with Introduction and Commentary.* Anchor Bible 11. Garden City, NY: Doubleday.

Coggins, R. J.

1975 *Samaritans and Jews: The Origins of Samaritanism Reconsidered.* Growing Points in Theology. Oxford: Blackwell.

1989 After the Exile. Pp. 229–49 in *Creating the Old Testament: The Emergence of the Hebrew Bible*, ed. S. Bigger. Oxford: Blackwell.

1991 The Samaritans and Northern Israelite Tradition. Pp. 99–108 in *Proceedings of the First International Congress of the Société d'Études Samaritaines*, ed. A. Tal and M. Florentin. *Tel Aviv*: Rosenberg School for Jewish Studies.

Cohen, S. J. D.

1979 *Josephus in Galilee and Rome: His Vita and Development as a Historian.* Leiden, the Netherlands: Brill.

1999 *The Beginnings of Jewishness: Boundaries, Varieties, Uncertainties.* Berkeley: University of California Press.

Cohn, R.

2000 *2 Kings.* Berit Olam. Collegeville, MN: Liturgical Press.

Cornelius, I.

2011 "A Tale of Two Cities": The Visual Symbol Systems of Yehud and Samaria and identity; Self-understanding in Persian-Period Palestine. Pp. 213–37 in *Texts, Contexts and Readings in Postexilic Literature: Explorations into Historiography and Identity Negotiation in Hebrew Bible and Related Texts*, ed. L. C. Jonker. Forschungen zum Alten Testament, 2nd ser., 53. Tübingen, Germany: Mohr Siebeck.

Crane, O. T.

1890 *The Samaritan Chronicle, or The Book of Joshua the Son of Nun.* New York: Alden. Translation of Juynboll 1848.

Crawford, S. W.

1995 4QDeut^n. Pp. 117–28 in *Qumran Cave 4. IX: Deuteronomy, Joshua, Judges, Kings*, ed. E. Ulrich, F. M. Cross, S. W. Crawford, J. A. Duncan, P. W. Skehan, E. Tov, and J. Trebolle Barrera. Discoveries in the Judaean Desert 14. Oxford: Clarendon.

2008 *Rewriting Scripture in Second Temple Times*. Grand Rapids, MI: Eerdmans.

Cross, F. M.

1961 The Development of the Jewish Scripts. Pp. 133–202 in *The Bible and the Ancient Near East: Essays in Honor of William Foxwell Albright*, ed. G. E. Wright. Garden City, NY: Doubleday.

1964 The History of the Biblical Text in the Light of the Discoveries in the Judaean Desert. *Harvard Theological Review* 57: 281–99.

1966 Aspects of Samaritan and Jewish History in Late Persian and Hellenistic Times. *Harvard Theological Review* 59: 201–11.

1971 Papyri of the Fourth Century B. C. from Daliyeh. Pp. 45–69 in *New Directions in Biblical Archaeology*, ed. D. N. Freedman and J. N. Greenfield. New York: Doubleday.

1973 *Canaanite Myth and Hebrew Epic: Essays in the History of the Religion of Israel*. Cambridge, MA: Harvard University Press.

1974 The Papyri and Their Historical Implications. Pp. 17–29 in *Discoveries in the Wâdî ed-Dâlîyeh*, ed. P. W. Lapp and N. L. Lapp. Annual of the American Schools of Oriental Research 41. Cambridge, MA: American Schools of Oriental Research.

1985 Samaria Papyrus 1: An Aramaic Slave Conveyance of 335 B.C.E. Found in the Wâdî ed-Dâlîyeh. *Eretz-Israel* 18:1–17.

1998 *From Epic to Canon: History and Literature in Ancient Israel*. Baltimore: Johns Hopkins University Press.

2006 Personal Names in the Samaria Papyri. *Bulletin of the American Schools of Oriental Research* 344: 75–90.

Crowfoot, J. W.

1942 Buildings round and below the Summit. Pp. 5–20 in Crowfoot, Kenyon, and Sukenik 1942.

1957a Introduction. Pp. 1–8 in Crowfoot, Crowfoot, and Kenyon 1957.

1957b Pottery: Imported Wares. Pp. 210–16 in Crowfoot, Crowfoot, and Kenyon 1957.

Crowfoot, J. W., G. M. Crowfoot, and K. M. Kenyon

1957 *The Objects from Samaria* (eds.). Samaria-Sebaste Reports of the Work of the Joint Expedition in 1931–1933 and of the British Expedition in 1935 3. London: Palestine Exploration Fund.

Crowfoot, J. W., K. M. Kenyon, and E. L. Sukenik

1942 *The Buildings at Samaria*. London: Palestine Exploration Fund.

Crown, A. D.

1974a The Date and Authenticity of the Samaritan Hebrew Book of Joshua as Seen in Its Territorial Allotments. *Palestine Exploration Quarterly* 96: 79–100.

1974b The Samaritan Diaspora to the End of the Byzantine Era. *Australian Journal of Biblical Archaeology* 2: 107–23.
1989a The Byzantine and Moslem Period. Pp. 55–81 in Crown 1989c.
1989b The Samaritan Diaspora. Pp. 195–217 in Crown 1989c.
1989c *The Samaritans* (ed.). Tübingen, Germany: Mohr.
1991 Redating the Schism between the Judaeans and the Samaritans. *Jewish Quarterly Review* 82: 17–50.
1994 Samaritan Literature and Its Manuscripts. *Bulletin of the John Rylands University Library* 76: 21–49.
1998 Was There a Samaritan Book of Joshua? Pp. 15–22 in *Ancient History in a Modern University, vol. 2, Early Christianity, Late Antiquity, and Beyond*, ed. T. W. Hillard, R. A. Kearsley, C. E. V. Nixon, and A. M. Nobbs. Grand Rapids, MI: Eerdmans.

Daise, M.
1998 Samaritans, Seleucids, and the Epic of Theodotus. *Journal for the Study of the Pseudepigrapha* 17: 25–51.

Dalley, S.
1985 Foreign Chariotry and Cavalry in the Armies of Tiglath-Pileser III and Sargon II. *Iraq* 47: 31–48.

Dandamaev, M. A.
2004 Twin Towns and Ethnic Minorities in First-Millennium Babylonia. Pp. 137–49 in *Commerce and Monetary Systems in the Ancient World: Means of Transmission and Cultural Interaction*, ed. R. Rollinger and C. Ulf. Melammu Symposia 5. Stuttgart: Franz Steiner.

Dar, S.
1986 *Landscape and Pattern, vol. 1*. BAR International Series 308/1. Oxford: BAR.
1992 Samaria; Archaeology of the Region. *Anchor Bible Dictionary* 5: 926–31.
2011 The Samaritans in Caesarea Maritima. Pp. 225–35 in Zsengellér 2011.

Day, J.
2000 *Yahweh and the Gods and Goddesses of Canaan*. Journal for the Study of the Old Testament Supplement 265. Sheffield, UK: Sheffield Academic Press.

Delavault, B., and A. Lemaire
1979 Les inscriptions phéniciennes de Palestine. *Rivista di Studi Fenici* 7: 5–12.

De Odorico, M.
1995 *The Use of Numbers and Quantifications in the Assyrian Royal Inscriptions*. State Archives of Assyria Studies 3. Helsinki: Neo-Assyrian Text Corpus Project, Department of Asian and African Studies, University of Helsinki.

Dever, W. G.
1997 Bethel. *Oxford Encyclopedia of Archaeology in the Near East* 1: 300–301.
2007 Archaeology and the Fall of the Northern Kingdom. Pp. 78–92 in *"Up to the Gates of Ekron": Essays on the Archaeology and History of the Eastern Mediterranean in Honor of Seymour Gitin*, ed. S. W. Crawford et al. Jerusalem: Israel Exploration Society.

De Vries, S. J.
1989 *1 and 2 Chronicles*. Forms of the Old Testament Literature 11. Grand Rapids, MI: Eerdmans.

De Wette, W. M. L.
1806–7 *Beiträge zur Einleitung in das Alten Testament*. 2 vols. Halle, Germany: Schimmelpfennig.

Dexinger, F.
1977 Das Garizimgebot im Dekalog der Samaritaner. Pp. 111–33 in *Studien zum Pentateuch: Walter Kornfeld zum 60. Geburtstag*, ed. G. Braulik. Vienna: Herder.

1981 Limits of Tolerance in Judaism: The Samaritan Example. Pp. 88–114 in *Jewish and Christian Self-Definition*, vol. 2, *Aspects of Judaism in the Graeco-Roman Period* ed. E. P. Sanders. Philadelphia: Fortress.

1992 Der Ursprung der Samaritaner im Spiegel der frühen Quellen. Pp. 76–103 in *Die Samaritaner*, ed. F. Dexinger and R. Pummer. Wege der Forschung 604. Darmstadt, Germany: Wissenschaftliche Buchgesellschaft.

Dietrich, W.
1972 *Prophetie und Geschichte: Eine redaktionsgeschichtliche Untersuchung zum deuteronomistischen Geschichtswerk*. Forschungen zur Religion und Literatur des Alten und Neuen Testaments 108. Göttingen, Germany: Vandenhoeck & Ruprecht.

2000 Prophetie im deuteronomistischen Geschichtswerk. Pp. 47–65 in *The Future of the Deuteronomistic History*, ed. T. Römer. Bibliotheca Ephemeridum Theologicarum Lovaniensium 147. Leuven, Belgium: Peeters.

Di Segni, L.
1990 The Church of Mary Theotokos on Mount Gerizim: The Inscriptions. Pp. 343–50 in *Christian Archaeology in the Holy Land: New Discoveries*, ed. G. C. Bottini, L. Di Segni, and E. Alliata. Jerusalem: Franciscan Press.

1993 The Greek Inscriptions in the Samaritan Synagogue at El Khirbe, with Some Considerations on the Function of the Samaritan Synagogue in the Late Roman Period. Pp. 231–39 in *Early Christianity in Context: Monuments and Documents*, ed. F. Manns and E. Alliata. Jerusalem: Franciscan Press.

Dobbs-Allsopp, F. W., J. J. M. Roberts, C. L. Seow, and R. E. Whitaker
2005 *Hebrew Inscriptions: Texts from the Biblical Period of the Monarchy with Concordance*. New Haven, CT: Yale University Press.

Donner, H.
1977 The Separate States of Israel and Judah. Pp. 381–434 in *Israelite and Judean History*, ed. J. H. Hayes and J. M. Miller. London: SCM.

1986 *Geschichte des Volkes Israel und seiner Nachbarn in Grundzügen*, vol. 2. Grundrisse zum Alten Testament 4/2. Göttingen, Germany: Vandenhoeck & Ruprecht.

1992 *The Mosaic Map of Madaba: An Introductory Guide*. Kampen, the Netherlands: Kok Pharos.

Dorsey, D. A.
1991 *The Roads and Highways of Ancient Israel*. Baltimore: Johns Hopkins University Press.

Dozeman, T. B., T. C. Römer, and K. Schmid
2011 *Pentateuch, Hexateuch, or Enneateuch? Identifying Literary Works in Genesis through Kings* (eds.). Atlanta, GA: Society of Biblical Literature.

Dubovský, P.
2006 *Hezekiah and the Assyrian Spies: Reconstruction of the Neo-Assyrian Intelligence Services and Its Significance for 2 Kings 18–1*. Biblica et Orientalia 49. Rome: Pontifical Biblical Institute.

Dumbrell, W. J.
1971 The Tell el-Maskhuṭa Bowls and the "Kingdom" of Qedar in the Persian Period. *Bulletin of the American Schools of Oriental Research* 203: 33–44.

Dušek, Jan
2007a *Les manuscrits araméens du Wadi Daliyeh et la Samarie vers 450–332 av. J.-C.* Culture and History of the Ancient Near East 30. Leiden, the Netherlands: Brill.
2007b Ruling of Inscriptions in Hellenistic Samaria. *Maarav* 14: 43–65.
2011 Administration of Samaria in the Hellenistic Period. Pp. 71–88 in Zsengellér 2011.
2012a *Aramaic and Hebrew Inscriptions from Mt. Gerizim and Samaria between Antiochus III and Antiochus IV Epiphanes*. Culture and History of the Ancient Near East 54. Leiden, the Netherlands: Brill.
2012b Archaeology and Texts in the Persian Period: Focus on Sanballat. Pp. 117–32 in Nissinen 2012.

Dutcher-Walls, P.
2007 Queen Mothers and Royal Politics of the Seventh Century BCE. Pp. 209–20 in *To Break Every Yoke: Essays in Honor of Marvin L. Chaney*, ed. R. B. Coote and N. K. Gottwald. Sheffield, UK: Sheffield Phoenix.

Dyck, J. E.
1996 The Ideology of Identity in Chronicles. Pp. 89–116 in *Ethnicity and the Bible*, ed. M. G. Brett. Leiden, the Netherlands: Brill.
1998 *The Theocratic Ideology of the Chronicler*. Biblical Interpretation 33. Leiden, the Netherlands: Brill.

Egger, R.
1986 *Josephus Flavius und die Samaritaner: Eine terminologische Untersuchung zur Identitätsklärung der Samaritäner*. Novum Testamentum et Orbis Antiquus 4. Fribourg, Switzerland: Universitätsverlag.

Eissfeldt, O.
1965 *The Old Testament: An Introduction*. New York: Harper & Row.

Ephʿal, I.
1991 "The Samarian(s)" in the Assyrian Sources. Pp. 36–45 in *Ah, Assyria: Studies in Assyrian History and Ancient Near Eastern Historiography Presented to Hayim*

Tadmor, ed. M. Cogan and I. Eph'al. Scripta Hierosolymitana 33. Jerusalem: Magnes.

1998 Changes in Palestine during the Persian Period in Light of Epigraphic Sources. *Israel Exploration Journal* 48: 106–19.

2006 The Babylonian Exile: The Survival of a National Minority in a Culturally Developed Foreign Milieu. Pp. 21–31 in *Gründungsfeier am. 16. Dezember 2005*. Göttingen, Germany: Akademie der Wissenschaften.

Eshel, E.

1991 4QDeut^n: A Text that has Undergone Harmonistic Editing. *Hebrew Union College Annual* 62: 117–54.

Eshel, E., and H. Eshel

2003 Dating the Samaritan Pentateuch's Compilation in Light of the Qumran Biblical Scrolls. Pp. 215–40 in *Emanuel: Studies in Hebrew Bible, Septuagint, and Dead Sea Scrolls in Honor of Emanuel Tov*, ed. S. M. Paul, R. A. Kraft, L. H. Schiffman, and W. W. Fields. Vetus Testamentum Supplement 94. Leiden, the Netherlands: Brill.

Eshel, H.

1994 The Samaritan Temple on Mt. Gerizim and Historical Research. *Beth Mikra* 39: 141–55 (Hebrew).

1996 Wâdi ed-Dâlîyeh Papyrus 14 and the Samaritan Temple. *Zion* 61: 125–36 (Hebrew).

1997 Israelite Names from Samaria in the Persian Period. Pp. 181–89 in *These Are the Names: Studies in Jewish Onomastics*, ed. A. Demsky, J. Tabory, Y. A. Raif, and E. D. Lawson. Ramat Gan, Israel: Bar-Ilan University Press (Hebrew).

2007 The Governors of Samaria in the Fifth and Fourth Centuries BCE. Pp. 223–34 in Lipschits, Knoppers, and Albertz 2007.

Eshel, H. And B. Zissu

2006 Two Notes on the History and Archaeology of Judea in the Persian Period. Pp. 823–31 in *"I Will Speak the Riddles of Ancient Times": Archaeological and Historical Studies in Honor of Amihai Mazar on the Occasion of his Sixtieth Birthday*, ed. A. M. Maeir and P. de Miroschedji. Winona Lake, IN: Eisenbrauns.

Eskenazi, T. C.

1988 *In an Age of Prose: A Literary Approach to Ezra-Nehemiah*. Society of Biblical Literature Monograph Series 36. Atlanta, GA: Scholars Press.

Esler, P. F.

2003 Ezra-Nehemiah as a Narrative of (Re-invented) Israelite Identity. *Biblical Interpretation* 11: 413–26.

Eynikel, E.

1996 *The Reform of King Josiah and the Composition of the Deuteronomistic History*. Oudtestamentische Studiën 33. Leiden, the Netherlands: Brill.

1997 The Portrait of Manasseh and the Deuteronomistic History. Pp. 233–61 in Vervenne and Lust 1997.

Fantalkin, A., and O. Tal
2009 Re-discovering the Iron Age Fortress at Tell Qudadi in the Context of Neo-Assyrian Imperialistic Policies. *Palestine Exploration Quarterly* 141: 188–206.

Faü, J.-F., and A. D. Crown.
2001 *Les Samaritains: Rescapés de 2700 ans d'histoire*. Paris: Maisonneuve & Larose.

Faust, A.
2001 Jerusalem's Countryside during the Iron II–Persian Period Transition. Pp. 83–89 in *New Studies on Jerusalem: Proceedings of the Fifth Conference*, ed. A. Faust and E. Baruch. Jerusalem: Rennert Center (Hebrew).

2003a The Farmstead in the Highlands of Iron III Israel. Pp. 91–104 in *The Rural Landscape of Ancient Israel*, ed. A. M. Maeir, S. Dar, and Z. Safrai. BAR International Series 1121. Oxford: Archaeopress.

2003b Judah in the Sixth Century BCE: A Rural Perspective. *Palestine Exploration Quarterly* 135: 37–53.

2004 Social and Cultural Changes in Judah during the 6th Century BCE and Their Implications for our Understanding of the Nature of the Neo-Babylonian Period. *Ugarit Forschungen* 36: 157–76.

2006 Farmsteads in the Foothills of Western Samaria. Pp. 477–504 in *"I Will Speak the Riddles of Ancient Times": Archaeological and Historical Studies in Honor of Amihai Mazar on the Occasion of his Sixtieth Birthday*, ed. A. M. Maeir and P. de Miroschedji. Winona Lake, IN: Eisenbrauns.

Feldman, L. H.
1965 *Josephus, Jewish Antiquities: Books XVIII–XIX*. Loeb Classical Library 433. Cambridge, MA: Harvard University Press.

1996 *Studies in Hellenistic Judaism*. Arbeiten zur Geschichte des Antiken Judentums und des Urchristentums 30. Leiden, the Netherlands: Brill.

1997 The Concept of Exile in Josephus. Pp. 145–72 in *Exile: Old Testament, Jewish, and Christian Conceptions*, ed. J. M. Scott. Supplements to the *Journal for the Study of Judaism* 56. Leiden, the Netherlands: Brill.

Fine, S.
2005 *Art and Judaism in the Greco-Roman World: Toward a New Jewish Archaeology*. Cambridge, UK: Cambridge University Press.

Finkelstein, I.
1988–89 The Land of Ephraim Survey, 1980–1987: Preliminary Report. *Tel Aviv* 15–16: 117–83.

1993a Environmental Archaeology and Social History: Demographic and Economic Aspects of the Monarchic Period. Pp. 56–66 in *Biblical Archaeology Today, 1990*, ed. A. Biran. Jerusalem: Israel Exploration Society.

1993b Southern Samarian Hills Survey. *New Encyclopaedia of Archaeological Excavations in the Holy Land* 4: 1313–14.

2008a Jerusalem in the Persian (and Early Hellenistic) Period and the Wall of Nehemiah. *Journal for the Study of the Old Testament* 32: 501–20.

2008b The Settlement History of Jerusalem in the Eighth and Seventh Centuries BCE. *Revue Biblique* 115: 499–515.

2010 The Territorial Extent and Demography of Yehud/Judea in the Persian and Early Hellenistic Periods. *Revue Biblique* 117: 39–54.

Finkelstein, I., Z. Lederman, and S. Bunimovitz

1997 *Highlands of Many Cultures*. 2 vols. Tel Aviv: Institute of Archaeology.

Finkelstein, I., and L. Singer-Avitz

2009 Reevaluating Bethel. *Zeitschrift des Deutschen Palästina-Vereins* 125: 33–48.

Finkelstein I., and D. Ussishkin

2000 Archaeological and Historical Conclusions. Pp. 576–605 in *Megiddo III: The 1992–1996 Seasons*, vol. 2, ed. I. Finkelstein, D. Ussishkin, and B. Halpern. Tel Aviv: Institute of Archaeology.

Finkelstein I., D. Ussishkin, and B. Halpern

2006 Archaeological and Historical Conclusions. Pp. 843–59 in *Megiddo IV: The 1998–2002 Seasons*, ed. I. Finkelstein, D. Ussishkin, and B. Halpern. Tel Aviv: Institute of Archaeology, Tel Aviv University.

Fishbane, M.

1985 *Biblical Interpretation in Ancient Israel*. Oxford: Clarendon.

Fleishman, J.

2009 To Stop Nehemiah from Building the Jerusalem Wall. Pp. 361–90 in *Homeland and Exile: Biblical and Ancient Near Eastern Studies in Honour of Bustenay Oded*, ed. G. Galil, M. Geller, and A. Millard. Vetus Testamentum Supplement 130. Leiden, the Netherlands: Brill.

Florentin, M.

1999 *The Tulida—A Samaritan Chronicle: Text, Translation, Commentary*. Jerusalem: Ben Zvi, 1999 (Hebrew).

2005 *Late Samaritan Hebrew: A Linguistic Analysis of Its Different Types*. Leiden, the Netherlands: Brill.

Floyd, M. H.

2006 The Production of Prophetic Books in the Early Second Temple Period. Pp. 276–97 in *Prophets, Prophecy, and Prophetic Texts in Second Temple Judaism*, ed. M. H. Floyd and R. D. Haak. Library of Hebrew Bible/Old Testament Studies 427. London: Clark.

Fossum, J.

1989 Sects and Movements. Pp. 293–389 in Crown 1989c.

Frame, G.

1999 The Inscription of Sargon II at Tang-I Var and the Chronology of Dynasty 25. *Orientalia* 68: 31–57.

Franklin, N.

1994 The Room V Reliefs at Dur-Sharrukin and Sargon II's Western Campaigns. *Tel Aviv* 21: 255–75.

2004 Samaria: From Bedrock to the Omride Palace. *Levant* 36: 189–202.

2005 Correlation and Chronology: Samaria and Megiddo Redux. Pp. 310–22 in *The Bible and Radiocarbon Dating: Archaeology, Text and Science*, ed. T. E. Levy and T. Higham. London: Equinox.

Fried, L. S.

2004 *The Priest and the Great King: Temple-Palace Relations in the Persian Empire*. Biblical and Judaic Studies 10. Winona Lake, IN: Eisenbrauns.

Friedman, R. E.

1981 *The Exile and Biblical Narrative: The Formation of the Deuteronomistic and Priestly Works*. Harvard Semitic Monographs 22. Chico, CA: Scholars Press.

Fritz, V.

2003 *1 & 2 Kings*. Minneapolis: Fortress.

2008 Tel Chinnereth. *New Encyclopaedia of Archaeological Excavations in the Holy Land* 5: 1684–85.

Fuchs, A.

1994 *Die Inschriften Sargons II. aus Khorsabad*. Göttingen, Germany: Cuvillier.

Fuller, M. E.

2006 *The Restoration of Israel: Israel's Re-Gathering and the Fate of the Nations in Early Jewish Literature and Luke-Acts*. Beihefte zur Zeitschrift für die Neutestamentliche Wissenschaft und die Kunde der Älteren Kirche 138. Berlin: de Gruyter.

Fulton, D. N.

2011 Mapping Early Jewish Traditions: The Case of MT and LXX Nehemiah 11–12. Ph.D. Diss., The Pennsylvania State University.

Gadd, C. J.

1954 Inscribed Prisms of Sargon II from Nimrud. *Iraq* 16: 173–201.

Gal, Z.

1992 *Lower Galilee during the Iron Age*. Translated by Marcia Reines Josephy. Winona Lake, IN: Eisenbrauns.

Gal, Z., and Y. Alexandre

2000 *Ḥorbat Rosh Zayit: An Iron Age Storage Fort and Village*. IAA Reports 8. Jerusalem: Israel Exploration Society.

Galil, G.

2000 A New Look at the Inscriptions of Tiglath-pileser III. *Biblica* 81: 511–20.

2007 *The Lower Stratum Families in the Neo-Assyrian Period*. Culture and History of the Ancient Near East 27. Leiden, the Netherlands: Brill.

2009 Israelite Exiles in Media: A New Look at ND 2443+. *Vetus Testamentum* 59: 71–79.

Gall, A., von.

1914–18 *Der hebräische Pentateuch der Samaritaner*. Giessen, Germany: Töpelmann.

Galling, K.

1935 Assyrische und persische Präfekten in Geser. *Palästina-jahrbuch* 31: 75–93.

1954 *Die Bücher der Chronik, Esra, Nehemia*. Alte Testament Deutsch 12. Göttingen, Germany: Vandenhoeck & Ruprecht.

Gaster, M.
1925 *The Samaritans: Their History, Doctrines, and Literature.* London: Oxford University Press.

Gesenius, W.
1815 *De Pentateuchi samaritani origine, indole, et auctoritate.* Halle, Germany: Impensis Librariae Rengerianae.

Ginsberg, H. L.
1982 *The Israelian Heritage of Judaism.* New York: Jewish Theological Seminary of America.

Gitler, H., and O. Tal
2006 *The Coinage of Philistia of the Fifth and Fourth Centuries BC: A Study of the Earliest Coins of Palestine.* Collezioni Numismatiche 6. Milan: Ennerre.

Glock, A. E.
1993 Taanach. *New Encyclopaedia of Archaeological Excavations in the Holy Land* 4: 1428–33.

Goldstein, J. A.
1976 *I Maccabees.* Anchor Bible 41. New York: Doubleday.
1983 *II Maccabees.* Anchor Bible 41A. New York: Doubleday.

Gomes, J. F.
2006 *The Sanctuary of Bethel and the Configuration of Israelite Identity.* Beihefte zur Zeitschrift für die Alttestamentliche Wissenschaft 368. Berlin: de Gruyter.

Goodblatt, D. M.
2006 *Elements of Ancient Jewish Nationalism.* Cambridge, UK: Cambridge University Press.

Goodman, M.
2008 *Rome and Jerusalem: The Clash of Ancient Civilizations.* New York: Vintage.

Gonen, R.
2002 *To the Ends of the Earth: The Quest for the Ten Lost Tribes of Israel.* Northvale, NJ: Aronson.

Grabbe, L. L.
1992 *Judaism from Cyrus to Hadrian.* 2 vols. Philadelphia: Fortress.
1995 Synagogues in Pre-70 Palestine: a Reassessment. Pp. 17–26 in *Ancient Synagogues: Historical Analysis and Archaeological Discovery*, vol. 1, ed. D. Urman and P. V. M. Flesher. Studia Post-Biblica 47. Leiden, the Netherlands: Brill.
1998 Triumph of the Pious or Failure of the Xenophobes? The Ezra/Nehemiah Reforms and their *Nachgeschichte*. Pp. 55–65 in *Jewish Local Patriotism and Self-Identification in the Graeco-Roman Period*, ed. S. Jones and S. Pearce. Journal for the Study of the Pseudepigrapha Supplement 31. Sheffield, UK: Sheffield Academic Press.
2000 *Judaic Religion in the Second Temple Period: Belief and Practice from the Exile to Yavneh.* London: Routledge.

2004 *A History of the Jews and Judaism in the Second Temple Period*. Vol. 1, *Yehud, a History of the Persian Province of Judah*. Library of Second Temple Studies 47. London: Clark.

2008 *A History of the Jews and Judaism in the Second Temple Period*. Vol. 2, *The Early Hellenistic Period (335–175 BCE)*. Library of Second Temple Studies 68. London: Clark.

Gray, J.

1970 *I & II Kings: A Commentary*. 2nd ed. Old Testament Library. Philadelphia: Westminster.

Grayson, A. K.

1975 *Assyrian and Babylonian Chronicles*. Texts from Cuneiform Sources 5. Locust Valley, NY: Augustin.

Greenberg, M.

2007 Nash Papyrus. Pp. 783–84 in *Encyclopaedia Judaica*, vol. 14, ed. Fred Skolnik. 2d ed. Detroit: Macmillan Reference USA.

Grelot, P.

1972 *Documents araméens d'Égypte*. Paris: Cerf.

Gropp, D. M.

1986 The Samaria Papyri from Wâdī ed-Dâliyeh. Ph.D. diss., Harvard University.

1990 The Language of the Samaria Papyri: A Preliminary Study. *Maarav* 5–6: 169–85.

2001 *Wadi Daliyeh II: The Samaria Papyri from Wadi Daliyeh*. Discoveries in the Judaean Desert 28. Oxford: Oxford University Press.

Gruen, E. S.

1998 *Heritage and Hellenism: The Reinvention of Jewish Tradition*. Berkeley: University of California Press.

Gunneweg, A. H. W.

1965 *Leviten und Priester: Hauptlinien der Traditionsbildung und Geschichte des israelitisch-jüdischen Kultpersonals*. Forschungen zur Religion und Literatur des Alten und Neuen Testaments 89. Göttingen, Germany: Vandenhoeck & Ruprecht.

Hachlili, R.

2001 *The Menorah, the Ancient Seven-Armed Candelabrum: Origin, Form, and Significance*. Leiden, the Netherlands: Brill.

2009 *Ancient Mosaic Pavements: Themes, Issues, and Trends*. Leiden, the Netherlands: Brill.

Hadjisavvas, S., A. Dupont-Sommer, and H. Lozachmeur

1984 Cinq stèles funéraires découvertes sur le site d'Ayios Georghios, à Larnaca-Kition, en 1979. *Report of the Department of Antiquities, Cyprus 1984: 101–15 (pls. xix–xxi)*.

Hall, B.

1989 From John Hyrcanus to Baba Rabbah. Pp. 32–53 in Crown 1989c.

Halpern, B.
1988 *The First Historians: The Hebrew Bible and History*. San Francisco: Harper & Row.
1998 Why Manasseh Is Blamed for the Babylonian Exile: The Evolution of a Biblical Tradition. *Vetus Testamentum* 48: 473–514.
2000 Centre and Sentry. Pp. 535–75 in *Megiddo III: The 1992–1996 Seasons*, vol. 2, ed. I. Finkelstein, D. Ussishkin, and B. Halpern. *Tel Aviv*: Institute of Archaeology.

Hanhart, R.
1982 Zu den ältesten Traditionen über das Samaritanische Schisma. *Eretz-Israel* 16: 106–15.

Haran, M.
1978 *Temples and Temple-Service in Ancient Israel: An Inquiry into the Character of Cult Phenomena and the Historical Setting of the Priestly School*. Oxford: Clarendon.

Harrington, D. J., and A. J. Saldarini
1987 *Targum Jonathan of the Former Prophets*. Aramaic Bible 10. Wilmington, DE: Glazier.

Headland, T. N., K. Pike, and M. Harris
1990 *Emics and Etics: The Insider/Outsider Debate* (eds). Newbury Park, CA: Sage.

Hendel, R. S.
1998 *The Text of Genesis 1–11: Textual Studies and Critical Edition*. New York: Oxford University Press.

Herrmann, S.
1981 *A History of Israel in Old Testament Times*. Translated by J. Bowden. Rev. ed. Philadelphia: Fortress.

Himbaza, I.
2004 *Le Décalogue et l'histoire du texte: Études des formes textuelles du decalogue et leurs implications dans l'histoire du texte de l'Ancien Testament*. Orbis Biblicus et Orientalis 207. Göttingen, Germany: Vandenhoeck & Ruprecht.

Hjelm, I.
2000 *The Samaritans and Early Judaism: A Literary Analysis*. Journal for the Study of the Old Testament Supplement 303. Sheffield, UK: Sheffield Academic Press.
2004 *Jerusalem's Rise to Sovereignty: Zion and Gerizim in Competition*. Journal for the Study of the Old Testament Supplement 404. London: Clark.

Hoffmann, H.-D.
1980 *Reform und Reformen: Untersuchungen zu einem Grundthema der deuteronomistischen Geschichtsschreibung*. Abhandlungen zur Theologie des Alten und Neuen Testaments 66. Zürich: Theologischer Verlag.

Holladay, J. S., Jr.
2004 Judaeans (and Phoenicians) in Egypt in the Late Seventh to Sixth Centuries B.C. Pp. 405–37 in *Egypt, Israel, and the Ancient Mediterranean World: Studies in Honor of Donald B. Redford*, ed. G. N. Knoppers and A. Hirsch. Probleme der Ägyptologie 20. Leiden, the Netherlands: Brill.

Holladay, W. L.
1989 *Jeremiah 2: A Commentary on the Book of the Prophet Jeremiah, Chapters 26–52*. Hermeneia. Philadelphia: Fortress.

Holloway, S. W.
2002 *Aššur is King! Aššur is King!: Religion in the Exercise of Power in the Neo-Assyrian Empire*. Culture and History of the Ancient Near East 10. Leiden, the Netherlands: Brill.

van der Horst, P. W.
1990 *Essays on the Jewish World of Early Christianity*. Novum Testamentum et Orbis Antiquus 14. Göttingen, Germany: Vandenhoeck & Ruprecht.
2006 *Jews and Christians in Their Graeco-Roman Context: Selected Essays on Early Judaism, Samaritanism, Hellenism, and Christianity*. Wissenschaftliche Untersuchungen zum Neuen Testament 196. Tübingen, Germany: Mohr Siebeck.

Ilan, T.
2002 *Lexicon of Jewish Names in Late Antiquity*. Vol. 1, *Palestine, 330 BCE–200 CE*. Texte und Studien zum Antiken Judentum 91. Tübingen, Germany: Mohr Siebeck.
2008 *Lexicon of Jewish Names in Late Antiquity*. Vol. 3, *The Western Diaspora, 330 BCE–650 CE*. Texte und Studien zum Antiken Judentum 126. Tübingen, Germany: Mohr Siebeck.

Japhet, S.
1968 The Supposed Common Authorship of Chronicles and Ezra-Nehemiah Investigated Anew. *Vetus Testamentum* 18: 330–71.
1983 People and Land in the Restoration Period. Pp. 103–25 in *Das Land Israel in biblischer Zeit*, ed. G. Strecker. Göttingen Theologische Arbeiten 25. Göttingen, Germany: Vandenhoeck & Ruprecht.
1989 *The Ideology of the Book of Chronicles and Its Place in Biblical Thought*. Beiträge zur Erforschung des Alten Testaments und des Antiken Judentums 9. Frankfurt am Main: Lang.
1993 *I & II Chronicles: A Commentary*. Old Testament Library. Louisville, KY: Westminster John Knox.

Jastram, N.
1998 A Comparison of Two "Proto-Samaritan" Texts from Qumran: 4QpaleoExod^m and 4QNum^b. *Dead Sea Discoveries* 5: 264–89.

Joannès, F., and A. Lemaire
1999 Trois tablettes cunéiformes à l'onomastique ouest-sémitique. *Transeuphratène* 17: 17–34.

Jobling, D.
2003 The Salvation of Israel in "The Book of the Divided Kingdoms," or, Was There any "Fall of the Northern Kingdom?" Pp. 50–61 in *Redirected Travel: Alternative Journeys and Places in Biblical Studies*, ed. R. Boer and E. W. Conrad. *Journal for the Study of the Old Testament Supplement* 382. London: Clark.

Joffe, A. H., E. H. Cline, and O. Lipschits
2000 Area H. Pp. 140–60 in *Megiddo III: The 1992–1996 Seasons*, vol. 2, ed. I. Finkelstein, D. Ussishkin, and B. Halpern. Tel Aviv: Institute of Archaeology.

Johnstone, W.
1997 *1 and 2 Chronicles*. Journal for the Study of the Old Testament Supplement 253/254. Sheffield, UK: Sheffield Academic Press.

Jonker, L. C.
2003 *Reflections of King Josiah in Chronicles: Late Stages of the Josiah Reception in II Chr. 34f.* Gütersloh, Germany: Gütersloher Verlagshaus.

Jones, G. H.
1984 *1 and 2 Kings*. 2 vols. New Century Bible Commentary. Grand Rapids, MI: Eerdmans.

Joosten, J.
2010 The Aramaic Background of the Seventy: Language, Culture and History. *Bulletin of the International Organization for Septuagint and Cognate Studies* 43: 53–72.
(Forthcoming) Septuagint and *Samareitikon*. In *From Author to Copyist: The Composition, Redaction and Transmission of the Hebrew Bible; Festschrift Zipora Talshir*. Winona Lake, IN: Eisenbrauns.

Joüon, P.
1923 *Grammaire de l'Hébreu biblique*. Rome: Pontifical Biblical Institute.

Juynboll, T. W. J.
1848 *Chronicon Samaritanum: Arabice conscriptum, cui titulus est Liber Josuae*. Leiden, the Netherlands: Luchtmans.

Kalimi, I.
1995 *Zur Geschichtsschreibung des Chronisten: Literarisch-historiographische Abweichungen der Chronik von ihren Paralleltexten in den Samuel- und Königsbüchern*. Beihefte zur Zeitschrift für die Alttestamentliche Wissenschaft 226. Berlin: de Gruyter.
2002 *Early Jewish Exegesis and Theological Controversy: Studies in Scriptures in the Shadow of Internal and External Controversies*. Jewish and Christian Heritage 2. Assen, the Netherlands: Van Gorcum.

Kallai, Z.
1986 *Historical Geography of the Bible: The Tribal Territories of Israel*. Jerusalem: Magnes.

Kaplan, Y.
2008 Recruitment of Foreign Soldiers into the Neo-Assyrian Army during the Reign of Tiglath-pileser III. Pp. 135–52 in *Treasures on Camels' Humps: Historical and Literary Studies from the Ancient Near East Presented to Israel Eph'al*, ed. M. Cogan and D. Kahn. Jerusalem: Magnes.

Kartveit, M.
1989 *Motive und Schichten der Landtheologie in I Chronik 1–9*. Coniectanea Biblica Old Testament Series 28. Stockholm: Almqvist & Wiksell.

2009 *The Origin of the Samaritans*. Vetus Testamentum Supplement 128. Leiden, the Netherlands: Brill.

Kaufmann, Y.

1960 *The Religion of Israel: From its Beginnings to the Babylonian Exile*. Translated and abridged by M. Greenberg. Chicago: University of Chicago Press.

Keel, O., and C. Uehlinger

1996 *Gods, Goddesses, and Images of God in Ancient Israel*. Minneapolis: Fortress.

Kelle, B. D.

2002 What's in a Name?: Neo-Assyrian Designations for the Northern Kingdom and Their Implications for Israelite History and Biblical Interpretation. *Journal of Biblical Literature* 121: 639–66.

Kellermann, U.

1967 *Nehemia: Quellen, Überlieferung und Geschichte*. Beihefte zur *Zeitschrift für die Alttestamentliche Wissenschaft* 102. Berlin: Töpelmann.

Kelly, B. E.

1996 *Retribution and Eschatology in Chronicles*. Journal for the Study of the Old Testament Supplement 211. Sheffield, UK: Sheffield Academic Press.

Kelso, J. L.

1968 *The Excavation of Bethel (1934–1960)*. Annual of the American Schools of Oriental Research 39. Cambridge, MA: American Schools of Oriental Research.

Kenyon, K. M.

1942 The Summit Buildings and Constructions. Pp. 91–120 in Crowfoot, Kenyon, and Sukenik 1942.

1957 Pottery: Early Bronze and Israelite. Pp. 91–209 in Crowfoot, Crowfoot, and Kenyon 1957.

Kessler, J.

2009 The Diaspora in Zechariah 1–8 and Ezra-Nehemiah: The Role of History, Social. Location, and Tradition in the Formulation of Identity. Pp. 119–45 in *Community Identity in Judean Historiography: Biblical and Comparative Perspectives*, ed. G. N. Knoppers and K. A. Ristau. Winona Lake, IN: Eisenbrauns.

van Keulen, P. S. F.

1996 *Manasseh through the Eyes of the Deuteronomists: The Manasseh Account (2 Kings 21: 1–18) and the Final Chapters of the Deuteronomistic History*. Oudtestamentische Studiën 38. Leiden, the Netherlands: Brill.

Kiefer, J.

2005 *Exil und Diaspora: Begrifflichkeit und Deutungen im antiken Judentum und in der Hebräischen Bibel*. Arbeiten zur Bibel und ihrer Geschichte 19. Leipzig: Evangelische Verlagsanstalt.

Kim, K.-R.

1994 Studies in the Relationship between the Samaritan Pentateuch and the Septuagint. Ph.D. diss., Hebrew University.

King, P. J., and L. E. Stager
2001 *Life in Biblical Israel.* Louisville, KY: Westminster John Knox.
Kippenberg, H. G.
1971 *Garizim und Synagoge: Traditionsgeschichtliche Untersuchungen zur samaritanischen Religion der aramäischen Periode.* Religionsgeschichtliche Versuche und Vorarbeiten 30. Berlin: de Gruyter.
Kirkman, J. S.
1957 The Evidence of the Coins. Pp. 43–70 in Crowfoot, Crowfoot, and Kenyon 1957.
Knauf, E.-A.
1994 *Die Umwelt des Alten Testaments.* Neuer Stuttgarter Kommentar—Altes Testament 29. Stuttgart: Katholisches Bibelwerk.
2002 Towards an Archaeology of the Hexateuch. Pp. 275–94 in *Abschied vom Jahwisten: Die Komposition des Hexateuch in der jüngsten Diskussion,* ed. J. C. Gertz, K. Schmid, and M. Witte. Beihefte zur *Zeitschrift für die Alttestamentliche Wissenschaft* 315. Berlin: de Gruyter.
2003 "Kinneret I" Revisted. Pp. 159–69 in *Saxa loquentur: Studien zur Archäologie Palästinas/Israels; Festschrift für Volkmar Fritz zum 65. Geburtstag,* ed. C. G. den Hertog, U. Hübner, and S. Münger. Münster, Germany: Ugarit-Verlag.
2006 Bethel: The Israelite Impact on Judean Language and Literature. Pp. 291–349 in Lipschits and Oeming 2006.
Knoppers, G. N.
1989 A Reunited Kingdom in Chronicles? *Proceedings: Eastern Great Lakes and Midwest Biblical Societies* 9: 74–88.
1990 Rehoboam in Chronicles: Villain or Victim? *Journal of Biblical Literature* 109: 423–40.
1992 "There Was None Like Him": Incomparability in the Book of Kings. *Catholic Biblical Quarterly* 54: 411–31.
1993a "Battling against Yahweh": Israel's War against Judah in 2 Chr 13:2–20. *Revue Biblique* 100: 511–32.
1993b *Two Nations under God: The Deuteronomistic History of Solomon and the Dual Monarchies.* Vol. 1, *The Reign of Solomon and the Rise of Jeroboam.* Harvard Semitic Monographs 52. Atlanta, GA: Scholars Press.
1994 *Two Nations under God: The Deuteronomistic History of Solomon and the Dual Monarchies.* Vol. 2, *The Reign of Jeroboam, the Fall of Israel, and the Reign of Josiah.* Harvard Semitic Monographs 53. Atlanta, GA: Scholars Press.
1995 Aaron's Calf and Jeroboam's Calves. Pp. 92–104 in *Fortunate the Eyes That See: Essays in Honor of David Noel Freedman in Celebration of His Seventieth Birthday,* ed. A. B. Beck, A. H. Bartelt, P. R. Raabe, and C. A. Franke. Grand Rapids, MI: Eerdmans.
1996 "Yhwh Is Not with Israel: Alliances as a Topos in Chronicles." *Catholic Biblical Quarterly* 58: 601–26.

1997 Historiography and History: The Royal Reforms. Pp. 178–203 in *The Chronicler as Historian*, ed. M. P. Graham, S. L. McKenzie, and K. Hoglund. Journal for the Study of the Old Testament Supplement 238. Sheffield, UK: Sheffield Academic Press.

1999a Hierodules, Priests, or Janitors? The Levites in Chronicles and the History of the Israelite Priesthood. *Journal of Biblical Literature* 118: 49–72.

1999b Treasures Won and Lost: Royal (Mis)appropriations in Kings and Chronicles. Pp. 181–208 in *The Chronicler as Author: Studies in Text and Texture*, ed. M. P. Graham and S. L. McKenzie. Journal for the Study of the Old Testament Supplement 263; Sheffield, UK: Sheffield Academic Press.

2000a "Great Among His Brothers," But Who Is He? Heterogeneity in the Composition of Judah. *Journal of Hebrew Scriptures* 3, available online at http://www.jhsonline.org/Articles/article_16.pdf.

2000b Sources, Revisions, and Editions: The Lists of Jerusalem's Residents in MT and LXX Nehemiah 11 and 1 Chronicles 9. *Textus* 20: 141–68.

2001 Intermarriage, Social Complexity, and Ethnic Diversity in the Genealogy of Judah. *Journal of Biblical Literature* 120: 15–30.

2004a *I Chronicles 1–9*. Anchor Bible 12. New York: Doubleday.

2004b *I Chronicles 10–29*. Anchor Bible 12A. New York: Doubleday.

2005 Mt. Gerizim and Mt. Zion: A Study in the Early History of the Samaritans and Jews. *Studies in Religion/Sciences Religieuses* 34: 307–36.

2006 Revisiting the Samarian Question in the Persian Period. Pp. 265–89 in Lipschits and Oeming 2006.

2007 Nehemiah and Sanballat: The Enemy Without or Within? Pp. 305–31 in Lipschits, Knoppers, and Albertz 2007.

2009 Ethnicity, Genealogy, Geography, and Change: The Judean Communities of Babylon and Jerusalem in the Story of Ezra. Pp. 147–71 in *Community Identity in Judean Historiography: Biblical and Comparative Perspectives*, ed. G. N. Knoppers and K. A. Ristau. Winona Lake, IN: Eisenbrauns.

2010 Some Aspects of Samaria's Religious Culture during the Early Hellenistic Period. Pp. 159–74 in *The Historian and the Bible: Essays in Honour of Lester L. Grabbe*, ed. P. R. Davies and D. V. Edelman. Library of Hebrew Bible/Old Testament Studies 530. London: Clark.

2011a Did Jacob Become Judah? Pp. 39–67 in Zsengellér 2011.

2011b Exile, Return, and Diaspora. Pp. 29–61 in *Texts, Contexts and Readings in Postexilic Literature: Explorations into Historiography and Identity Negotiation in Hebrew Bible and Related Texts*, ed. L. Jonker. Forschungen zum Alten Testament, 2nd ser., 53. Tübingen, Germany: Mohr Siebeck.

2011c Parallel Torahs and Inner-Scriptural Interpretation: The Jewish and Samaritan Pentateuchs in Historical Perspective. Pp. 507–31 in *The Pentateuch: International Perspectives on Current Research*, ed. T. Dozeman, K. Schmid, and B. Schwartz. Forschungen zum Alten Testament 78. Tübingen, Germany: Mohr Siebeck.

2012a Periodization in Ancient Israelite Historiography: Three Case Studies. Pp. 121–45 in *Periodisierung und Epochenbewusstsein im Alten Testament und in seinem Umfeld*, ed. J. Wiesehöfer and T. Krüger. Oriens et Occidens 20. Stuttgart: Steiner.

2012b Samaritan Conceptions of Jewish Origins and Jewish Conceptions of Samaritan Origins: Any Common Ground? Pp. 81–118 in *Die Samaritaner und die Bibel: Historische und literarische Wechselwirkungen zwischen biblischen und samaritanischen Traditionen*, ed. J. Frey, U. Schattner-Rieser, and K. Schmid. Studia Samaritana 7. Berlin: de Gruyter.

2012c The Samaritan Schism or the Judaization of Samaria? Reassessing Josephus's Account of the Mt. Gerizim Temple. Pp. 163–78 in *Making a Difference: Essays on the Bible and Judaism in Honour of Tamara Cohn Eskenazi*, ed. D. J. A. Clines, K. Richards, and J. L. Wright. Hebrew Bible Monographs 49. Sheffield, U.K.: Sheffield Phoenix.

2012d Who or What Is Israel in Third Isaiah? Pp. 153–65 in *Let Us Go Up to Zion: Essays in Honour of H. G. M. Williamson on the Occasion of his Sixty-Fifth Birthday* ed. I. Provan and M. J. Boda. Supplements to Vetus Testamentum 153. Leiden, the Netherlands: Brill.

(Forthcoming a) The Altar at the Central Sanctuary and the Altar on Mt. Gerizim: One and the Same? *Zeitschrift für Altorientalische und Biblische Rechtsgeschichte*.

(Forthcoming b) Archenemies or Affiliates? Samarians and Judeans in the Early Persian Period. In *The Samaritan Pentateuch and Samaritan Literature*, ed. S. Schorch. Studia Samaritana. Berlin: de Gruyter.

Knoppers, G. N., and B. M. Levinson

2007 *The Pentateuch as Torah: New Models for Understanding Its Promulgation and Acceptance* (eds.). Winona Lake, IN: Eisenbrauns.

Koenen, K.

2003 *Bethel: Geschichte, Kult und Theologie*. Orbis Biblicus et Orientalis 192. Göttingen, Germany: Vandenhoeck & Ruprecht.

Köhlmoos, M.

2006 *Bet-El, Erinnerungen an eine Stadt: Perspektiven der alttestamentlichen Bet-El-Überlieferung*. Forschungen zum Alten Testament 49. Tübingen, Germany: Mohr Siebeck.

van der Kooij, A.

2007 The Septuagint of the Pentateuch and Ptolemaic Rule. Pp. 289–300 in Knoppers and Levinson 2007.

Kottsieper, I.

2007 "And They Did Not Care to Speak Yehudit": On Linguistic Change in Judah during the Late Persian Era. Pp. 95–124 in Lipschits, Knoppers, and Albertz 2007.

Kratz, R. G.

2006a Israel in the Book of Isaiah. *Journal for the Study of the Old Testament* 31: 103–28.

2006b The Temple of Jeb and of Jerusalem. Pp. 247–64 in Lipschits and Oeming 2006.

2008 "The Place Which He Has Chosen": The Identification of the Cult Place of Deut. 12 and Lev. 17 in 4QMMT. *Megillot* 5–6: *57–*68.

Kuenen, A.

1875 *The Religion of Israel to the Fall of the Jewish State, vol. 2.* Translated by A. H. May. London: Williams & Norgate.

Kugel, J. L.

2001 Ancient Biblical Interpretation and the Biblical Sage. Pp. 1–26 in *Studies in Ancient Midrash*, ed. J. L. Kugel. Cambridge, MA: Harvard University Press.

Kuhrt, A.

1995 *The Ancient Near East, c. 3000–330 BC.* 2 vols. London: Routledge.

Laato, A.

1994 The Levitical Genealogies in 1 Chronicles 5–6 and the Formation of Levitical Ideology in Post-Exilic Judah. *Journal for the Study of the Old Testament* 62: 77–99.

Lanfranchi, G. B.

1997 Consensus to Empire: Some Aspects of Sargon II's Foreign Policy. Pp. 81–87 in *Assyrien im Wandel der Zeiten*, ed. H. Waetzoldt and H. Hauptmann. Heidelberg, Germany: Heidelberg Orientverlag.

Lapp, N. L.

2008 *Shechem IV: The Persian-Hellenistic Pottery of Shechem/Tell Balâṭah.* Boston: American Schools of Oriental Research.

Lapp, N. L., and G. W. E. Nickelsburg

1974 The Roman Occupation and Pottery of ʿArâq en-Naʿsâneh. Pp. 49–54 in Lapp and Lapp 1974.

Lapp, P. M., and N. L. Lapp

1974 *Discoveries in the Wâdī ed-Dâlīyeh.* Annual of the American Schools of Oriental Research 41. Cambridge, MA: American Schools of Oriental Research.

Law, D. A.

1992 *From Samaria to Samarkand: The Ten Lost Tribes of Israel.* Lanham, MD: University Press of America.

Layton, S.

1990 *Archaic Features of Canaanite Personal Names in the Hebrew Bible.* Harvard Semitic Monographs 47. Atlanta, GA: Scholars Press.

Lehmann, G.

1998 Trends in Local Pottery Development of the Late Iron Age and Persian Period in Syria and Lebanon, ca. 700 to 300 B.C. *Bulletin of the American Schools of Oriental Research* 311: 7–37.

Leith, M. J. W.

1997 *Wadi Daliyeh I: The Seal Impressions.* Oxford: Oxford University Press.

1998 Israel among the Nations: The Persian Period. Pp. 276–316 in *The Oxford History of the Biblical World*, ed. M. D. Coogan. New York: Oxford University Press.

2000 Seals and Coins in Persian Period Samaria. Pp. 691–707 in Schiffman, Tov, and VanderKam 2000.

Lemaire, A.

1977 *Inscriptions hébraïques. Vol. 1, Les ostraca*. Paris: Cerf.

1990 Populations et territoires de la Palestine à l'époque perse. *Transeuphratène* 3: 31–74.

1995 Ashdodien et judéen à l'époque perse: Ne 13: 24. Pp. 153–63 in *Immigration and Emigration within the Ancient Near East: Festschrift E. Lipiński*, ed. K. Van Lerberghe and A. Schoors. Orientalia Lovaniensia Analecta 65. Leuven, Belgium: Peeters.

1999 MGBY/Menbigî, monétaire de Transeuphratène avant Alexandre? Pp. 215–19 in *Travaux de numismatique grecque offerts à Georges Le Rider*, ed. M. Amandry and S. Hurter. London: Spink.

2001 Épigraphie et religion en Palestine à l'époque achéménide. *Transeuphratène* 22: 97–113.

2003–6 Graffito hébreu sur tétradrachme pseudo-athénien. *Israel Numismatic Journal* 15: 24–27.

2004 Nouveau Temple de Yahô (IVe S. av. J.-C.). Pp. 265–73 in *"Basel und Bibel": Collected Communications to the XVIIth Congress of the International Organization for the Study of the Old Testament, Basel 2001*, ed. M. Augustin and H. M. Niemann. Beiträge zur Erforschung des Alten Testaments und des antiken Judentums 51. Frankfurt am Main: Peter Lang.

2006 New Aramaic Ostraca from Idumea and Their Historical Interpretation. Pp. 413–56 in Lipschits and Oeming 2006.

2007 Administration in Fourth-Century B.C.E. Judah in Light of Epigraphy and Numismatics. Pp. 53–74 in Lipschits, Knoppers, and Albertz 2007.

2011 Judean Identity in Elephantine: Everyday Life According to the Ostraca. Pp. 365–74 in Lispschits, Knoppers, and Oeming 2011.

2012 A Reference to the Covenant Code in 2 Kings 17:24–41? Pp. 395–405 in *Let Us Go Up to Zion: Essays in Honour of H. G. M. Williamson on the Occasion of his Sixty-Fifth Birthday*, ed. I. Provan and M. J. Boda. Supplements to Vetus Testamentum 153. Leiden, the Netherlands: Brill.

Levine, L. I.

2000 *The Ancient Synagogue: The First Thousand Years*. New Haven, CT: Yale University Press.

2003 The First Century CE Synagogue in Historical Perspective. Pp. 1–24 in Olsson and Zetterholm 2003.

Levinson, B. M.

1995 "But You Shall Surely Kill Him!": The Text-Critical and Neo-Assyrian Evidence for MT Deut 13:10. Pp. 37–64 in *Bundesdokument und Gesetz: Studien zum Deuteronomium*, ed. G. Braulik. Freiburg, Germany: Herder.

1996 Recovering the Lost Original Meaning of ולא תכסה עליו (Deut 13:9). *Journal of Biblical Literature* 115: 601–20.

1997 *Deuteronomy and the Hermeneutics of Legal Innovation*. New York: Oxford University Press.

2001 Textual Criticism, Assyriology, and the History of Interpretation: Deuteronomy 13:7a as a Test Case in Method. *Journal of Biblical Literature* 120: 211–43.

2008 *"The Right Chorale": Studies in Biblical Law and Interpretation*. Forschungen zum Alten Testament 54. Tübingen, Germany: Mohr Siebeck.

Liddell, H. G., and R. Scott

1996 *A Greek-English Lexicon*. 9th ed. Oxford: Clarendon.

Limet, H.

1995 L'émigré dans la société mésopotamienne. Pp. 165–79 in *Immigration and Emigration within the Ancient Near East: Festschrift E. Lipiński*, ed. K. van Lerberghe and A. Schoors. Orientalia Lovaniensia Analecta 65. Leuven, Belgium: Peeters.

Linder, A.

2006 The Legal Status of Jews in the Roman Empire. Pp. 128–73 in *The Cambridge History of Judaism. Vol. 4, The Late Roman–Rabbinic Period*, ed. S. T. Katz. Cambridge, UK: Cambridge University Press.

Linville, J. R.

1998 *Israel in the Book of Kings: The Past as a Project of Social Identity*. Journal for the Study of the Old Testament Supplement 272. Sheffield, UK: Sheffield Academic Press.

Lipiński, E.

1990 Géographique linguistique de la Transeuphratène à l'époque achéménide. *Transeuphratène* 3: 95–107.

Lipschits, O.

1998 Nebuchadrezzar's Policy in "Ḫattu-Land" and the Fate of the Kingdom of Judah. *Ugarit Forschungen* 30: 467–87.

1999 The History of the Benjamin Region under Babylonian Rule. *Tel Aviv* 26: 155–90.

2001 Judah, Jerusalem, and the Temple, 586–539 B.C. *Transeuphratène* 22: 129–42.

2003 Demographic Changes in Judah between the Seventh and Fifth Centuries BCE. Pp. 323–76 in Lipschits and Blenkinsopp 2003.

2005 *The Fall and Rise of Jerusalem: Judah under Babylonian Rule*. Winona Lake, IN: Eisenbrauns.

2006 Achaemenid Imperial Policy, Settlement Processes in Palestine, and the Status of Jerusalem in the Middle of the Fifth Century BCE. Pp. 19–52 in Lipschits and Oeming 2006.

2011 A New Look on the Archaeology of Persian Period Judah. Pp. 187–211 in *Texts, Contexts and Readings in Postexilic Literature: Explorations Into Historiography and Identity Negotiation in Hebrew Bible and Related Texts*, ed. L. C. Jonker. Forschungen zum Alten Testament, 2nd ser., 53. Tübingen, Germany: Mohr Siebeck.

2012 Between Archaeology and Text: A Reevaluation of the Development Process of Jerusalem in the Persian Period. Pp. 145–65 in Nissinen 2012.

Lipschits O., and J. Blenkinsopp
2003 *Judah and the Judeans in the Neo-Babylonian Period* (eds.). Winona Lake, IN: Eisenbrauns.

Lipschits, O., Y. Gadot, B. Arubas, and M. Oeming
2011 Palace and Village, Paradise and Oblivion: Unraveling the Riddles of Ramat Raḥel. *Near Eastern Archaeology* 74: 2–49.

Lipschits, O., G. N. Knoppers, and R. Albertz
2007 *Judah and the Judeans in the Fourth Century B.C.E.* (eds.). Winona Lake, IN: Eisenbrauns.

Lipschits, O., G. N. Knoppers, and M. Oeming
2011 *Judah and the Judeans in the Achaemenid Period: Negotiating Identity in an International Context* (eds.). Winona Lake, IN: Eisenbrauns.

Lipschits, O., and M. Oeming
2006 *Judah and the Judeans in the Persian Period* (eds.). Winona Lake, IN: Eisenbrauns.

Lipschits, O., and O. Tal
2007 The Settlement Archaeology of the Province of Judah: A Case Study. Pp. 33–52 in Lipschits, Knoppers, and Albertz 2007.

Liverani, M.
2005 Imperialism. Pp. 223–43 in *Archaeologies of the Middle East: Critical Perspectives*, ed. S. Pollack and R. Bernbeck. Malden, MA: Blackwell.

London, G.
1992 Reply to A. Zertal's "The Wedge-Shaped Decorated Bowl and the Origin of the Samaritans." *Bulletin of the American Schools of Oriental Research* 286: 89–90.

Long, B. O.
1991 *2 Kings*. Forms of the Old Testament Literature 10. Grand Rapids, MI: Eerdmans.

Lozachmeur, H.
2006 *La collection Clermont-Ganneau: Ostraca, épigraphes sur jarre, étiquettes de bois*. 2 vols. Paris: Boccard.

McCarter, P. K.
1984 *II Samuel*. Anchor Bible 8A. Garden City, NY: Doubleday.

McCarthy, C.
2004 Samaritan Pentateuch Readings in Deuteronomy. Pp. 118–30 in *Biblical and Near Eastern Essays: Studies in Honour of Kevin J. Cathcart*, ed. C. McCarthy and J. F. Healey. Journal for the Study of the Old Testament Supplement 375. London: Clark.

2007 אלה הדברים; *Deuteronomy*. Biblia Hebraica Quinta 5. Stuttgart: Deutsche Bibelgesellschaft.

Macchi, J.-D.

1992 Les controversies théologiques dans le judaïsme de l'époque postexilique: L'example de 2 Rois 17,24–41. *Transeuphratène* 5: 85–93.

1994a *Les Samaritains: Histoire d'une legend—Israël et la province de Samarie.* Le Monde de la Bible 30. Geneva: Labor et Fides.

1994b Megiddo à l'époque assyrienne. *Transeuphratène* 7: 9–31.

1999 *Israël et ses tribus selon Genèse 49.* Orbis Biblicus et Orientalis 171. Göttingen, Germany: Vandenhoeck & Ruprecht.

Macdonald, J.

1964 *The Theology of the Samaritans.* New Testament Library. Philadelphia: Westminster.

1969–70 The Structure of II Kings xvii. *Transactions of the Glasgow University Oriental Society* 23: 29–41.

Macdonald, M. C. A.

1999 Personal Names in the Nabataean Realm: A Review Article. *Journal of Semitic Studies* 44: 251–89.

Machinist, P. B.

1994 The First Coins of Judah and Samaria: Numismatics and History in the Achaemenid and Early Hellenistic Periods. Pp. 365–80 in *Continuity and Change: Proceedings of the Last Achaemenid History Workshop, April 6–8 1990, Ann Arbor*, ed. H. Sancisi-Weerdenburg, A. Kuhrt, and M. C. Root. Achaemenid History 8. Leiden, the Netherlands: Nederlands Instituut voor het Nabije Oosten.

McKay, J. W.

1973 *Religion in Judah under the Assyrians, 732–609 B.C.* Studies in Biblical Theology, 2nd ser., 26. Naperville, IL: Allenson.

McKenzie, S. L.

1985 *The Chronicler's Use of the Deuteronomistic History.* Harvard Semitic Monographs 33. Atlanta: Scholars Press.

1991 *The Trouble with Kings: The Composition of the Book of Kings in the Deuteronomistic History.* Vetus Testamentum Supplement 42. Leiden, the Netherlands: Brill.

Magen, Y.

1990 Mount Gerizim—A Temple City. *Qadmoniot* 23.3–4: 70–96 (Hebrew).

2000 Mount Gerizim—A Temple City. *Qadmoniot* 33.2: 74–118 (Hebrew).

2007 The Dating of the First Phase of the Samaritan Temple at Mount Gerizim in Light of the Archaeological Evidence. Pp. 157–211 in Lipschits, Knoppers, and Albertz 2007.

2008a *Judea and Samaria: Researches and Discoveries.* Translated by Edward Levin and Michael Guggenheimer. Judea and Samaria Publications 6. Jerusalem: Israel Antiquities Authority.

2008b *Mount Gerizim Excavations. Vol. 2, A Temple City.* Judea and Samaria Publications 8. Jerusalem: Israel Antiquities Authority.

2008c *The Samaritans and the Good Samaritan*. Edited by N. Carmin. Translated by E. Levin. Judea and Samaria Publications 7. Jerusalem: Israel Antiquities Authority.

2009 *Flavia Neapolis: Shechem in the Roman Period*. 2 vols. Judea and Samaria Publications 11. Jerusalem: Israel Antiquities Authority.

Magen, Y., D. T. Ariel, G. Bijovsky, Y. Tzionit, and O. Sirkis.

2004 *The Land of Benjamin*. Judea and Samaria Publications 3. Jerusalem: Israel Antiquities Authority.

Magen, Y., H. Misgav, and L. Tsfania

2004 *Mount Gerizim Excavations. Vol. 1, The Aramaic, Hebrew and Samaritan Inscriptions*. Judea and Samaria Publications 2. Jerusalem: Israel Antiquities Authority.

Magen, Y., L. Tsfania, and H. Misgav

2000 The Hebrew and Aramaic Inscriptions from Mt. Gerizim. *Qadmoniot* 33.2: 125–32 (Hebrew).

Magness, J.

2001 The Cults of Isis and Kore at Samaria-Sebaste in the Hellenistic and Roman Periods. *Harvard Theological Review* 94: 157–77.

Mazar, A.

1990 *Archaeology of the Land of the Bible 10,000–586 BCE*. Anchor Bible Reference Library. Garden City, NY: Doubleday.

2008 Beth-Shean. *New Encyclopaedia of Archaeological Excavations in the Holy Land* 5: 1616–22.

Mazar, B.

1957 The Tobiads. *Israel Exploration Journal* 7: 137–45, 229–38.

1993 Kinneret. *New Encyclopaedia of Archaeological Excavations in the Holy Land* 2: 872–73.

van der Meer, M. N.

2004 *Formation and Reformulation: The Redaction of the Book of Joshua in the Light of the Oldest Textual Witnesses*. Vetus Testamentum Supplement 102. Leiden, the Netherlands: Brill.

Mendels, D.

1992 *The Rise and Fall of Jewish Nationalism: Jewish and Christian Ethnicity in Ancient Palestine*. Anchor Bible Reference Library. New York: Doubleday.

Meshorer Y.

1982 *Ancient Jewish Coinage. Vol. 1, Persian Period through Hasmoneans*. New York: Amphora.

2000 *TestiMoney*. Jerusalem: Israel Museum.

2001 *A Treasury of Jewish Coins: From the Persian Period to Bar Kokhba*. Jerusalem: Yad Ben-Zvi.

Meshorer Y., and S. Qedar

1991 *The Coinage of Samaria in the Fourth Century BCE*. Beverly Hills, CA: Numismatics Fine Arts International.

1999 *Samarian Coinage*. Numismatics Studies and Researches 9. Jerusalem: Israel Numismatics Society.
2002 Samaritan Coins in the Persian Period. Pp. 71–81 in *The Samaritans*, ed. E. Stern and H. Eshel. Jerusalem: Yad Ben-Zvi (Hebrew).

Meyers, C. L., and E. M. Meyers
1987 *Haggai, Zechariah 1–8: A New Translation with Introduction and Commentary*. Anchor Bible 25b. Garden City, NY: Doubleday.

Middlemas, J.
2005 *The Troubles of Templeless Judah*. Oxford: Oxford University Press.

Mikoláŝek, A.
1995 The Samaritans: Guardians of the Law against the Prophets. Pp. 85–94 in *Essays in Honour of G. D. Sixdenier: New Samaritan Studies of the Société d'Études Samaritaines*, ed. A. D. Crown and L. Davey. Sydney: Mandelbaum.

Mildenberg, L.
1996 *yĕhûd* und *šmryn*: Über das Geld der persischen Provinz Juda und Samaria im 4. Jahrhundert. Pp. 119–46 in *Geschichte–Tradition–Reflexion: Festschrift für Martin Hengel zum 70. Geburtstag*, vol. 1 *Judentum*, ed. H. Cancik, H. Lichtenberger, and P. Schäfer. Tübingen, Germany: J. C. B. Mohr.
1997 On the Imagery of the Philisto-Arabian Coinage: A Preview. *Transeuphratène* 13: 9–16.
1998 *Vestigia Leonis: Studien zur antiken Numismatik Israels, Palästinas und der östlichen Mittelmeerwelt*. Novum Testamentum et Orbis Antiquus 36. Göttingen, Germany: Vandenhoeck & Ruprecht.
2000 Über die Münzbildnisse in Palästina und Nordwestarabien zur Perserzeit. Pp. 375–91 in *Images as Media: Sources for the Cultural History of the Near East and the Eastern Mediterranean—1st millenium BCE*, ed. C. Uehlinger. Orbis Biblicus et Orientalis 175. Göttingen, Germany: Vandenhoeck & Ruprecht.

Milgrom, J.
1990 *Numbers: The Traditional Hebrew Text with the New JPS Translation*. JPS Torah Commentary. Philadelphia: Jewish Publication Society.

Milgrom, J., L. Harper, and H.-J. Fabry
1998 תרמשמ; *mišmeret*. *Theological Dictionary of the Old Testament* 9: 72–78.

Miller J. M., and J. H. Hayes
2006 *A History of Ancient Israel and Judah*. 2nd ed. Louisville, KY: Westminster John Knox.

Mitchell, C.
1999 The Dialogism of Chronicles. Pp. 311–26 in *The Chronicler as Author: Studies in Text and Texture*, ed. M. P. Graham and S. L. McKenzie. Journal for the Study of the Old Testament Supplement 263. Sheffield, UK: Sheffield Academic Press.
2006 The Ironic Death of Josiah in 2 Chronicles. *Catholic Biblical Quarterly* 68: 421–35.

2010 Otherness and Historiography in Chronicles. Pp. 93–112 in *Historiography and Identity (Re)formulation in Second Temple Historiographical Literature*, ed. L. C. Jonker. Library of Hebrew Bible/Old Testament Studies 534. New York: Clark.

Mitchell, T. C.

1991 Israel and Judah from the Coming of the Assyrian Domination until the Fall of Samaria, and the Struggle for Independence in Judah (c. 750–700 B.C.). Pp. 322–70 in *The Cambridge Ancient History*, Vol. 3, pt. 2, *Assyrian and Babylonian Empires and Other States of the Near East from the Eighth to the Sixth Centuries B.C.*, ed. J. Boardman. 2nd ed. Cambridge, UK: Cambridge University Press.

Mittmann, S.

2000 Tobia, Sanballat und die Persische Provinz Juda. *Journal of Northwest Semitic Languages* 26: 1–50.

Montgomery, J. A.

1907 *The Samaritans: The Earliest Jewish Sect—Their History, Theology, and Literature. Bohlen Lectures 1906.* Philadelphia: John C. Winston.

Montgomery, J. A., and H. S. Gehman

1951 *A Critical and Exegetical Commentary on the Book of Kings.* International Critical Commentary. Edinburgh: Clark.

Mor, M.

1989a The Persian, Hellenistic, and Hasmonaean Period. Pp. 1–18 in Crown 1989c.

1989b The Samaritans and the Bar Kokhbah Revolt. Pp. 19–31 in Crown 1989c.

2003 *From Samaria to Shechem: The Samaritan Community in Antiquity.* Jerusalem: Zalman Shazar Center (Hebrew).

2005 Putting the Puzzle Together: Papyri, Inscriptions, Coins and Josephus in Relation to Samaritan History in the Persian Period. Pp. 41–54 in *Proceedings of the Fifth International Congress of the Société d'Études Samaritaines*, ed. H. Shehadeh and H. Tawa. Paris: Geuthner.

2011a The Building of the Samaritan Temple and the Samaritan Governors—Again. Pp. 89–108 in Zsengellér 2011.

2011b The Samaritans in Transition from the Persian to the Greek Period. Pp. 176–98 in *Judah between East and West: The Transition from Persian to Greek Rule (ca. 400–200 BCE)*, ed. L. L. Grabbe and O. Lipschits. London: Clark.

Mor, M., and F. V. Reiterer

2010 *Samaritans: Past and Present—Current Studies* (eds.). Studia Samaritana 5. Berlin: de Gruyter.

Mosis, R.

1973 *Untersuchungen zur Theologie des chronistischen Geschichtswerkes.* Freiburg, Germany: Herder.

Mowinckel, S.
1964 *Studien zu dem Buche Ezra-Nehemia*. Vol. 1, *Die nachchronische Redaktion des Buches: Die Listen*. Oslo: Universitetsforlaget.
Mulder, M. J.
1975 בַּעַל; *baʿal*. *Theological Dictionary of the Old Testament* 2: 181–200.
Myers, J. M.
1965 *II Chronicles*. Anchor Bible 13. Garden City, NY: Doubleday.
Naʾaman, N.
1990 The Historical Background to the Conquest of Samaria (720 BC). *Biblica* 71: 206–25.
1993 Population Changes Following the Assyrian Deportations. *Tel Aviv* 20: 104–24.
1995a Province System and Settlement Pattern in Southern Syria and Palestine in the Neo-Assyrian Period. Pp. 103–15 in *Neo-Assyrian Geography*, ed. M. Liverani. Quaderni di Geografia Storica 5. Rome: Università di Roma.
1995b Rezin of Damascus and the Land of Gilead. *Zeitschrift des Deutschen Palästina-Vereins* 111: 105–17.
1995c Tiglath-pileser III's Campaigns against Tyre and Israel (734–732 BCE). *Tel Aviv* 22: 271–77.
2005 *Ancient Israel and its Neighbors: Interaction and Counteraction*. Winona Lake, IN: Eisenbrauns.
2006 *Ancient Israel's History and Historiography: The First Temple Period*. Winona Lake, IN: Eisenbrauns.
2007 When and How Did Jerusalem Become a Great City? *Bulletin of the American Schools of Oriental Research* 347: 21–56.
2009a The Growth and Development of Judah and Jerusalem in the Eighth Century BCE: A Rejoinder. *Revue Biblique* 116: 321–35.
2009b Was Dor the Capital of an Assyrian Province? *Tel Aviv* 36: 95–109.
2010 Does Archaeology Really Deserve the Status of a "High Court" in Biblical Historical Research? Pp. 165–83 in *Between Evidence and Ideology: Essays on the History of Ancient Israel Read at the Joint Meeting of the Society for Old Testament Study and the Oud Testamentisch Werkgezelschap, Lincoln, July 2009*, ed. B. Becking and L. L. Grabbe. Oudtestamentische Studiën 59. Leiden, the Netherlands: Brill.
Naʾaman N., and R. Zadok
1988 Sargon II's Deportations to Israel and Philistia (716–708 B.C.). *Journal of Cuneiform Studies* 40: 36–46.
2000 Assyrian Deportations to the Province of Samerina in the Light of Two Cuneiform Tablets from Tel Haddid. *Tel Aviv* 27: 159–88.
Naveh, J.
1971 Hebrew Texts in Aramaic Script in the Persian Period? *Bulletin of the American Schools of Oriental Research* 203: 27–32.

1998 Scripts and Inscriptions in Ancient Samaria. *Israel Exploration Journal* 48: 91–100.

Naveh, J., and Y. Magen

1997 Aramaic and Hebrew Inscriptions of the Second-Century BCE at Mount Gerizim. *'Atiqot* 32: 9*–17*.

Nelson, R. D.

1981 *The Double Redaction of the Deuteronomistic History.* Journal for the Study of the Old Testament Supplement 18. Sheffield, UK: JSOT Press.

Nickelsburg, G. W. E.

1974 Miscellaneous Small Finds. Pp. 101–2 in Lapp and Lapp 1974.

Nihan, C.

2007a *From Priestly Torah to Pentateuch: A Study in the Composition of the Book of Leviticus.* Forschungen zum Alten Testament, 2nd ser., 25. Tübingen, Germany: Mohr Siebeck.

2007b The Torah between Samaria and Judah: Shechem and Gerizim in Deuteronomy and Joshua. Pp. 187–223 in Knoppers and Levinson 2007.

2012 Garizim et Ébal dans le Pentateuque: Quelques remarques en marge de la publication d'un nouveau fragment du Deutéronome. *Semitica* 54: 185–210.

Nissinen, M.

2012 *Congress Volume, Helsinki 2010 (ed.).* Vetus Testamentum Supplement 148. Leiden, the Netherlands: Brill.

Nitzan, B.

1999 Repentance in the Dead Sea Scrolls. Pp. 145–70 in *The Dead Sea Scrolls after Fifty Years: A Comprehensive Assessment, vol. 2,* ed. P. W. Flint and J. C. VanderKam. Leiden, the Netherlands: Brill.

Nodet, E.

1997 *A Search for the Origins of Judaism: From Joshua to the Mishnah.* Translated by E. Crowley. Journal for the Study of the Old Testament Supplement 248. Sheffield, UK: Sheffield Academic Press.

2011 Israelites, Samaritans, Temples, Jews. Pp. 121–71 in Zsengellér 2011.

Noja, S.

1967 Les préceptes des Samaritains dans le manuscrit Sam 10 de la Bibliothèque Nationale. *Revue Biblique* 74: 255–59.

Noth, M.

1943 *Überlieferungsgeschichtliche Studien.* Tübingen, Germany: Max Niemeyer.

Noy, D., A. Panayotov, and H. Bloedhorn

2004 *Inscriptiones Judaicae Orientis.* 3 vols. Texte und Studien zum Antiken Judentum 99, 101–2. Tübingen, Germany: Mohr Siebeck.

O'Brien, Mark A.

1989 *The Deuteronomistic History Hypothesis: A Reassessment.* Orbis Biblicus et Orientalis 92. Göttingen, Germany: Vandenhoeck & Ruprecht.

Oded, B.
1979 *Mass Deportations and Deportees in the Neo-Assyrian Empire.* Wiesbaden, Germany: Reichert.
1987 II Kings 17: Between History and Polemic. *Jewish History* 2: 37–47.
1992 *War, Peace, and Empire: Justifications for War in Assyrian Royal Inscriptions.* Wiesbaden, Germany: Reichert.
1995 Observations on the Israelite/Judaean Exiles in Mesopotamia during the Eighth–Sixth Centuries BCE. Pp. 205–12 in *Immigration and Emigration within the Ancient Near East: Festschrift E. Lipiński,* ed. K. van Lerberghe and A. Schoors. Orientalia Lovaniensia Analecta 65. Leuven, Belgium: Peeters.
1997 The Inscriptions of Tiglath-pileser III: Review Article. *Israel Exploration Journal* 47: 110–11.
2000 The Settlements of the Israelite and the Judean Exiles in Mesopotamia in the 8th–6th Centuries BCE. Pp. 91–103 in *Studies in Historical Geography and Biblical Historiography Presented to Zecharia Kallai,* ed. G. Galil and M. Weinfeld. Vetus Testamentum Supplement 81. Leiden, the Netherlands: Brill.
2003 Where is the "Myth of the Empty Land" to Be Found? History versus Myth. Pp. 55–74 in Lipschits and Blenkinsopp 2003.

Oeming, M.
1990 *Das wahre Israel: Die "genealogische Vorhalle" 1 Chronik 1–9.* Beiträge zur Wissenschaft vom Alten und Neuen Testament 128. Stuttgart: Kohlhammer.

Olsson, B.
2003 The Origins of the Synagogue: An Evaluation. Pp. 27–36 in Olsson and Zetterholm 2003.

Olsson, B., and M. Zetterholm.
2003 *The Ancient Synagogue from Its Origins until 200 CE* (eds.). Coniectanea Biblica New Testament Series 39. Stockholm: Almqvist & Wiksell.

Olyan, S. M.
2000 *Rites and Rank: Hierarchy in Biblical Representations of Cult.* Princeton, NJ: Princeton University Press.
2004 Purity Ideology in Ezra-Nehemiah as a Tool to Reconstitute the Community. *Journal for the Study of Judaism* 35: 4–10.

Orlinsky, H. M.
1960 *Ancient Israel.* 2nd ed. Ithaca, NY: Cornell University Press.

Otto, E.
1979 *Jakob in Sichem: überlieferungsgeschichtl., archäolog. u. territorialgeschichtl. Studien zur Entstehungsgeschichte Israels.* Stuttgart: Kohlhammer.
2009 *Die Tora: Studien zum Pentateuch—Gesammelte Schriften.* Beihefte zur Zeitschrift für Altorientalische und Biblische Rechtsgeschichte 9. Wiesbaden, Germany: Harrasowitz.

Parker, B. J.
1997 Garrisoning the Empire: Aspects of the Construction and Maintenance of Forts on the Assyrian Frontier. *Iraq* 59: 77–87.
2001 *The Mechanics of Empire: The Northern Frontier of Assyria as a Case Study in Imperial Dynamics.* Helsinki: Neo-Assyrian Text Corpus Project.

Parpola, S.
2003 Assyria's Expansion in the 8th and 7th Centuries and Its Long-Term Repercussions in the West. Pp. 99–111 in *Symbiosis, Symbolism, and the Power of the Past: Canaan, Ancient Israel, and Their Neighbors from the Late Bronze Age Through Roman Palaestina*, ed. W. G. Dever and S. Gitin. Winona Lake, IN: Eisenbrauns.

Paul, S. M.
1991 *Amos*. Hermeneia. Philadelphia: Fortress.

Pearce, L. E.
2006 New Evidence for Judeans in Babylonia. Pp. 397–408 in Lipschits and Oeming 2006.
2010 Sealed Identities. Pp. 301–28 in *Opening the Tablet Box: Near Eastern Studies in Honor of Benjamin R. Foster*, ed. S. C. Melville and A. L. Slotsky. Culture and History of the Ancient Near East 42. Leiden, the Netherlands: Brill.

Peersmann, J.
2000 Assyrian Magiddu: The Town Planning of Stratum III. Pp. 524–34 in *Megiddo III: The 1992–1996 Seasons*, vol. 2, ed. I. Finkelstein, D. Ussishkin, and B. Halpern. *Tel Aviv*: Institute of Archaeology.

Person, R. F.
1997 The Kings-Isaiah and Kings-Jeremiah Recensions. Beihefte zur *Zeitschrift für die Alttestamentliche Wissenschaft* 252. Berlin: de Gruyter.

Pfeiffer, R. H.
1948 *Introduction to the Old Testament.* 2nd ed. New York: Harper.
1961 *Religion in the Old Testament: The History of a Spiritual Triumph.* 2nd ed. New York: Harper.

Plöger, O.
1968 *Theocracy and Eschatology*. Oxford: Blackwell.

Porten, B.
1968 *Archives from Elephantine: The Life of an Ancient Jewish Military Colony.* Berkeley: University of California Press.
2001 Judeans of Yeb Named after Their Ancestors. Pp. 332–61 in *Homage to Shmuel: Studies in the World of the Bible*, ed. Z. Talshir, S. Yonah, and D. Sivan. Beersheba, Israel: Ben Gurion University (Hebrew).

Pummer, R.
1982 Genesis 34 in Jewish Writings of the Hellenistic and Roman Periods. *Harvard Theological Review* 75: 177–88.
1987a ΑΡΓΑΡΙΖΙΝ: A Criterion for Samaritan Provenance? *Journal for the Study of Judaism* 18: 18–25.

1987b *The Samaritans*. Iconography of Religions, sect. 23, Judaism, 5. Leiden, the Netherlands: Brill.

1989a Samaritan Material Remains. Pp. 135–77 in Crown 1989c.

1989b Samaritan Rituals and Customs. Pp. 650–89 in Crown 1989c.

1998a How to Tell a Samaritan Synagogue from a Jewish Synagogue. *Biblical Archaeology Review* 24.3: 24–35.

1998b The Greek Bible and the Samaritans. *Revue des Études Juives* 157: 269–358.

1998c The Samaritans in Egypt. Pp. 213–32 in *Études sémitiques et samaritaines offertes à Jean Margain*. Paris: Éditions du Zèbre.

1999 Samaritan Synagogues and Jewish Synagogues: Similarities and Differences. Pp. 118–60 in *Jews, Christians, and Polytheists in the Ancient Synagogue: Cultural Interaction during the Greco-Roman Period*, ed. S. Fine. London: Routledge.

2000 Samaritanism in Caesarea Maritima. Pp. 181–202 in *Religious Rivalries and the Struggle for Success in Caesarea Maritima*, ed. T. L. Donaldson. Waterloo, ON: Wilfrid Laurier University Press.

2002 *Early Christian Authors on Samaritans and Samaritanism: Texts, Translations, and Commentary*. Texte und Studien zum Antiken Judentum 92. Tübingen, Germany: Mohr Siebeck.

2007 The Samaritans and Their Pentateuch. Pp. 237–69 in Knoppers and Levinson 2007.

2009 *The Samaritans in Flavius Josephus*. Texte und Studien zum Antiken Judentum 129. Tübingen, Germany: Mohr Siebeck.

2012 Alexander und die Samaritaner nach Josephus und nach samaritanischen Quellen. Pp. 157–80 in *Die Samaritaner und die Bibel: Historische und literarische Wechselwirkungen zwischen biblischen und samaritanischen Traditionen*, ed. J. Frey, U. Schattner-Rieser, and K. Schmid. Studia Samaritana 7. Berlin: de Gruyter.

Purvis, J. D.

1968 *The Samaritan Pentateuch and the Origins of the Samaritan Sect*. Harvard Semitic Monographs 2. Cambridge, MA: Harvard University Press.

1981 The Samaritan Problem: A Case Study in Jewish Sectarianism in the Roman Era. Pp. 323–50 in *Traditions in Transformation: Turning Points in Biblical Faith*, ed. B. Halpern and J. D. Levenson. Winona Lake, IN: Eisenbrauns.

1986 The Samaritans and Judaism. Pp. 81–98 in *Early Judaism and Its Modern Interpreters*, ed. R. A. Kraft and G. W. E. Nickelsburg. Atlanta, GA: Scholars Press.

Qimron, E., and J. Strugnell

1994 *Qumran Cave 4. V: Miqṣat Maʿaśe ha-Torah*. Discoveries in the Judaean Desert 10. Oxford: Clarendon.

Rad, G. von
1930 *Das Geschichtsbild des chronistischen Werkes*. Stuttgart: Kohlhammer.

Rainey, A. F., and R. S. Notley
2006 *The Sacred Bridge: Carta's Atlas of the Biblical World*. Jerusalem: Carta.

Rappaport, U.
1995 The Samaritans in the Hellenistic Period. Pp. 281–88 in *Essays in Honour of G. D. Sixdenier: New Samaritan Studies of the Société d'Études Samaritaines*, ed. A. D. Crown and L. Davey. Studies in Judaica 5. Sydney: Mandelbaum.

Reich, R.
1988 A Note on Samaritan Ritual Baths. Pp. 242–44 in *Jews, Samaritans, and Christians in Byzantine Palestine*, ed. D. Jacoby and Y. Tsafrir. Jerusalem: Ben Zvi (Hebrew).

1995 The Synagogue and the *Miqweh* in Eretz-Israel in the Second-Temple, Mishnaic, and Talmudic Periods. Pp. 289–97 in *Ancient Synagogues: Historical Analysis and Archaeological Discovery*, vol. 1, ed. D. Urman and P. V. M. Flesher. Studia Post-Biblica 47. Leiden, the Netherlands: Brill.

Reisner, G. A., C. S. Fisher, and D. G. Lyon
1924 *Harvard Excavations at Samaria, 1908–1910*. 2 vols. Cambridge, MA: Harvard University Press.

Rendsburg, G. A.
1990 *Linguistic Evidence for the Northern Origin of Selected Psalms*. Society of Biblical Literature Monograph Series 43. Atlanta, GA: Scholars Press.

1991a The Northern Origin of Nehemiah 9. *Biblica* 72: 348–66.

1991b The Strata of Biblical Hebrew. *Journal of Northwest Semitic Languages* 17: 81–99.

2002 *Israelian Hebrew in the Book of Kings*. Bethesda, MD: CDL.

Richardson, P.
2003 An Architectural Case for Synagogues as Associations. Pp. 90–117 in Olsson and Zetterholm 2003.

Richter, S. L.
2002 *The Deuteronomistic History and the Name Theology: lešakkēn šemô šām in the Bible and the Ancient Near East*. Beihefte zur *Zeitschrift für die Alttestamentliche Wissenschaft* 318. Berlin: de Gruyter.

Ringgren, H.
1975 *Israelite Religion*. Philadelphia: Fortress.

Rofé, A.
2002 *Deuteronomy: Issues and Interpretations*. London: Clark.

Römer, T.
2002 Le pentateuque toujours en question. Pp. 343–74 in *Congress Volume: Basel, 2001*, ed. A. Lemaire. Vetus Testamentum Supplement 92. Leiden, the Netherlands: Brill.

2011 How Many Books (*Teuchs*): Pentateuch, Hexateuch, Deuteronomistic History, or Enneateuch? Pp. 25–42 in Dozeman, Römer, and Schmid 2011.

Rösel, H. N.

2009 Why 2 Kings 17 Does Not Constitute a Chapter of Reflection in the "Deuteronomistic History." *Journal of Biblical Literature* 128: 95–90.

Rothstein, J. W.

1908 *Juden und Samaritaner: Die grundlegende Scheidung von Judentum und Heidentum*. Beiträge zur Wissenschaft vom Alten Testament 3. Leipzig: Hinrichs.

Rowley, H. H.

1955–56 Sanballat and the Samaritan Temple. *Bulletin of the John Rylands University Library* 38: 166–98.

1962 The Samaritan Schism in Legend and History. Pp. 208–22 in *Israel's Prophetic Heritage: Essays in Honor of James Muilenburg*, ed. B. W. Anderson and W. Harrelson. New York: Harper.

Rudolph, W.

1949 *Esra und Nehemia samt 3. Esra*. Handbuch zum Alten Testament 20. Tübingen, Germany: Mohr.

1951 Zum Text der Königsbücher. *Zeitschrift für die Alttestamentliche Wissenschaft* 61: 201–15.

1955 *Chronikbücher*. Handbuch zum Alten Testament 21. Tübingen, Germany: Mohr.

Runesson, A.

2001 The Synagogue at Ancient Ostia: The Building and its History from the First to the Fifth Century. Pp. 29–99 in *The Synagogue of Ancient Ostia and the Jews of Rome: Interdisciplinary Studies*, ed. B. Olsson, D. Mitternacht, and O. Brandt. Stockholm: Åström.

2003 Persian Imperial Politics, the Beginnings of Public Torah Readings, and the Origins of the Synagogues. Pp. 63–89 in in Olsson and Zetterholm 2003.

Runesson, A., D. D. Binder, and B. Olsson

2008 *The Ancient Synagogue from its Origins to 200 CE: A Source Book*. Leiden, the Netherlands: Brill.

Sanderson, J. E.

1986 *An Exodus Scroll from Qumran: 4QpaleoExodm and the Samaritan Tradition*. Harvard Semitic Studies 30. Atlanta, GA: Scholars Press.

Scatolini Apóstolo, S. S.

2006 On the Elusiveness and Malleability of "Israel." *Journal of Hebrew Scriptures* 6, available online at http://www.jhsonline.org/Articles/article_57.pdf.

Schaper, J.

2007 The "Publication" of Legal Texts in Ancient Judah. Pp. 225–36 in Knoppers and Levinson 2007.

Schenker, A.

2000 *Septante et texte massorétique dans l'histoire la plus ancienne du texte de 1 Rois 2–14*. Cahiers de la *Revue Biblique* 48. Paris: Gabalda.

2005 La cause de la chute du royaume d'Israël selon le texte massorétique et selon la Septante ancienne. Pp. 151–71 in *Traduire la Bible hébraïque: De la Septante á la Nouvelle Bible Segond*, ed. R. David and M. Jinbachian. Sciences Bibliques 15. Montreal: Médiaspaul.

2008 Le Seigneur choisira-t-il le lieu de son nom ou l'a-t-il choisi? L'apport de la Bible Grecque ancienne á l'histoire du texte Samaritain et Massorétique. Pp. 339–51 in *Scripture in Transition: Essays on Septuagint, Hebrew Bible, and Dead Sea Scrolls in Honour of Raija Sollamo*, ed. A. Voitila and J. Jokiranta. Supplements to the *Journal for the Study of Judaism* 126. Leiden, the Netherlands: Brill.

2010 Textgeschichtliches zum Samaritanischen Pentateuch und Samareitikon. Pp. 105–20 in Mor and Reiterer 2010.

Schiffman, L. H.

1985 The Samaritans in Tannaitic Halakah. *Jewish Quarterly Review* 75: 323–50.

2000 Phylacteries and Mezuzot. EDSS 2: 675–77.

Schiffman, L. H., E. Tov, and J. C. VanderKam

2000 *The Dead Sea Scrolls: Fifty Years after Their Discovery* (eds.). Jerusalem: Israel Exploration Society.

Schmid, K.

1999 *Erzväter und Exodus: Untersuchungen zur doppelten Begründung der Ursprünge Israels innerhalb der Geschichtsbücher des Alten Testaments*. Wissenschaftliche Monographien zum Alten und Neuen Testament 81. Neukirchen-Vluyn, Germany: Neukirchener Verlag. Translated by James Nogalski as *Moses and the Genesis Story: Israel's Dual Origins in the Hebrew Bible* (Winona Lake, IN: Eisenbrauns 2010).

2011 The Emergence and Disappearance of the Separation between the Pentateuch and the Deuteronomistic History in Biblical Studies. Pp. 11–24 in Dozeman, Römer, and Schmid 2011.

Schmitt, R.

2003 Gab es einen Bildersturm nach dem Exil? Einige Bemerkungen zur Verwendung von Terrakottafigurinen im nachexilischen Israel. Pp. 186–98 in *Yahwism After the Exile: Perspectives on Israelite Religion in the Persian Era*, ed. R. Albertz and B. Becking. Studies in Theology and Religion 5. Assen, the Netherlands: Royal Van Gorcum.

Schoors, A.

1998 *Die Königreiche Israel und Juda im 8. und 7. Jahrhundert v. Chr.: Die assyrische Krise*. Biblische Enzyklopädie 5. Stuttgart: Kohlhammer.

Schorch, S.

1997 Die Bedeutung der samaritanischen mündlichen Tradition für die Textgeschichte des Pentateuch (II). *Mitteilungen und Beiträge der Forschungsstelle Judentum, Theologische Fakultät Leipzig* 12–13: 53–64.

1999 Die Bedeutung der samaritanischen mündlichen Tradition für die Exegese des Pentateuch. *Wort und Dienst* 25: 77–91.

2004 *Die Vokale des Gesetzes: Die samaritanische Lesetradition als Textzeugin der Tora*. Vol. 1, *Das Buch Genesis*. Beihefte zur *Zeitschrift für die Alttestamentliche Wissenschaft* 339. Berlin: de Gruyter.

2007 La formation de la communauté samaritaine au 2e siècle avant J.-Chr. et la culture de lecture du Judaïsme. Pp. 5–20 in *Un carrefour dans l'histoire de la Bible: Du texte à la théologie au IIe siècle avant J.-C.*, ed. I. Himbaza and A. Schenker. Orbis Biblicus et Orientalis 233. Göttingen, Germany: Vandenhoeck & Ruprecht.

2010 The Latent Masorah of the Samaritans. Pp. 123–32 in Mor and Reiterer 2010.

2011 The Samaritan Version of Deuteronomy and the Origin of Deuteronomy. Pp. 23–37 in Zsengellér 2011.

Schuller, E. M.

1990 4Q372 1: A Text about Joseph. *Revue de Qumran* 14: 349–76.

1992 The Psalm of 4Q372 within the Context of Second Temple Prayer. *Catholic Biblical Quarterly* 54: 67–79.

Schur, N.

1989 *History of the Samaritans*. Beiträge zur Erforschung des Alten Testaments und des antiken Judentums 18. Frankfurt am Main: Lang.

Schwartz, D. R.

2007 "Judean" or "Jew"? How Should We Translate IOUDAIOS in Josephus? Pp. 3–27 in *Jewish Identity in the Greco-Roman World*, ed. J. Frey, D. R. Schwartz, and S. Gripentrog. Ancient Judaism and Early Christianity 71. Leiden, the Netherlands: Brill.

2008 *2 Maccabees*. Commentaries on Early Jewish Literature. Berlin: de Gruyter.

Schwartz, S.

1989 The "Judaism" of Samaria and Galilee in Josephus's Version of the Letter of Demetrius I to Jonathan (Antiquities 13.48–57). *Harvard Theological Review* 82: 377–91.

1991 Israel and the Nations Roundabout: I Maccabees and the Hasmonean Expansion. *Journal of Jewish Studies* 42: 16–38.

1993 John Hyrcanus I's Destruction of the Gerizim Temple and Judaean-Samaritan Relations. *Jewish History* 7: 9–25.

2001 *Imperialism and Jewish Society, 200 B.C.E. to 640 C.E.* Princeton, NJ: Princeton University Press.

Schweitzer, S. J.

2007 *Reading Utopia in Chronicles*. Library of Hebrew Bible/Old Testament Studies 442. London: Clark.

Seeligman, I. L.

1978 Die Auffassung von der Prophetie in der deuteronomistischen und chronistischen Geschichtsschreibung. Pp. 254–84 in *Congress Volume, Göttingen 1977*, ed. J. A. Emerton. Vetus Testamentum Supplement 29. Leiden, the Netherlands: Brill.

1980 The Beginnings of Midrash in the Book of Chronicles. *Tarbiz* 49: 14–32 (Hebrew).

Segal, M.
2000 4QReworked Pentateuch or 4QPentateuch? Pp. 391–99 in Schiffmann, Tov, and VanderKam 2000.

Sellin, E.
1917 *Gilgal: Ein Beitrag zur Geschichte der Einwanderung Israels in Palästina.* Leipzig: Deichert.

Shehadeh, H.
1977 The Arabic Translation of the Pentateuch. PhD diss. Jerusalem: Hebrew University.

Shepherd, D.
2005 Prophetaphobia: Fear and False Prophecy in Nehemiah VI. *Vetus Testamentum* 55: 232–50.

Smith, G. A.
1897 *The Historical Geography of the Holy Land.* London: Hodder & Stoughton.

Smith, J. Z.
1985 What a Difference a Difference Makes. Pp. 3–48 in *"To See Ourselves as Others See Us": Christians, Jews, "Others" in Late Antiquity,* ed. J. Neusner and E. S. Frerichs. Chico, CA: Scholars Press.

Smith, M.
1982 *Juda unter Assur in der Sargonidenzeit.* Forschungen zur Religion und Literatur des Alten und Neuen Testaments 129. Göttingen, Germany: Vandenhoeck & Ruprecht.
1987 *Palestinian Parties and Politics that Shaped the Old Testament.* 2nd ed. London: SCM.

Spieckermann, H.
1982 *Juda unter Assur in der Sargonidenzeit.* Forschungen zur Religion und Literatur des Alten und Neuen Testaments 129. Göttingen, Germany: Vandenhoeck & Ruprecht.

Stade, B.
1886 Miscellen 16: Anmerkungen zu 2 Kö. 15–21. *Zeitschrift für die Alttestamentliche Wissenschaft* 6: 156–89.

Steiner, M. L.
1997 Two Popular Cult Sites of Ancient Palestine. *Scandinavian Journal of the Old Testament* 11: 16–28.

Steiner, R. C.
1997 The Aramaic Text in Demotic Script (1.99). Pp. 309–27 in *The Context of Scripture,* vol. 1, *Canonical Inscriptions from the Biblical World,* ed. W. W. Hallo and K. L. Younger, Jr. Leiden, the Netherlands: Brill.

Steins, G.
1995 *Die Chronik als kanonisches Abschlussphänomen: Studien zur Entstehung und Theologie von 1/2 Chronik.* Bonner Biblische Beiträge 93. Weinheim, Germany: Beltz Athenäum.

Stenhouse, P. L.
1985 *The 'Kitāb al-tarīkh' of Abū 'l Fatḥ*. Sydney: Mandelbaum.
1989 Samaritan Chronicles. Pp. 218–65 in Crown 1989c.
Stern, E.
1989 What Happened to the Cult Figurines? Israelite Religion Purified after the Exile. *Biblical Archaeology Review* 15.4: 22–29, 53–54.
1994a *Dor, Ruler of the Seas: Twelve Years of Excavations at the Israelite-Phoenician Harbor Town on the Carmel Coast*. Jerusalem: Israel Exploration Society.
1994b Notes on the Development of Stamp-Glyptic Art in Palestine during the Assyrian and Persian Periods. Pp. 135–46 in *Uncovering Ancient Stones: Essays in Memory of H. Neil Richardson*, ed. L. M. Hopfe. Winona Lake, IN: Eisenbrauns.
2001 *Archaeology of the Land of the Bible*. Vol. 2, *The Assyrian, Babylonian, and Persian Periods, 732–332 BCE*. Anchor Bible Reference Library. New York: Doubleday.
2002 A Hoard of Persian Period Bullae from the Vicinity of Samaria. Pp. 82–103 in *The Samaritans*, ed. E. Stern and H. Eshel. Jerusalem: Yad Ben-Zvi (Hebrew).
2006 The Religious Revolution in Persian-Period Judah. Pp. 199–205 in Lipschits and Oeming 2006.
Stern, E., and Y. Magen
1984 A Pottery Group of the Persian Period from Qadum in Samaria. *Bulletin of the American Schools of Oriental Research* 253: 9–27.
Strange, J. F.
2003 Archaeology and Ancient Synagogues up to about 200 CE. Pp. 37–62 in Olsson and Zetterholm 2003.
Strawn, B. A.
2005 *What Is Stronger than a Lion?: Leonine Image and Metaphor in the Hebrew Bible and the Ancient Near East*. Orbis Biblicus et Orientalis 212. Göttingen, Germany: Vandenhoeck & Ruprecht.
Sukenik, E. L.
1942 An Israelite Shrine. Pp. 23–24 in Crowfoot, Kenyon, and Sukenik 1942.
1949 The Samaritan Synagogue at Salbit: Preliminary Report. *Bulletin of the Louis M. Rabinowitz Fund for the Exploration of Ancient Synagogues* 1: 26–30.
Sweeney, M. A.
2001 *King Josiah of Judah: The Lost Messiah of Israel*. New York: Oxford University Press.
Tadmor, H.
1958 The Campaigns of Sargon II of Assur: A Chronological-Historical Study. *Journal of Cuneiform Studies* 12: 22–40, 77–100.
1994a *The Inscriptions of Tiglath-pileser III, King of Assyria*. Jerusalem: Israel Academy of Sciences and Humanities.
1994b Judah. Pp. 261–96 in *The Cambridge Ancient History*. Vol. 6, *The Fourth Century B.C.*, ed. D. M. Lewis, J. Boardman, S. Hornblower, and M. Ostwald. 2nd ed. Cambridge, UK: Cambridge University Press.

1999 World-Dominion: The Expanding Horizon of the Assyrian Empire. Pp. 55–62 in *Landscapes: Territories, Frontiers and Horizons in the Ancient Near East*, vol. 1, ed. L. Milano. History of the Ancient Near East Monographs 3/1. Padua, Italy: Sargon.

Tadmor, M.

1979 Fragments of an Achaemenid Throne from Samaria. *Israel Exploration Journal* 24: 37–43.

Tal, A.

1980–83 *The Samaritan Targum of the Pentateuch* (ed.). 3 vols. Texts and Studies in the Hebrew Language and Related Subjects 4–6. *Tel Aviv*: Tel Aviv University.

1988 The Samaritan Targum of the Pentateuch. Pp. 189–216 in *Mikra: Text, Translation, Reading, and Interpretation of the Hebrew Bible in Ancient Judaism and Early Christianity*, ed. M. J. Mulder. Compendia Rerum Iudaicarum ad Novum Testamentum section 2, Literature of the Jewish People in the Period of the Second Temple and the Talmud 1. Assen, the Netherlands: Van Gorcum.

1994 *The Samaritan Pentateuch Edited According to MS 6 [C] of the Shekhem Synagogue*. Texts and Studies in the Hebrew Language and Related Subjects 8. Tel Aviv University: Rosenberg School (Hebrew).

2011 "Hebrew Language" and "Holy Language" between Judea and Samaria. Pp. 187–201 in Zsengellér 2011.

Talmon, S.

1958 Divergencies in Calendar Reckoning in Ephraim and Judah. *Vetus Testamentum* 8: 58–63.

1981 Polemics and Apology in Biblical Historiography: 2 Kings 17: 24–41. Pp. 57–68 in *The Creation of Sacred Literature: Composition and Redaction of the Biblical Text*, ed. R. E. Friedman. Near Eastern Studies 22. Berkeley: University of California Press.

1999 A Papyrus Fragment Inscribed in Palaeo-Hebrew Script. Pp. 18–49 in *Masada: The Yigael Yadin Excavations, 1963–1965—Final Reports*, vol. 6, ed. S. Talmon and Y. Yadin. Jerusalem: Israel Exploration Society.

Talshir, Z.

2001 *1 Esdras: From Origin to Translation*. Septuagint and Cognate Studies 50. Atlanta, GA: Society of Biblical Literature.

Tappy, R.

2001 *The Archaeology of Israelite Samaria*. Vol. 2, *The Eighth Century BCE*. Harvard Semitic Studies 50. Winona Lake, IN: Eisenbrauns.

2007 The Final Years of Israelite Samaria: Toward a Dialogue between Texts and Archaeology. Pp. 258–79 in *"Up to the Gates of Ekron": Essays on the Archaeology and History of the Eastern Mediterranean in Honor of Seymour Gitin*, ed. S. W. Crawford. Jerusalem: Israel Exploration Society.

Thompson, T. L.

2001 The Exile in History and Myth: A Response to Hans Barstad. Pp. 101–18 in *Leading Captivity Captive: "The Exile" as History and Ideology*, ed. L. L. Grabbe. Journal for the Study of the Old Testament Supplement 278. Sheffield, UK: Sheffield Academic Press.

Throntveit, M. A.

2003 The Relationship of Hezekiah to David and Solomon. Pp. 105–21 in *The Chronicler as Theologian: Essays in Honor of Ralph W. Klein*, ed. M. P. Graham, S. L. McKenzie, and G. N. Knoppers. Journal for the Study of the Old Testament Supplement 371. London: Clark.

Tigay, J. H.

1985 Conflation as a Redactional Technique. Pp. 53–95 in *Empirical Models for Biblical Criticism*, ed. J. H. Tigay. Philadelphia: University of Pennsylvania Press.

1986 *You Shall Have No Other Gods: Israelite Religion in the Light of Hebrew Inscriptions*. Harvard Semitic Studies 31. Atlanta, GA: Scholars Press.

1987 Israelite Religion: The Onomastic and Epigraphic Evidence. Pp. 157–94 in *Ancient Israelite Religion: Essays in Honor of Frank Moore Cross*, ed. P. D. Miller, P. D. Hanson, and S. D. McBride. Philadelphia: Fortress.

1996 *Deuteronomy: The Traditional Hebrew Text with the New JPS Translation*. JPS Torah Commentary. Philadelphia: Jewish Publication Society.

Timm, S.

1989–90 Die Eroberung Samarias aus assyrisch-babylonischer Sicht. *Welt des Orients* 20/21: 62–82.

2002 Ein assyrisch bezeugter Tempel in Samaria? Pp. 126–33 in *Kein Land für sich allein: Studien zum Kulturkontakt in Kanaan, Israel-Palästina und Ebirnâri für Manfred Weippert zum 65. Geburtstag*, ed. U. Hübner and E. A. Knauf. Orbis Biblicus et Orientalis 186. Göttingen, Germany: Vandenhoeck & Ruprecht.

Tod, M. N.

1951 On the Greek Inscription in the Samaritan Synagogue at Salbit. *Bulletin of the Louis M. Rabinowitz Fund for the Exploration of Ancient Synagogues* 2: 27–28.

Torrey, C. C.

1909 The Chronicler as Editor and as Independent Narrator. *American Journal of Semitic Languages and Literatures* 25: 157–73, 188–217.

1954 *The Chronicler's History of Israel: Chronicles-Ezra-Nehemiah Restored to Its Original Form*. New Haven, CT: Yale University Press.

Tov, E.

1989 The Proto-Samaritan Texts and the Samaritan Pentateuch. Pp. 397–407 in Crown 1989c.

1990 The Samaritan Pentateuch and the So-Called "Proto-Samaritan" Texts. Pp. 136–46 in *Studies on Hebrew and Other Semitic Languages Presented to Professor Chaim Rabin on the Occasion of his Seventy-Fifth Birthday*, ed. M. H. Goshen-Gottstein, S. Morag, and S. Kogut. Jerusalem: Academon (Hebrew).

2001 *Textual Criticism of the Hebrew Bible*. 2nd ed. Assen, the Netherlands: Van Gorcum.
2010 From 4QReworked Pentateuch to 4QPentateuch (?). Pp. 73–92 in *Authoritative Scriptures in Ancient Judaism*, ed. M. Popović. Supplements to the *Journal for the Study of Judaism* 141. Leiden, the Netherlands: Brill.
2012 *Textual Criticism of the Hebrew Bible*. 3rd ed. Minneapolis: Fortress.

Tov, E., and S. White (Crawford)
1994 Reworked Pentateuch. Pp. 187–352 in *Qumrân Cave 4. VIII: Parabiblical Texts, Part 1*, ed. E. Tov. Discoveries in the Judaean Desert 13. Oxford: Clarendon.

Trebolle Barrera, J. C.
1989 *Centena in libros Samuelis et Regum: Variantes textuales y composición literaria en los libros de Samuel y Reyes*. Textos y Estudios "Cardenal Cisneros" 47. Madrid: CSIC.
1998 *The Jewish Bible and the Christian Bible: An Introduction to the History of the Bible*. Leiden, the Netherlands: Brill.

Uehlinger, C.
1999 Powerful Persianisms in Glyptic Iconography of Persian Period Palestine. Pp. 134–82 in *The Crisis of Israelite Religion: Transformation of Religious Tradition in Exilic and Post-Exilic Times*, ed. B. Becking and M. Korpel. Leiden, the Netherlands: Brill.

Ulrich, E. C.
1994 4QJoshua^a and Joshua's First Altar in the Promised Land. Pp. 89–104 in *New Qumran Texts and Studies: Proceedings of the First Meeting of the International Organization for Qumran Studies, Paris, 1992*, ed. G. J. Brooke. Studies on the Texts of the Desert of Judah 15. Leiden, the Netherlands: Brill.
1995 4QJoshua (Pls. XXXII–XXXIV). Pp. 143–52 in *Qumran Cave 4. Vol. 9, Deuteronomy, Joshua, Judges, Kings*, ed. E. C. Ulrich. Discoveries in the Judaean Desert 14. Oxford: Clarendon.
1999 *The Dead Sea Scrolls and the Origins of the Bible*. Grand Rapids, MI: Eerdmans.
2010 *The Biblical Qumran Scrolls: Transcriptions and Textual Variants*. Vetus Testamentum Supplement 138. Leiden, the Netherlands: Brill.
2012 The Old Latin, Mount Gerizim, and 4QJosh^a. Pp. 361–75 in *Textual Criticism and Dead Sea Scrolls Studies in Honour of Julio Trebolle Barrera: Florilegium Complutense*, ed. A. Piquer Otero and P. A. Torijano Morales. Supplements to the *Journal for the Study of Judaism* 157. Leiden, the Netherlands: Brill.

Ussishkin, D., and J. Woodhead
2008 Tel Jezreel. *New Encyclopaedia of Archaeological Excavations in the Holy Land* 5: 1837–39.

Vanderhooft, D. S.
1999 *The Neo-Babylonian Empire and Babylon in the Latter Prophets*. Harvard Semitic Monographs 59. Atlanta, GA: Scholars Press.

2003 New Evidence Pertaining to the Transition from Neo-Babylonian to Achaemenid Administration in Palestine. Pp. 219–35 in *Yahwism after the Exile: Perspectives on Israelite Religion in the Persian Era*, ed. R. Albertz and B. Becking. Assen, the Netherlands: Van Gorcum.

VanderKam, J. C.

2004 *From Joshua to Caiaphas: High Priests after the Exile*. Minneapolis: Fortress Press.

Van Houten, C.

1991 *The Alien in Israelite Law*. Journal for the Study of the Old Testament Supplement 107. Sheffield, UK: JSOT.

Van Seters, J.

2000 The Deuteronomistic History: Can It Avoid Death by Redaction? Pp. 119–34 in *The Future of the Deuteronomistic History*, ed. T. Römer. Bibliotheca Ephemeridum Theologicarum Lovaniensium 147. Leuven, Belgium: Peeters.

Vaux, R. de

1965 *Ancient Israel*. 2 vols. New York: McGraw-Hill.

Vervenne, M., and J. Lust

1997 *Deuteronomy and Deuteronomic Literature: Festschrift C. H. W. Brekelmans* (eds.). Bibliotheca Ephemeridum Theologicarum Lovaniensium 133. Leuven, Belgium: Peeters.

Vilmar, E.

1865 *Abulfathi Annales Samaritani: Quos Arabice edidit cum prolegomenis*. Gotha, Germany: Perthes.

Vincent, A.

1937 *La Religion des Judéo-Araméens d'Éléphantine*. Paris: Geuthner.

Viviano, P. A.

1987 2 Kings 17: A Rhetorical and Form-Critical Analysis. *Catholic Biblical Quarterly* 49: 548–59.

Wagenaar, J. A.

2007 "Someone came from Baal Shalisha": The Significance of the Topography in 2 Kgs 4.42–44. *Biblische Notizen* 135: 35–42.

Walsh, J. T.

2000 2 Kings 17: The Deuteronomist and the Samaritans. Pp. 315–23 in *Past, Present, Future: The Deuteronomistic History and the Prophets*, ed. J. C. de Moor and H. F. Van Rooy. Leiden, the Netherlands: Brill.

Waltke, B. K., and M. O'Connor

1990 *An Introduction to Biblical Hebrew Syntax*. Winona Lake, IN: Eisenbrauns.

Watkins, L.

1997 Survey of Southern Samaria. *Oxford Encyclopedia of Archaeology in the Near East* 5: 66–68.

Watts, J. W.

2007 The Torah as the Rhetoric of Priesthood. Pp. 319–31 in Knoppers and Levinson 2007.

Weinfeld, M.
1972 *Deuteronomy and the Deuteronomic School*. Oxford: Clarendon.
1991 *Deuteronomy 1–11: A New Translation with Introduction and Commentary*. Anchor Bible 5. New York: Doubleday.

Wellhausen, J.
1885 *Prolegomena to the History of Ancient Israel*. Translated by J. S. Black and A. Menzies Edinburgh: Adam & Charles Black.

Werlitz, J.
2002 *Die Bücher der Könige*. Neuer Stuttgarter Kommentar Altes Testament 8. Stuttgart: Katholisches Bibelwerk.

Wevers, J. W.
1990 *Notes on the Greek Text of Exodus*. Septuagint and Cognate Studies 30. Atlanta, GA: Scholars Press.
1998 *Notes on the Greek Text of Numbers*. Septuagint and Cognate Studies 46. Atlanta, GA: Scholars Press.

White, L. M.
1987 The Delos Synagogue Revisited: Recent Fieldwork in the Graeco-Roman Diaspora. *Harvard Theological Review* 80: 133–60.

Wilkinson, T. J., E. B. Wilkinson, J. Ur, and M. Altaweel
2005 Landscape and Settlement in the Neo-Assyrian Empire. *Bulletin of the American Schools of Oriental Research* 340: 23–56.

Willi, T.
1994 Late Persian Period Judaism and Its Conception of an Integral Israel according to Chronicles. Pp. 146–62 in *Second Temple Studies*, vol. 2, *Temple and Community in the Persian Period*. ed. T. C. Eskenazi and K. H. Richards. Journal for the Study of the Old Testament Supplement 175. Sheffield, UK: JSOT.
1995 *Juda—Jehud—Israel: Studien zum Selbstverständnis des Judentums in persischer Zeit*. Forschungen zum Alten Testament 12. Tübingen, Germany: Mohr.

Williamson, H. G. M.
1977a The Historical Value of Josephus' Jewish Antiquities XI. 297–301. *Journal of Theological Studies* 28: 49–66.
1977b *Israel in the Books of Chronicles*. Cambridge, UK: Cambridge University Press.
1982 *1 and 2 Chronicles*. New Century Bible Commentary. Grand Rapids, MI: Eerdmans.
1985 *Ezra, Nehemiah*. Word Biblical Commentary 16. Waco, TX: Word.
1989 The Concept of Israel in Transition. Pp. 141–60 in *The World of Ancient Israel: Sociological, Anthropological, and Political Perspectives*, ed. R. E. Clements. Cambridge, UK: Cambridge University Press.

Wolff, S.
2008 'En Haggit. *New Encyclopaedia of Archaeological Excavations in the Holy Land* 5: 1726–27.

Wright, G. E.
1965 *Shechem: The Biography of a Biblical City*. New York: McGraw-Hill.
Wright, G. R. H.
2002 *Shechem III: The Stratigraphy and Architecture of Shechem/Tell Balâṭah*. 2 vols. Boston: American Schools of Oriental Research.
Wright, J. L.
2004 *Rebuilding Identity: The Nehemiah-Memoir and Its Earliest Readers*. Beihefte zur *Zeitschrift für die Alttestamentliche Wissenschaft* 348. Berlin: de Gruyter.
Würthwein, E.
1984 *Die Bücher der Könige*. Vol. 2, *1 Kön. 17–2 Kön. 25*. Alte Testament Deutsch 11/2. Göttingen, Germany: Vandenhoeck & Ruprecht.
Younger, K. L., Jr.
1998 The Deportations of the Israelites. *Journal of Biblical Literature* 117: 201–27.
1999 The Fall of Samaria in the Light of Recent Research. *Catholic Biblical Quarterly* 61: 461–82.
2000a Sargon II: The Annals (2.118). Pp. 293–94 in *The Context of Scripture*, vol. 2, *Monumental Inscriptions from the Biblical World*, ed. W. W. Hallo and K. L. Younger, Jr. Leiden, the Netherlands: Brill.
2000b Sargon II: Nimrud Prisms D & E (2.118D). Pp. 295–96 in *The Context of Scripture*, vol. 2, *Monumental Inscriptions from the Biblical World*, ed. W. W. Hallo and K. L. Younger, Jr. Leiden, the Netherlands: Brill.
2000c Tiglath-pileser III: Summary Inscription 4 (2.117C). Pp. 287–88 in *The Context of Scripture*, vol. 2, *Monumental Inscriptions from the Biblical World*, ed. W. W. Hallo and K. L. Younger, Jr. Leiden, the Netherlands: Brill.
2003a Assyrian Involvement in the Southern Levant at the End of the Eighth Century B.C.E. Pp. 235–63 in *Jerusalem in Bible and Archaeology: The First Temple Period*, ed. A. Killebrew and A. Vaughn. Society of Biblical Literature Symposium Series18. Atlanta, GA: Society of Biblical Literature.
2003b Give Us Our Daily Bread. Pp. 271–80 in *Life and Culture in the Ancient Near East*, ed. R. E. Averbeck, M. W. Chavalas, and D. S. Weisberg. Bethesda, MD: CDL.
Zadok, R.
1985 Samarian Notes. *Bibliotheca Orientalis* 42: 657–72.
1986 Die nichthebräischen Namen der Israeliten vor dem hellenistischer Zeitalter. *Ugarit Forschungen* 17: 387–98.
1988 *The Pre-Hellenistic Israelite Anthroponymy and Prosopography*. Orientalia Lovaniensia Analecta 28. Leuven, Belgium: Peeters.
1998 A Prosopography of Samaria and Edom/Idumea. *Ugarit Forschungen* 30: 781–828.
1995 Foreigners and Linguistic Material in Mesopotamia and Egypt. Pp. 431–47 in *Immigration and Emigration within the Ancient Near East: Festschrift E. Lipiński*, ed. K. van Lerberghe and A. Schoors. Orientalia Lovaniensia Analecta 65. Leuven, Belgium: Peeters.

2002 *The Earliest Diaspora: Israelites and Judeans in Pre-Hellenistic Mesopotamia.* Publications of the Diaspora Research Institute 151. Tel Aviv: Tel Aviv University.

2008 Neo-Assyrian Notes. Pp. 312–30 in *Treasures on Camels' Humps: Historical and Literary Studies from the Ancient Near East Presented to Israel Eph'al,* ed. M. Cogan and D. Kahn. Jerusalem: Magnes.

Zahn, M. M.

2008 The Problem of Categorizing the 4QReworked Pentateuch Manuscripts. *Dead Sea Discoveries* 15: 315–39.

2011 *Rethinking Rewritten Scripture: Composition and Exegesis in the 4Q Reworked Pentateuch Manuscripts.* Studies on the Texts of the Desert of Judah 95. Leiden, the Netherlands: Brill.

Zakovitch, Y.

1999 The First Stages of Jerusalem's Sanctification under David: A Literary and Ideological Analysis. Pp. 16–35 in *Jerusalem: Its Sanctity and Centrality to Judaism, Christianity, and Islam,* ed. L. I. Levine. New York: Continuum.

Zangenberg, J.

1994 *ΣAMAPEIA: Antike Quellen zur Geschichte und Kultur der Samaritaner in deutscher Übersetzung. Texte und Arbeiten zum Neutestamentlichen Zeitalter 15.* Tübingen, Germany: Francke.

Zertal, A.

1988 The Water Factor during the Israelite Settlement Process in Canaan. Pp. 341–52 in *Society and Economy in the Eastern Mediterranean, c. 1500–1000 B.C,* ed. M. Heltzer and E. Lipiński. Orientalia Lovaniensia Analecta 23. Leuven, Belgium: Peeters.

1989 The Wedge-Shaped Decorated Bowl and the Origin of the Samaritans. *Bulletin of the American Schools of Oriental Research* 276: 77–84.

1990 The Pahwah of Samaria (Northern Israel) during the Persian Period: Types of Settlement, Economy, History and New Discoveries. *Transeuphratène* 3: 9–30.

1991 Israel Enters Canaan: Following the Pottery Trail. *Biblical Archaeology Review* 17.5: 38–45.

1993 Khirbet el-Hammam. *New Encyclopaedia of Archaeological Excavations in the Holy Land* 2: 563–65.

1997 Survey of Northern Samaria. *Oxford Encyclopedia of Archaeology in the Near East* 4: 164–66.

1999 The Province of Samaria during the Persian and Hellenistic Periods. Pp. 75*–98* in *Michael: Historical, Epigraphical and Biblical Studies in Honor of Professor Michael Heltzer,* ed. Y. Avishur and R. Deutsch. Tel Aviv: Archaeological Centre Publications (Hebrew).

2001 The Heart of the Monarchy: Pattern of Settlement and New Historical Considerations of the Israelite Kingdom of Samaria. Pp. 38–64 in *Studies in the Archaeology of the Iron Age in Israel and Jordan,* ed. A. Mazar. *Journal for the Study of the Old Testament* Supplement 331. Sheffield, UK: Sheffield Academic Press.

2003 The Province of Samaria (Assyrian *Samerina*) in the Late Iron Age (Iron Age III). Pp. 377–412 in Lipschits and Blenkinsopp 2003.

2004 *The Manasseh Hill Country Survey*. Vol. *1, The Shechem Syncline*. Culture and History of the Ancient Near East 21/1. Leiden, the Netherlands: Brill.

2008 *The Manasseh Hill Country Survey*. Vol. 2, *The Eastern Valleys and the Fringes of the Desert*. Culture and History of the Ancient Near East 21/2. Leiden, the Netherlands: Brill.

Zimhoni, O.

1990 Two Ceramic Assemblages from Lachish Levels III and II. *Tel Aviv* 17: 3–52.

Zorn, J. R.

2003 Tell en-Naṣbeh and the Problem of the Material Culture of the Sixth Century. Pp. 413–47 in Lipschits and Blenkinsopp 2003.

Zsengellér, J.

1996 Personal Names in the Wadi ed-Daliyeh Papyri. *Zeitschrift für Althebräistik* 9: 181–89.

1998 *Gerizim as Israel: Northern Tradition of the Old Testament and the Early History of the Samaritans*. Utrechtse Theologische Reeks 38. Utrecht, the Netherlands: University of Utrecht.

2011 *Samaria, Samarians, Samaritans: Studies on Bible, History and Linguistics* (ed.). Studia Samaritana 6. Berlin: de Gruyter.

Jewish Scriptures

Genesis
1–11, 181
5:19–31, 181
8:1–22, 181
9:23, 156n59
11:10–26, 181
12:6, 200, 210
12:6–8, 194, 209
12:8, 194
12:9, 194
13:3, 194
14:18, 206n92
21:14, 194
21:25–34, 194
22:2, 200n77
22:19, 194
23:2, 194
23:19, 194
26:5, 16n21
26:23–33, 194
28:10, 194
28:10–22, 194
30:23–24, 194
31:13, 194
31:46–52, 180
33:18, 3, 206n92
33:18–20, 194
34, 97n55
35:1–12, 61
35:1–15, 194

35:27, 194
35:4, 200
37:14, 194
46:1, 194
48:3, 194

Exodus
2:1–27, 85n32
12:1–13, 90n41
12:21–27, 90n41
12:43–51, 90n41
13:3–10, 85n32
13:11a, 184
15:1–18, 205
15:18, 231n39
20:1–17, 184
20:4, 232
20:11, 182
20:13, 200n7, 201, 219
20:18, 182
20:18–21, 184n39
20:24–26, 207–211
21:2–11, 79
21:33, 156n59
25:33–38, 232
26:13, 156n59
26:31–35, 232
32:1–35, 54n18
32:10, 181
32:20, 64

33:7–11, 186
34, 88
34:6–7, 87
34:11–16, 164n80
38:15, 156n59
40:33–38, 186

Leviticus
7:19–21, 90n41
8:35, 16n21
9:24, 207n93
17:3–4, 187n49
18:30, 16n21
21:10, 129n60
22:9, 16n21
23:5–6, 85n32
23:5–8, 90n41
23:40, 231
24:1–4, 232n44
25:39–46, 79
26, 6n13
26:42–45, 88n38

Numbers
4:9, 156n59, 232n44
4:15, 156n59
6:24–26, 234
9:1–14, 84n31, 85n32, 90n41
9:19, 16n21
9:21–23, 180
9:23, 16n21
10:1–10, 231n36
10:10, 151n45
10:34–36, 180
12:2, 207n93
12:6–7, 207n93
13:29, 200
13:33, 180
15:35, 180
18:7–8, 16n21
22:5, 156n59
22:11, 156n59

25:12–13, 192
28:16–17, 85n32
28:16–25, 90n41
31:54, 151n45
35:25, 129n60
35:28, 129n60

Deuteronomy
1:5, 203n84
1:35, 46
3:25, 46
4:8, 203n84
4:10, 60n36
4:13, 184n40
4:21–22, 46
4:25, 6n13
4:25–28, 47n3
4:25–31, 87, 88n38
4:44, 203n84
5:1–18, 184n40
5:6–5:7, 232
5:6–22, 233
5:15, 182
5:17, 200n77, 201, 219
5:18, 184
5:19–28, 184n37
5:22, 136n5
5:28–29, 182
6:4–9, 233–234
6:6, 233
6:9, 233
6:13–15, 47n3
6:18, 46
7:1–4, 164n80
8:10, 46
9:13–21, 54n18
9:16, 46
9:20, 181
9:21, 64
11:1, 16n21
11:13–21, 234
11:17, 46

11:20, 233
11:26–30, 198, 201
11:26–32, 197
11:29, 210
11:29–30, 184, 197n73, 199, 206
11:30, 184, 199–201
11:31–12:1, 198
12, 1, 64
12:1–13:1, 195. 214
12:1–26:15, 197–199
12:2–26:19, 201
12:2–3, 91
12:4–12, 91
12:5, 184n41, 185nn42–43, 187n49, 196, 209
12:5–7, 208
12:9, 211
12:10, 211
12:11, 185n45, 196, 212
12:13–14, 208
12:14, 196, 211
12:18, 196
12:21, 196
12:26, 196
12:26–27, 91
12:27, 208–209
12:29–31, 91
13:2–12, 64
13:10, 184n40
13:13–17, 212n99
14:23, 60n36, 185n45
14:25, 185n42
15:4, 46
15:12–18, 79
16:1–8, 85n32
16:2, 185n45
16:6, 185n45
16:11, 185n45
16:18–18:22, 195
17:19, 60n36
18:18–22, 182
18:22, 158n65

19:10, 46
20:1–18, 64n46
20:10–18 138n16
20:10–14, 79
20:16, 46
21:23, 46
23:2–3, 136n4
23:4–7, 146n28
23:4–9, 164n80
23:14, 156n59
24:4, 46
25:19, 46
26:1, 46
27:1–3, 202
27:1–26, 199, 208
27:2–7, 184
27:2–26, 204
27:4, 188n51, 202–203, 205, 210, 215
27:4–6, 202
27:4–8, 196n69
27:5–7, 202, 207–209, 211
27:8, 202
27:9–10, 202, 210
27:11–13, 196n69, 202
27:14–26, 202
28:1–68, 199n75
28:36–37, 47n3
28:37, 46
28:63–68, 47n3
28:37, 46
28:63, 47n3
29:17–27, 47n3
29:26–27, 47n3
29:27, 7
30:1–3, 145n25
30:1–4, 185n43
30:1–10, 6n13, 87–88
31:12–13, 60n36
31:30, 136n5
32:10, 234n50
32:21, 174n15

33:4, 136n5

Joshua
4:19, 204
4:19–20, 200
4:24, 60n36
5:9–10, 204
5:19, 211
8:1–29, 205
8:30–35, 203–204
9:1–27, 204
9:27, 184n41, 186
10:1–12:24, 204
11:1, 21n7
11:5, 21n7
11:23, 200, 212n98
13:1–21, 40, 205
13:1b–6, 212n98
14:7–10, 205n89
16:3, 147
16:5, 147
18:13, 147
19:14, 21n7
19:21, 221
20:6, 129n60
21:22, 147
21:43–45, 212n98
22:3, 16n21
23:13, 46, 47n3
23:15–16, 46, 47n3
24:7, 156n59
24:26, 200

Judges
1, 46
3:19, 200
4:19, 156n59
9:37, 200
10:16–11:33, 61

1 Samuel
1:3, 129n59
2:34, 129n59
4:4, 129n59
4:11, 129n59
4:17, 129n59
4:19, 129n59
7:1, 129n58
7:3–14, 61
12:14, 60n36
12:24, 60n36
12:25, 47n3
14:3 129n59

2 Samuel
2:8, 112n17
7:7–16, 186
13:19, 94n48
19:16, 200
19:41, 200
23:29, 129n58
24:18–26, 207n93

1 Kings
2:3, 16n21
5:2, 94n48
5:18, 212n98
6:1, 212n98
6:1–9:3, 53
8, 54
8:11, 186
8:16, 185–186, 187n49
8:22–53, 87n36, 224n18
8:36, 46
8:40, 60n36
8:43, 60n36
8:44, 185–187
8:46–52, 87
8:48–51, 88
9:1–9, 128
9:2–9, 87n36
9:7, 46, 47n43
11:1, 187
11:1–13, 80,

11:13, 187
11:32, 187
11:36, 187
11:26–22:53, 118n31
11:29–38, 5
11:31–38, 80
12:1–18, 151
12:15, 80
12:16, 151
12:26–28, 53
12:28, 53–54
12:30, 53n15
12:31, 53, 55n21
12:32, 53n15, 55n21
12:33–13:33, 62n42
13:1–3, 63
13:1–9, 53
13:2, 56
13:11–32, 54
13:20, 52
13:24, 52
13:31–32, 56
13:32, 53, 55
13:32–34, 63
13:33, 54
14:9, 55
14:10, 53
14:11, 47n3
14:15, 46, 47n3
14:16, 54n19
14:21, 187
15:26, 54n19
15:30, 54n19
15:34, 54n19
16:13, 54n19
16:19, 54n19
16:24, 15n19
16:26; 54n19
16:33, 50n8
20:35–36, 52
21:1, 55n23
22:53, 54n19

2 Kings
1:3, 55n23
2:1, 201
2:18, 201
3, 73
3:3, 54n19
3:3–23:15, 118n31
4:38, 201
6:23, 94n48
10:29, 53, 54n19
10:31, 54n19
10:32–33, 51n10
12:4, 54n19
12:11, 129n60
13:2, 54n19
13:3–5, 51n10
13:6, 54n19
13:11, 54n19
13:13, 118
13:22–23, 51n10
14:4, 54n19
14:16, 118n31
14:23, 118n31
14:24, 54n19
14:25–27, 51n10
14:27, 118n31
14:29, 118n31
15:1, 118n31
15:4, 54n19
15:8, 118n31
15:9, 54n19
15:18, 54n19
15:19, 21
15:24, 54n19
15:27–29, 46
15:28, 54n19
15:29, 21, 46, 75n8, 147n31
15:35, 54n19
16:1–2a, 77
16:2b–3a, 77
16:3b–4, 77
16:5, 76n16

16:5–9, 21
16:6, 77
16:8, 76n14
16:10, 75n8
17, 3, 5, 21, 44, 45n1, 46, 54
17:1–6, 45
17:3, 48
17:5–6, 18, 148n31
17:5–41, 24
17:5, 23n15
17:6, 36, 48, 51n10, 57, 68
17:7, 60n36
17:7–23, 18, 28n24, 45
17:7–17, 45n1
17:15, 23
17:18, 51n10, 68
17:19, 52
17:19–20, 45n1,
17:20, 51n10, 68
17:21, 54n19
17:22, 54n19
17:23, 51n10, 59, 68, 81
17:23–34a, 48, 59, 81
17:24, 3, 40, 45, 62n41, 65–67, 71
17:24–26, 47, 51, 57
17:24–34a, 32, 49, 56n25, 57–58, 60n36, 61n39, 62, 64–65, 66n48, 67–68, 71
17:24–41, 10, 18, 21n5, 24, 28n24, 45
17:25, 52
17:25–28, 4
17:27, 52
17:27–28, 56n25
17:27–33, 56
17:27–34, 47
17:28, 52, 56
17:29, 15, 55, 60, 85n33
17:32, 55, 60
17:34b–40, 47–48, 56n25, 57–60, 61n38, 62, 65, 66n48, 67n50, 68, 81n25
17:35–36, 58

17:35–39, 60
17:39, 61
17:40, 61
17:41, 57n26, 59n34, 60n36, 63, 66n48
18, 45n1
18:1–3, 83
18:4, 83
18:5–6, 83
18:7, 83
18:8, 83
18:9–12, 24, 48n5, 51n10, 83–84
18:11, 15
18:13–19:37, 82
18:13–20:19, 83
18:14–16, 83
18:22, 83
18:31–32, 24
20:20, 83
21–23, 45n1
21:1–18, 75n10
21:4–9, 52n12
21:7, 185, 187
21:9, 51
21:11, 52
21:19, 21n7, 63n44, 163n76
22:1, 93
22:2, 92–93
22:3, 92–93
22:3–7, 93
22:4, 94, 129n60
22:8, 129n60
22:8–13, 93
22:13, 95
22:14–20, 93
22:19, 46
23:1–3, 93, 95n49
23:3, 92
23:4–20, 93, 129n60
23:4–9, 95n49
23:4–14, 62,
23:4–20, 64
23:8, 95

23:15, 54n19
23:15–20, 10, 48, 62, 64, 66n48, 67, 95n49
23:17–18, 63
23:19, 55n21
23:21–23, 93
23:22, 96n52
23:26, 21n7
23:26–27, 47
23:36, 63n44, 163n76
24:2, 47
24:3, 47
25, 46
25:27–30, 47

1 Chronicles
2:3–8:40, 72
3:20, 159n62
3:22, 157n64
4:37, 157n64
5:4, 157n64
5:6, 21, 75n8
5:17, 118n31
5:25, 137n10
5:25–26, 21, 92n44
5:26, 75
5:29–41, 162
5:31, 192
5:6, 21, 75n8
6:13, 96n52
6:18, 96n52
6:39, 159n62
6:53, 147
7:24, 148
8:33, 112n17
9:3, 6, 89n40, 147
9:7, 127n55
9:14, 157n64
9:16, 157n64, 159n62
9:22, 96n52
9:23–34, 233n46
11:1–12:41, 92

11:1–3, 77
11:3, 96n52
11:12, 129n58
12:6, 112n17
12:38, 76n13
13:1–4, 77
13:2, 94n48
15:8, 157n64
15:11, 158n64
15:17, 159n62
15:23, 159n62
17:12–14, 93
21:1–22:1, 207n93
21:2, 84n30
22:2, 94, 137n10
22:6, 207n93
24:6, 158n64
24:7, 214n104
26:4, 157n64
26:6–7, 157n64
26:28, 96n52
27:24, 129n58
28:3–8, 187n49
29:1–9, 96
29:15, 137n10
29:29, 96n52

2 Chronicles
2:16, 94, 137n10
6:5, 186n48, 187n49
6:12–42, 87n36, 224n18
6:33, 137n10
6:36–40, 87
6:37–38, 156n57
6:38–39, 88
7:11–22, 128
7:12–14, 95
7:12, 187n49
7:12–22, 87n36
7:12b–16a, 87
7:14, 90
7:16, 87, 187n49

9:29–13:20, 118n31
10:1, 79n22,
10:1–17, 151
10:16, 151
11:2, 157n64
11:13–14, 79n22
11:15, 157n64
12:5, 157n64
12:5–6, 77
12:7, 157n64
12:13, 187n49
13:4–11, 16n21
13:4–12, 72, 79n22, 90
13:5, 93
13:9, 137n10
13:11, 16n21
14:10, 76n15
17:8, 158n64
18:31, 76n15
19:5, 84
19:18, 84
20:5–12, 224n18
21:4, 77
21:8–11, 75n11
21:16–17, 75n11
22:4–10, 75n11
23:2, 77
23:16, 16n21
23:17, 75
23:18, 75n11
24:6, 158n64
24:7, 75
24:15, 75n11
25:7–10, 72
25:8, 76n15
25:13, 148
26:7, 76n15
26:15, 76n15
28:1b–2a, 77
28:2, 75
28:2b–4, 77
28:5, 76–77
28:6, 76
28:6–8, 77
28:7, 76
28:8, 76
28:8–15, 74, 100
28:9, 76n12
28:9–11, 76n12
28:9–15, 72, 77–78
28:10, 78–79
28:10–16, 75
28:11, 78
28:12, 77, 159
28:13, 80
28:14, 77
28:17, 76–77
28:18, 76
28:20, 75n8
28:20–21, 76
28:23, 76n15
28:24, 75
29:1–2, 83
29:1–32:33, 82
29:3–19, 83
29:3–36, 84
29:7, 75
29:10, 90
29:14, 158n64
29:17, 84
29:18, 75
29:20–36, 83
29:24, 84, 90
29:27, 90
30:1, 84, 90
30:1–9, 83
30:1–26, 74
30:2 86
30:2–3, 84
30:3, 84n31
30:4, 86
30:5, 84, 90
30:6, 85–87, 90
30:6–9, 85, 87

30:7–8, 86
30:8, 87, 89
30:9, 87n37, 89
30:10, 90
30:10–12, 83
30:11–12, 86
30:13–14, 83–84
30:15, 84
30:15–20, 83
30:18, 86
30:18–19, 90
30:20, 90
30:21, 90
30:21–23, 83
30:23–25, 90
30:24–27, 83
30:25, 86, 90, 94, 137n10
30:26, 90
31:1, 83–84 90–91
31:2–21, 83
31:5, 90
31:6, 90
31:8, 90
31:15, 158n64
32:1–8, 83
32:1–23, 92n45
32:8, 76n15
32:9–23, 83
32:13, 137n10
32:19, 137n10
32:20, 224n18
33:1, 75
33:7, 187n49
34:1, 74, 93
34:1–35:19, 74
34:2, 92–93
34:3–7, 93
34:4–5, 94
34:6–7, 94
34:7, 94, 97n53
34:8–12a, 93
34:9, 94, 129n60

34:12b–14, 93
34:15–21, 93
34:21, 95
34:22–28, 93
34:24, 95
34:27, 95
34:28, 95
34:29–32, 93
34:31, 95
34:33, 93, 95–96, 97n53
35:1–19, 85n32, 93, 96
35:3, 97n53
35:7–9, 96
35:9, 158n64
35:10, 96
35:16–18, 96
35:17–18, 97n53
35:20–24, 97
35:25, 97n53
36:15, 78
36:20–21, 99
36:21, 88n38
36:22–23, 5n11

Ezra
1–6, 140n16, 143, 146, 155n56
1:1–4, 5n11
1:1–11, 139
1:5, 137, 143
1:11, 135n2
2, 148n39
2:1, 135n2
2:1–2, 136n4
2:1–6:22, 139
2:1–70, 5n11, 114n21, 130n63, 136
2:2, 164
2:5, 159
2:33, 147n34
2:36, 164
2:53, 127
2:60, 147n31
2:70, 136n4

3–6, 165
3:1, 136n4
3:2, 162
3:3, 137n11, 151n49
3:9, 127n55
4:1, 121n36, 135n2, 137, 143, 145
4:1–3, 72
4:2, 25n21, 67n50
4:3, 136n4
4:4, 137n11, 150
4:7–11, 72
4:7–23, 140n17
4:8–6:18, 136n9
4:10, 25n21, 67n50, 147n33
4:12, 136n9
4:12–14, 121n36
4:17, 147n33
4:23, 136n9
5:1, 136n9
5:1–2, 158
5:3, 72
5:5, 136n9
5:6, 72
5:13–16, 5n11, 139
6:6, 72
6:7, 136n9
6:8, 136n9
6:14, 136n9
6:16, 135n2, 136n4
6:17, 136n7
6:19–20, 135n2
6:19–22, 85n32
6:21, 136n4, 136n7, 137n11
7:1–10:44, 139
7:1–28, 5n11
7:4, 192
7:10, 136n4
7:12–26, 136n9
7:13, 136n4
7:28, 136n4
8:1–14, 5n11, 136
8:13, 157n64

8:16, 158n64
8:25, 136n4
8:29, 136n4
8:33, 129n58
8:35, 135n2, 136n7
9:1, 136n4, 137n11, 155
9:1–2, 163–164
9:2, 136, 137n11
9:4, 135n2, 136n4
9:5, 136n4
9:9, 94n47
9:11, 137n11, 164
9:12, 164
9:14, 137n11, 145n25
10:1, 136nn4–5
10:2, 136n4, 137n11, 164n80
10:5, 136n2
10:6, 135n2
10:7, 135n2
10:8, 136n4
10:9, 137, 143
10:10, 136n4
10:11, 137n11, 164n80
10:12–16, 136
10:16, 135n2
10:17, 164n80
10:18–23, 164
10:21, 158n64
10:23, 127n55
10:25, 129n58, 135n4
10:31, 157n64
10:35, 115n24
10:36, 115n25
10:44, 164n80

Nehemiah
1:1, 147
1:1–2:11, 5n11
1:1–7:72a, 139
1:2, 143
1:3, 141, 143
1:5–11, 146n29

1:6–9, 136n4
1:6 146
1:8, 145
1:9, 185n43
2:3, 143
2:7–9, 144
2:10, 136, 144–145
2:11–18, 141
2:16, 142
2:19, 144, 150
2:20, 150
3:1, 129,
3:1–32, 152n50
3:1–4:17, 141
3:4, 159
3:5, 154n53
3:29, 158n67
3:30, 159
3:33, 142
3:33–34, 121n36, 151
3:33–35, 144
3:34, 118, 142, 147, 151n48
3:35, 144, 152
3:36, 108n10
3:36–37, 156
3:38, 142
4:1, 144, 155n55
4:1–2, 121n36, 152
4:3, 152
4:4, 143
4:5, 145, 152
4:6, 142, 143n20, 157
4:7, 142, 152
4:9, 145, 152
4:10, 143, 152
4:11, 152
4:16, 142
5:1, 142
5:1–19, 154n53
5:5, 79
5:8, 142, 143n20, 145
5:9, 145

5:13, 142
5:14, 154
5:14–16, 5n11, 141n19
5:14–18, 154n52
5:15, 139, 142
5:17, 142, 145
5:18, 142
5:19, 142, 165
6:1, 144–145, 153
6:2, 144, 147n34, 153
6:3, 153
6:5, 155
6:6, 142, 144–145, 155
6:8, 150
6:9, 150
6:10–11, 157
6:10–14, 154n53
6:12, 144
6:12–13, 157
6:14, 144, 158, 165
6:15, 153
6:16, 137n11, 145
6:17–19, 154n53, 158
6:18, 146n28, 158n67
6:19, 144n23
7:1–7:3, 141, 153
7:4, 153
7:4–5, 142, 153n52
7:5–72, 114n21, 130n63, 136
7:6, 135n2
7:7, 136n4
7:10, 159
7:33, 147n34
7:45, 130
7:46, 130
7:57, 130
7:62, 147n31
7.72b–8:18, 139
7:73, 136n4
8:1, 136n4
9:1–2, 136n4
9:1–12:26, 139

9:2, 136n4
9:10, 145n25
9:17, 87n37
9:22, 145n25
9:24, 137n11
9:27, 145
9:28, 145
9:30, 137n11
9:31, 87n37
9:36, 138n13
10:1–37, 139
10:2, 139
10:9, 158n64
10:17, 114n22
10:21–22, 159
10:29, 137n11
10:31–32, 137n11
10:34, 136n4
11:1, 143
11:1–2, 153n52
11:1–24, 136
11:4, 137, 143, 147n30
11:7, 143
11:9, 127n55
11:15, 158n64
11:20, 143
11:24, 159
11:25, 137, 143
11:31, 143
11:34, 147n34
11:35, 137
11:36, 143
12:1–26, 136
12:6, 158n64
12:8, 127n55
12:10, 162
12:12–21, 214n104
12:18, 158n64
12:27–47, 153
12:27–13:3, 139
12:34, 127n55
12:34–36, 158n64

12:36, 127n55
12:42, 129n58
12:45, 16n21
13:1, 136, 142, 146n28
13:4, 144n23, 161
13:4–5, 154n53
13:4–7, 146n28
13:4–31, 139, 160–161
13:5, 161
13:6–7, 144
13:6, 161
13:7, 144n23, 154n53
13:7–9, 161
13:8, 144n23, 161
13:12, 143
13:14, 165
13:16, 143
13:17–18, 154n53
13:20–21, 154n53
13:22, 165
13:23, 142, 155
13:23–28, 154n53
13:24, 145
13:26, 145–146
13:28, 121n36, 162, 163n78
13:29, 163
13:30, 163
13:31, 165

Esther
2:5, 143n20
2:7, 148

Job
9:24, 156n59
31:33, 156n59
36:30, 156n59

Psalms
32:1, 156n58
32:5, 156nn59, 61
35, 156n60

51:3, 156n61
58, 156n60
59, 156n60
69, 156n60
76:3, 206n92
78:68, 187n49
81:6, 127
85:3, 156n59
86:15, 87n37
103:8, 87n37
109, 156n60
111:4, 87n37
112:4, 87n37
132:12–13, 187n49
137, 156n59
145:8, 87n37

Proverbs
10:18, 156n59
11:13, 156n59
17:9, 156n59
28:13, 156n59

Isaiah
6:13, 136n3
7:1–8:15, 76n16
15:5, 147n32
36:1–39:8, 83
36:16–17, 24
44:24–28, 5n11
45:1–8, 5n11

Jeremiah
3:6–11, 48n5
7:15, 48n5
7:34, 94n47
18:23, 156n60
22:5, 94n47
25:11, 94n47
30:10, 156n57
31:5, 55n23
34:8–16, 79

41:4–8, 122
41:5, 121n36
46:27, 156n57
48:3, 147n32

Ezekiel
1:1–27, 56
4:1–8, 48n5
8:1–19:14, 56
16:44–63, 48n5
23:1–49, 48n5
25:13, 94n47
27:17, 94n48
36:10, 94n47
36:33, 94n47
40:2; 94n48
44:16; 16n21
45:21, 85n32
47:18, 94n48
48:11, 16n21

Daniel
6:10, 224n18
9:2, 94n47

Hosea
1:1 118n31
4:15, 53n17, 201
9:15, 53n17
10:5, 53n17
10:7, 55n23
12:12, 53n17
13:2, 53n17

Joel
2:13, 87n37

Amos
1:1, 118n31
3:9, 55n23
4:1, 55n23
4:4–5, 53n17, 201

5:4–5, 53n17
6:1, 55n23
7:9–11, 118n31
7:13, 86n35

Obadiah
19, 55n23

Jonah
4:2, 87n37

Haggai
1:1, 129n60, 162
1:12, 129n60, 162
1:14, 129n60
2:2, 129n60, 162
2:4, 129n60

Zechariah
3:1, 129n60
3:7, 16n21
3:8, 129n60
6:11, 129n60, 162
6:14, 150

Malachi
1:4, 94n47
3:14, 16n 21

Christian Scriptures

Matthew
10:5–6, 220
15:21– 24, 221n9
23:5, 234
28:19, 221n9

Luke
10:25–37, 81n26

John
4:1–43, 227
4:5–6, 3

4:8, 228
4:9, 1, 3, 217
4:20, 1, 224
4:22, 228
4:27, 3
4:43, 228

Acts
27:1, 221n10
15, 235n51

Galatians
2, 235n51

Other Ancient Sources

Abū 'l Fath, 191, 205, 220n6, 230nn28, 35, 235n52, 237
Adler–Séligsohn, 15n20, 191nn60–61, 230, 235, 237

Babylonian Chronicle, 21, 23n15, 36

Chronicon Samaritanum (Sam Josh), 191, 195, 205, 220n6, 237

Dead Sea Scrolls (DSS), 9, 13, 177, 179, 181–184, 185n42, 189, 202, 205
Didascalia Apostolorum, 235n51

Elephantine papyri, 12, 110, 114, 115n25, 119, 120, 148
Epiphanius, 16n21, 201n80, 215n105, 229n27
Eusebius, 16n21, 63n44, 169, 170, 201n80, 206n92

Herodotus, 149

Jerome, 16n21, 63n44, 169, 201n80
Josephus, 3, 11–12, 51n11, 52n13, 56n25, 62n41, 64n45, 75n9, 107,

114n19, 123, 140, 143n20, 148n37, 162n75, 164n79, 164n81, 167n85, 169–176, 190–191, 204–205, 206n92, 208, 212n98, 213, 220–224, 226–227, 231n36, 232n42, 234, 235n54
Josippon, 191

Letter of Aristeas, 170, 193n65, 218n4, 234

Maccabees, 148nn41, 167n85, 170, 171n7, 172–173, 176, 213, 214n104
Macdonald II, 15n20
Masoretic text (MT), 13, 15, 52n12, 55n21, 56n25, 58n28, 59n33, 61n37, 62n41, 63n44, 78n20, 94n47, 112n117, 114n22, 115n25, 127n55, 136n3, 151n48, 152n51, 155n55, 156n57, 163n77, 164n80, 177, 179–189, 192, 195–196, 200nn76–77, 201n81, 202–205, 206n92, 207, 208n96, 209–211, 232, 233n47
Mishnah, 4, 7, 15, 224, 227n22, 236
Mt. Gerizim inscriptions, 123, 125–132

Old Latin (OL), 52n12, 185, 202
Origen, 16n21, 215n105, 222n16

Philo, 234
Procopius of Gaza, 201n80

Quintus Curtius Rufus, 107, 169
Qumran texts (4Q), 86n34, 174n15, 179, 181–183, 185n43, 187n49, 188, 203n83, 204, 234

Samaria papyri (WDSP), 9, 79, 109–111, 113–115, 117, 122n39, 126–127, 129–130, 145n26, 169
Samaritan Liturgy (SL), 235n52
Samaritan Pentateuch (SP), 13–14, *72*, 177, 179–185, 187–190, 192, 193n63, 195–196, 197n73, 198n74, 200nn76–78, 201–202, 203n83, 206, 208n96, 209–210, 215, 218n4, 219, 231n39, 232, 233n47
Samaritan Targum, 206, 238
Septuagint (LXX), 13, 15, 52n12, 55n21, 56n25, 59n33, 61n37, 63n44, 78n20, 94n47, 112n17, 114n22, 115n25, 129n58, 136n3, 151n47, 152n51, 155n55, 163nn77–78, 164n80, 173n14, 177, 179–181, 185, 186n49, 189, 192–193, 196, 200n76, 200n78, 201n81, 202, 203n86, 204–206, 209n97, 210, 218n4, 233n47, 234n48

Tacitus, 221–222
Talmud, 4, 7, 15, 225, 227nn21–22, 236
Targum, 14–15, 58n28
Tulida, 191–192, 235n52, 237

Author Index

(The author of this book has been excluded)

Abel, F.-M., 170n5
Abraham, K., 5n11, 143n20
Achenbach, R., 189n52, 207n93
Ackroyd, P.R., 83
Aejmelaeus, A., 183n35
Aharoni, Y., 63n44
Ahlström, G.W., 19n1
Albertz, R., 162, 193n64
Albright, W.F., 63n44, 108, 234
Alexandre, Y., 22n11
Allen, L.C., 81n26
Alt, A., 27, 29n25, 67, 146n27, 147n33, 155n56, 176n23
Amiran, R., 39
Applebaum, A., 105, 170n4
Arav, R., 33n34
Arnold, W., 136n9
Asa-El, A., 7
Astour, M.C., 50, 52n14
Auld, A.G., 50n9
Avi-Yonah, M., 170n5
Avigad, N., 35, 106, 111, 112n16, 114n19, 119, 127

Baillet, M., 239
Barag, D., 117, 130n62
Barkay, G., 26, 103n2
Barrick, W.B., 50, 63n44

Barstad, H.M., 19n3
Bartlett, J.R., 218n4
Beaulieu, P.-A., 113
Becking, B., 36n40, 45n1, 112, 114n21, 128
Bedford, P.R., 137
Beentjes, P.C., 59
Beit-Arieh, I., 34n36
Ben Zvi, E., 58, 75, 97n54, 131n64, 135n1, 137n12
Ben-Hayyim, Z., 184n37, 234n50, 238n61
Ben-Tor, A., 22n13, 35
Benjamin, J.M., 7
Berlejung, A., 32n32
Berlin, A.M., 170
Berman, J.A., 136n9
Bernstein, M.J., 182n33, 183n36
Bewer, J.A., 50, 72
Binder, D.D., 171, 225n27, 229n25, 230
Birnbaum, S.A., 106
Blenkinsopp, J., 14, 53n17, 69, 108, 122n38, 143n20, 145n25, 146nn27–28, 152n50, 163, 168, 185n43
Bloch-Smith, E., 23, 32, 39
Bloedhorn, H., 171

Blum, E., 189n52
Boda, M.J., 145n25
Bolin, T.M., 125
Botterweck, G.J., 156
Brett, M.G., 138n16
Brettler, M.Z., 29n25, 45n1, 58, 65
Brewer, D.I., 197n72
Briant, P., 149
Bright, J., 19n1
Broshi, M., 23, 29n26, 30, 35n39, 37
Bruneau, P., 171
Bunimovitz, S., 38, 104, 170
Burney, C.F., 29n25, 50, 58n27

Campbell, E.F., 34n35, 107n8, 173, 175n19, 201n79, 206n92
Capponi, L., 213n100
Carr, D.M., 190n54
Carroll, R.P., 19n3
Carter, C.E., 108
Chambon, A., 34
Charlesworth, J.H., 202
Clements, R.E., 156
Clines, D.J.A., 141
Cogan, M., 22, 23n17, 27n23, 32n32, 46n2, 58, 63n44, 64n45, 66n49, 77, 200
Coggins, R.J., 6, 26–29, 50, 67, 86, 102
Cohen, S.J.D., 14, 143n20, 221n10
Cohn, R., 52, 59n35
Cornelius, I., 119, 132
Crane, O.T., 191n58, 205n89
Crawford, S.W., 182, 183n36, 189
Cross, F.M., 25, 52n12, 85, 102n1, 111–116, 189, 193n63
Crowfoot, G.M., 170
Crowfoot, J.W., 36, 105–106, 124n46, 170
Crown, A.D., 14n18, 61n40, 102, 132, 171, 191, 196n68, 220n7, 223, 237

Daise, M., 176n21
Dalley, S., 24, 30n28, 32n32, 35–36

Dandamaev, M.A., 112
Dar, S., 38, 105, 223
Day, J., 32n32
De Odorico, M., 30n29
De Vries, S.J., 76n12
De Wette, W.M.L., 72
Delavault, B., 119n32
Dever, W.G., 24n20, 43n49
Dexinger, F., 20, 184n37, 203n83, 234n50
Di Segni, L., 230
Dietrich, W., 45n1
Dobbs-Allsopp, F.W., 119n32
Donner, H., 19n1, 201n80
Dorsey, D.A., 105
Dubovský, P., 23n14, 31
Dumbrell, W.J., 144n21
Dupont-Sommer, A., 136n6
Dušek, J., 14n18, 16, 111, 113–114, 115n23, 122n39, 123, 125, 126n51, 127n56, 129, 148n37, 169–170, 171n7, 172n9, 176n23, 186n46, 193n64, 203n83
Dutcher-Walls, P., 63n44
Dyck, J.E., 75, 135n1

Egger, R., 14n18, 170n2, 175n19
Eissfeldt, O., 180
Eshel, E., 180, 182
Eshel, H., 111n15, 113–114, 115n23, 121, 122n39, 144n24, 180
Eskenazi, T.C., 152n50
Esler, P.F., 160
Eusebius, 16n21, 63n44, 169–170, 201n80, 206n92
Eynikel, E., 52n12, 58n29

Fabry, H.J., 16n21
Fantalkin, A., 31
Faü, J.-F., 14n18, 61n40
Faust, A., 37–38, 44, 108
Feldman, L.H., 175n18, 220n6
Fine, S., 2n3

Finkelstein, I., 23, 29n26, 30, 34–35, 37–38, 53n17, 104, 108, 170
Fishbane, M., 96, 164n80
Fisher, C.S., 105–107, 223n17
Florentin, M., 191, 239
Floyd, M.H., 138n14
Fossum, J., 227, 232n43
Franklin, N., 24, 105–106
Fried, L.S., 157n63, 163n78
Friedman, R.E., 64
Fritz, V., 23n14, 45n1, 47n4, 50, 58n29
Fuchs, A., 23n16, 30n28, 36
Fuller, M.E., 6, 137
Fulton, D.N., 194n66

Gadd, C.J., 24
Gal, Z., 22–23, 235n51
Galil, G., 6, 22n10, 37
Galling, K., 71n1, 147n32
Gaster, M., 14n18
Gehman, H.S., 50, 58n29, 62
Ginsberg, H.L., 29, 67, 207
Gitler, H., 107n9, 118n30, 119
Glock, A.E., 35
Goldstein, J.A., 173, 176
Gomes, J.F., 53n17
Gonen, R., 7–8
Goodblatt, D.M., 137
Goodman, M., 220n5, 226–227
Grabbe, L.L., 19n3, 141, 155n56, 157, 158n64, 167n85, 225n20, 236
Gray, J., 30n29, 58n27, 58n29
Grayson, A.K., 23n15, 36n40
Greenberg, M., 234
Grelot, P., 120n34, 136n6
Gropp, D.M., 110, 113, 115n23, 122n39, 169

Hachlili, R., 2n3, 231n36, 231n40, 232–233
Hadjisavvas, S., 136n6

Haggai, 100, 155, 158, 168
Hall, B., 220n5, 222n13
Halpern, B., 35, 52n12, 53n16
Haran, M., 147n32, 186n47
Harper, L., 16n21
Harrington, D.J., 58n28
Harris, M., 238
Hayes, J.H., 21n6, 74n7, 108
Headland, T.N., 238
Hendel, R.S., 181, 189
Herrmann, S., 19n1
Himbaza, I., 184n37
Hjelm, I., 4n9, 14n18, 19n2, 20, 61n40, 132, 191, 196n68
Hoffman, H.-D., 50
Holladay, J.S., 136n6
Horst, P.W. van der, 171, 174, 225n20, 232n43

Ilan, T., 132n66

Japhet, S., 27n23, 72, 75, 78, 85–86, 96, 102n1, 135n1, 137, 147n30
Jastram, N., 183
Joannès, F., 5n11, 143n20
Jobling, D., 50, 65
Joffe, A.H., 35
Johnstone, W., 75
Jones, G.H., 45n1, 58nn27–28
Jonker, L.C., 96
Joosten, J., 185n44, 218
Josephus, 3, 11–12, 51n11, 52n33, 56n25, 62n41, 64n45, 75n9, 107, 114n19, 123, 140, 143n20, 148n37, 162n75, 164n79, 164n81, 167n85, 169–176, 190–191, 204–205, 206n92, 208, 212n98, 213, 220–224, 226–227, 231n36, 232n42, 234, 235n54
Juynboll, T.W.J., 191n58

Kalimi, I., 197n72, 200n77
Kallai, Z., 63n44

Kaplan, Y., 37
Kartveit, M., 14n18, 19n2, 20, 73n5, 123n40, 123n42, 170n2, 171n6, 175n16, 184n37, 203n83
Kaufman, Y., 66n49
Keel, O., 120
Kelle, B.D., 26, 55n23
Kellermann, U., 146n27, 147n32, 160n71
Kelly, B.E., 75n10, 78
Kelso, J.L., 34
Kenyon, K.M., 35–36, 105–106, 124n46, 170
Kessler, J., 137n12
Keulen, P.S.F. van, 52n12
Kiefer, J., 19n3
Kim, K.-R., 180
King, P.J., 109
Kippenberg, H.G., 121, 170n2, 176n23, 225, 234n50
Kirkman, J.S., 106
Knauf, E.-A., 23n14, 29n25, 53n17, 69, 121, 193n64
Koenen, K., 53n17, 121
Köhlmoos, M., 121
Kooij, A. van der, 192n62
Kottsieper, I., 110n13
Kratz, R.G., 121, 125, 133n67, 136n6, 187n49
Kuenen, A., 66n49
Kugel, J.L., 183
Kuhrt, A., 19n1

Lanfranchi, G. B., 37
Lapp, N.L., 175n19
Law, D.A., 7n14
Layton, S.S., 113
Lederman, Z., 38, 104, 170
Lehmann, G., 39
Leith, M.J.W., 111, 112n16, 113, 117, 122n39, 169

Lemaire, A., 5n11, 100n59, 107n9, 110n13, 111, 113, 116–117, 119n32, 125, 136n6, 143n20, 145n26, 155n56, 194n66
Levine, L.I., 229, 230n33, 231, 232nn41–43, 236nn57–58
Levinson, B.M., 64, 85n32, 96, 183n35, 195, 207, 209
Liddell, H.G., 230n31
Limet, H., 30
Linder, A., 223n16
Linville, J.R., 65
Lipiński, E, 110
Lipschits, O., 19n3, 35, 44, 69n55, 104n4, 106, 108, 121, 149n42, 155n56
Liverani, M., 41–42
London, G., 40
Long, B.O., 45n1
Lozachmeur, H., 5n11, 136n6, 143n20
Lyon, D.G., 105–107, 223n17

Macchi, J.-D., 14n18, 35, 58nn29–30, 62n42, 65, 132, 193n64
Macdonald, J., 14n18, 16n20, 45n1, 215
Macdonald, M.C.A., 112
Machinist, P.B., 111
Magen, Y., 2n3, 38, 107n8, 109, 111n14, 116n28, 123–126, 128–129, 171, 173, 176n23, 193n64, 212n99, 213–214, 220n5, 225n20, 229–230, 231n36, 232n41, 232nn43–44, 233n46, 234n50, 235–236
Magness, J., 170
Mazar, A., 24, 33
Mazar, B., 23n14, 24, 33, 146n27, 151n45
McCarter, P.K., 112n17
McCarthy, C., 203
McKay, J.W., 32n32
McKenzie, S.L., 58n27, 96n52

Meer, M.N. van der, 204
Mendels, D., 220n5, 222n13, 223
Meshorer, Y., 107n9, 111, 113n18, 115–118, 122n39, 130n61
Meyers, C.L., 151n45
Middlemas, J., 19n3
Mikolášek, A., 131n64
Mildenberg, L., 107n9, 111, 115, 117
Milgrom, J., 16n21, 231n36
Miller, J.M., 21n6, 74n7, 108
Misgav, H., 109, 111n14, 123, 125–126, 128–129, 171, 173n13
Mitchell, C., 88n39, 97n54, 135
Mitchell, T.C., 24
Mittmann, S., 147nn32–33
Montgomery, J.A., 4n9, 14n18, 16n21, 50, 58n28, 62, 220n7, 225n20
Mor, M., 114n20, 115, 130n62, 172, 176n21, 176n23
Mosis, R., 71n1
Mowinckel, S., 160n71
Mulder, M.J., 112
Myers, J.M., 27n23, 86

Na'aman, N., 21nn6–7, 23, 25n22, 26, 29n26, 30–31, 35, 36n40, 53n17, 69, 121, 138n15
Naveh, J., 110–111, 112n16, 115n25, 116n28, 123
Nelson, R.D., 58n27
Nihan, C., 187, 193n64, 196n69, 197n73, 199n75, 202–203, 207
Nitzan, B., 86n34
Nodet, E., 14n18, 175, 176n23
Noja, S., 239
Noth, M., 45, 47n4, 58n27, 58n29
Notley, R.S., 149
Noy, D., 171

O'Brien, M.A., 58n29
O'Connor, M., 187n50

Oded, B., 21n8, 30, 41–42, 63n44, 68
Oeming, M., 73n5
Olsson, B., 171, 229n25
Olyan, S.M., 163
Orlinsky, H.M., 19n1
Otto, E., 29n25, 189n52

Panayotov, A., 171
Parker, B.J., 31, 40n48
Parpola, S., 32n32
Paul, S.M., 86n35
Pearce, L.E., 5n11, 112, 143n20
Peersmann, J., 35
Person, R.F., 83
Pfeiffer, R.H., 50, 71–72
Pike, K., 238
Plöger, O., 71n1
Porten, B., 5n11, 119, 125, 136n6
Pummer, R., 2n3, 3n6, 14n18, 15, 16n21, 52n13, 61n40, 62n41, 97n55, 123n40, 123n42, 131n64, 140n18, 167n85, 170n12, 171, 173n14, 174, 175n16, 175n19, 176, 184n37, 184n41, 191n55, 191n58, 193n64, 201n80, 202n82, 215n105, 218n4, 222n16, 225n20, 229, 230n32, 231, 234n49, 238–239
Purvis, J.D., 102, 188–189, 193n63, 215, 234n50

Qedar, S., 107n9, 111, 113n18, 115–118, 122n39
Qimron, E., 187n49

Rad, G. von, 71
Rainey, A.F., 149
Rappaport, U., 176n23
Reich, R., 236
Reisner, G.A., 105–107, 223n17
Rendsburg, G.A., 29, 218n3
Richardson, P., 229n25

Richter, S.L., 185n45
Ringgren, H., 50
Rofé, A., 206
Römer, T.C., 189n52
Rösel, H.N., 45n1
Rothstein, J.W., 102
Rowley, H.H., 71n1, 102
Rudolph, W., 58n31, 146n27, 147n32, 151n47
Runesson, A., 171, 229n25, 233n46

Saldarini, A.J., 58n28
Sanderson, J.E., 184n37, 188
Sass, B., 111, 112n16, 114n19, 119, 127
Scatolini Apóstolo, S. S., 135n1
Schaper, J., 189n52
Schenker, A., 52n12, 55n21, 185–186
Schiffman, L.H., 4, 224n19, 225, 234n48
Schmid, K., 189n52
Schoors, A., 76n15
Schorch, S., 29n25, 67, 181n29, 187n49, 188, 207
Schuller, E.M., 174
Schur, N., 26–27, 50, 67
Schwartz, D.R., 175–176
Schwartz, S., 172–173, 175–176, 213, 220, 222, 224
Schweitzer, S.J., 73n6
Scott, R., 230n30
Seeligman, I.L., 96
Segal, M., 183n36
Sellin, E., 200
Shehadeh, H., 239n64
Shepherd, D., 158n65
Singer-Avitz, L., 34, 53n17
Smith, G.A, 200
Smith, J.Z., 138n16, 238
Smith, M., 67n53
Spieckermann, H., 32n32, 76n16
Stade, B., 58n27, 58n29
Stager, L.E., 109
Steiner, M.L., 122

Steiner, R.C., 167n84
Steins, G., 84n29
Stenhouse, P.L., 191, 196n68, 205n89, 237n61
Stern, E., 21–22, 24–25, 30, 33n33, 34n36, 38n46, 40, 43, 69n55, 106–107, 112n16, 116n28, 117, 120–121, 149n42, 175n19
Strange, J.F., 229
Strawn, B.A., 52
Strugnell, J., 187n49
Sukenik, E.L., 122, 124, 231

Tadmor, H., 21–22, 23nn16–17, 30n27, 46n2, 58, 63n44, 77, 121n36, 200
Tadmor, M., 26, 106
Tal, A., 4n10, 31, 107n9, 108, 118n30, 119, 200n77, 238–239
Talmon, S., 50, 55n21, 62n42, 84n31, 202n82
Talshir, Z., 164n79
Tappy, R., 20n4, 23n17, 30, 35–36, 106
Thompson, T.L., 41
Throntveit, M.A., 82n17
Tigay, J.H., 113, 183, 200, 234
Timm, S., 20n4, 23n16, 122
Tod, M.N., 229
Torrey, C.C., 71n1
Tov, E., 179–180, 181n30, 181n32, 182n34, 183–184, 188–189, 202, 209
Trebolle Barrera, J.C., 52n12, 193n63
Tsfania, L., 109, 111n14, 123, 125–126, 128–129, 171, 173n13

Uehlinger, C., 118, 120
Ulrich, E.C., 179, 185n42, 203n83, 204
Ussishkin, D., 34–35, 38n46

Van Houten, C., 143
Van Seters, J., 62n42

Vanderhooft, D., 44, 143n20
VanderKam, J.S., 167n85, 172, 213n100
Vaux, R. de, 30
Vilmar, E., 191n59
Vincent, A., 119, 125
Viviano, P.A., 45n1

Wagenaar, J.A., 201
Walsh, J.T., 58n27, 59
Waltke, B.K., 187n50
Watkins, L., 38
Watts, J.W., 192
Weinfeld, M., 45–47, 60n36, 91n43, 184n41, 185n45, 198n74, 199, 203
Wellhausen, J., 71
Wevers, J.W., 180, 209n97
White, L.M., 171, 183
Willi, T., 27n23, 72, 94n48, 102n1, 135n1
Williamson, H.G.M., 27n23, 72, 84n27, 86, 102n1, 133n67, 135n1, 151n48, 152, 155n56, 156n60, 159, 161n71, 163, 185n43
Wolff, S., 23

Woodhead, J., 34
Wright, G.E., 175
Wright, G.R.H., 175
Wright, J.L., 72, 145n25, 146n29, 160, 161n71
Würthwein, E., 22n10, 46n2, 58n29

Younger, K.L., 6, 21n8, 23nn16–17, 24n18, 25n22, 26, 30nn28–29, 36n40, 41

Zadok, R., 6, 23, 26, 31, 112, 114, 115n24, 116–117, 147n32, 148n39, 159n70
Zahn, M.M., 180n28, 181n29, 182n33, 183nn35–36
Zakovitch, Y., 151
Zangenberg, J., 174n15
Zertal, A., 31n30, 34, 35n39, 37, 39–40, 103n2, 104–105, 107–109, 170, 200
Zimhoni, O., 29
Zissu, B., 144n24
Zorn, J.R., 108
Zsengellér, J., 14n18, 113

Subject Index

'Aqbun V, 237
Aaron, 2, 54n18, 129, 162, 164, 181, 190–192, 218
Abijah, 90
Abraham, 2, 209–210
Ahaz, 74–76, 77n17, 80, 82
Alexander Balas, 172
Alexander Jannaeus, 213
Alexander the Great, 105, 107, 123n40, 169, 172n11, 175, 176n23, 190–191
Ammonites, 47, 137, 144–146, 149, 152, 158, 164n80
Andromachus, 169
Antiochus III, 123, 170
Antiochus IV, 176
Apollonius the Mysarch, 170
Arabah, 199–200
Araḥ, 158–159
Arsames, 110, 120, 167
Artaxerxes I, 114, 138–139, 143–144
Ashdodites, 137, 145, 152, 155
Asher, 86, 90, 91n42, 202
Ashurbanipal, 25
Assyrians
  greater empire of, 40–41
  Israel and, 18–25, 45–46, 49–50, 85–86, 91–92, 97
  Judah and, 41, 82
  Samaria and, 2–3, 9, 15, 18–44, 46–59, 66–68, 104
  Transjordan and, 9, 21–22, 33, 38, 42

Baba Rabba, 230n25, 235, 237
Bagavahya. *See* Bagohi
Bagohi, 114, 120
Benjamin region, 20, 71, 73n5, 90–91, 94, 108, 137, 143, 147
Berechiah, 159
Beth Horon (lower and upper), 147, 148n36
Bethel
  archaeological evidence from, 24, 34, 38
  Assyrian rule and, 32, 52
  prophets from, 54–55
  sanctuary at, 52–54, 56, 62–64, 69, 121

Caesarea, slaughter at, 223
Cerealis, Sextus Vettulenus, 223
Chaldeans, 40, 47
Chronicon Samaritanum, 191, 205, 220n6
coins. *See* numismatics
Commodus, 237n59
Coponius, 220
Covenant Code, 79, 208–209, 211
Cumanus, Ventidius, 221

Cutheans, 3, 19, 49, 62n41
Cyrus I, 138

Damascus, 23, 42, 76
Dan, 21, 34, 53, 55
Darius I, 138
David, 96, 151, 186, 207n93, 211
Dead Sea Scrolls (DSS). *See under* Pentateuch
Decalogue, 184, 196, 197n73, 214, 219, 232–234
Delaiah, 114–115, 120, 148, 167
Delos, 171
Demetrius I, 107, 170, 173n12
Demetrius II Nicator, 172
Dor, 22, 25, 34, 149n42
Dothan, 24, 34
Dothan Valley, 104, 170

Edomites, 47, 76–77, 164n80
El-Ḥirbe, 214, 230, 232, 235
Elam, 40–41
Elephantine Temple, 119–120, 125, 167
Eli, 191
Eliashib, 161–162
Elijah, 69
Elisha, 69
Ephraim (settlement), 5, 9, 38, 40, 42, 84, 86, 90–91, 94, 98
Ephraim, tribe of, 2, 20, 146–148
Ephraimites, 77–78, 80–81, 147–148
Esarhaddon, 25
Essenes, 226
Ezekiel, 6, 27–28, 100–101, 137, 158

Fifth Legion of Macedonia (*Legio quinta Macedonica*), 223
Fourth Philosophy, 226–227

Galilee
　Assyrian conquest and, 9, 21–23, 33, 37–38, 42–43, 46

Maccabees and, 12, 173
Gashmu. *See* Geshem
Geshem, 141, 144, 149–150, 152–156
Gibeonites, 186, 204
Gilead, 21–22, 25, 43, 46
Gilgal, 199–201, 203–205, 211
Great Revolt, 222–224

Haggai, 158, 168
Hezekiah
　Assyrians and, 83
　Passover and, 74, 83–90, 94, 96, 98–99
　priests and, 84
　religious reforms by, 82–84, 90–92, 94, 98
　Solomon's prayer and, 87–88
Holiness Code, 79
Hosea, 29, 69
Hoshea, 18, 75, 77n17
Huldah, 93, 95
Hyrcanus, John, 1, 12, 107, 173, 212–214

Idoumea, 12, 99, 125, 172, 222, 224
Israel. *See also* Judah; Samaria
　ancestral lineage and, 12, 135–136
　Assyrian conquest and, 18–25, 45–46, 49–50, 85–86, 91–92, 97
　Babylonian exile and, 5, 20, 136–137
　foreign settlers of, 49–50, 56, 97
　Josiah's religious reforms and, 74, 94–99
　Judah and, 75–82, 86–91, 97, 99–101, 142–143
　land and, 46, 51–52, 65, 199, 211
　Nehemiah and, 134, 146, 150–151, 166–167
　Passover and, 84–90, 96, 204
　population transfers and, 91–92, 97
　prophets and, 77–78
　religious practices and, 198–199, 202–209, 211–212

slavery and, 79
unity and, 72–73, 84–86, 89, 97, 122–123, 137, 193
Yahwism and, 65, 69–70, 78, 80, 84–88, 91, 97–98
Yhwh and, 51–52, 59–61, 78, 210–212

Jacob, patriarchal status of, 2, 10, 12, 48, 57–58, 60–61, 66, 68, 72, 97, 100, 135, 162, 166–167, 193–194, 217–218
Jaddua, 190
Jedaniah, 120
Jehoḥanan, 159
Jehoiachin, 47
Jehozadak, 162
Jeremiah, 6, 27–28, 101, 137, 156, 158
Jeroboam I, 18, 45n1, 50n8, 53–57, 62–63, 90
Jeroboam II, 119
Jerusalem
    archeological evidence from, 44, 109
    Babylonian conquest and, 44
    Deuteronomistic centralization and, 195, 206–207
    temple in, 1, 11, 64, 75, 85, 87–89, 91, 93–94, 120–122, 138–139, 168, 206–207, 220
Jeshua, 162, 164
Jesus, 1–3, 217, 220–221, 227–228
Jewish Wars, 222–223, 225, 237
Jews. *See also* Judah; Judeans
    ancestral lineage of, 2, 218
    definition of terminology regarding, 14–15, 17
    diasporic communities and, 218, 226
    Great Revolt and, 222–224
    Hellenistic Era and, 218
    mezuzot and, 234–235
    miqva'ot and, 235–237
    Roman Era and, 16, 218–228
    Samaritans and, 1–4, 13, 17, 71, 102, 188, 217–229, 233, 237–239
    synagogues and, 228–229, 231, 237–238
Joiada, 162–163
Jonathan Maccabeus, 172, 213
Jordan River, 200, 202–203
Joseph (son of Jacob), 2–3, 20
Josiah of Judah
    David and, 92
    Huldah and, 95
    Israel and, 74, 94–99
    Passover and, 96, 98
    religious reforms of, 10, 48–49, 62, 74, 92–99
    Samaria and, 48–50, 62–65, 67–69
    Torah and, 95
Judah
    Aramaic language and, 111
    Assyrians and, 41, 82
    Babylonian conquest and, 2, 19–20, 43–44, 47, 108, 122
    Deuteronomic principle of centralization and, 177, 194–195, 197, 199, 207–212, 215, 218
    Ephraim and, 73
    Hasmonean Period, 172, 174, 238
    Hellenistic Period and, 11–12, 14–16, 108, 168, 170–171
    Israel and, 75–82, 86–91, 97, 99–101, 142–143
    Maccabean Era, 12, 168, 172, 178, 213–214
    monarchy in, 47, 75, 77, 80, 82, 98–99
    Nehemiah and, 134, 136, 142–143, 145–146, 151, 153–154, 156–157, 159–160, 164–168
    Neo-Babylonian Period in, 11, 14–16, 108, 213
    non-Yahwistic worship and, 75, 77, 80
    numismatics and, 111, 117–119

Pentateuch and, 13, 177–178, 181, 184, 189–190, 192–197, 214–216, 218
Persian Era and, 11, 14–16, 107–108, 119, 145, 149, 160, 168, 172, 213
population transfers and, 69, 76
priests in, 80, 164, 192
religious syncretism in, 50–52
Yehud, 11–12, 16, 19, 74–75, 88, 98–100, 103, 108–109, 111, 114, 116–117, 119–121, 131–134, 142, 146, 155, 164, 166–168, 193
Yhwh and, 78
Judas Maccabeus, 170
Judea, Roman province of, 222, 224, 226–227, 235
Judeans. *See* Judah

Kethuvim, 15
Kh. Ǧilǧiliye, 200–201
Kh. Samara, 214, 230, 232, 235
Khirbet el-Qôm, 125

Levi, tribe of, 2, 20, 53, 147, 191–192, 202, 237
Levites, 80, 84, 96, 129–130, 202
Lost Tribes. *See* Northern Tribes of Israel

Maccabees, 12–13, 168, 212n10, 214n104, 218
Manasseh (king), 51–52, 75n10
Manasseh (Samarian priest), 190–191
Manasseh (settlement), 5, 9, 37–38, 40, 42, 86, 90–91, 94, 98
Manasseh, tribe of, 2, 20, 146
Masoretic Text (MT). *See under* Pentateuch
Megiddo, 22, 25, 30, 35, 42, 82, 119, 125n48, 149n42
Menippos of Herakeion, 171
Meshezabel, 159

Meshullam, 159
mezuzot, 13, 228, 233–235, 237
miqva'ot (ritual baths), 228, 235–237
Moabites, 47, 137, 145, 155, 164n80
Moreh, 200–201
Moses
  golden calf and, 64, 181
  instructions of, 182, 198–199, 203–204, 208
  Mount Sinai and, 87–88
  Yahwism and, 14, 178, 215
Mount Ebal, 198–206, 210, 215
Mount Gerizim temple
  Abraham's altar and, 209–210
  archeological evidence from, 9, 11, 103, 123–124, 171, 213
  construction of, 120–122
  destruction of, 1, 12, 173, 212–214, 218–219
  Deuteronomic centralization and, 195, 198–199, 206–211, 214–215, 219
  expansion of, 124–125, 170–171
  faunal remains at, 124–125
  inscriptions at, 103, 125–132, 171
  Jewish wars and, 223
  priests and, 128–130, 190–192
  questions regarding location of, 199–203
Mount Zion, 1, 88, 98, 100, 176, 190, 192, 218, 231
Mountains of Manasseh, 104, 109
Murabba'at, 110

Naḥal Ḥever deed, 110
Nash Papyrus, 234
Nebuchadnezzar, 43, 89n40, 121
Nehemiah (governor of Judah)
  Ataxerxes I and, 143–144
  building campaign of, 139–142, 149–155, 157, 165, 168

Israel and, 134, 146, 150–151, 166–167
Judean society and, 134, 136, 142–143, 145–146, 151, 153–154, 156–157, 159–160, 164–168
priests and, 140, 161–163
prophets and, 158
religious reforms of, 161–162, 167
Samaria and, 12, 140, 144–145
Sanballat and, 19, 134, 140–142, 144–147, 149–156, 160, 162–163, 165–166, 174
Tobiah and, 141, 144–146, 149–150, 152–156, 158–162, 165–167
Nevi'im, 15, 178
Noadiah, 158
Northern Kingdom of Israel. *See* Samaria
Northern Tribes of Israel. *See also* Samaria
exile of, 4–6, 18–19, 21–26, 45–46, 85–86
prophecies regarding, 6, 8n17, 27–29, 137, 158
search for, 5–8, 24, 26, 42–44
surviving in the land, 26–42, 49, 57–65, 84–92, 94–97
numismatics
Judah and, 111, 117–119
Samaria and, 9, 109–111, 115–119, 124, 130, 132

Oded, 77–80, 97
Omri, House of, 21, 41, 43
onomastics. *See* personal names (PNs)
Ostanes, 114

Passover
Hezekiah and, 74, 83–90, 94, 96, 98–99
Israel and, 84–90, 96, 204
Josiah and, 96, 98

Pentateuchal statues and, 195
Pekah, 75–76, 77n17
Pentateuch
altar legislation and, 207–208
Dead Sea Scrolls (DSS) and, 177, 181–184, 189, 202, 205–206
Deuteronomic principle of centralization and, 64, 185, 194–199, 205–212, 215, 219
festival prescriptions and, 195
Judah and, 13, 177–178, 181, 184, 189–190, 192–197, 214–216
liturgical prescriptions and, 198–199, 202
Masoretic Text (MT) and, 179–182, 184–185, 187–189, 192, 195–196, 202–207, 209–211
Old Latin (OL) and, 185, 202
pan-Israelite viewpoint in, 193–194
Qumran texts and, 179, 181–184, 188, 204
Samaria and, 13, 177–178, 181, 184, 189–190, 192–197, 205, 214–216, 219, 231
Samarian/Samaritan Pentateuch (SP) and, 179–185, 187–189, 192, 195–196, 201–202, 209–210, 215–216, 219, 231
sectarian additions and, 184, 188–189, 196
Septuagint (LXX) and, 179–181, 185, 189, 192, 196, 202, 204–206, 210
Peraea, 172, 173n12
Perdikkas, 169
Persian Empire
Egyptian uprising and, 149
Judah and, 11, 14–16, 107–108, 119, 145, 149, 160, 168, 172, 213
Samaria and, 2, 11, 14, 16, 37–38, 103–108, 110–111, 117–124, 126, 132–133, 144–145, 168, 172, 213

personal names (PNs), 11, 112–117,
    126–132
Petaḥiah, 159
Pharisees, 226
Philistines, 41, 76, 83, 173
Phinehas, 2, 191–192
Pompey, 107
priesthood
    Aaron and, 164, 190–192, 212, 214
    Judah and, 80, 192
    Mount Gerizim temple and, 128–130,
        190–192
    Samaria and, 10, 47, 52, 54, 56, 63–64,
        174–175, 190–192, 214, 237
Ptolemies, 107, 170

Qedarite kingdom, 144
Qumran texts. *See under* Pentateuch

Rabban ben Gamaliel, 225
Rabbi Aqiba, 7
Rabbi Eliezer, 7
Rabbi Judah the Prince, 225
Rehoboam, 151
ritual baths. *See miqva'ot*

Sadducees, 226
Samaria. *See also* Israel
    Achaemenid Era, 38, 73, 103–105,
        107, 109, 112, 133
    Aramaic language and, 110–112, 116,
        126, 131
    archeological evidence from, 8–9,
        11, 20, 24, 26, 30–39, 42–43, 103,
        105–107, 109, 121
    Assyrians and, 2–3, 9, 15, 18–44,
        46–59, 66–68, 104
    Babylonian campaigns and, 2, 108,
        121–122
    Byzantine period and, 124, 228
    Deuteronomic principles of
        centralization and, 64, 177,
        194–198, 205–206, 208–212, 215,
        218–219
    foreign settlers in, 10, 18, 24, 27,
        39–41, 47–49, 51–52, 54–57, 61,
        63, 65, 67–68, 85, 169–170
    Greek temples in, 170
    Hasmonean Period, 172, 174, 224,
        236, 238
    Hebrew language and, 2, 29, 63, 110–
        112, 126, 131
    Hellenistic Period and, 11–12, 14, 16,
        38, 103–107, 110, 112, 117, 123–
        126, 128–133, 168–171, 218
    heterodox worship in, 48–51, 53–58,
        60–62, 64, 81
    inscriptions and, 106, 109–110
    Josiah and, 48–49, 62–65, 67–69
    Judah's relations with, 12–13, 70–74,
        81, 100, 102, 108, 119–122, 132–
        134, 138–142, 144–145, 163–164,
        167–168, 172–178, 188, 197,
        215–216
    lions and, 4, 47, 52, 57
    Maccabean Era and, 11–12, 172–173,
        178, 213–214, 218
    Neo-Assyrian Period and, 103, 105
    Neo-Babylonian Period and, 2, 11, 14,
        16, 103, 105–106, 112, 120–121,
        132, 214
    numismatics and, 9, 107, 109–111,
        115–119, 124, 130, 132
    Pentateuch and, 13, 177–178, 181,
        184, 189–190, 192–197, 205,
        214–216, 218–219, 231
    Persian Era, 2, 11, 14, 16, 37–38,
        103–108, 110–111, 117–124, 126,
        132–133, 144–145, 168, 172, 213
    personal names (PNs) in, 112–117,
        126–132
    population transfers and, 10, 18–30,
        32–34, 36, 38–43, 48–49, 57–58,
        65–69, 108

priests in, 10, 47, 52, 54, 56, 63–64, 164, 174–175, 190–192, 214, 237
prophets from, 10, 69, 77–81, 97
Roman Era and, 13–14, 107
Samaria papyri and, 109–111, 113–114
Seleucid period, 170, 172
Yahwism in, 10–13, 16–17, 27, 48–49, 52, 56–59, 63–65, 67–70, 74, 80, 86, 99–100, 117, 120–123, 125–126, 130–134, 161, 171, 174, 176–177, 194, 215, 217–218
Yahwistic names in, 113–117, 127–131
Samarian/Samaritan Pentateuch (SP). *See under* Pentateuch
Samarians. *See* Samaria
Samaritans. *See also* Samaria
ancestral lineage of, 2–3, 10, 68 100, 218
as Cutheans, 3, 19
as descendants of Joseph, 2, 3, 20, 61n40, 127, 132, 174n15
as "guardians" of the Torah, 16
calendar, 2, 215, 224
chronicles of, 20, 191–192, 196n68, 205, 212n98, 235, 237
Decalogue, 184, 196, 197n73, 214, 219, 232, 234
definition of terminology regarding, 14–16
diasporic communities and, 218, 226, 230
Hebrew language and, 2, 239
Israel and, 1–2, 14–15, 16n20, 217, 220, 228, 232–233
Jesus and, 1, 3, 217, 220–221, 227–228
Jewish Wars and, 222–223, 225
Jews and, 1–4, 13, 17, 71, 102, 188, 217–229, 233, 237–239
mezuzot and, 228, 233–235

miqva'ot and, 228, 235–237
Moses, beliefs regarding, 14, 215
Roman Era and, 16, 218–220, 222–224, 226
synagogues and, 228–233, 236–237
Yahwism and, 4, 14, 17, 232–234
Samaritis, 16, 170n2, 170n5
Sanballat
Alexander the Great and, 175
Ephraimite status of, 148
the Horonite, 147–149
Israelite status of, 155–156, 162–163
Judah and, 102, 152, 155, 157, 167
Nehemiah and, 19, 134, 140–142, 144–147, 149–156, 160, 162–163, 165–166, 174
sons of, 120, 148
Yahwism of, 165
Sanballat II, 111, 114
Sargon II, 9, 20, 23–27, 30–33, 35–41, 43, 82
Seleucids, 170
Sennacherib, 25, 30, 41, 82–83
Serapion of Knossos, 171
Shalmaneser III, 30
Shalmaneser V, 9, 20, 23, 25, 36, 42–43, 82
Shecaniah, 158
Shechem
altar at, 204, 209–210
archeological discoveries at, 9, 11, 34
convocation at, 151
Samarians/Samaritans and, 173–176, 200–201, 237
Shelemiah, 111, 115, 120, 148
Shema, 233–234
Shemaiah ben Delaiah ben Mehetab'el, 157
Shiloh sanctuary, 191
Simeon ben Gamaliel II, 225
Simon Maccabee, 213
slavery, 79, 114–115

Solomon, 87–88, 90, 95, 128, 186–187
synagogues, 2, 13, 228–237

Tanakh, 15, 178, 215
Tel el-Balaṭah, 200
Tel el-ʿUnuq, 200–201
Tetragrammaton, 128, 130–131
Tiglath-pileser III, 9, 21–23, 25, 30–33, 35–36, 40n47, 41–42, 46, 75–76
Tobiah
    Judah and, 157–159, 161, 167
    Nehemiah and, 141, 144–146, 149–150, 152–156, 158–162, 165–167
    Yahwism of, 147, 150–151, 155, 161, 165
Torah. *See* Pentateuch
Transjordan
    Assyrian conquest and, 9, 21–22, 33, 38, 42
    Maccabees and, 12

Uzzi, 191–192

Yehud. *See under* Judah

Zechariah, 6, 100–101, 158, 168
Zerah, 159
Zichri, 77

www.ingramcontent.com/pod-product-compliance
Ingram Content Group UK Ltd.
Pitfield, Milton Keynes, MK11 3LW, UK
UKHW042005230426
12048UKWH00009B/572